Lelant Ferry: *Tom Watty with one of the praam-type ferryboats built by his father for the Lelant crossing. Date c. 1902.*
Sketch – Terry Duggan.

Malpas Passage: *Malpas Ferry about 1892 at St. Michael Penkivel, with horse and trap side-loaded.*
Sketch – Terry Duggan.

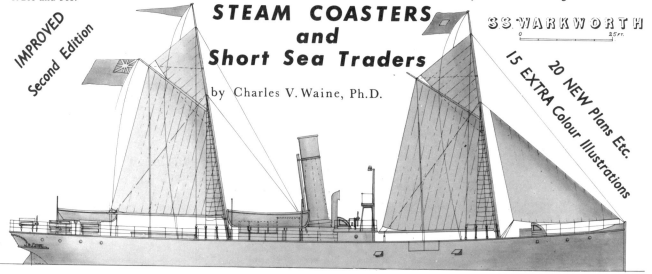

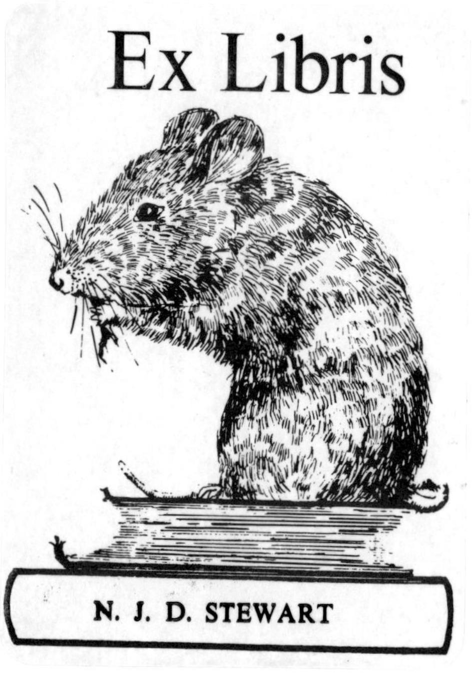
Ex Libris
N. J. D. STEWART

*Sandbanks – Shell Bay, Poole Harbour. The steam chain ferry **No.1.** loads cars at Shell Bay on the 21st of April 1958 a few weeks before she was replaced by a new ferry.*

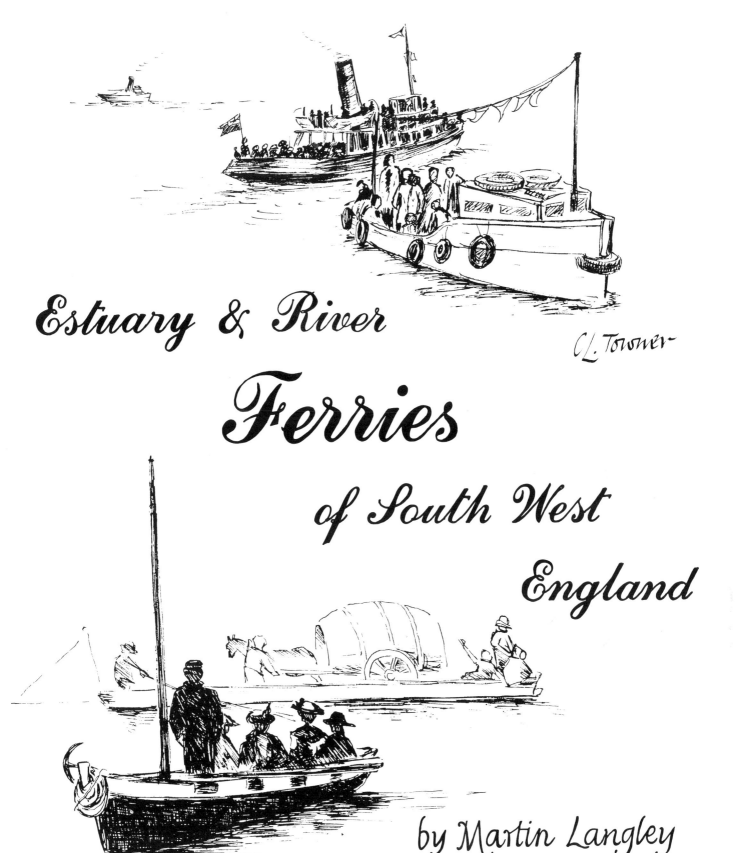

Estuary & River

Ferries

of South West

England

by Martin Langley
& Edwina Small

WAINE Research Publications

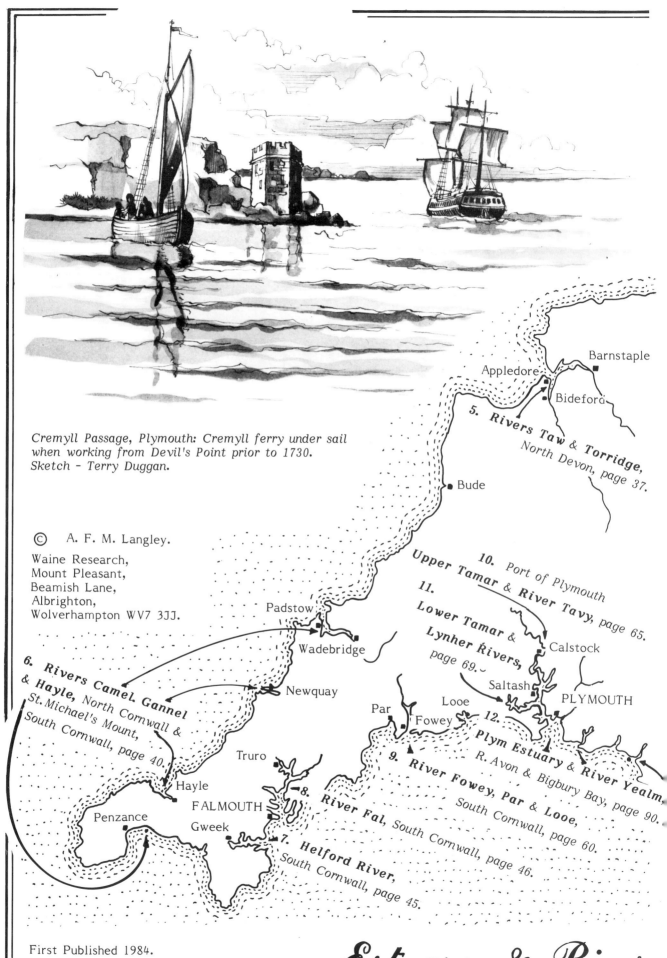

Cremyll Passage, Plymouth: Cremyll ferry under sail when working from Devil's Point prior to 1730. Sketch - Terry Duggan.

© A. F. M. Langley.

Waine Research,
Mount Pleasant,
Beamish Lane,
Albrighton,
Wolverhampton WV7 3JJ.

Barnstaple

Appledore

Bideford

5. Rivers Taw & Torridge, North Devon, page 37.

Bude

10. Port of Plymouth

Upper Tamar & River Tavy, page 65.

11.

Lower Tamar & Lynher Rivers, page 69.

Calstock

Padstow

Wadebridge

Saltash

PLYMOUTH

Newquay

Looe

Par

Fowey

12.

Plym Estuary & River Yealm,

6. Rivers Camel, Gannel & Hayle, North Cornwall & St. Michael's Mount, South Cornwall, page 40.

Truro

9. River Fowey, Par & Looe, South Cornwall, page 60.

R. Avon & Bigbury Bay, page 90.

Hayle

FALMOUTH

Penzance

Gweek

8.

River Fal, South Cornwall, page 46.

7. Helford River, South Cornwall, page 45.

First Published 1984.
ISBN 0 905184 08 4.
Printed & Bound in England.

Estuary & River

CONTENTS

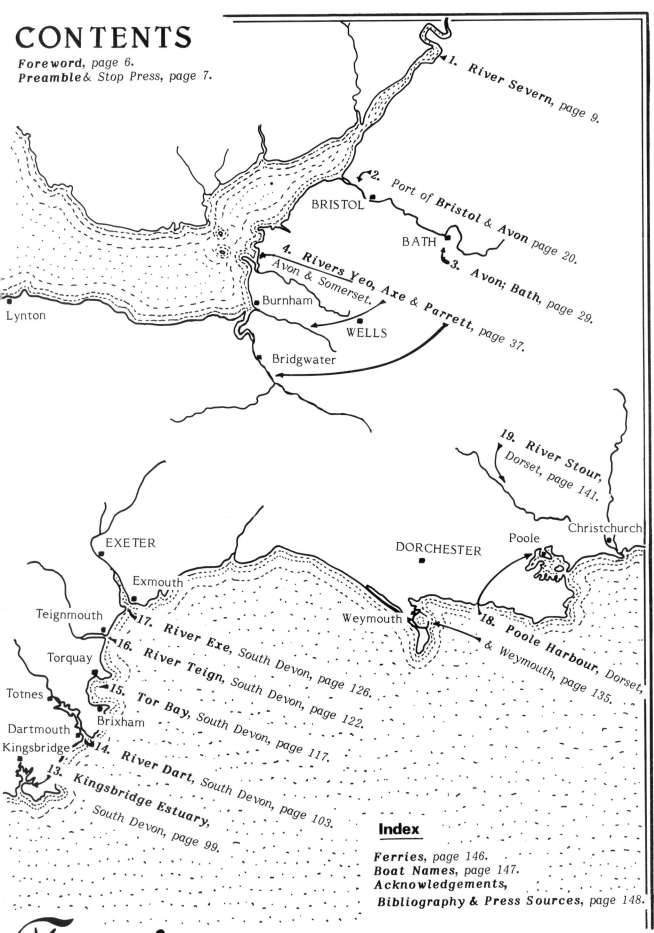

BRISTOL
BATH
Lynton
Burnham
WELLS
Bridgwater
EXETER
Exmouth
Teignmouth
Torquay
Totnes
Brixham
Dartmouth
Kingsbridge
DORCHESTER
Weymouth
Poole
Christchurch

Index

Ferries of South West England

Bernard Watts (left) and Martin Finlay aboard **Weston Maid**, *1980 at Mayflower Steps.*

Foreword

My first experience of ferries, as a small boy, was on holiday at Teignmouth, where for one and a half pence one could cross the estuary to Shaldon in the broad-beamed motor ferries with their painted ports. Our family crossings were infrequent, but I drew youthful pleasure simply from watching the boats arrive and depart.

One year, however, we went to Exmouth, via Starcross. This involved a much more ambitious Ferry passage of 15 minutes in one of three small steamers - **Prince, Melita,** or **Zulu.** I was much impressed, and rated Exmouth Dock steps, where one could watch the ferries negotiating the entrance, second only to the pier and excursion steamers, among the town's major attractions.

As a teenager in Plymouth, which was my home for 23 years, I came to love the Oreston and Turnchapel ferries, known to locals as the 'P. & O. Liners'. For 6d one could voyage from Phoenix Wharf to Turnchapel and Oreston, and return, with often a call at R.A.F. Mt. Batten thrown in for good measure. This gave one about 45 minutes afloat in the Cattewater, and I have always considered it the best 'tanner's worth' in pre-war Plymouth. My friends and I would repair on board the ferry most summer Saturdays, armed with bathing costumes and towels so that we could disembark at Turnchapel if the mood took us, for a swim at Jennycliffe. How we argued about the merits of the steamers - **Dart, Lively, May Queen, Swift,** and **Rapid! Swift** was the general favourite, being reputedly slightly faster than the others.

When on my own, I would make for the Barbican and spend hours aboard the steam trawlers, helping to 'paint ship' and yarning with the crews. I knew that the sea was calling me and I had every intention of answering the call. The other side of Sutton Harbour accommodated merchant steamers and one could avoid the long walk round by taking the rowboat ferry from Mayflower jetty. It must have been one of the shortest ferry passages on record and the fare was only 1d. The boat plied as needed and if on your arrival it was on the other side, one had only to raise an arm and shout 'Ferry ahoy!' I nicknamed the boatman Charon after the ferryman of Hades in Greek mythology and he did not seem to resent this doubtful honour. Probably this was an area of literature which had passed him by.

An alternative resort on Saturdays was the Stonehouse ferry from Admirals' Hard to Cremyll, aboard one of the Emmet-like steamers **Shuttlecock** and **Armadillo.** From Cremyll one could skirt the foreshore to the creepy - and surely haunted? - Picklecombe Fort with its derelict pier. An added attraction was that the Cremyll ferryman allowed us to sprawl on the open stern, which was strictly forbidden on the Turnchapel boats.

Wonderful days! Certainly they gave me an interest in ferries which has lasted my lifetime.

Martin Langley

Wells, 1984.

What is a ferry? The media today regularly misapply the word to packet and cross-channel services, and the latest editions of some dictionaries are stretching the definition of the word in deference to this contemporary habit. We prefer the definition given in the Encyclopaedia Britannica (11th Edition), viz - "a place where boats ply regularly across a river or arm of the sea for the convenience of goods and persons".

A right of ferry is an exclusive right to convey persons or goods (or both) over a river or arm of the sea and to charge reasonable tolls for the service. These exclusive rights generally pertained to ferries which were integral parts of the highway system. The origin of a right of ferry is usually ancient - often, indeed, "from time immemorial" - but such right was invariably conferred by Royal Grant or Act of Parliament. With that right went an obligation to provide and maintain a safe and adequate service, without interfering with ordinary navigation. Such a ferry is legally established and cannot be suspended nor closed down at the discretion of the proprietor or his lessee. All such ferries were originally owned by private people, but the Ferries (Acquisition by Local Authorities) Act, 1919, empowered local authorities to purchase or accept transfer of a legally established ferry and thereafter be fully responsible for the service.

Other ferries may be regarded as vested in a property. Only the landowner can exercise right of ferry because the landing-places on either side are within his property.

Some ferries are vested by Act of Parliament in a railway company or harbour authority. Other ferries have been a commercial venture, where the need has been recognised, but these have no monopoly and live daily with the possibility of competition.

Most ferries operate within "smooth water limits", and with the exception of chain ferries, which are excluded from the operation of the Merchant Shipping Acts, require a Department of Trade Passenger Certificate (Form St.5). The Turnchapel steam ferry at Plymouth was an example. There are, however, certain ferries worked within "partially smooth water limits", for which a Passenger Certificate Form St.4 is required; e.g. Torbay Ferry, and Aust-Beachley passage. The 'St.' stands for steamer and the regulations state that this "includes a ship propelled by electricity or other mechanical power".

A great many ferries, especially in the higher reaches of rivers, never developed beyond a rowboat service (e.g. Calstock passage), perhaps latterly expedited by an outboard motor (e.g. Topsham-Exminster), usually a waterman's boat, essentially any strong boat with fairly full lines aft able to carry a number of passengers. They could be carvel or clinker built depending on the district. Most of these have now gone, but they enjoyed virtual freedom from the law and its supervision until a Merchant Shipping Notice following the **Darlwyn** boat disaster in 1967 enjoined the provision of safety equipment for the ferryboat, and the licensing of a competent ferryman by the local authority.

STOP PRESS

SOUTH CORNWALL - River Fal
RESTRONGUET PASSAGE: The model of H.M.S. **Pandora** formerly on view at the Pandora Inn on the Mylor side, has, sadly, now been sold out of the district.

MALPAS PASSAGE: The estate workboat **Duckweed** is now fully restored and has replaced the dinghy on the service.

PORT OF PLYMOUTH - River Tamar.

CREMYLL PASSAGE: The Millbrook Steamboat & Trading Company were acquired by Mr. Bob Cruse of Dartmouth in 1982 but the company name has been retained.

PORT OF PLYMOUTH - River Plym.

CAWSAND FERRY: This service has been taken over by Mr. Fred Doidge of Millbrook, and one boat only, the **Weston Maid**, is now running.

DRAKE'S ISLAND FERRY: The public ferry. This service has now been taken over by the Millbrook Steamboat Company. **Queen Boadicea I** (from Dartmouth) temporarily succeeded the **Edgcumbe Belle** but has now been scrapped and the latter vessel has resumed the duty.

The staff ferry. During the stormy night of 25/26 January 1984 the staff ferryboat **Sir Egbert Cadbury** broke away from its moorings and was found in the morning on the rocks in Barn Pool. The 30-capacity boat was badly damaged and repair is problematical.

SOUTH DEVON - River Dart

TOTNES BOATS: In 1982 **Compton Castle** was purchased by her present owner, David Worlledge, but her engine was sold to the Blackgang China Bazaar, where it is on display. Towed by a Plymouth tug from Looe to Truro, the ship has been restored for use as a floating restaurant at a cost of £170,000, and is now moored at Lemon Quay in the city centre.

In mid-November 1982 **Kingswear Castle** (2), her restoration complete by the Paddle Steamer Preservation Society, steamed again, in the River Medway. Captain David Neill of **Waverley** was in command.

HIGHER FERRY: On Wednesday, 9th February 1984 the **Philip** was torn from its cables in a gale and swept downstream out of control. Skipper Simon Deacon and fare-collector John Leyland let go the emergency anchor but the ferry struck 12 moored yachts before her progress was arrested. On the runaway, besides pedestrian passengers, there were 5 cars and an ambulance taking a sick woman to hospital.

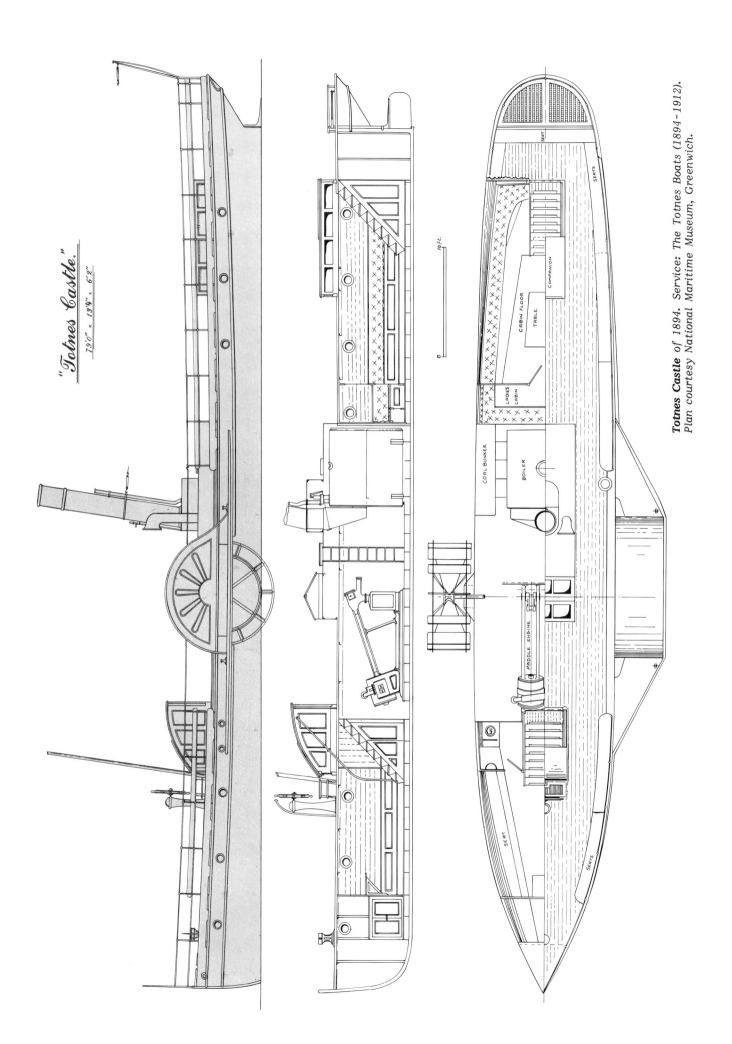

"Totnes Castle."

79'0" x 13'4" x 6'2"

Totnes Castle of 1894. Service: The Totnes Boats (1894-1912). Plan courtesy National Maritime Museum, Greenwich.

CORAL BUNKER

BOILER

PADDLE ENGINE

LADIES CABIN

CABIN FLOOR

TABLE

COMPANION

SEATS

SEAT

SEATS

10 ft.

0

1.

River Severn

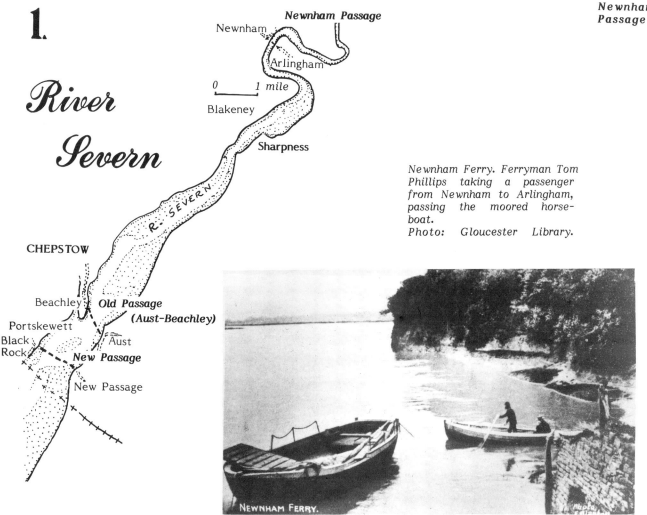

Newnham Passage

Newnham
Arlingham

0   1 mile

Blakeney

Sharpness

R. SEVERN

CHEPSTOW

Beachley   **Old Passage**
        (Aust-Beachley)
Portskewett
Black   Aust
Rock   **New Passage**

New Passage

Newnham Ferry. Ferryman Tom Phillips taking a passenger from Newnham to Arlingham, passing the moored horse-boat.
Photo: Gloucester Library.

NEWNHAM FERRY.

NEWNHAM PASSAGE: In the higher reaches of the Severn estuary, where today the village of Newnham, on the A48, stands opposite to the Arlingham peninsular on the east bank, there was an important ford from the earliest times until the shifting of a sandbank in 1802 made the crossing no longer fordable. A busy tidal ford required the complement of a boat at high water, and no doubt a ferry of sorts existed at Newnham from time immemorial.

The earliest actual reference we have to the ferry is from the thirteenth century. The following is found in the Close Rolls, 22 Henry III 1238:- "De Quercu data - It is commanded to the Constable of St. Briavell that he cause the woman keeping the passage of Nyweham to have one oak in the forest of St. Briavell to make a certain boat thereof, of the gift of the King". Clearly the poorer women of Plantagenet times included some formidable characters! Women have throughout the ages pulled or sculled or poled ferries across rivers, but the implication here is that the Newnham ferrywoman built her own boats.

In 1570 we learn of legislation to prevent the ferry being used by criminals to avoid capture. In 23 Henry VIII Chapter 12 it is recorded that malefactors were accustomed to take refuge in the forest of Dean after committing crimes in Gloucester and district, and warning was given to any person who kept ferries at Aust, Newnham and other places who conveyed horses, cattle or oxen before sunrise or after sunset should be liable to fine or imprisonment.

In 1779 (reign of George III) there is a reference by Rudder to the ford "over which at low water wagons and people on horseback, of more reputation than prudence, sometimes pass, for many have lost their lives in the attempt". Before the end of the eighteenth century we find Rudge writing: "From this town (Newnham) is one of the passages over the river which is perfectly safe, and can be made in almost every state of the tide, for men, horses, and carriages. Near to this place a rock rises so near to the surface of the water that horses and carriages are conducted with great safety by a guide without a boat. But to those who are unacquainted with the line of the ridge, the attempt is attended with extreme danger, as the rocks precipitate suddenly to a great depth on either side". However, by 1802 the ford had become unusable, probably for good. An article in "The Gloucestershire Chronicle" for 15th September 1866 mentions the "clumsy, yet picturesque ferry boat crossing, slowly moved by labouring oars, creaking and splashing".

A writer in the Austin Magazine of November 1927 describes a typical crossing from Newnham to Arlingham at that time. "...the tide has come up in great style from the Bristol Channel and the sturdy boatman has something to do to stem the flow. He makes a zig-zag course, however, and gets across to a point about 50 yards from the bank....and now for the excitement: Old Charon... puts on an enormous pair of wading boots, and breaks the news gently that, from this point, we must be carried ashore; the water is too shallow to take the boat in further! And so - greatly to the delight of an appreciative audience of children...we are, one after the other hoisted on to Charon's broad shoulders, "pick-a-back" style, and transported by man power to the bank!"

In 1939 there was a public announcement that the Old Passage Severn Ferry Co. had bought the ferry rights at Newnham, and intended to provide for vehicular traffic by establishing a chain-ferry. This would have involved:- the blasting of rock from the west bank to make a landing-slip; the building of an approach road on the Arlingham side by the New Inn; and the putting down of ferry chains and sprung anchorages. On 3rd September that year World War II broke out and all these plans had to be shelved.

The Old Passage Severn Ferry Co. was managed by Enoch Williams, the pioneer of vehicle-carrying motor-ferries between Aust and Beachley. When the war ended Enoch Williams turned his attention again to the Newnham passage and resolved to experiment with the invention of a man named Ronald Hamilton. Hamilton's idea has been conceived during the war and was a novel form of floating platform capable of rapid assembly and adaptable for use by aircraft or road vehicles. The intention had been to use the invention, code-named 'LILY', in the onslaught on Japan. Hiroshima made this irrelevant, and no operational use had been made of the idea when the war ended.

After the war, Hamilton recovered his patent rights from the Government and endeavoured to exploit his invention financially in various parts of the world, but without success. Enoch Williams however felt it had possibilities for the Severn, and in 1948 announced that the plans for a chain ferry had been abandoned in favour of a shore-to-shore floating bridge. Hamilton designed six-feet wide hexagonal floats which had a depth of thirty inches. The floats or cans were linked by loose bolting so that the platform could conform to the undulations or swell of the river surface. On either side of the river, at Newnham and Arlingham large concrete anchorage bays were constructed to secure the ends of the floating bridge. In February 1949 the anticipation was expressed that the bridge would be ready for the summer traffic. But it was not to be. In practice it was found that the strong tide looped the bridge up or downstream at an unacceptable angle; that the anchoring cables were liable to part or give a dangerous tilt to the 'pontoon'; and that only at slack water did the bridge behave as its designer had intended.

Enoch Williams had to cut his losses - thought by some to be as high as £35,000 - and abandon the scheme. The pontoon floats, which had become known as "Lily Cans" were towed in strings from Arlingham in 1956 to be used for a floating jetty for Chepstow Yacht Club at St. Pierre. However by this time the old-established orthodox ferry had ceased to ply.

Thomas Phillips had been ferryman before the nineteenth century ended, and did not retire until 1929 after more than 30 years service. His son-in-law William Hayward succeeded him for the 19 years that followed, including the World War II period. A single rowing-boat was maintained for passengers, and if an overload of passengers was waiting, a second crossing had to be made. During busy times other members of the ferrymans' family helped out with their own boats. There was always a horseboat, but its use required assistance, chiefly by members of the family. Muscle-power prevailed to the end, motor boats never coming into use on Newnham ferry. For many years a heavy rowing-boat named **Dorothy** had been in use but this was eventually retired and left to rot quietly away on the river bank. In later years a lighter type of boat was used, of approximately 16 ft. length.

There was tragedy in 1899, when ferryman Tom Phillip's two little sons, Thomas, 8, and Reginald, 7, were drowned on 17th July. Their tombstone can be seen in Newnham Churchyard. Mrs. Askew, grand-daughter of Tom Phillips and daughter of William Hayward, recalls having to bang a metal bucket to give direction signs when the ferry was crossing in dense fog - a hazardous undertaking. Sometimes there was rescue work to do. One summer in the 1930s, a woman swimmer got into difficulties and shouted for help. Ferryman Hayward ran down the slipway - gashing a bare foot in the process, jumped fully clothed into the river and hauled the woman to safety. Her husband had sat throughout on the sands wearing his swimming costume, and upbraided her on her return for shouting and making a fuss!

Mrs. Askew can remember her father conveying 16 cyclists on one occasion. He recruited one of his family with another boat, piled the 16 bikes in one boat and the 16 cyclists in the other! Amongst well-known personalities who sometimes made the crossing must be mentioned, Sir Lionel Durrell and family from Frethern in Gloucestershire who used the Newnham ferry from time to time.

William Hayward died in November 1948 and Newnham ferry came officially to a close with his passing. For awhile crossings were made by other boat owners, upon special request, but these became fewer and today Newnham Passage has been abandoned. William Haywards' ferryboat gradually decayed on the beach and all that can be seen today is the dilapidated concrete slipway on the Newnham side built with such misplaced optimism by Enoch Williams' contractors.

SEVERN, OLD PASSAGE (Aust-Beachley): Throughout its long and chequered history the Old Passage across the Severn presented a formidable challenge to the skill of those whose livelihood was to work it, and to the fortitude of those whose necessity was to use it. G. Bernard Wood in "Ferries and Ferrymen" (1969) remarks "...it was regarded as one of the natural hazards of life in this part of England.... to be taken with as much philosophy as one could muster". Indeed. For here the turbulent waters of Britain's longest river merge with the ocean waters of the Bristol Channel in a fast-flowing and temperamental estuary.

There was a crossing in the vicinity of Aust, probably upstream from the eventual passage, in Roman times, and historians seem agreed that here the Propraetor Ostorius ferried his legions in his campaign against the Silures, c. AD 48. The legend that the seven Welsh bishops crossed here to meet Augustine, for their abortive conference in c. 600 AD, is oft-repeated, but rejected by most authorities. From 748 until the Reformation the overlordship of Aust was held by the Priory of Worcester and Bishop of Worcester, and the rights of Ferry were for a while ecclesiastical. About 910 AD Edward the Elder crossed here, with his warlike sister Ethelfleda, to a meeting with the unruly Llewelyn, a South Wales chieftain who would not admit Saxon suzerainty. Not until 1131 however do we get a definite reference to the Ferry, when it is recorded that Winebold de Bolan held the rights from the Crown, but allowed the Abbot and monks of Tintern Abbey to use the Ferry free of charge at 'Austre-Clive'.

It is believed that Hubert de Burgh used the Old Passage when escaping in 1233 from the wrath of the ungrateful Henry III: and that John Wycliffe (translator of the Bible into English) crossed here a number of times between 1362 and 1375. In 1370 it is recorded that William de Mareschal, Earl of Pembroke, was granted by the Crown the right to ferry himself, his family, and livestock in his own craft. The bestowal of this privilege entitled the Earl's family to cross in greater comfort of their own provision, but is evidence that the ferry rights were ancient, and independent of his position. From the time of Richard II, if not earlier, the ferry operated as a common law company of unlimited liability with 24 shares variously distributed: and by 1400 the Churchman Family's involvement with the ferry, had begun. Off and on, they were to be associated actively with its working for about 300 years, and were probably responsible for its transfer to its latter site, in Stuart times.

The exposed site, the vagaries of weather, and the Famous Severn Bore were not the only perils of those far-off days. The shores of the estuary had acquired an evil reputation for murders and felonies; and by Henry VIII's reign the situation was so bad that the Ferries were forbidden to run in the hours of darkness, while in daylight the Ferrymen were instructed to carry only passengers with whose credentials they were satisfied. An Act imposed these regulations, under penalty. In James I's reign it is recorded that there were 12 Ferrymen, all based in Aust; but it seems that the Ferry-landing at what is now called The Folly was then in use. It is claimed by local historians that 'Tovey's Folly', inhabited by "John Tovey, gentleman", in Civil War days, had previously been the Ferry Inn. In 1645 New Passage was peremptorily closed by Cromwell after the incident of the drowned troopers, and the operators of the Old Passage enjoyed over 70 years free from competition. Aust Manor was acquired by Sir Samuel Astry in 1652; he bought up all the shares and thus became owner of the Ferry. The irrepressible Churchmans managed the Ferry for Sir Samuel in his lifetime; and on his death, in conjunction with the Baker and Bonson Families of Aust, rented the Ferry at a high rental. They owned and operated four inns (two on each side of the river) and may well have foreseen the benefits to their business from the inevitable delays resulting from a much less practical passage than the Ferry was then using. It is alleged, and may well be true that they contrived to transfer the Ferry from Old Aust to what we now call Old Passage. Up to this time, it is said, (Old) Passage House, which they had built, was their private residence, and did not become the Ferry hotel until after 1650.

The re-siting of the Ferry did nothing to enhance the safety of the crossing, nor gain the goodwill of a long-suffering public. Daniel Defoe (later to be the author of 'Robinson Crusoe') was a reluctant passenger in 1703 and later described the drowning of one of the Churchmans and his son, while trying to save a barge and its crew in a maelstrom of water on the Benches. The following year Sir Samuel Astry died; the estate was divided, and the Ferry passed to Mrs. Diana Orlebar. In 1725 Daniel Defoe was at Aust again, but he found "the boats to carry over man and beast so mean that we did not venture the passage". No doubt his experience of 20 years earlier had made a lasting impression. John Wesley, who usually travelled by New Passage, recorded in his journal for February 1748 that he crossed from Aust to Beachley on Tuesday the 16th on his way to Chepstow. From about this time traffic at Old Passage declined greatly and its owner was soon in such grave difficulties that the Parish Clerk of Aust was installed as Receiver. In 1780 the Ferry was up for sale at Exchange Coffee Tavern, Bristol, and thereafter passed from private ownership to a quadruple partnership and then again to a common-law company. There was a grim interlude in the Ferry story in 1782. Two drovers, who had stolen some cattle in Wales and sold them in Bristol, quarrelled over the sharing of the money on their return on the Ferry, and one, Jenkyns Prothero, murdered his companion. He was soon arrested, and was hung in chains from a gibbet on Clifton Downs. The Churchman family had quitted the ferry scene just after the accession of George I, and since 1765 the service had been worked by the Whitchurch family, who were associated with the Old Passage till 1861. It had now become the mail route to Wales, and in 1802 the Union post coach was advertised as running from Bristol every Sunday, Wednesday and Friday morning via the Old Passage to Chepstow, Monmouth and Hereford.

The sail-and-oar Ferryboats of the time being subject to wind and tide, made the timing of the Royal Mails erratic. Meanwhile about 1820 a group of Welsh MPs and businessmen had bought the Ferry rights and founded the Old Passage Ferry Association. To counter the competition of New Passage they were putting the approach roads in order and building the two stone piers, at Aust and Beachley, 30 ft. wide and several hundred feet long, which are the ones we see today. The Post Office however was less than satisfied with the carriage of the mails, and in 1825 the Association met to consider the purchase of a steam vessel. The decision they made was to buy up the New Passage and eliminate competition for the mail. But in this they were rebuffed and their initiative served only to provoke the New Passage into forestalling them by acquiring a steamboat that same year.

In June 1827 the Old Passage met the challenge by introducing on to the Ferry the wooden paddle steamer **Worcester**, built at Bristol. She was a slightly larger vessel than the New Passage's **St. Pierre**, and probably faster, for by 1831 the Post Office had transferred all mail to the Old Passage. The triumph had been hard-won, and the fierce competition brought the Old Passage Ferry Association to the verge of bankruptcy. On a March day in 1829 an auction was attempted of the Ferry lease and assets:

Lot 1. The Improved Old Passage Ferry with the Steam Packet and large and small sailing and row boats.

Lot 2. The Inn at Aust with standing for six carriages, stabling for 36 horses, and a bowling green.

There was not a single bid for Ferry or inn!

Somehow the business was carried on. Indeed, in 1832 a second steam Ferry was acquired, the wooden paddler **Beaufort**. This proved to have been a good move when in 1837 the **Worcester** caught fire and was put ashore at Beachley, a blazing wreck. She never returned to the Ferry service, although her remains were bought by a ship-builder named Davies and rebuilt as a schooner-rigged

**Severn,
Old Passage
(Aust – Beachley)**

sailing collier. In Felix Farley's Journal for June 1836 it is recorded: 'The two sons of the Prince of Orange and their retinue crossed the Severn at Old Passage Ferry on Thursday and after express-ing their satisfaction at the attention paid to them by the superintendent and boatmen, they ordered dinner at the Beachley Inn". They were by no means the first royalty to use the crossing, nor yet the last. The following year two Monmouthshire families took over the financially ailing Ferry, trading as the Aust Ferry Association.

The potential dangers of the passage were re-emphasised in 1839 when the sailing Ferry **Jane** was lost with all hands, swept on to the Lady Bench reef in a gale. One of the Crawshays, the great South Wales coal and ironmasters, was among those drowned. The previous year the Association had taken delivery of a new steam ferry. Named **Worcester** like her predecessor, she was a 60-ton iron vessel purpose-built by Napiers of Glasgow. Neither she nor the **Beaufort** were working during the gale in which the **Jane** had sunk. Apparently it was policy to use only the sailing vessels in very bad weather, but there was a great deal of adverse public criticism. Tragedy struck again in 1855 when the 20-ton sailing Ferry **Dispatch** was lost on 30th of March. Built of elm, quarter-decked aft to provide cabin shelter for passengers, and designed to carry a deck load of 14 tons, the **Dispatch** was crowded with Littleton, Aust, and Olveston folk returning from Chepstow Market. In addition to her crew of two were 12 passengers and 56 livestock. As she neared Aust Pier a sudden swell dashed her against some heavy wooden piling used for mooring the steam ferries. She was badly holed and sank rapidly. Seven passengers were drowned: five others, with the crew, saved themselves by clinging to the tails of the cattle as they swam ashore. The press was sharply critical, Felix Farley's Journal declaring that the Ferry "needed to be looked into", especially the "crazy old steam-kettle which still did duty when its engines could be induced to run". Accounts of this incident are confusing and contradictory. One report says that the steamer captains had refused to run in the conditions prevailing: another that it was a fine day, and the breeze was gentle.

The steam Ferries appear to have been withdrawn and scrapped by the end of 1861, and the service reverted to sail. After 1864 the importance of Old Passage declined, because New Passage had been adopted for the railway Ferry service. Even so, Old Passage still handled most of the livestock to and from Chepstow market, and continued to do so even after the G.W.R. had opened the Severn Tunnel in 1886. The Passage House, Aust, had long been a popular hostelry: and drovers used to leave their animals in the sheds, stables and pen at the bottom of the hill and stay at the inn if tide was delaying the ferry. With the steamboats gone, shipboard conditions were once again primitive. The horse-boats were open, two-masted craft - the aftermast just a short mizzen. The motley collection on board must often have been most uncomfortable, well-dressed travellers finding themselves cheek by jowl with country folk from the markets, and livestock everywhere on deck. As the nineteenth century drew to a close, pedestrian and animal traffic alike gradually dwindled away, and by 1900 the Ferry had closed down, though up to 1914 it was possible to get a boat to take one across.

But, just as the rise of rail-travel had given new birth to the New Passage, so the return to road transport brought about by the petrol engine was to give new life to the Old Passage. In 1920, with the Great War over, all that was needed was for the hour to bring forth the man. This it duly did, in the person of Enoch Williams.

Enoch Williams, a 32-year old Welshman of Swansea, had served in the Royal Engineers during the Great War and had been concerned with the Richborough-Dieppe ammunition train ferry. In 1920 he was talking to a friend named Walter Watts who had spent the war lorry-driving between Newport and Bristol. Watts complained of the long detour via Gloucester, and said there ought to be a bridge or a ferry further downstream. Enoch's keen commercial sense was alerted by this remark, and there and then he decided that this was a need he would try to supply. He was at this time an architect for Newport Council, but that same year he inspected several sites on the Severn with his wife, Ida, and made up his mind to re-work the Old Passage between Aust and Beachley. Terms were agreed with the ninth Duke of Beaufort for lease of the Ferry rights by a consortium of Enoch Williams, Walter Watts, and another backer, S.D. Williams. The legal work involved had, as ever, taken a considerable time and the date from which the lease ran was eventually 31 July 1924.

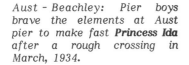

*Aust – Beachley: Pier boys brave the elements at Aust pier to make fast **Princess Ida** after a rough crossing in March, 1934.*

Arrangements were now made with Olney Bros. of Barry to supply a ferryboat and build a 200 ft. wooden extension to the old stone piers at Aust. This work was under way when the General Strike threatened. Enoch saw at once that this would be an ideal time to start the service, because with rail and bus services at a standstill his Ferry would enjoy a monopoly. He redoubled his efforts to get started, but in the event the strike lasted only 8 days, and it was not possible to be ready in time.

Olney Bros. supplied the **Silver Queen** for the first Williams' Ferry. She was a single-screw open motor boat with a mast for'ard to which a derrick for handling motor-bikes, etc. was later fitted. She had been built in Appledore in 1922, was 48 ft. long, and had a passenger capacity of 70. Meanwhile arrangements were made with Bristol Tramways to meet the Ferry hourly at Aust pier, and a widespread distribution of handbills was carried out. An official opening of the service took place on 6 July 1926, attended by the Lord Mayor of Bristol. Shortly after, the Ferry was being advertised as follows:

> 'A preliminary Service across the Severn by Swift
> Motor Craft carrying Passengers, Cycles,
> and Side Cars - but NOT Motor Cars YET'.

Subject to the vagaries of tide and weather the service operated successfully and daily for more than two years when disaster struck. A storm destroyed the pier extension at Aust and the Ferry came to a close in October 1928. Enoch Williams continued his career as an architect, and Olneys repossessed the **Silver Queen** and later sold her to Lowestoft. Three years elapsed when there was no ferry. However in 1931, with the backing of the Beauchamp family, Enoch was able to form a new company - the Old Passage Severn Ferry Company Limited - to underlease the ferry rights, reinstate the piers, and order a purpose-built Ferryboat able to transport cars.

The service recommenced on Monday, 18 May 1931, with a 26 ft. motor boat named the **May Queen**, which had originally been a Thames Police launch. Her capacity was 30 passengers but permission was shortly obtained for motorbikes and cycles to be loaded. The **May Queen** was a stop-gap until delivery of the new car ferry; but in fact she continued to be used, when only pedestrians had to be crossed, until January 1936, when a gale tore her from her moorings at Beachley and she was never seen again. The new ferry, which was introduced on 30 July, was named **Princess Ida**, in tribute to Mrs. Williams. Indeed, no tribute was more deserved, for the vessel incorporated an ingenious idea of her namesake which was of vital importance - a turntable in the deck. By this means more cars and vans could be accommodated. So far as we can discover, there has been no similar ferry in the British Isles, the nearest approach to Ida's turntable (it came to her in a dream!) being the swivel deck of the Ballachulish Ferry in Scotland. Built of wood, at Chepstow, the **Princess Ida** was 60 ft. in length, and fitted with an Elwe single-cylinder diesel engine which gave her a speed of about 6 knots. The first skipper was Geoff Groves, later followed by his river-pilot brother, Bill Groves: Bob Jones (later promoted to skipper) was the mate, and Bert Blatchford and Percy Palmer were deckhands. Bert Blatchford skippered the **May Queen** when required; Percy Palmer was to achieve 31 years service on the Ferry. An early mishap was the stranding of **Princess Ida** on Beachley Pier, necessitating dry-docking for repairs. Not long after, she was aground at Beachley again, but this time on the mud - in the following circumstances. Enoch had given up his work as an architect to become a full-time Ferry operator, and was on board the **Ida** on this occasion. Skipper Geoff Groves had loaded two cars and was away and heading for Aust when Enoch noticed some further passengers had arrived at Beachley just too late. Anxious to oblige his public, he ordered Geoff Groves to put about and pick them up. This the skipper was unwilling to do, as he feared grounding on the rapidly-falling tide. There were some sharp verbal exchanges before he complied; and then, as he had feared the **Princess Ida** stuck fast. They missed the tide and the two irate motorists had to be expensively compensated.

The first year of profitable operation was 1932, when despite low figures in winter, an overall 25,070 passengers and 5,837 cars were ferried. Over 1,000 cars were carried by **Princess Ida** on the August Bank Holiday. It was clear that the Ferry had a future, and that the service must be expanded. The challenge was met by ordering two new vessels from Woodward & Scarr of Beverley, Yorkshire, which were to have twin screws for greater manoeuvrability and power. While the new vessels were building, Beachley stone pier was strengthened, and a heavy timber pier was constructed at Aust. Two lorries bringing stone to Aust pier one day had their ignition systems soaked by spray and were overtaken by the rising tide. Both slid off the pier into the river, and were only recovered with difficulty! Before the new Ferryboats arrived **Princess Ida** suffered another stranding. On a very wild day in February 1934 she was swept on to the pier as she was coming astern. Fortunately no damage was done. The two new Ferries were named **Severn Queen** and **Severn King**. The **Queen** arrived in November 1934; the **King** in August 1935. Bob Jones became skipper of the **Queen** and Bill Groves skipper of the **King**. The **Princess Ida** was relegated to reserve Ferry. The new boats had similar hulls and engines: but whereas the **Queen** had an island wheelhouse like the **Ida's**, the **King** had the wheelhouse on a bridge which spanned the deck and thus allowed the full length of the deck to be used for stowing cars. Some seating for pedestrian passengers was provided aft, but shelter from the elements was minimal, and conditions were undoubtedly spartan.

The first Royal passenger in the new era of the Ferry was Prince Paul of Greece, who crossed in **Severn Queen** on a visit to Lord Tredegar in April 1935. The years following saw the rise to power of Hitler in Germany, and a growing threat of war. As Britain belatedly re-armed, plans for a Severn Bridge - which had always overshadowed the Ferry undertaking - were laid aside indefinitely, while traffic continued to increase. There were two incidents of life-saving by the Ferry during this period; one when skipper Charlie Savage fell overboard and was nearly drowned: the other when a dinghy manned by a father and son was seen to capsize on a sandbank. The hero of rescue on both occasions was Percy Palmer.

Came September 1939, and the outbreak of World War II. Military vehicles and service personnel now represented the major part of the traffic - mostly American after 1942. Royal passengers, undeterred by hostilities, were not unusual. Queen Mary crossed several times on visits to Lord and Lady Bledisloe: the teenage princesses Elizabeth and Margaret Rose were frequent passengers, as was Haile Selassie, the refugee Emperor of Ethiopia. Beachley pier boasted its own gun emplace-ment. Passengers often witnessed aerial combat over the estuary in close-up. In 1941 the **Princess Ida** was requisitioned by the Admiralty for war work with experimental weapons, and was renamed **Birnbeck**. She never returned to the Ferry and after the war rotted away in Castle Pill, Milford Haven. The war had no sooner ended in 1945 than autumn gales wrecked Aust pier. This time the Ministry of War Transport, mindful of the Ferry's contribution to the war effort, arranged for Royal Engineers to carry out repairs. The service now depended on two boats, and in the early morning of 24 January 1952 it seemed they might be left with only one. Fire broke out on the **Severn King** while she was at anchor below Chepstow Bridge. A train driver, seeing flames, reported to the signalman at Lydney Box, and the fire brigade were able to suppress the fire before much damage had been done. The trouble was believed due to an overheated exhaust system, and the **King** was later given twin funnels in place of her former single stack, to reduce the likelihood of a repetition.

In 1951 the figures for both passengers (166,649) and vehicles (110,831) were in six figures, and the growth of traffic continued. Considering the amount of traffic handled in the swift, swirling currents and mists of the estuary, the exposure of the passage to gales, and the menace of mud at the landings, it was remarkable that so few accidents occurred and no passenger's life was ever lost. It is a record that reflects great credit on the skill and diligence of the Ferry staff. However, the 'Fifties did not pass without incident.

One day a car with two occupants went over the edge at Beachley pier. 'Pier boys' were employed at both piers to sweep them clear of silt and muddy water as the tides receded, but care was still needed when driving on or off the Ferry. On this occasion an elderly couple in a Daimler Conquest reversed in a semi-circle right off the pier, dropping 12 feet into 3 feet of water! Fortun-ately the car remained upright, and Undermanager John Williams (Enoch's son) dashed down the pier, plunged in, and made the car secure with a rope to the rear bumper. The tide was falling fast and the couple, with head and shoulders just above water decided to stay put until it was easier to open the doors. They were then extricated and well cared for at the Ferry Inn, neither they nor their car coming to any harm: but the incident attracted considerable attention. Questions were asked in the Press and even in the House of Commons as to the safety of the Ferry.

There was more adverse publicity of a different kind when a girl holidaymaker was found stabbed to death behind the Ferry Inn at Beachley and her assailant proved to be one of the Ferry 'pier boys'. He was committed to Broadmoor. Again there was tragedy when Lionel Sims, a 60 year old deckhand, was lost overboard from the **Severn Queen** one summer's evening in the late 'Fifties at Aust pier. The Ferry had just arrived with racegoers from Chepstow, when Lionel was missed. He was later found drowned and it was thought he perhaps lost his footing while walking outboard on the rubbing strake to get for'ard past the cars. Despite these events, the service was undeniably efficient. Enoch Williams was not an absentee boss: he was daily at the Beachley Office or travelling on the Ferries. Mac Knapp, who was Booking Clerk in the Aust Office for 21 years, recalls the boss's voice on the phone if he could see from across the river, that Aust pier had no cars at low tide: "Izzat you, Knapp? Get those cars down on the pier, will you? I want t'see a continuous line of cars, closed up, ready! Get them down, will you?"

Many travellers regarded a trip on the Aust-Beachley Ferry as an adventure, an experience. Motorist Ken White of Wells recalls: "There were stories of dreadful happenings at Aust, cars slipping off the routeway down to the Ferry because of the mud, but I never witnessed such an event. There were two ferryboats operating from opposite sides. They were small and took only 17 or 18 vehicles plus a few push bikes and a number of foot passengers, so the vehicle queue moved slowly. When your turn came the men in control signalled furiously. You drove on to a turn-table, which whisked you round into the required position and you drove tightly into the allotted space. This was done at great speed so that the boat could move off as quickly as possible. You sat in the car and the fee was then collected. The current was swift and the little boat seemed to be swept downstream and you wondered if you would get to the opposite side, but they knew what they were doing". 24th April 1957 was a red-letter day for the Ferry and a great personal satisfaction to Enoch. The Queen and Prince Philip who had been paying an official visit to Worcestershire and Herefordshire crossed from Beachley that day for the three day event at Badminton. The **Severn King**, immaculately prepared and carrying a double crew and a doctor, flew the Royal Standard for the crossing, and HMS **Venturer** lay in midstream as guardship. By 1958 the need for a more frequent service at peak periods had decided Enoch Williams on placing an order for a third vessel. The work was entrusted to the Yorkshire Dry-Dock Company, Hull, and the new ferry **Severn Princess** was launched with full ceremony on 23 May 1959 and brought round the coast with William's own man in charge. Her deck space could accommodate 18 cars and her ramps were mechanically power-ed. She was fitted with £3,500 Leyland marine diesel engines, and the other ferries afterward were sent in turn to Sharpness, to have similar engines installed. The usual 30-minute service maintained by two boats could now be stepped up when needed to every twenty minutes with the three boats, and the service was then handling 60 cars an hour each way.

Officially the weight-limit per vehicle was 5 tons, but coaches - and on one occasion a double-decker bus - had been handled. Each of the latter three Ferries carried about 15-18 cars. The skippers became skilled at estimating their next load on sight. Percy Palmer told me "We could look over the queue of vehicles on the pier we were approaching, and could say confidently - for example "We can get 16 on this time". But stowing the cars was an art. You had to place them rightly, and you had to be smart in slewing the turntable."

The three latter Ferries were originally licensed for 48 passengers, a number sometimes exceeded. Bill Groves was skipper one day when a Board of Trade Inspector counted 12 passengers in excess, and a fine of £12 was imposed. Later, the matter of passenger capacity was reviewed, and the Ferries were permitted to carry over 90 passengers. Concession Fares of 25% reduction were allowed to CTC and YHA cyclists - 1/9 instead of 2/- for cyclist and bike. A young CTC cyclist argued one day that 25% reduction meant he should be paying 1/6 not 1/9d. Enoch Williams who was standing

Last day of the Aust-Beachley ferry; 8th September 1966. **Severn Princess** *dressed over-all at Beachley Pier, her turntable obscured by the cars lying athwartships.*
Photo: C. Jordan.

nearby corrected the youth: "You're a member of CTC but your bike isn't, so only you get the reduction!" Even so, there were some anomalies. A hearse was charged 7/6 if crossing empty, but 10/6 if carrying a body in a coffin. This appealed to Percy Palmer's sense of humour, who used to quip: "You're worth 1/- to the Ferry if you're alive, but 3/- if you're dead".

Among the more romantic vehicles remembered to have crossed was a colourful horse-drawn gipsy caravan. The exploit of the Daimler which went over the pier at Beachley was emulated by a mini which plunged into the water while leaving the Ferry at Aust. Again, the passengers were safe and the car was quickly secured and later retrieved.

A most important part of the Ferry organisation was the advance circulation of timetables showing the effect of tide on the service. A large number were posted to regular commuters and the Police, RAC, and AA always had copies. Not everyone knew this, and others did not take the precaution of phoning before starting for the pier. Some motorists had long waits. Andy Pickford of Street recalls: "The only time I used the Ferry as a driver was shortly before the Severn Bridge opened. I wanted to get to South Wales early on a Saturday, and the first sailing was at 7.30 a.m. I arrived in what I thought was good time only to see a very long queue. I waited, eventually bought my ticket and boarded the Ferry. The crossing was uneventful, except that I realised that in the time I had waited I could have driven via Gloucester and the cost of the ticket was more than the cost of petrol I would have used! Needless to say, I returned via Gloucester and waited for the bridge to open before I went that way again."

Tide periodically interrupted the service. John Williams, the Undermanager, who still lives near the scene of the Ferry, explained to us "A big spring tide would mean about three hours at low water when the Ferry could not run, because the boats could not reach the pier at either side. On the other hand, at neap tides it was often possible to run continuously". Weather also could interfere with the service, for the Severn can take on a frightening aspect. A Parkinson's butter-scotch delivery van spent lost hours at Aust one wild day when the driver, thinking he had missed a ferry and must be the first in the next queue decided to have a nap at the wheel. On awaking some hours later, everywhere was still deserted and he saw a notice he had missed before: "Ferry suspended for the day".

Not only the passengers, but the crew had their moments. Deckhand John Reeks relieved skipper Ben Brown at the helm one evening, as the **Queen** was moving up the Wye to her mooring at the end of the day. Unfortunately he fouled a reef and the **Queen** suffered a broken A-bracket which put the propeller shaft on that side out of commission. "And" Ben Brown says ruefully today, "of course it had to be Whit-weekend when every boat was needed! On a number of occasions the Ferries acted as lifeboats, and lives were saved which otherwise must certainly have been lost. These rescues included: Skipper Charlie Savage, who once fell overboard; a boatload of boys in danger of overturning; three workers of Howards (concrete workers on the bridge), and a father and son from Huddersfield adrift in a dinghy. On each of these occasions Percy Palmer was the skipper who accomplished the rescue. Distinguished passengers were many. In addition to the Royalty mentioned previously, Percy Palmer recalls the Duke of Beaufort, Lord Roseberry, Amy Johnson, Charlie Coombs, Richard Dimbleby and David Niven.

From its inception of course, the Williams Ferry had operated under the certain threat of a Severn Bridge at some future date. World War II and the economic recession that followed extended the Ferry's lease of life but the writing was always on the wall. Eventually construction of the bridge began and it looked doubtful whether the Ferry could continue to operate at the same time. When Messrs. Howard, the bridge-builders started work on the Welsh shore, the Ferries passed under the line of the bridge, and had to use the upstream side of Beachley pier. This meant depth of water problems, and Howard's had to construct a breakwater to the Beachley lighthouse, and carry out some dredging.

The Severn Bridge was opened by the Queen on Thursday, 8th September 1966, and Enoch Williams was one of the official guests to meet Her Majesty. The last Ferry run was made by the **Severn Princess**, crew and passengers joining hands and singing "Auld Lang Syne". Compensation of £90,000 was paid to the Company, and the three boats were taken to their moorings in the Wye. Although it seemed likely that they would soon find buyers, in fact this did not happen, and Enoch re-assembled the crews (of whom a number were now toll officers on the bridge) to move them to the security of Cardiff East Dock. Negotiations took place with Ferry operators in Cornwall, Ireland, Switzerland, Portugal and Spain without success. At the end of 1967 the boats were taken to Charles Hill's shipyard at Bristol but the intended refitting was found to be more costly than anticipated, and was not carried out.

In April 1968 the **Severn King** was sold as she lay, to British Rail for £3,250, and converted to a crane-ship. In July the following year she was badly damaged when working on the demolition of the Sharpness railway bridge, and was scrapped. Her remains are probably still visible on the Severn bank above the outer basin at Sharpness. In June 1969 the **Severn Queen** and **Severn Princess** were sold to West of Ireland Fisheries Ltd. The **Queen** was re-sold for breaking to Cashmores of Newport, and was de-registered in January 1970. The **Princess** was re-sold in 1975 to Oceanic Services Ltd., Galway, for a salvage tender and may be still in use. At Aust and Beachley the piers, somewhat decayed, can still be seen, but the buildings which housed the ticket offices and cafes are ruinous, having been vandalised. In The Five-Alls Inn, Chepstow, where Mine Host is Former Ferry Skipper Ben Brown, is exhibited the maker's name-plate from the **Severn Queen**.

Enoch Williams lived to the ripe old age of 91, and died in September 1979. Ben Brown penned the following ode to his memory:

FAREWELL TO THE FERRY BOSS

His stature was small, but his heart was big;
He excelled in everything he did:
From architect to the Ferry Boss,
We, and his family, know the loss.
Where he has gone, to a better place,
To his Maker, whom he will face.
There he will find another Severn,
Another Ferry, up there in Heaven.
He was the Father of the Ferrymen:
Goodbye, Enoch! God bless! Amen.

SEVERN, NEW PASSAGE: New Passage may be said to be on the disputed Roman route between Venta Silurum (Caerwent) and Aqua Sulis (Bath): but there is no evidence of the use of this crossing until much later. The likelihood is that it was established early in the seventeenth century in preference to Old Passage, which possibly went out of use for several decades. The New Passage ferry rights were held by the manor of St. Pierre.

During the Civil War, Charles I held council at Crick House near Chepstow in 1645; and his nephew Prince Rupert used the New Passage when travelling from Bristol Castle to meet him. Later that year the King found himself in a desperate position. His army, outnumbered two to one, had been defeated at Naseby, and he was being hunted by his enemies. Raglan Castle, where he had been taking refuge, had fallen, and he needed to cross the Severn. On 24th July the King and his aides, tired and dishevelled, arrived on horseback at the ferry landing at Black Rock, Portskewett. The ferrymen were staunch Royalists and eager to help. Soon after, the King and his men were landed safely on the Gloucester shore: but when the ferry crew returned to Black Rock an unpleasant surprise awaited them. Sixty of Cromwell's red-coated troopers, hot on the King's trail, were demanding passage. In vain the ferryman protested that they were too tired to handle such a load in the prevailing conditions of offshore wind and ebb tide: the Parliamentary captain was not disposed to take 'No' for an answer. He demanded the crossing be made immediately and threatened the crew with cold steel. Fearfully and resentfully the ferry men got their overladen boat under way; but on reaching the English Stones reef they explained they could get the boat no further on a falling tide: the troopers must disembark, but would find solid rock all the way to the Gloucestershire shore. What they did not tell them was that the fast flood tide having already begun, they had no hope of reaching the shore alive. One can picture the irate troopers, slipping, stumbling and cursing on the slimy rocks, and realising that their chance of overtaking the King was now slim indeed. It would not have been long before they were aware of their own desperate plight; but the ferry was then beyond recall and beyond musket shot. All sixty troopers, weighed down by their helmets and breastplates, were swept to their deaths. When the story reached Cromwell's ears, he was enraged, and ordered the ferry to be closed down for good. It did not reopen till 1718, when the St. Pierre family managed to restore the service in spite of a lawsuit brought by the Beauforts, whose Old Passage ferry had been profiting greatly from its 73-year monopoly.

In 1743 Charles Wesley was fortunate to escape shipwreck when crossing at New Passage in wild weather. On Monday, 15th February 1749 his brother, John Wesley, the evangelist, came to New Passage. He recorded in his diary "We came to the New Passage at ten. After waiting about five hours, we found (which they did not care to confess) that the boatmen did not dare to venture out; it blew a storm...." On this occasion he got across the next day via the Old Passage, but on his many visits to Wales and Ireland he seems to have used the New Passage invariably.

In 1825 the Post Office appear to have been pressing for more expeditious and reliable carriage of the mails across the Severn. That year the New Passage operators received a bid from the rival Old Passage Association to buy them out! Thus galvanised into action, they purchased a steamboat, the 30 ton **St. Pierre**, and entered on a period of increased prosperity. Advertised as a "fine and elegant new steam packet" the **St. Pierre** was purpose-built by Pride & Williams of Newport, and boasted a woman bust figurehead. All mails between England and Wales with one exception, now took the New Passage route. From an annual handbook for travellers published from 1771 to 1832 by a Lieut.-Colonel Paterson, we learn that the New Passage ferry tolls at this time were:-

4-wheeled carriage	2/-	Equestrian	1/6
2-wheeled carriage	1/-	Pedestrian	9d.
Each horse	1/-	Cattle, each	6d.

Sheep, pigs, lambs ..... 3/4 per 20

New Passage: The paddle ferry **Christopher Thomas** *lies off Portskewett pier, 1880. To-day her remains are rusting on a West African sandbank. Drawing: Terry Duggan.*

The same publication tells us that a small boat could be hired to take a pedestrian across for 5/- and 9d. for any passengers accompanying the hirer. By 1832 the small boat rates increased to 6/- and 1/- respectively.

From 1827 the **St. Pierre** was in competition with a larger and faster vessel on the Old Passage, to which the mail coaches were gradually being diverted. She was sold to Neath Abbey in 1831 and the New Passage experienced a period of decline for more than 30 years. Its heyday however was yet to come, though not until hopes had three times been raised and dashed.

In 1836 J.M. Rendel, inventor of the floating bridge ferries at Dartmouth and Torpoint, surveyed the New Passage on behalf of the Post Office with a view to installing his system: but he had to report that the Severn Tidal currents were too strong for chain ferries to be used. In 1845 the South Wales Junction Railway endeavoured to establish a rail-link across the Severn: they acquired the ferry rights of both Old and New Passages and permission to lay down rail connections to both crossings on both sides of the river. These dreams remained unfulfilled when the company was wound up in 1853. In 1854 an attempt was made to interest investors in a steam ferry to transport trains, but public support was not forthcoming.

To understand the difficulties confronting the engineers of the day, it is necessary to consider the nature of the river at New Passage. The Severn is here two miles wide, with an extreme tidal range (50 feet at the mouth of the Wye). Moreover the river bed is irregular. From the eastern side there is a considerable distance of very shallow water, which at low tide exposes the English Stones, a reef of hard marl. On the Welsh side is a corresponding rock shelf called Lady Bench, reaching out half a mile to the Gruggy reef. Between the two come the Shoots, a channel 400 yards wide with a maximum depth of 95 feet at spring high tides, and a 10 knot current on the ebb.

In 1857 the Bristol & South Wales Union Railway obtained an Act of Parliament similar to that of 1845, and work commenced on both sides of the river in October 1858. On the Gloucestershire side an 11½ mile branch from South Wales Junction, Bristol, led to a 1,635 ft. long pier at New Passage, built out over the rocks to deep water, on which trains moved out to the steamer pontoon. The pier deck bearing the railway track was carried on 70 rows of massive, creosoted timber piles, which the workmen of Rowland Brotherhood had been hammering into the rock for months past between tides. Buildings at the pierhead comprised an island-platform terminal station, Marine Superintendent's office, passenger shelter and goods store. The Marine Superintendent was Captain Peake, ex-P. & O. liner captain. An employee described him as "A veritable stickler for efficiency and perfection in every detail". After unloading at the pier station, trains ran into a turntable yard for the return trip to Bristol.

At the end of the pier, where the rise and fall of tide could be 46 ft., iron staircases gave access to the steamer pontoon. This was the wooden hulk of a former sea-going sailing ship, reprieved from the shipbreakers to serve in this humble yet necessary capacity. The pier hand in charge of the hulk was a French-Canadian who loved to regale passengers with reminiscences of pioneer life in the Far West, and odd adventures at sea. His comrade for company and guard-duty was a black retriever. Also at the pierhead was a steam-powered lift for handling passengers' luggage, merchandise, and livestock, in which there was considerable traffic.

Immediately north of the pier was erected the New Passage Hotel. It provided luxury accommodation for passengers waiting to make the crossing, but was also intended to establish New Passage village as a resort. Nearby was a small hospital for sea-sick passengers, a three-storey home for the ferryboat's captain, a row of terraced cottages for railway company employees, and a gasworks.

Across the river at Black Rock the railway line ran down to the pier from Portskewett station. The pier here was 708 ft. long, and it was the custom for the trains to back on to it. The hulk pontoon at the pierhead was a former Indian-trade clipper, whose graceful lines invariably drew admiring comments from seafaring passengers. As at New Passage there were freight lifts, both piers having been designed on similar lines by Charles Richardson, the resident engineer. The hotel was named Black Rock after the offshore islet with a lighthouse which guards the approach. As at New Passage, workers' cottages and a gasworks were also provided.

Pending delivery of a purpose-built vessel, three paddle steam ferries had been obtained to work the service, which commenced on 1st January 1864. These were: the **Gem**, an iron six year old ex-Mersey ferry of 100 tons gross; the **Relief**, an iron, two year old 163 ton tug/excursion boat from Liverpool; and the **President**, a 25 year old, 179 ton wooden tug/ferry from South Wales. The **Gem** was rather an ugly duckling - a double ended, mastless vessel, with poor cabin accommodation, but a 'river' certificate for 417 passengers. She worked for only a year at New Passage, and was then sold back to the Mersey ferry, where she was involved in the worst accident on that service, in 1878. Her chequered career came to an end on 21st November 1881, when she was wrecked at Porthlow in the Scilly Isles. The **Relief**, which had a 'river' certificate for 563, came to New Passage 'on approval', but was purchased before the ferry opened, and continued in service until June 1874, when she also returned to the Mersey. The **President**, tall-funnelled and single-masted, was employed as relief vessel, until in 1865 she was sold to Morris of Bristol for breaking up.

The purpose-built ferry steamer ordered for the passage arrived in 1864, and was named **Christopher Thomas** after the chairman of the company. An iron paddler of 159 tons gross, she was very well-appointed in cabin accommodation and catering facilities. In 1868 the B. & S.W.U.R. was taken over by the Great Western Railway, who in 1875 replaced the **Relief** by the **Chepstow**, which was slightly larger than the **Christopher Thomas**, two-funnelled, and had a similar 100 n.h.p. diagonal engine. The late Alfred Whitchurch, former carpenters' mate on the **Christopher Thomas** reminisced about these steamers in an article published by the Times & Mirror press in 1927:- "the whole of the space abaft the engine-room was devoted to 1st and 2nd-class accommodation. On the lower deck was a spacious saloon, and abaft that, a refreshment bar and dining accommodation. Amidships, over the full length of the engine and boilers, was a boat deck with four lifeboats always swung outboard when in service. The forward end of this deck formed the navigating bridge with its conspicuous brass speaking trumpets, forerunners of Chadburn and his engine-room telegraphs. The space under this deck gave abundant shelter for first-class passengers, and was very ornate in its period, bemirrored and upholstered in red plush. The space forward on the main deck with bulwarks three feet in height and stanchions with chains, was devoted to cattle, horses, livestock, and luggage and merchandise in trolleys ready for running straight off into the lift cages. In these pre-Campbell days quite a big business was done in the summer by the P.S. **Chepstow** in trips to Ilfracombe, Swansea, Weston and Clevedon. On Bank Holidays both boats would be kept busy on the Portskewett-New Passage run. On those days both the piers and the boats would be gay with bunting. Each boat would be in commission for four months, and when relieved would proceed to moorings in front of the New Passage Hotel. Annually both boats would dry-dock at Bristol (their port of registry) for Board of Trade survey.

The men who commanded these ferries were held in high regard by the regular travellers and by their own crews. The late Archie Powell, one-time cook/steward on the **Christopher Thomas**, wrote as follows to the Western Daily Press in 1956:- "I retain fond memories of Captain Roberts, master of the **Christopher Thomas**, and his family. Notwithstanding my humble position on the steamer, they made me welcome at their home on Sundays and with them I attended every service at the Methodist Chapel...After supper the family settled down in the good old fashioned way to sing Sankey and Moody's hymns, with one of the daughters at the piano. Captain Aitken, master of the **Chepstow**, reserve ship to the **Christopher Thomas**, is also held in pleasant remembrance. He was a bluff old sea-dog, but I still retain a book on elementary navigation he gave me".

The commencement of the regular ferry service was preceded some four months earlier by an official opening conducted with all the pomp and ceremony considered necessary in those days. The first train from Paddington arrived at Temple Meads at 11 am., its engine, named 'Pyracman', garlanded with flowers and evergreens. All the principal Bristolians and their ladies were waiting to take their seats. The local Volunteers were on parade; the band of the Artillery played stirring music; and the pioneer train steamed out of the station to enthusiastic cheers. Between Lawrence Hill and Stapleton Road a triumphal arch had been erected with the word 'WELCOME'; while at New Passage a huge crowd had assembled to see the opening of this rail and ferry link that would bring South Wales "to our doors", as one of the speakers said at the time. On the pierhead Artillerymen fired two field guns in noisy salute as the **Gem** steamed away with the privileged passengers on the first crossing. Unfortunately the weather did not co-operate with the well-laid plans for a great day. It was wet and stormy throughout, and many of the passengers and most of the spectators got a soaking for their trouble. Even so, the event marked a new era in the crossing of the Severn, and few could have guessed that most who took part that day would live to see the ferries withdrawn and the great piers dismantled. Yet so it was to happen, as within 25 years passenger trains were running through the Severn Tunnel.

The Great Western Railway conduct of the New Passage ferry was described by a passenger of the time as "beyond reproach"; while steamer crewman Alfred Whitchurch later testified: "There was no stint of capital outlay or personnel by the G.W.R. to make the service as efficient and safe as humanly possible." In fact the passage maintained to the end absolute immunity from loss of life to its credit, despite the fact that it was a crossing demanding the fullest measure of seamanship. Here again is Archie Powell, describing life on board the **Christopher Thomas**:- "In the summer the ferry crossing was a pleasant interlude in the rail journey, but in the winter "when the stormy winds did blow" it was not so good! Meals were available during the crossing and it was my job to cook and serve them. On a Monday morning, commercial travellers clamoured for hot coffee. At midday many passengers took the chance of a hot lunch cooked in the steamer's galley, and later in the afternoon lady passengers were glad of a cup of tea handed round by my assistants - one being the son of the village police sergeant, and the other, the son of the pier railway station master.

Interesting personalities crossed in the old **Christopher Thomas** in those long ago years. One day when I was standing at the head of the lunch table ready to carve the joint, a noisy company clattered down the saloon stairway, leading them being a big man with a black beard. It was Dr. W.G.Grace taking the Gloucestershire team to play Wales". Over again to Alfred Whitchurch, describing departure from Portskewett Pier: "When leaving Portskewett on the flood the boat would head into the tide, and striking the full force of the stream, would be swung towards Aust. The stream in a big tide would always overcome the helm on approacing New Passage, and she would always round the Chequer Buoy (or House Buoy) in order to stem the flood to moor".

The establishment of the ferry service created lively village communities at New Passage and Black Rock: and since virtually everyone was an employee of the railway company, comradeship developed and social life flourished. Among New Passage personalities were the Norris family. Old John kept the village store and was a stalwart member of the Methodist Chapel. His son, Charles controlled the salmon fishing and lived in a house opposite the hotel. While Oliver, Charles' brother, (known as 'Look-ee Norris' because he constantly said 'Look-ee' in conversation), was a popular figure involved with most local activities - farming, the hotel, and later a contractor working on the Severn Tunnel. This began in 1873, and the navvies employed on the work would crowd into the New Passage Hotel on Saturday evenings and have uproarious and impromptu sing-songs. At Portskewett there was a cricket club strong enough to play Cardiff or Newport, and near the pier were cricket nets - often used by cricketing members of the steamer crews if their ferry was alongside for a few hours. Sometimes on a Sunday the ferry crews were required to lower the ships' lifeboats and carry out a rowing exercise. On these occasions a shotgun was usually concealed in the equipment, as there were plenty of rabbits up Chepstow way!

During the night of 23rd May 1881 fire broke out at the seaward end of the Portskewett Pier. The alert nightwatchman at New Passage aroused some members of the crew of the **Christopher Thomas** and rowed them out to her. Fortunately she had steam and was quickly across the river where she pumped water on to the burning pierhead and pontoon. The freight lift was destroyed and the pierhead too badly damaged for the ferries to berth. The following day the **Christopher Thomas** took rail passengers direct to Chepstow, but this does not seem to have been a satisfactory alternative, and traffic ceased till 16th June, by which date repairs to the pier had been completed. Possibly despite the repairs it was felt that the pier had been weakened by the fire; at any rate it appears that the trains did not use the pier track after the fire, and a temporary platform was constructed by the hotel at the shore end.

Although the railway ferry had shortened passengers' journeys between Bristol and Cardiff from 94 miles via Gloucester to 38, there were no heavy-freight facilities, and G.W.R. coal trains still had to make the time-consuming detour. Thus it was that the Company adopted the recommendation of the engineer Charles Richardson to construct the Severn Tunnel. Work began in 1873 and after many vicissitudes was completed in 1886. On 1st December that year the first passenger trains ran through and the **Christopher Thomas** made the final ferry crossing. She and the **Chepstow** were retained awhile for excursion work but eventually were sold to W.S. Ogden, a Cardiff timber merchant, in 1890. Ogden had them re-engined and converted to twin-screw propulsion. The **Chepstow** renamed **Rover**, was sold to another Cardiff owner in 1895 but was wrecked four years later at Youghal, Ireland. Meanwhile the **Christopher Thomas** had driven ashore in a gale on the north Irish coast in 1894 and suffered considerable damage. However, she was salved, repaired, and sold to the African Association of Liverpool who sent her 4,000 miles to Nigeria - a considerable voyage for a Severn Ferry! Here she traded on the rivers until about 1902 when, 38 years old, she was bought by a trading firm to be sunk as a breakwater at their factory on the banks of the River Opobo. On the way she parted her tow in a gale and went ashore on a mudbank. Her rusting remains are still there today.

The piers at New Passage and Black Rock were dismantled, and the pontoon hulks broken up on New Passage beach. At Portskewett the branch line to the pier was retained as a siding for many years, and in World War II the Royal Train rested here overnight when the late King George VI and Queen Elizabeth were visiting the bombed cities of South Wales. The siding was similarly used again for our present Queen when Princess Elizabeth, and for Mr. Winston Churchill on one of his visits. Today the track has long been lifted, and the road bridge which crossed it now spans a wildly-overgrown dell. Black Rock Hotel survived as a private house until eventually destroyed by fire. One house remains, in use as a farm; also the stone shoreward end of the railway pier, much dilapidated.

At New Passage the hotel, though sold off, remained in business, and enjoyed a new heyday in the 1950s and 60s, when landlady Mollie Bracey and her elderly husband Wilf were mine hosts. In their days 500 people would crowd the ballroom in the evenings, dancing the night away. In 1973 the Braceys sold the hotel for £69,000 to Galmanian, a Bristol property-development company The new owners planned to convert the hotel into 18 luxury flats, but they encountered many frustrations and planning delays, while thieves, vandals, and the weather made the building derelict. It has now been pulled down, and the site is marked only by rubble. New houses are appearing beside the grassy embankment which once carried the railway branch to the pier. As at Black Rock, the stone end of the pier can still be seen: for long it has acted as a windbreak for sunbathers and picnickers, and a storm shield for property. In 1965 the stonework was disintegrating, and the Council requested the private owner to repair or demolish it. On our visit in 1980 we found it not only restored, but paved and railed, which has not enhanced its archaeological interest. One building alone survives from the ferry days - the hospital for seasick passengers: identifiable by its wide balconies and wrought iron supports, it is in use as a private house. In 1953 an elderly pensioner who had grown up at New Passage in the days of the ferry reminisced in a letter: "as a boy I used to go to the pierhead and watch the ferry steamers come and go. I saw the first passenger train enter the Severn Tunnel, also, and I remember what a dead place New Passage became after the ferry was closed".

Thus the railway, which had given to the New Passage its greatest hour, had also brought about its abandonment and demise.

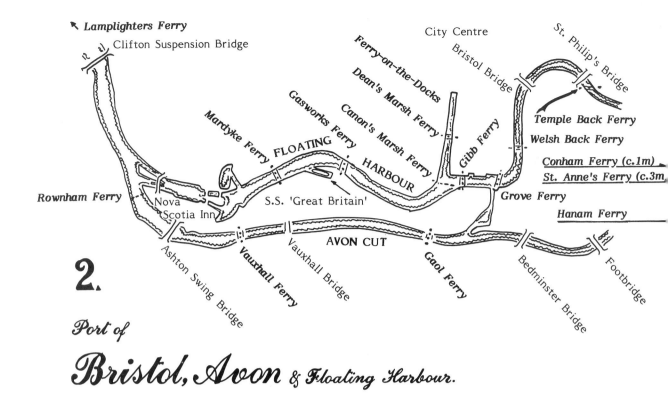

Lamplighters Ferry
Clifton Suspension Bridge
Rownham Ferry
Nova Scotia Inn
Mardyke Ferry
Gasworks Ferry
FLOATING
Canon's Marsh Ferry
Dean's Marsh Ferry
Ferry-on-the-Docks
City Centre
Bristol Bridge
St. Philip's Bridge
Temple Back Ferry
Welsh Back Ferry
Conham Ferry (c.1m)
St. Anne's Ferry (c.3m)
Gibb Ferry
HARBOUR
S.S. 'Great Britain'
Grove Ferry
Hanam Ferry
AVON CUT
Ashton Swing Bridge
Vauxhall Ferry
Vauxhall Bridge
Gaol Ferry
Bedminster Bridge
Footbridge

2.

Port of

Bristol, Avon & Floating Harbour.

THE LAMPLIGHTERS FERRY: The ferry between Pill and Shirehampton has a long history. The monopoly was anciently owned by the squire of Easton-in-Gordano, and in the early seventeenth century there was a clash of rights between this worthy and the city of Bristol over the ferry passage. Bristol merchants maintained mooring posts along the bank, and it seems that in 1604 Thomas Morgan, the squire and proprietor of the ferry, was prosecuted for moving some of the posts and 'interfering with the navigation of the Avon'. He was found guilty and imprisoned; but the lords of the manor remained defiant. In 1634 Richard Morgan was prosecuted for building houses so close to the river that the towpath (probably maintained by Bristol merchants) was encroached on and had collapsed. This time the squire was ordered to pull down all the houses - except one for use as the ferry house.

A map which is still in existence bears a record that King William III used Pill ferry on 6th September, 1690. The occasion was the King's return from the Battle of the Boyne and the siege of Limerick. The story, perhaps apocryphal, goes that in the 1850s a doctor who was a general practitioner in Shirehampton, crossed by the ferry regularly with his horse, to drink in the 'Duke of Cornwall' at Pill. Here he became enchanted with the innkeeper's daughter, seduced her and eloped with her. In keeping with Victorian melodrama it is said that he later deserted his young bride, and she came home in her shame and heartbreak to die. Later the brash and heartless doctor also returned, as ever on his horse, to see his wife's grave. Perhaps he was filled with remorse, as he stepped out of the ferry and remounted. But if so, his horse was not impressed; he threw his master heavily on to the cobbles outside the 'Duke of Cornwall', and he did not rise again.

This ferry became known as 'The Lamplighters' in the eighteenth century. This was on account of the inn of that name on the Shirehampton side, which had been built from the profits made by a contractor who provided oil lamps for Bristol streets. During the Regency days this hostelry enjoyed a vogue as a fashionable weekend resort - according to J. Latimer in his 'Annals of Bristol in the nineteenth century'.

From early times and until the end of World War II there was a horseboat, described by one writer as "distinctly reminiscent of the ark"; it had a covered shed amidships. The last horseboat lay derelict on the Shirehampton bank up to 1956 and perhaps later, but had probably not been used since the war. Like most Avon and Somerset rivers, the Bristol Avon had a great rise and fall of tide, and is troubled by heavy deposits of mud on the slips. Local youngsters could earn a little money brooming the slips clean. Frank Stennor of Bristol wrote to the Evening Post on 18th February 1982: "Like other lads I was paid to keep the slip clear of mud. When the pilots on board the vessels coming up the river sounded their sirens to advise their relatives they would be home, we lads would chase off to advise".

During the Great War and the years immediately following, the ferryman was Walter Rice, the father of James Rice who was to be tragically drowned in 1952. For many years the ferry was the property of the Porter family of Pill, the last member of the family to operate it being the late Captain R.J. Porter, senior surveyor to the Board of Trade at Bristol, who lived in the old Watch House and so was able to keep a weather eye on his investment.

Came World War II, and in 1939 the Pill Ferry was requisitioned by the Ministry of Transport, and operated by the Port of Bristol Authority till 1946. In that year it was returned to its owners, the Porter family, who however were not disposed to resume operating, and it thus came on to the market. In December that year the rights and the boats were acquired by C.J. King and Sons Ltd., the tug owners and stevedores, who took over the running on 21st December and advertised the lease. The tenancy was taken up by James Rice, a B.A.C. policeman, and his wife. 1st January

1953 had been planned as the takeover date, but because Kings were having difficulty manning

the boats, Rice agreed to run the ferry as from 1st December 1952. It was then that tragedy struck.
Two days later he tried to jump into a ferryboat which had gone adrift, to secure it; missed his
footing, was pulled under in the icy tide, and drowned. Mrs. Rice was left a widow with seven
children - and a ferry. For many weeks she lost the will to live, while her two year old son nearly
died, pining for his father. But Mrs. Rice triumphed bravely over her sorrows and determined to
make a success of the ferry to enable her to provide for her young family.

King and Sons had provided an additional boat, retained some of Porter's boatmen, and were
considering erecting a passenger shelter. The ferry prospered and by 1957 there were three motorboats in use - the **Nova**, the **Pillshire** and the **Nexas**. (**Nova** was Avon spelt backwards, **Pillshire**
commemorated the two landing points; the origin of **Nexas** we have failed to discover). At five
o'clock one day in 1958 Mrs. Rice gave an interview to an Evening Post reporter in the little paybox
at the top of Shirehampton slip.... "Coppers rattled across the counter as the fourpences - for a
single trip - came rolling in." "It's not as busy as this all the day", Mrs. Rice pointed out "and you
need a lot of fourpences to meet the overheads". In fact at the time the ferry was costing nearly
£100 a week to run. Wages were almost £60 and then there were rent, rates, a heavy insurance,
lighting and heating. The principal ferrymen at this time were Royston Rice (one of Mrs. Rice's
sons), Albert Sharp (eventually served over 20 years), and his son Bert. The hours were 5 am. to
10.40 pm. (!) and the men worked in three shifts.

There were moments of comedy and drama alike. One intending passenger who had imbibed too
much strong liquor argued about the fare, then announced he would swim for it. Divesting himself
of most of his clothes (into the ferry!) he dived in and struck out strongly. The ferry followed
anxiously in his wake, like a "parent" boat with a Channel swimmer, and a great cheer greeted
his safe arrival on the other side. Here he crawled out through the cloying mud and without drying
himself, dressed again in his clothes and announced triumphantly to all and sundry "I saved the
fare!".

But there was one dramatic day when a man who had been working on top of the Avonmouth
oil tanks was brought home by ferry after the disastrous fire there. By some miracle this man had
been blown off the tank and still lived; and he came back over the ferry with clothes in burnt
shreds, to the silent crowd of waiting women who did not know the fate of their own husbands in
the same holocaust. The ferry, too, was very much a part of the district's social life. In 1962 the
Pill Rag Queen came down the River Avon by the ferry and stepped daintily ashore in crown and red
robe, accompanied by her attendant maids and some noisy revellers swigging beer from the bottle.

In 1966 the ferry was seriously threatened with closure when the Company announced in January
that the service was to be suspended. This was due to an impending High Court action brought
by the local boatmen, who claimed an 800 year old right to use the slipway which the ferry company
denied. The Company wished to restrict access to the ferry slipway and charge a toll for the use
of it. A meeting of the Pill parish council, attended by a representative of the County legal department, and the solicitors of the parties at variance, was convened by the parish council chairman,
Bertram Short, at Bristol.

As a result of this meeting the ferry, due to have shut down on the 17th January continued
to operate, and the appalling inconvenience of a 10 mile detour to the hundreds who used the ferry
daily to get to work, was averted. A director of the ferry company, Mr. Bill Hunt, stated: "the
Company will now be able to close off the slipway and use the turnstiles which have been going
rusty since they were put up two years ago at a cost of £500. We shall now have proper control and
this will enable us to run the service properly". A Pill man who worked at Avonmouth said: "Thank
goodness the ferry is still running. It would have cost me eight shillings each day by bus, and three
hours travelling time". While Mrs. Florence Sharp, as she collected the tolls in her pay box, agreed
"Everyone is very pleased". The Sharps had taken over the tenancy from the Rice family, and Albert
('Oggy') Sharp eventually served more than twenty years on the ferry.

In 1968 King and Sons sold the ferry rights to the landlord of the Star Inn at Pill, Bob Brown,
but the tenancy remained with the Sharp family. In 1970 one of the ferry launches was made available to the Royal National Lifeboat Institution as a rescue craft, until a R.N.L.I. boat could be
supplied for Pill. By 1972 the completion of the M5 Avon Bridge was clearly imminent, and the
future of the ferry was doubtful. With traffic lanes, cycle track and pedestrian way, the bridge was
only a few minutes' walk from the ferry slip, and clearly was going to be a formidable rival. Assisting Albert Sharp at this time were ferrymen Barry Jackman, Tim Parsons and P. Rugman; and
the hours were then 5.30 am. to 10.30 pm. "Oggy" and his men maintained the service for another
two years, and preserved to the end the Pill ferry's accident-free record within living memory. The
Avon motorway bridge opened in the autumn of 1974, and the last Lamplighters' ferry ran at 8.30 pm
on 31st October that year. The ferry rights, though no longer exercised, were acquired by the
Portishead Cruising Club.

ROWNHAM FERRY: Of all Bristol's ferries, Rownham had the longest recorded history. It replaced,
and at one time supplemented, a ford across the Avon used in Roman times. This ford was from
the foot of the slope below Clifton Camp (now Observatory Hill) to a spot close to the mouth of
Nightingale Valley. It appears that the Romans at least partially paved the riverbed at this point to
give them a surer footing. It is not possible to say when the ferry superseded the ford, but we
know that it crossed at the same point until difficulties of access on both sides of the river brought
about its removal upstream toward the eventual site of the Cumberland Basin.

As long ago as 1148 the passage belonged to the Abbot of St. Augustine, and was a means of
approach to his residence at Leigh. For years the abbots of Bristol used to ride to the crossing
and be ferried, man and horse, across the river. Later the ferry became the property of the Abbot's
successors, the Dean and Chapter of Bristol Cathedral. It was always a rather hazardous crossing, and
over the years a number of tragedies occurred. It was here, in 1610, that John Snigge, eldest son of
Sir John Snigge, was carried away by the strong tide and drowned. Yet he was on horseback, and had
been trying to negotiate the ford while on his way to Sir Hugh Smyth's at Ashton.

The Ecclesiastical Commissioners became the new lords of the manor of Blackswarth in 1835, and thus acquired the ferry from the Dean and Chapter. Until 1864 when the Clifton Suspension Bridge was built, and before there was any bridge at Hotwells, Rownham Ferry provided a very important service, for there was no nearer crossing than that at Bristol Bridge. When Hotwells was almost a rival to Bath by reason of its fashionable visitors, the ferry was much used for picnics and excursions to Leigh Woods. There is a William Randall photograph in the Avon County Reference Library which shows the ferry scene in Victorian times. Young women are having to cope with stiff unyielding outdoor wear and straw boaters held in place by hatpins. Almost as encumbered are the men, wearing stiff, high collars and bowler hats. Little boys, on a weekend excursion over the ferry, are wearing knickerbocker suits, long stockings, lace-up boots and Eton collars.

In 1865 or 66 (records vary) the Commissioners sold out to the Bristol City Corporation for £10,000 - a good deal for the Commissioners, it would seem, seeing that the ferry had been working at a loss for some time previously. The Corporation moved the ferry crossing 100 yards downstream, and advertised the lease. Their first tenant was Bristolian George Wort, and in fact the ferry was to remain with his family for the rest of its existence. Apart from a brief spell when the Dockmaster was in charge, George Wort ran the ferry from March 1867 till his death eleven years later. His son John Wort succeeded him as lessee and carried on the ferry for 48 years till he died in 1926. He in turn was succeeded by his brother-in-law, W.C. Woodward, who ran this ferry - and others - until closure in 1933. Considering that it was always recognised as a rather dangerous crossing to work, it is much to the credit of the Wort family that only two fatalities occurred during their regime.

At the turn of the century the New Inn at Rownham was widely known, and so were the tea gardens. A popular jaunt for Bristolians on a Saturday afternoon was over the Suspension Bridge to Leigh Woods, then a stroll down Nightingale Valley to the riverside, and then on to the tea gardens. The Rownham Ferry was also very popular with railway passengers to and from Portishead using Clifton Bridge Station. Retired boatman Bert Roach, who used to keep the ferry slip clear of mud, recalls: "Rownham was a chain-ferry utilising current and tiller. At the top of the tide the boat was disconnected from the chain and rowed across. At low water passage was via three gangways over two ferryboats - both aground".

A former passenger, reminiscing in the local press after the closure of the ferry wrote: "I have many times had breakfast at Adelaide Terrace at Portishead, finished my meal at 8.50 am., caught the 8.55 am. from Possett to Clifton Bridge Station, then over the Rownham ferry to the Rose of Denmark. Here a tram was usually soon caught and the journey into the city completed inside forty minutes. Passengers usually preferred getting out at Clifton Bridge (to catch the ferry) even if they had booked to Temple Meads. The reason for this was that if they went on they were usually held up for some minutes for tickets to be collected at Bedminster Station, and very often later held up again by trains waiting in front for Temple Meads".

During John Wort's managership, in 1873, the ferry was moved back to its former site owing to alterations to the Cumberland Basin entrance. In the course of time, the opening of the Ashton Swing Bridge in 1906 and the increasing bus services, gradually devalued the ferry's usefulness and viability. A much-reproduced picture (of which the original is in the Bristol Art Gallery) portrays the Rownham Ferry scene in the 1890s, looking towards the south bank and the New Inn. On Christmas Eve 1932 the Evening Post gave notice of the closure within seven days of both the Rownham and Canon's Marsh ferries, but according to some reports Rownham Ferry finally closed after New Years Day 1933. Three of the ferrymen working Rownham in the last days were named Morgan, Smith and Wright.

At low water, the remnants of the roadway at Rownham ferry can still be seen, leading down into the river above Brunel's lock.

VAUXHALL FERRY: The Vauxhall Ferry, so called after the works of that name, was opened by E.F. Fox in 1862, by permission of the Bristol Corporation. It crossed the Avon Cut between Cumberland Road and Corporation Road, and was slightly downstream of the site of the footbridge which eventually replaced it.

Charles Lamoon, writing to the Bristol Weekend in December 1961 reminisced: "I used to go from Hotwells via Avon Crescent and Cumberland Road, over Vauxhall Ferry to St. John's Lane to see South End and Bristol City". No doubt football supporters helped to keep the ferry in business at weekends but in the working week a good proportion of the passengers were employees of the nearby John Payne's Shipyard.

This ferry did not remain in private ownership, being eventually acquired by the Corporation and run under the Docks Committee. They closed it down in 1900 when the Ashton Swing Bridge was opened. It would seem that the closure was premature, as not long after, the 270 ft. Greenway Bush Lane footbridge was erected near the ferry crossing. The now disused ferry path and slip are still discernible on the south side.

The bed of the river at the point of this erstwhile ferry, being opposite the Underfall Sluices where the New Cut commences, is an absolute gold mine for beachcombers. This is because anything thrown or dropped into the floating harbour is eventually dredged and deposited through the sluices.

GAOL FERRY: Across the Avon 'cut' between Cumberland Road and Coronation Road, is today a footbridge which in 1935 replaced the old Gaol Ferry. This crossing was established by John Acraman in 1828 and remained the property of his family for many years. Although sometimes known as the Southville ferry, the popular name was due to the fact that the ferry plied from right outside the Bristol gaol, of which only the imposing gateway is standing today. The remains were sold prior to the war to the Great Western Railway, and the stones that made the gaol were widely distributed for various uses. Up to a few years ago there were elderly Bristolians who claimed to remember the last execution there. I think this is doubtful, but they would certainly recall handcuffed passengers in the ferry with their police escort!

For the Acraman family the ferry proved a money-spinner. It brought Southville people near to the heart of the city, and was well patronised to the last. More than a million passengers were carried between 1828 and 1854. In that year the ferry was acquired from representatives of John Acraman's widow for £200. For the ferrymen it was hard graft for a low wage, and one regular passenger on the ferry has since said "I remember many a tempestuous crossing with half a gale blowing". On one occasion he was wearing a new bowler hat, which was swept off his head into the Avon. The compassionate ferryman lent him his own furry chapeau with huge ear flaps - it was long before the days of the hatless brigade. Thus attired, he made his way to a menswear shop in Redcliffe Street to buy a new bowler. The shop assistant, endeavouring to be sociable, said "I expect you don't think much of our winter, sir, after what you've been used to in Canada".

On the ebb tide the ferryboat was manipulated by a wire in the bows attached to a chain anchored to the river-bed. At night the ferry closed at 11 pm: so did the public houses, and many a thirsty soul had to decide whether he would have a 'last one' or catch the ferry. If he missed the last ferry it meant a walk round via Bedminster Bridge and he probably came to the conclusion that the last drink wasn't worth the trouble.

In later years owing to changes in the river bed there was insufficient water to enable the ferry to work for a considerable period each day. It was estimated that during the time the ferry could not be used, six thousand workers had to travel many extra miles to work. In 1935 immediately after Whitsun, the erection of a long-proposed footbridge began. It was in use two months later and had cost £2,600. Now the river could be crossed at any time without delay and without charge. Romance had given place to convenience and yet another of Bristol's city ferries had passed into history. The last ferryman at Gaol Ferry was Bert Roach, and he conveyed the final boatload on 10th October 1935. Making a nostalgic crossing on that last trip was "Old George", former Gaol ferryman for 42 years, a record service there surpassed only by Dick Thomas (50 years) who died in 1954 aged 84.

MARDYKE FERRY: The Mardyke Ferry was named after the district it served, and not after a local public house, as has been supposed by many. It was certainly in existence as early as 1854, and was the westernmost ferry of Bristol's floating harbour, plying between Hotwells Road and the timber yards. In the late nineteenth century it was reported 'very little used' but it was later well patronised, and indeed was the last of the Bristol city ferries to survive, until 1967.

By the turn of the century it was a commuter-route for white-collar workers and artisans alike. Bristolian Charles Lamoon wrote to the local press in 1961 "When I started in an office at Prince's Wharf Granary, in 1894, I used the Mardyke Ferry four times a day"; while the manual workers were mostly from the shipyards, the Bedminster tobacco factory, and the timber yards on the quay. The ferry was run by the Docks Committee of the Port of Bristol Authority, who issued special workers' two trips-a-day or four trips-a-day weekly tickets.

By the 1960s the position was less cheerful. Although there were 300 users a day the ferry was making an annual loss of £900. The toll was raised from 2d. to 3d., but this timid move was insufficient to give viability, and the Docks Committee decided to close the ferry down after 30th June, 1962. Tobacco worker Irene Glass organised a petition to go to the city council, and the 'Evening Post' conducted an on-the-spot opinion poll among ferry-users. This poll showed that ten in twelve regular passengers were quite willing for the fares to be doubled, and some preferred a still higher increase rather than lose the ferry. Petition-organiser Irene Glass said: "Closure would mean hardship for a lot of people.... It is a very long walk round without the ferry working. Bus fares are always going up". Reginald Gould of Clifton explained "The snag with the bus is that if the Ashton swing bridge closes it can put workers twenty minutes late". Jim Archer of Knowle declared: "Sixpence a trip would be well worth it".

Ferryman Bert Derrick, who had been on the crossing since 1946, dreaded the impending closure as much as anyone. "I know most of my regulars by name, and could tell you where they all work. The ferry has been my life, and I just don't know what I shall do now. When I first became ferryman we used to row the people across, and it was three years before we got a motor boat".

At a meeting of the Docks Committee on 19th June, a bid to take over the ferry was accepted from Harold Hoskins, partner in an Avon pleasure-boat firm; who with Alan Hoskins, his son, took over the service on 22nd June on a three-month trial basis. Fares were increased by a penny and the ferry entered on a new lease of life.

This was the only one of Bristol's old ferries to be motorised, the first motor ferry being put into service in 1949. Two of the boats used on the service during the years following were named **Brandon** and **Vauxhall**, but information about them is lacking. It is believed that Bert Green was the last Mardyke ferryman when the service closed in 1967, and the ferryboat **Vauxhall** was acquired by the Docks Committee. In 1980 she was being re-engined at Underfall Yard as a Docks workboat.

GAS WORKS FERRY: This ferry which ran for about a hundred years between the oil gas works, Canons Marsh, and the Albion Dockyard, Wapping, had interesting origins. It was opened about the time of Queen Victoria's accession to convey workers to the shipyard where Brunel's **Great Western**, the first trans-Atlantic liner, was being built. This 1,340 ton wooden paddle steamer was the pride of Bristol at the time, and one can imagine that on the day of her launch the ferry must have been worked to the limit of capacity. And how full of expectation and conjecture must the conversation on the ferry have been that morning in 1838 when the **Great Western** was to begin her first crossing of the Atlantic! Finding herself engaged in an unofficial race with the smaller steamer **Sirius** which had left five days earlier, Brunel's vessel averaged 8.2 knots on the crossing to reach New York the same day, and may be considered the first winner of the 'Blue Riband'. It was a great achievement, and the daily passengers of the Gasworks Ferry were fully conscious of their share in it.

Five years later the ferry was carrying more rivetters and blacksmiths than shipwrights, for Brunel's second great steamship was under construction and she had an iron hull. This was the **Great Britain**, of 3,618 tons. The shipyard workers were now truly making history, for this was the first sea-going iron vessel, the first ocean-going screw steamer, and the first ship to have a double bottom and transverse watertight bulkheads. Today she is back in the dock where she was built, and is being lovingly restored to something of her former glory.

J. Williams, Esq., the owner of Gasworks Ferry, sold the rights to Bristol Corporation in 1903. A sketch by S. Loxton in 1905 shows a beamy, end-loading ferryboat, with a felt-hatted ferryman rowing three passengers across. The service was not withdrawn until 1936 - the longest surviving Bristol ferry apart from the Mardyke. Today its landing-places on either side are served by the new motor ferry when occasion demands.

We visited the scene in August 1980. Sitting by a window in the "Great Britain" tea-room we looked across to the derelict gas works building and the ferry steps. Suddenly the figure of a youth appeared furtively from the ruins and began to climb to the roof of the adjoining quayside shed. Looking anxiously around him, he began to pick his way gingerly across the tin roof, and disappeared at the far end. A few minutes later a police car screamed to a halt at the ferry steps, the crew jumping out and searching the gas works ruins. We did not see the outcome, but the thought persisted that had the ferry still been plying, the miscreant's movements would have been more easily observed and the police more easily directed. Every ferry lost has been the loss of another vantage-point of society.

CANON'S MARSH FERRY: Compared with some of Bristol's older ferries, Canon's Marsh was a mere baby. It was instituted by the Docks Committee in 1906, and controlled by them throughout its life of 26 years. Working between Canon's Road and Princes Wharf, it became popularly known as "Long Reach". Today the ferry steps on both sides are still maintained as public landings, and are served when requested by the present-day Ferry on the Docks. In the past, dockers and office-workers found it a convenient short cut from Prince Street to Canon's Marsh.

Just prior to the Great War the rights of this ferry and Dean's Marsh were let to John Wort for £25 per annum. John Wort died in the nineteen-twenties, and a Mr. Woodward took over. Woodward's manager was Walter Close, a Baltonsborough man of many parts. He was an accomplished gardener, trained in Lord Portman's gardens and greenhouses: he was also a Great War mariner, having served aboard H.M.S. **New Zealand** at the Battle of Jutland. After a while in charge of Canon's Marsh he was appointed manager of all the Dock authority's ferries.

Canon's Marsh ferries were governed by the port regulations and unless more passengers were waiting to embark, were required to leave when two passengers had boarded. Ferrymen were not permitted to pick up passengers en route from ships or other quay steps, unless they had the consent of their fares.

The decline of the city docks hastened the end of Canon's Marsh ferry which the Corporation closed in 1932.

DEAN'S MARSH FERRY: This passage, often known to Bristolians as 'Short Reach', ran between Narrow Quay and Dean's Marsh, making a handy crossing over the harbour near the city centre. It was one of the later Bristol ferries, having been established by the Corporation's Docks Committee in 1906 and was among the last to survive, being finally closed by 1960. The ferry steps on either side are still maintained as public landings, and signposted accordingly.

In common with Canon's Marsh it was much used by dock workers and from about 1913 to 1922 was let by the Corporation to John Wort. The bye-law that decreed that ferrymen need not proceed with only one passenger unless such passenger paid double, did not apply at Dean's Marsh, where the trip across the Frome was a short one.

At one time there were ferries upstream of Dean's Marsh. The city docks once extended into St. Augustine's Parade and Colston Avenue, this land being filled in and reclaimed during the present century. Until the building of St. Augustine's Bridge, a ferry plied from The Butts to Broad Quay, where the Neptune statue stands today. And it is certain that until the mid-thirteenth century a ferry preceded the earliest bridge between St. Nicholas Gate and St. Thomas, close to where Bristol Bridge (original built 1248) stands today.

The 1896 harbour regulations required the boats at Dean's Marsh to be painted conspicuously with their number and the owner's surname. Not more than eight boats were allowed to ply simultaneously from a slip, and turns were to be taken strictly in order of arrival. No one less than 16 years of age was allowed in charge of a ferryboat.

There is a photograph of this ferry in Reece-Winston's "Bristol as it was 1939-1944", showing the ferryman rowing standing, and carrying three passengers, dated 21 March 1934.

GIBB FERRY: One of Bristol's most ancient ferries plied between Prince Street and Princess Wharf and was known latterly as Gibb or Gibbs Ferry. Originally known as Gybb Tailleur, and mentioned as early as 1247, it was one of three ferries owned by Bristol Abbey and it worked near the site of the present Prince Street bridge. From Bristol Abbey the ownership passed in the sixteenth century to the Dean and Chapter.

Shipyard workers were among the most regular users. At the Gibb, the Royal Naval frigate H.M.S. **St. Patrick** (52 guns) was launched in 1666 - the year of the Great Fire of London. Early in the nineteenth century the Floating Harbour was formed and the Avon Cut completed. The Dock Company then built a wooden bridge at the site of the passage, the Church authorities retaining the tolls from foot passengers, while the Company took those derived from vehicular traffic. This was Prince Street Bridge, erected in 1809, and the ferry closed that year.

Subsequently the Great Western Railway acquired the pedestrian tolls, but were bought in 1878 by the Corporation. A swing bridge was erected by the City in place of the wooden structure, and it was opened, free of toll, on 27th January, 1879. It will no doubt have a number of successors before the Gibb Ferry's six hundred years of service are equalled.

GROVE FERRY: Probably the oldest of Bristol's city ferries, the Grove ferry plied between Guinea Street (in Redcliffe), and the Grove, by the Coach and Horses. Like Rownham, it belonged to the Dean and Chapter, until they sold the rights in 1869 to Messrs. R.J. Poole King and W.T.Poole King. Thirty years later their successor Mervyn K. King sold out to Bristol Corporation, who ran the ferry under the Estates Committee from 1901 to 1931. From the mid-nineteenth century until closure the ferry was worked by successive generations of the George family. Grandfather William George was tenant of the Dean and Chapter, his son James George (Snr.) worked for the King family, while Jim George (Jnr.) was the last ferryman on the run.

But the Grove Ferry's chief claim to fame was its boat, which (on one side only) had a hand cranked paddle wheel. A steering oar was used on the other side. There has never been a manually worked paddle ferry elsewhere in the West country and possibly nowhere in Britain. This boat had an extraordinary record, when the ferry closed down in 1931, of having been in continual use (refitting excepted) for 76 years. Many passengers were pleased to work the handle while the ferry-man used his scull for steering. Arthur Baker and Harry Below were among well-known Bristolians who were always willing to 'work their passage' in an honorary capacity. In the 1870s there was a boy who spent many a $\frac{1}{2}$ d. travelling to and fro for the sheer pleasure of operating the paddle!

An incident from the 1920s is perhaps worth re-cording. A well-known Bristol businessman made a journey several times a week from his office in Queen Square to Victoria Street. Most often he walked - always with his dog - via Bristol Bridge, but on this occasion he decided to use the Grove Ferry and Mitchell Lane. The dog however had his doubts about the boat, and was still undecided when the ferry left the slip. "Come on, old chap" called his master, and the dog made a jump for the boat, but landed in the water. After swimming behind for a couple of yards the dog returned to shore. His master hurried on to his appointment and was astonished, on arrival, to find his dog sitting on the doorstep. He remember-ed where the 'boss' was going, and got there first.

The private car, the telephone, and the taxi between them destroyed the custom of Grove Ferry. In 1926, Ferryman James George told a 'Western Daily Press' reporter "I can recall the time when business was so good that I could afford to pay a rental of £3 for the ferry: now I got as much as I can do to pay 4 bob and the rates". The ferry ran for the last time in 1931, but it is a misfor-tune that the unique ferryboat was not preserved.

WELSH BACK FERRY: Welsh Back ferry plied to Redcliffe Back, but long predated the floating harbour. An entry in a local chronology tells us that a slip was constructed for this ferry in 1717. It began life as a private concern and Bristol records refer to it again in 1794. Before 1854 it had become the property of Bristol Corporation and was run by the Docks Committee.

The ferry bye-laws, revised in 1896, set the limits of working at 5 am. to 11 pm. in summer and 6 am. - 8 pm. in winter. They prohibited the use of sail(s), and laid down that refusal to convey a passenger, delay, abusive language, drunkenness, insolence to the dockmaster, or refusal to give details of self and boat to a passenger on request, were all punishable offences for the ferryman. A book recording the bye-laws and the scale of fares had to be kept in a tin in the boat, available for inspection.

During the years between the wars traffic on the Welsh Back ferry declined considerably, and closure came in 1930, after a life of over two hundred years.

TEMPLE FERRY: The ferry at Temple Back, once called the Bathavon Ferry, was one of Bristol's mediaeval passages which closed down in Victorian times. It derived its name from its original owners, the Knights Templar, a religious order of knights, founded in 1118 to protect Christians who were on pilgrimage to Jerusalem. About 1140 Robert, Earl of Gloucester, Lord of the manor of Bedminster, gave a piece of land, afterwards called Temple Fee, to the Knights Templar at Bristol. The ferry which they established gave access to the great water-gate of Bristol Castle. An effigy in stone of St. Christopher, patron saint of travellers, once crowned the shaft of one of the Templars' wayside crosses near here, until demolished by bombing in 1940. The gutted Temple Church alone stands to remind us of the Knights Templar and their days. The order was suppressed at the end of the thirteenth century, and their properties in Bristol were handed over to the Order of St. John of Jerusalem, the Knights Hospitaler. The ferry rights passed to them until the mid-eighteenth century, when the picture becomes unclear.

It is possible that the ferry then lapsed, until a boatman set up a ferry unauthorised by the Corporation, who put a stop to his enterprise - and started a ferry of their own. At all events, Temple Ferry passed to the Corporation, who leased it to tenant ferrymen at £2 a year. An old book in the Council House archives records that in 1741 law charges of £107.12s.4d. were paid for setting up a ferry at Temple Backs. By the nineteenth century it had become generally known as Counterslip, a corruption of "Countess-slip", the landing point at Temple Back.

Ferry-on-the-Docks
St. Anne's
Ferry

Eventually the ferry was superseded by St. Philip's Bridge. The need for a bridge at this point on the Avon became so great, that in November 1837 a meeting of traders and other citizens determined that a bridge should be built. A company was formed for the purpose, Parliamentary powers obtained, and the new bridge opened on 1st December 1841. The ferry, which had been carrying 115,000 passengers a year, was bought up by the Bridge Company. Tolls on the bridge were abolished on 31st July, 1875.

FERRY-ON-THE-DOCKS: The inception of this new ferry service was an imaginative venture of private enterprise. Working between Neptune Steps and the City centre and the Nova Scotia Inn at Cumberland Basin, it covers the greater part of the floating harbour, calling as required at all practicable public slips and landing-stages. In effect therefore it revives the services of four long-abandoned ferries - Dean's Marsh, Canon's Marsh, Gasworks and Mardyke. At these places bills are posted requesting intending passengers to stand on the ferry steps and make a clear signal to the ferryman, as the boat does not necessarily call unless there are passengers to be set down or embarked.

It is a summer-only service, operating daily from April to September from 11am. to 6 pm. The late start each day means that the ferry does not cater for work-bound commuters, but skipper Jim Newman told me that quite a number use the ferry to return home from work. The service in fact is principally used by people at leisure as a cruise in the harbour, and as a convenient means of visiting the preserved **Great Britain** in the Albion Dock. An approximately forty minute schedule is maintained, times of which are posted at each landing stage. This arrangement enables the boat to call at the S.S. **Great Britain** every twenty minutes. At weekends and on fine, hot summer evenings the operators have shown their willingness to extend the running time if there is a demand.

The service is operated by the motor launch **Margaret**, which has an interesting history. She was built in Appledore after the Lynton/Lynmouth flood disaster, for use at Lynmouth harbour where all craft had been destroyed. She was used for embarking and landing passengers from P. & A. Campbell's paddle steamers. A larger 'sister' boat, the **Donald** (36 ft.) is still at Lynmouth. From Lynmouth the **Margaret** was acquired for the ferry between Shirehampton and Pill. On closure of the Pill ferry the **Margaret** was lying abandoned on the grass bank at Shirehampton until purchased and refitted in 1978 by City Docks Ventures Ltd. for the new Bristol ferry service. Her hull painted yellow, with the legend 'FERRY' on either bow, and fitted with a midships awning, she has a crew of two and is licensed for 22 passengers.

ST. ANNE'S FERRY: The first authentic reference to this ferry was in 1540, but it is certainly much longer-established than the sixteenth century, and is probably older than any of Bristol's ferries except those at Pill and Rownham. The excavation of 1500 Roman coins near the crossing in 1937 suggests that the Romans had a ferry here - perhaps chiefly for the convenience of those who lived in the Roman villa which has been dug up in Wick Road, Brislington. In Norman times the ferry lay within the manor of Blackswarth, which was given by Robert Fitzwarren to the Augustinian canons of College Green. The ferry thus came under the jurisdiction of Bristol Abbey, and was let to successive tenants for a nominal rent.

The importance of the passage was certainly enhanced when, probably late in the twelfth century, the little chapel of St. Anne in the Wood was erected by one of the lords of the manor of Brislington (the de la Warr family), and quickly became a highly popular place of pilgrimage. Evidence of the ferry occurs in 1476 in the will of Robert Hynde (Bristol goldsmith and burgess) in which he left a legacy to "the chapel of St. Anthony opposite the chapel of St. Anne". In the record of rents entered in 1540 by the King's bailiff reference is made to a certain Thomas Newman, who paid "12d. for the passage of St. Anne". About this time John Leland, Henry VIII's antiquary, came this way on his itinerary, and recorded: "Saint Anne's Ferrye is about a myle and half above the town of Brightstowe". Later he added "A 2 myles above Bristow was a commune Trajectus by bote, where was a chapelle of S. Anne".

Ere long, however, the Chapel of St. Anne suffered the fate of hundreds of religious buildings as the abbeys and monasteries were suppressed; and with its destruction the 'great pilgrimage to S.Anne' which Leland mentioned, came to an end, and the glory of 'S. Anne's Ferrye' was no more. The chapel was dismantled and the wooden effigy of St. Anne, enriched with gold and precious gifts, was torn roughly from its seating and presumably sent to Smithfield with other venerated images to be burned. Thirty-two 'ships and little ships' (models maybe of the St. Anne ferryboat), and the five ships in silver on the altar used for holding incense were melted down for the King's Exchequer. But the ferry, now in secular hands, continued to function. For the next four hundred years its history was for the most part placid and uneventful. Workmen and other commoners still used the ferry, paying their toll of one ha'penny to the boatman; but the chapel had long been roofless and derelict.

Ferry-on-the-Docks: The ex-Lamplighters ferry **Margaret** *enjoying a new lease of life in Bristol Floating harbour, July 1980.*
Photo: Edwina Small.

By the nineteenth century the working of the ferry had been linked with the adjacent St. Anne's Mill, the miller having to accept responsibility for the passage. Until 1809 this was worked as a tidal ferry; that is, at low tide the ferryboat was turned into a kind of floating bridge in the middle of the stream, with foot-planks to the shore on either side. After Netham Dam was built in 1809, the river at St. Anne's was only partially tidal, and the reduced water power available caused the value of the mill to decline. The ferry was then a great help financially to the miller, who from 1817 to 1822 was John Roach. In the year 1817 he employed a boy of 14, a relative of his, Thomas Webley, to assist with the mill and the ferry. On Sundays his 5 year old grandson John Webley came to see him, and was made useful collecting the $\frac{1}{2}$d. tolls from the passengers ferried across by his cousin. Later, Roach employed a man named Abel Hibbs as ferryman. Hibbs, an ex-Navy man, was something of a celebrity as one of the few who had escaped from the **Royal George** when Admiral Kempenfelt's flagship sank in 1782 at Spithead with the loss of 900 lives.

The miller who succeeded Roach was named Gregory. On Whit Monday 1826 his son Daniel was engaged all day in working the ferry, and at the end of the day the $\frac{1}{2}$d. tolls amounted to almost £1. The next miller-ferryman of whom we know was James Fear, 1832-1841. In 1836 he noted that many of the navvies constructing the earthworks of the Great Western Railway used the ferry daily to get to work, so he had part of the mill converted into a public house, and until 1842 this served as a 'passage house inn' for the ferry. In 1842, the railway being completed, James Fear gave up the mill and public house, and the ferry rights became attached to St. Anne's farm. The farm had a new owner, a Mr. Ring, and he was desirous of stopping the ferry and closing the paths across his land leading to it. He instructed his 26 year old son, R.C. Ring, to explore the legal possibilities. The result of these enquiries was that he abandoned his plans to get the ferry discontinued, but re-sited it in a less convenient place 100 yards upstream near his farmhouse. This had the effect of reducing the numbers using the ferry, but not substantially. However it was more than 40 years before the ferry returned to its original site. Meanwhile the mill had not worked again since its closure by James Fear. A sketch of 1880 shows only the lower portion of two walls remaining of St. Anne's Chapel. The peacefulness of this sylvan scene was to be rudely interrupted in 1891 when St.Anne's ferry hit the headlines of the public press.

It was an August morning in 1887 when Charles Bishop, a young fitter at the Bristol Wagon Works, set off to work from his home in Brislington. His route took him daily through St.Anne's Woods and across the Avon by the ferry, whence he walked to Lawrence Hill. But this morning he was in for a shock: the gate to the pleasant, leafy paths of St. Anne's Wood was padlocked, and the ferry was not plying. Indignantly the young man had to plod his weary way round via Bath Bridge. It entailed an extra three miles walking each day. He then learned that St. Anne's Woods had recently been purchased by a Bristol solicitor names James Sinnot, who was determined to exclude the public. Charles Bishop was a young man of spirit, and he never doubted that a public right of way existed to the ferry: so he laid a complaint before the Bristol Footpath Preservation Society, who took up the case with considerable fervour. Battle had been joined, but it was to be four years before it was lost and won.

Twice members of the Society led by their secretary, Mr. Richard Tuckett (who, like Sinnot, was a lawyer) prised open the padlocks, removed the chains, and walked unhindered through the woods, "so" (in Bishop's own words, later) "publicly challenging the owner of St. Anne's to bring an action". But Sinnot would not be drawn. He simply ignored the trespass. Time passed by, and still there was no ferry. Bishop later wrote "As no action was brought, I determined to place a boat at the site of an ancient ferry and use it myself and invite the public to do the same". Accordingly a boat was placed at the original crossing-place on 22 June, 1889, and an advertisement of the fact was inserted in the Bristol newspapers. The Footpath Society's president and a number of committee members were among the first to cross.

Thus prodded into action, Sinnot - in conjunction with W.A. Pillers, occupier of St. Anne's Farm, applied for and obtained from Mr. Justice Kay an injunction restraining Mr. Richard Tuckett (and by inference, anyone else) from using the paths and the ferry. The Judge then ordered the case to be tried in Bristol by an Official Referee. The trial of the action commenced on 17 June 1890 before H.W. Verey, Esq. Sixty-seven witnesses were called by the Plaintiffs, and a hundred and twenty by the Defendant. The trial itself opened after the New Year and the final speeches of Counsel were concluded on 31 January 1891. The Official Referee's decision rejected the claims of the plaintiffs, and established the rights of the public to the footpaths and the ferry. As soon as the decision was made known, Charles Bishop restarted the ferry service, which remained in regular operation for 66 years. A small wooden shack on the Crews Hole side served as the ferry shelter. The ferryman for many years was Fred Ashmead, and in the winter months he cheered himself with a coke brazier fire outside, which was likewise popular with his passengers.

At the turn of the century St.Anne's Board Mill Company acquired the land on the river bank and thereby inherited responsibility for the ferry. The principal users were now employees of the company, although many local housewives also crossed regularly from Blacksworth Road to St. Anne's or vice-versa to do their shopping. Under the Company, the ferry operated from 5.30 am. to 10.30 pm., and was at its busiest when shifts were changing at the works. This continued until 1957, when the Company, who were carrying out an ambitious and expensive rebuilding programme, decided to erect a footbridge in place of the ferry, and entrusted the work to contractors John Lysaught Ltd. On the 8th of September that year crowds of local residents gathered on the bank to watch the 22 ton, 125 ft. span of the new footbridge slide inch by inch into place from the barge **Hermatic**. A few weeks later the bridge was opened to the public, and the ferry ran for the last time. The Company's uniformed ferrymen, Mervyn Vincent, Michael Boyle, and J.P. Ferrier were found jobs elsewhere in the board mills. A 2d. crossing had now become a free one, but many felt sad that after eight hundred years St. Anne's ferry was passing into history.

CONHAM FERRY: In these days when so many once busy ferries are now only memories, especially in rural settings, it is good to report that Conham ferry is alive and well. This success story is due entirely to the determination of the present owner, Mrs. Alma Brockwell, and Conham ferry is now experiencing a second heyday.

The early history of the ferry is unknown, but it is marked on a one-inch Ordnance Survey Map published in 1830. It is likely that the rights anciently belonged to the abbots of Keynsham. Later they must have been vested in the Earl of Temple, as he is mentioned in an abstract of title as conveying the ferry cottage, in 1925. The age of the house is not known but it was certainly in being by 1846, for it was then that Mrs. Mary-Anne Beese came to live there, and it is with her name that this ferry will always be associated.

The Great Western Railway had been completed between London and Bristol in 1841 and St. Anne's Park station beside the Avon was opened about four years later. The possibilities were not lost on Mrs. Beese and in 1845 she started her tea gardens at the ferry house. Mary-Anne Beese worked the tea-gardens in connection with the ferry till 1879. She was followed by a Mrs. Beese (junior) until 1909. The name had become so well known to many generations of Bristolians, that nobody has ever wanted to change it, and as Bees Ferry (but note the mis-spelling!) it is still known today. The Plumpton family followed, as tenants until 1925, when they bought house and ferry, and as owners till 1946. Their long tenure had seen the ferry through both world wars.

In 1946 they sold out to a Mr. and Mrs. Percy Labdan. On Mr. Labdan's death in December 1960 the ferry became disused until his son took over, but the tea gardens closed. In May 1962 a Mr. and Mrs. Stephen Barling took over from Mrs. Labdan, and announced that the ferry was to reopen. The Evening Post reported enthusiastically "regular ferry services linking St. George to Brislington and St. Anne's.... will save up to an hour's travelling time on a single journey for office and factory workers". Mrs. Caroline Barling, who planned to share the sculling chores with her husband, declared "This is a new venture for us, but we have always dreamed of owning a ferry".

Unfortunately, the hopes and dreams proved to be short-lived. Possibly the response of the public to the reopened tea-gardens had been underestimated, and Mrs. Barling who was doing most of the ferrying, had two young children at home. Whatever the reason, a month after announcing the re-opening the Evening Post was reporting its closure: "Last weekend crowds of picnickers streamed down to the ferry only to be told that it was no longer running. This morning passengers stood hopefully on the far side of the river and rang the old bell, but no one came to scull the ferry over". For two years the tea-gardens remained closed and the ferry failed to run.

It was in 1964 that the Brockwells came to Conham. Mr. Brockwell was an area production manager for a firm of mixed concrete manufacturers, but he met his German-born wife while he was in the Forces in Germany and she was working for the Control Commission. Alma Brockwell took over the run-down concern and has revitalised it. By this time people were driving to the seaside rather than walk from Bristol to Beese's.

The ferry was restarted almost at once. It is sculled over the stern, or rowed with two oars, or worked across by a rope, depending on how many people are waiting and how quickly they need to be ferried across. The ferry has, so far as is known, always been pedestrian-only: there is no record of a horse-and-cattle boat. The tea-gardens were restarted in 1977, and beer is now provided as well as tea. The chief users of the ferry have always been folk going to and from work during the week, and visitors to the tea-gardens at the weekends. Today in winter there is not much demand, but in spring and summer people use it to cross over to the tow path on the other side, and to visit the tea and beer gardens. Alma Brockwell told me "I am told that during the 28 years of the Plumptons' occupancy they twice took £10 in ferry tolls, when it cost a farthing to use the ferry!"

Perhaps more information will yet come to light about the earlier history of this crossing. Certainly the site of the ferry house and tea-garden have seen many years of occupation. In 1979 a wall was found about 5 inches below the turf, constructed of blocks such as those made by a smelting works, and the following year, above the site of this wall, was found a coin dated 1722.

HANHAM FERRY: This crossing of the Avon Navigation was known variously as the Hanham or Chequers Ferry. It is almost certainly an ancient passage, the Priory on the Hanham side and the Abbey on the Keynsham side making it logical to assume that a ferry had to be maintained here. Its origins are obscure and probably untraceable but with the land at Hanham Mills being originally in the ownership of Hanham Priory, it seems likely that this was for years an ecclesiastical ferry.

When and to whom the ownership of the ferry passed from the Church into secular control is also unknown. It is reasonable to suppose that it came into the hands of the Geswick family, the local squires of Hanham Court. Francis Geswick in 1685 supported the Duke of Monmouth's ill-fated rebellion and helped the rebels when they camped in Sydenham Meadow where the ferry ran. He was charged with treason and spent many years in Gloucester gaol. According to Ellecombe's 'History of Bitton Parish', Queen Anne, on a visit, granted a charter for the ferry to operate in perpetuity. If so, this brings the story of the ferry up to about 1710. Later owners may have been Squire Whittuck and his successors at Hanham Court, the de Carterets, or John Couch, a well known local landowner at about the time of Waterloo.

Eventually ownership passed to the owner of the original Chequers Inn. In later years when the present inn was built (c.1901) and the original building became a boatbuilders' residence, the ferry was run by the boatbuilder's family, and the owners of the boatyard continued to run it until the ferry was abandoned. Older residents recall that the boat was usually propelled by sculling over the stern, but when numbers (i.e. weight) demanded it, the boat was rowed by oars. Jim Oates, a partner in the boatyard, ran the ferry for some years: while several young men who fancied themselves as ferrymen, would help out during weekends and on summer evenings.

The last owner was a Mr. Arters, who owned the Old Chequers Boatyard until his death in 1966. His family continued to work the ferry when required for a few months afterward. The ferryboat was then sunk by 'yobbo' vandals and damaged beyond economic repair. The cost of a new boat was weighed against the declining number of customers (almost nil except at weekends) and it was reluctantly decided to terminate the ferry. The fare during the 1940-50 period was 2d. each way. A large bell was fixed to a wooden post on the Keynsham side for summoning the ferryman, but has long since disappeared. The ferry slipway on the Keynsham side, though silted badly and over-grown, is still discernible.

3. River Avon; Bath.

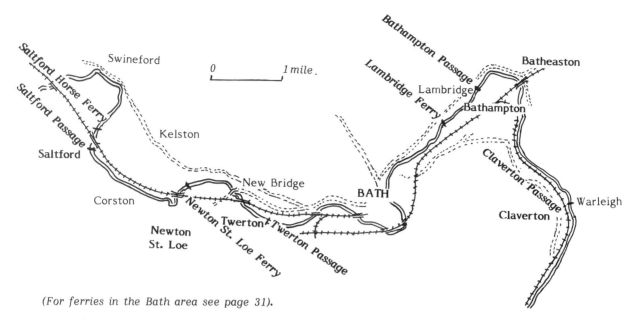

(For ferries in the Bath area see page 31).

SALTFORD HORSE FERRY: The tow path of the Avon Navigation changed from one bank to the other just near the Jolly Sailor Inn, and this ferry was used to cross the barge horses over, as at Newton St. Loe. There was no ferryhouse nor any ferryman employed, and the bargees worked the boat as needed. The boat ran on a submerged chain which passed over sheaves on the side of the craft. There was room for two horses to stand side-by-side. The ferry must have operated from the original canalisation of the river in 1728, and was working for more than 200 years. It continued until horsedrawn river traffic was phased out, probably as late as the 1930s. Mr. Frank Vine of Saltford thinks the ferry may even have survived into early post-war years. The ferry was really a canal service and not primarily intended for pedestrians. However, a small community lived at nearby Kelston Mills who could have made use of it to reach Saltford.

An unauthorised use of the ferry is described in Chapter 7 of S.G. Kendall's 'Farming Memoirs of a Westcountry Yeoman' (Faber, 1944). It appears that when the bargees had ferried their horses across to the towpath on the opposite side and unloaded them, they were supposed to leave the boat secured by a padlock through one of the chain links. Often, however, by oversight or indolence, the boat was not properly secured and Farmer Kendall relates how in his youth he and other mischievous boys would be on the watch for this occurring:- "on such an occasion we pulled the horseboat backwards and forward over the deep river until we were tired and exhausted with the work, or a barge loomed ahoy coming up or down the river....then we left the boat over the wrong side, ran up to the nearest railway bridge and crossed over, back and down - then awaited the tide of events; to hear the deep-voiced language of the rough bargees....because one of the men had either to do as we had done, find the nearest railway bridge to retrieve their boat, or do as they more often did, strip and swim over for it: while we were....enjoying their discomfiture immensely".

He goes on to relate that on one such occasion when they were moving the ferry, his younger brother fell overboard into deep water, coming up under the horseboat twice before surfacing alongside and being grabbed by his curly hair and dragged aboard. It had been a near thing. Today the timbers of that heavy horseboat must be rotting somewhere: and could they but speak they would have tales to tell.

SALTFORD PASSAGE: As with so many passages, the origins of the ferry at Saltford have gone unrecorded. The area was thinly populated, and it is probable that this crossing was not in regular use prior to the popularity of Lansdown Racecourse and the revival of Avon regattas in the late nineteenth century. In 'A History of Saltford Village' (Sims and Mawdett, 1976), the late Percy Sims tells us that for 22 years, from 1886 to 1908, the ferry was worked by Hannah Gregory, whose husband Charles Gregory was afflicted with the palsy. Earlier in the same book it is recorded that the ferryman, Charles Gregory and his wife lived in the cottage nearest to the mill, about 100 yards from the ferry crossing. So it is not clear whether Charles Gregory had earlier worked the ferry himself, or simply that the lease was in his name.

The ferry provided a direct route between Saltford and Kelston; on landing from Saltford one crossed a field and then passed through an arch in the Midland Railway embankment. For the greater part of the year there were not enough passengers to justify the ferry being constantly manned and those who wanted to cross knocked on the ferryman's door at Saltford, or shouted 'Ferry!' from the other bank. Saltford regattas, however, restarted in 1870 after a lapse of many years, kept the ferry very busy; and even more so did the Race Meetings at Lansdowne, the racecourse being about a two mile walk from the ferry landing. Many racegoers came from Bristol by a Midland Railway train which reached Kelston Station at 12 noon, but more arrived at Saltford Station by the Great Western Railway and crossed by ferry. While Hannah Gregory worked the ferry, her disabled husband made 'hulleys' (eel trap-baskets) and caught and sold eels.

**Newton
St. Loe
Twerton
Ferry**

William Hill and his wife took over the ferry from the Gregorys in 1908. They lived in a cottage close to the ferry which has since been demolished, but a public seat now marks the site. Their daughter, Mrs. Brookman, still lives in the district, and she recalls:- "In the summer we were kept busy on weekends, also on Bath Race days, when people came from Saltford G.W.R. Station....On those days, which were only twice a year, my father borrowed a much larger boat, and also strung a rope across the river. This made it easier for him to work the ferry while mother sat at a table on the bank taking the money (1d. toll). My father had other work so my mother, two brothers and I also had to work the ferry. It was hard work because it was a flat-bottomed boat with a square bow and you had to stand near the bow and paddle first one side, then the other".

A photo exists showing Mrs. Hill, wearing a cap, seated in the ferry with two passengers, and apparently waiting for others. The Misses Kelland of Saltford recall that the local blacksmith was on the Kelston side of the river, and that children used the ferry to buy iron hoops at the forge. The ferry ceased to be viable as cars and motor coaches proliferated after the Great War, and eventually closed in 1923. Mrs. Brookman says that no one can remember the eventual fate of the ferryboat, but she believes it broke away in a flood, and was damaged beyond repair.

NEWTON ST. LOE: The site of this ferry was at Calvary field, north of the A.36, opposite the Globe Inn. This was an unattended horseboat, on a waist-high wire, and was principally for the use of bargees transferring barge-towing horses from one side to the other. But it was there for all to use, and Mrs. Clutterbuck of Rackfield Place, Twerton, can recall that when she was a child she and other children often amused themselves on the ferry. It was a flat-bottomed and heavy craft, and she says that they sometimes stuck in midstream. Newton St. Loe ferry lasted about as long as Twerton ferry, finally closing down in the early 1930s.

TWERTON FERRY: The site of this passage is just north of the A.36 road on the east side of a present day scrapyard. The small landing-stage here once used by the ferry has long disappeared. A rowboat was used, sculled over the stern or pulled by oars: Twerton was always a pedestrian only ferry, and the fare was still a $\frac{1}{2}$d. within the memory of the oldest inhabitants. The ferryman from about 1820 till just after 1860 was named Branch. Many years later his grandson (then aged 83) would tell folks that his own first acquaintance with the ferry was when he was but a fortnight old and his grandparents had to have him aboard one busy day! Twerton ferry had long been in the possession of the Kitt family, but was sold by them about the turn of the century to the Weston Bridge Company. The sale was negotiated by Mr. Benjamin Kitt, of Sydney Lodge, Bathwick, and he also sold the site of the ferryman's house to a Mr. J.D. Taylor.

In 1885 the last Twerton ferryman, E.H. Lye, took over from his grandfather, and supplemented his income by hiring out boats on the river. In a May 1896 issue of the 'Bath & County Graphic' is a reproduction of a sketch by Maud Tyler entitled 'The Royal Old Ferry', showing the picturesque Ferry House in the background. It probably owed this name, found also on a 1903 map, to having been used by royalty in the heyday of Bath when the city was no stranger to Royal visitors. On 25 March, 1905, Ferryman Lye was served with a notice by the Weston Bridge Company, requiring him, under penalty, to close the ferry within twelve months. A year later an announcement appeared in the 'Bath Herald' of 12th April, that Twerton ferry was about to be closed down. The papers commented 'The disappearance of the old flat-bottomed chain-propelled ferry boat will be a source of regret to many, to whom both the ferry and the well-kept garden of the ferryman on the Twerton side of the river were well-known!'

The newspaper certainly misled the public in this announcement for although up to that time the ferry may have been chain-worked, it certainly did not cease running that year: and the 'well-kept garden' referred to must have been the lock-keeper's cottage on the west bank, the ferry house having been sold several years before. The Bridge Company offered to purchase the ferryboat from Lye, but he named a prohibitive price. We have been unable to discover why the Bridge Company wanted the ferry shut down, or whether the matter went to litigation, or whether public opinion applied pressure. But certainly ferryman Lye, who lived at River Place about half a mile from the ferry, kept the service going until the early 1930s, and is well remembered by many erstwhile passengers.

An impression of Twerton Ferry on the Avon by the artist Nattes showing the ferry cottage. No date is given.
Photo: Bath Reference Library.

*Bristol
Roads Ferry
Southgate
Ferry
Parade
Ferry*

*Ferries at Bath.
(River Avon).*

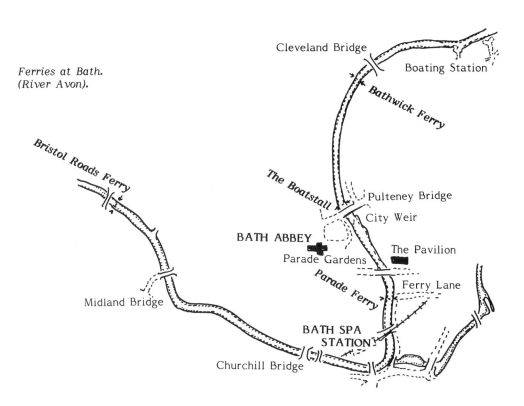

BRISTOL ROADS FERRY: Of the Bath city ferries between Old Bridge and Twerton, probably the last to survive was the passage connecting the Upper and Lower Bristol Roads, where Victoria Bridge stands today. Its customary name we have failed to discover. Its use probably increased after the opening of Royal Victoria Park nearby in 1830. The ferry presumably closed in 1837 when the bridge was completed.

SOUTHGATE FERRY: This was possibly the oldest of all Bath's ferries, and almost certainly the first to close down. The building of what came to be known as Old Bridge must have brought about its demise.

PARADE FERRY: This passage provided access from the city to the once famous Spring Gardens and other parts of Bathwick and Widcombe. About the year 1824 it was the scene of the worst ferry tragedy on the Avon. The following title is extracted from Emanuel Green's 'Bibliotheca Somersetensis' (1902), though no copies of the paper itself are known to survive:- "A particular account of the most dreadful accident which occurred in Bath, yesterday afternoon, by the upsetting the ferry boat, which contained thirty persons, who had assembled to witness the return of the Mayor and Corporation from processioning, out of which number ten or twelve perished. Bath,(182-)." A first-hand account of the disaster is given in the memoirs of the Rev. Robert Kilvert, published some years ago by the Kilvert Society, and reproduced here with their kind permission. At the time Kilvert was a youth, and lived at 7, Caroline Buildings in Widcombe.

"It was the custom on Ascension Day for the Corporation of the city to go by water from one point where the Bath parishes meet, that of Walcot, to another where they join again - thus beating the river bounds, the bounds on the land side being beaten by another party. A vast crowd on the bank always witnessed the progress of the river party, who amused themselves with flinging buns to be scrambled for on the banks. This caused a good deal of rough play. I have seen a boy in the act of seizing a bun, tossed into the river from the steep bank by another who was scrambling for it, and fished out with some difficulty amidst roars of laughter from the guardians of order and justice on board. On one of these celebrations a terrible accident occurred. There used to be a ferry boat from the South Parade to the Widcombe side of the river. It seldom carried more than a single passenger or a very small party, but the banks of the river on that occasion being crowded, and people impatient to get across, more got into the boat than it would safely carry. All went well for a time, but in one of the transits, when it was weighted almost to the level of the water, something made the boat roll a little, and it shipped a small quantity of water. The people rushed to the other side and swamped the boat in mid-stream, throwing the twenty or thirty who were in it, clinging together like a swarm of bees, into water far beyond their depth. Boats were quickly at hand. Some, buoyed up by those who were underneath them, were quickly saved; others were got up from below in good time to restore them; but six of the number were not found till it was too late. The news spread like wildfire, and the population of the city streamed out till the banks were densely crowded above and below the scene of the accident. I went down to the place, having missed my brother Edward, then a small boy, and I suppose I showed some symptoms of alarm. A poor young fellow had been fished up, and just as I glimpsed the poor, dank, livid corpse, someone sickened me by enquiring "Is that your brother?" Happily it was not. But until Edward, who had not been in the boat, turned up safely, I did not know whether the next might not be he......" This account is taken from 'More Chapters from the Kilvert Saga', published by the Kilvert Society.

In the last years of Parade ferry, according to the 'Bath & County Graphic' of May 1896, it "was presided over by a dame, who we have been told, lived to a great age". This ferry survived

The
Boatstall
Bathwick
Ferry
Lambridge
Ferry
Bathampton
Passage
Claverton-
Warleigh
Ferry

the opening of the North Parade bridge (built 1835-6 slightly upstream of the ferry site) and did not close until September 1838. Ferry lane, connecting the ferry landing with Pulteney Road, still bears its name today.

THE BOATSTALL: The most central of Bath's old ferry services, the City ferry, was operated by a rope, whereas the other Bath ferries were rowed. it was commonly called 'the boat-stall', and the west bank of the river at that point was known as Boatstall Lane (now covered by later buildings). This ferry ceased in 1774 with the completion of Pulteney Bridge (1769-74).

BATHWICK FERRY: The Walcot-Bathwick passage is mentioned in an advertisement of 1783, by which time it was becoming an increasingly important crossing. A sketch of the ferry by J.C. Nottes appeared in the 'Bath Illustrated' of 1805. It was eventually replaced by the Cleveland Bridge in 1827, but the bridge is a little way up stream from the site of the old ferry.

LAMBRIDGE FERRY: A minor ferry of which little information can be gleaned today crossed the Avon in the extreme north-east of Bath. it is mentioned in an 1896 issue of the 'Bath and County Gazette', but not by name, and although we have identified it here as 'Lambridge Ferry', we have failed to discover the name by which it was known in its time. It is presumed that it closed down after the completion of the Grosvenor Suspension Bridge in 1830.

BATHAMPTON PASSAGE: Bathampton Passage was the first crossing of the Avon east of Bath, and provided both a pedestrian and horseboat service. The earliest reference we have encountered to this ferry is in J. Collison's 'History and Antiquities of Somerset' (1791), volume 1, where one reads: "On the river is a mill at which a ferryboat is kept, and there is a pleasing waterfall near it from a high weir". A map of 1742 by Thomas Thorpe, generally regarded as reliable and accurate, does not show a ferry at Bathampton at that date. In the seeming absence of other documentary evidence, one cannot therefore date the ferry more precisely than sometime between 1742 and 1791.

The Bathampton mill features in a number of extant pictures of the ferry in Victorian times. Described in 1824 as ancient, it was rebuilt about 1857-8 by its owner, Major Allen of Bathampton Manor. The new building, oblong and three storeys high, was gutted by fire on Saturday night, 16th November 1861. An account of the fire is given in the "Bath Chronicle" for 21st November, 1861, where we learn that at the time it was a flour mill operated by Thomas Spackman of Batheaston. A knowledge of these varying fortunes of the mill helps in dating pictures of the ferry.

A local historian of Batheaston, on the opposite bank of the Avon, has checked the parish records regarding the ferry. It appears that at one time Ralph Allen claimed to be Lord of the manor there, but was proved to be claiming falsely, and we do not know who was Lord of Batheaston manor when the ferry started. It seems probable that the ferry rights were vested in Bathampton manor, and that possibly the tenancy was held by the mill. The ferry closed in 1871, having since

Bathampton Passage: The chain-worked horseboat prior to 1824 when the mill was rebuilt.
Photo: Bath Reference Library.

been superseded by a bridge. The last ferryman was Tom Smith, familiarly known as "Old Tom" and he may well have had an assistant, as vehicles were being transported by the horseboat till the bridge opened.

The Bath Chronicle of 8th October, 1938 reproduced a copperplate engraving dated 1824, by Thomas Falconer of Bath. This shows the pedestrian ferry being poled across in front of the earlier Bathampton mill building. In Bath Reference library is an undated print of the horseboat at work (32) with the old mill in the background; and a photograph dated c.1870 showing a bewhiskered ferryman holding the chest-high wire as the boat waits at Bathampton. This photograph shows Bathampton mill apparently restored after the fire.

CLAVERTON - WARLEIGH FERRY: This now disused passage in a very picturesque situation was for generations attached to Warleigh manor. The site is just below the junction of the Avon with the Frome near the weirs at Warleigh, some four miles from Bath, and at the reputed location of a Roman ford. In nearby Claverton churchyard lie buried three soldiers of the Parliament and one Royalist, who lost their lives in a skirmish near the ferry in 1643. Sir William Basset, Lord of the manor of Claverton was dining with Royalist officers in Claverton Manor house when a canon ball fired from Monkton Farleigh Down, crashed into the room. In the skirmish which followed, Royalist cavalry and Cornish infantry clashed with Waller's Parliamentarian advance guard in the Ham meadow where the ferry lands on the Claverton side. The Parliamentarians were chased into Batheaston, and the episode developed the following day into the Battle of Lansdowne.

*Claverton Passage: A scene about
1890 as the rope-worked ferry
nears Warleigh Steps with 8
passengers. The river was not
always as placid as this.*

For many years the ferry was owned by the Skrine family of Warleigh Manor, where the cannon ball which had started the 1643 skirmish could be seen for many years on one of the posts at the bottom of the steps. Claverton House no longer stands; it was situated at the top of the 'Elizabethan steps' in the centre of the village. After demolition about 1820 it was replaced by the building now housing the American Museum. What happened to the ferryman during this encounter is not known; in modern parlance he probably kept a 'low profile'. There are two trenches supposedly used by the Civil War combatants in Ferry Field either side of the ferry steps but the depressions become shallower with the passing years.

A lease dated September 1882 is in existence, bestowing on one Joseph Garraway the tenancy of ferry cottage and garden, ferry, and island, for an annual rent of £8 and signed by Henry Duncan Skrine of Warleigh. The Skrine family owned both Claverton and Warleigh manors and most of the valley. A 'tied' cottage, which still stands, was provided for the ferryman. A letter to the 'Somerset Countryman' in 1951 reported that a new boat, the **Queen Mary** had recently been brought into use to replace an older craft which had been wrecked by flood waters that year. The correspondent, a Mr. Donald Mullins, referred to a photograph which showed the ferry being navigated by ferryman John Byrne; and declared "the facilities of the crossing are much valued by pedestrians and cyclists who wish to cross between the pleasant surroundings of Claverton and the attractively wooded slopes of Warleigh - the rose gardens of whose manor are opened to the public at stated times, teas being provided".

At the time the ferry fee ($\frac{1}{2}$d. within living memory) was 2d. As many as 200 passengers a day were being carried during the busy season. Mrs. Bayliss of Claverton can recall two ferrymen who served in the latter days of the Skrine family - Messrs. Jones and Trebble. When Miss Dorothea Skrine died in 1956 the estate was sold. The manor house became a school, and the ferry rights were vested in the ownership of Ferry Cottage. Until then the ferry had been available at any time; and the ferryman could be summoned to the Claverton side by pulling on a wire suspended from a tree near the ferry steps. This rang a large $\frac{3}{4}$ cwt. bell in the ferryhouse garden on the Warleigh side.

The first occupiers after the sale of 1956 were George Cornell and his wife, and they continued to maintain the ferry between 6 am. and 9 pm. daily. Traffic was good from spring until well into autumn, local people regularly crossing morning and evening, many anglers during the fishing season, and afternoon visitors attracted to the tea gardens by Mrs. Cornell's renowned freshly-baked scones and strawberry teas. The peaceful scene which Claverton passage normally presents gives no idea of the river in flood. George Cornell recalls: "Normally from the cottage one could hear the water rushing and tumbling over the weir, and on several occasions wakened to complete silence, and rushing to the bedroom windows, we would find that the river was in a complete flood; no garden, completely under water, no island, again submerged, and alas no ferryboat! On one occasion the boat was found nearly into Bath, but fortunately was recognised as the Warleigh ferry and was towed back at a later date by the Sea Scouts from Bristol, who camped at Warleigh for many years. On other occasions of flooding, the boat reached Batheaston, and I retrieved it with the help of an outboard motor. On a couple of occasions it travelled a few hundred yards down the river and became entangled with a fallen tree."

And there were other frustrations. On a number of occasions the Cornells, having dressed in seaboots and warm clothing to answer the ferry bell on a winter's night, would then see, across the river, "some cattle rapturously rubbing themselves on the bell wire posts, and thereby ringing the bell!"

The Cornells left Warleigh in 1960 and were succeeded at the ferry cottage by John Guilfoyle, who says that in his time the ferry was largely used by work people from the estate. This however proved to be the last year of the ferry, for there was severe flooding in the December. George Cornell was at hand at the time and John Guilfoyle recalls "The flood of 1960 was the last straw. All day 4th December George Cornell and I tried to keep the ferry cable clear. All kinds of rubbish collected on the wire. At one time there must have been at least thirty tons of rubbish on the cable, and each time we cleared it, it would fill up again. The last time we cleared the wire was midnight on 4th December. The Avon was then running really high, and the risk too great. At about 1 am. on 5th December the cable broke, and this was the end of the Warleigh ferry". As is clear from this account, the boat was worked on the rope system, and the chain and anchor which secured the wire on the Claverton side can still be seen today beside the waterwheel pumping-house which serves the nearby Kennet and Avon canal. The ferryboat itself is still in existence, and was last noted at the Bathford paper mill.

4.

Rivers Yeo, Axe & Parrett

Avon & Somerset.

KINGSTON SEYMOUR - WICK ST. LAWRENCE: It seems to be a matter of doubt as to when, or even if, there was a ferry across the mouth of the Yeo. Retired farmer and local historian Ken Stuckey tells me he is not convinced that there was any other ferry than a possible constructor's boat when the Weston, Clevedon and Portishead Railway was bridging the Yeo 1896/7.

Until the later years of the nineteenth century, however, there was no means of crossing the river except by ford at low water, until the erection of Phipp's Bridge, a light structure which can take cattle (in file) besides pedestrians. It would seem therefore that in earlier times there must have been some arrangement for crossing by boat.

In the 'Somerset County Herald' newspaper in 1938 a reader enquired about ferries in Somerset. On 19th March a correspondent replied, enumerating several, and stating clearly that there was a passage across the 'Yeo':- "On the Yeo, near its mouth and connecting Kingston Seymour and Wick St. Lawrence, there is what might be called an "occasional ferry" for crossing the river." This may have taken the form of a local farmer who was willing to cross people on request if he was available, or an unmanned boat left at the bank for a 'do it yourself' service. There are said to have been a number of such 'convenience boats' at Somerset farm crossings. When the M5 motorway was built across the Yeo valley, the river was dammed just below the ferry site, so is no longer tidal above that point.

BREAN - UPHILL FERRY: Although the origin of Uphill ferry, as with most ancient passages, is lost in the mists of time, there is certainly no doubt that the crossing was much used in the days of the Roman Occupation. The Romans built a temple on Brean Down, roofed with pennant stone, probably quarried in the Midsomer-Norton area. This had to be brought across the Axe at some point near the present ferry. The Romans must have established a regular crossing for the temple builders and their materials; and when the building was completed the ferry would still have been required for visitors and worshippers. Moreover at Uphill there was a small Roman port for the export of iron and lead from Wookey Hole, while a small Roman garrison was maintained at Brean Down.

At the time of the Norman survey the manor of Brean belonged to Walter of Douai. The ferry would have been in his possession, although it is not named in Domesday Book. Collinson in his 'History of Somerset' traces the history of Brean manor, quoting from the deed of 1637 where it is stated that Thomas Bond had already conveyed to Henry, Lord Danvers and others "a newly built house, part of the manor..... also the down or warren called Brean Down and the passage or ferry belonging to the said manor....."

After this first specific reference to Uphill ferry in the seventeenth century, there is not another until the nineteenth, and we cannot be sure that there is a continuous history of passage at this point of the river. In the early eighteenth century there was a crossing at Hobb's Boat, Lympsham, suggesting the ferry had been moved upstream to meet the needs of the time and it belonged to an Axbridge family named Andrews. In 1808 when the bridge was built over the Axe, flood-gates installed, and the river courses diverted, the then owners of the ferry, Popham & Petheram, claimed £675 in compensation from the Commissioners of Sewers. Whether Hobb's Boat itself got its name from a former ferryman, or from Hubba, the Danish pirate menace of the Bristol Channel, is uncertain, but the closure of the ferry at Hobbs' Boat occurred in the same year as the first hotel opened in Weston-super-Mare; and the rapid rise of Weston as a seaside resort would have recreated the need for the ferry at Uphill. The map attached to the Uphill Enclosure Award of 1818 shows the ferry in approximately its present-day position, but there is no mention of the ferry in the text.

In L.M. Dutton's 'Brean Down' (1921) we read: "From March to October the ferryman is at the river from 9.30 am. to 5 pm; but by arrangement, and for the payment of 9d. instead of the usual 6d. per return fare, he will take passengers back until 7 o'clock."

From October to March so few people cross by the ferry at all that it is necessary to write to Mr. A.E. Pople, 4 Church Road, Uphill, to make an appointment beforehand. The present ferryman holds a Board of Trade monopoly and has made steps and board walks up the muddy banks for use at low tide." Mr. Walter Hillman of Weston (then 81 years of age) recalled in 1951 that his uncle, a local preacher, always contacted ferryman Pople in this way when he had to take a service at Brean. But Mr. Hillman also pointed out, in a letter to the 'Bristol Evening Post': "Not so many years ago 700 people would use the ferry on a Bank Holiday, and the service would have to be augmented by two motor boats. On an ordinary summer day 200-300 people would cross to the Down". Mr. Hillman had cause to know, for many of those ferry passengers had tea at the old fort which he bought, converted into a cafe, and operated for thirty years.

At the turn of the century the ferry was held by Wm. Pople (elder brother of A.E. Pople) whose widow in 1926 sold the boats, tackle, and interest in the two landings for the sum of approximately £30 to Leonard Smart of Uphill. Always known as "Cap'n", Smart was granted a crown lease on 11th March 1927 to maintain landing-stages, etc. Ruddy complexioned, white-moustached, wearing heavy gold earrings, and always dressed in navy blue jersey and uniform cap, Smart was a colourful, explosive seafaring character. Edward Hutton in his "Highways and Byways in Somerset" (last edition 1955) wrote: "I went over the difficult estuary of the Axe by ferry, and the ferryman was more like Charon than any other I am likely to meet before I see the great original and cross the Styx". Clearly, Hutton had encountered "Cap'n" Smart. In October 1928 the Board of Trade convened a private conference at Uphill to restore peace between the formidable Captain and the local fishermen who complained that Smart was unjustifiably claiming exclusive rights to the Uphill landing. At the conference, Smart modified his claims, saying "I do not and would not object to anyone using the landing, except for ferrying and provided they do not obstruct me in my business, or damage the steps". The Board of Trade expressed themselves satisfied with this declaration but requested Uphill Parish Council to report annually on Smart's use and maintenance of the landing "in so far as the interests of the public may be affected thereby".

Cap'n Smart died in 1936, and the lease was thereafter held by his widow Mrs. Mary Smart, who employed men to work the 15 foot boat, which her husband had named **Mary** after her. A.E. Pople and Len Patch ("Patchy") in turn managed the ferry for Mrs. Smart in the following years.

Brean Down was requisitioned by the Army in World War II, and the ferry fell into disuse. Hostilities over, the Bird Preservation Society "closed up" the Down, and holidaymakers were discouraged, so there was little business for the ferry. From 1950 to 1951 Mrs. Smart was unable to get a ferryman, and between then and 1957 Jim Brueford, Dick Gross and 'Dicky' Dykes in turn managed the ferry for her. During this time the ferry landings were resited 150 yards SE, to the present site. (During the present century the river has widened as its muddy banks have collapsed, and the site of the ferry had been moved once before). 'Dicky' Dykes was the first to work from the present site: on his retirement in 1956, Mrs. Smart decided to surrender the lease, due to expire on 1st January 1957.

Messrs. Hartnell and Taylor auctioned the ferry rights for the Crown on 17th July at the Dolphin Inn, Uphill. It was pointed out that the tenancy was subject to the payment of £1 a year to the Board of Trade and £20 to Mr. Vowles of Brean Farm, for the right for ferry passengers to cross his land on the Brean side. The auction was enlivened when Mr. H.W. Hayden of the Weston Marine Co., suggested that purchase would not give the tenant exclusive ferry rights. This was hotly refuted by Mr. Hartnell, who pointed out that Uphill ferry was a public service and there was an obligation to run it. It later transpired however that the tenant would not be under obligation but would have exclusive rights to operate whenever he desired. Eventually the ferry was purchased by Frank Watts, a member of Weston lifeboat crew, who paid only £6 for the residue of the expiring lease. Commented Mr. Hartnell, as he slammed down his gavel, "I have sold a few things cheaply in my time, but I do not think I have ever sold anything quite as cheaply as this". The ferryboat **Mary** was sold to another bidder for £56.

Although the ferry was shown (as it still is) in Ordnance Survey Maps, and was mentioned in the Weston Guide, it was no longer a 24 hour, 12 month service because it was not economically viable; but Weston's Council received numerous complaints from people who found no ferryman at hand when they wanted one; and criticisms of the running of the ferry were made at a meeting of the Highways & Works Committee, in June 1962. But Frank Watts was unmoved. "It's ridiculous" he said "to expect someone to be on hand all day, at this time of the year, costing between £10-£15 a week, just to collect a few shillings". He pointed out that the ferry had paid well enough when the old fort café was working at Brean Down, and suggested that Weston Council, as owners of the Down, should provide there some attraction for visitors. The Council however were not disposed to do this, and Frank Watts sub-let the ferry later that year. His tenants were the Bruefords - Frank and Jim till 1962, and thereafter Bill and Reg. Reg Brueford found that on average the ferry carried between 120 and 150 people a day at the height of the season. He kept going till 1970, by which time the landing-stages were in a state of collapse and the cost of rebuilding them seemed prohibitive. 5 years then elapsed when the ferry did not run. Eventually Reg Brueford and Gordon Gillam began renovating the landing stages at a cost of nearly £300 and acquired a new ferro-concrete motor-ferry for a cost of £850, the **Macboat**.

In 1975 Uphill ferry resumed operation under Gordon Ferryman (what better name?) who is still in charge today. It is still, of course, a summertime-only service, but runs as required, and the fare (6d. in 1927) is still only 15p. Three boats are available for the service: the **Macboat**, engined with an 8hp. diesel and having a passenger capacity of 12; the **Skylark**, a fibreglass dinghy with a capacity of 10; and an unnamed wooden punt (capacity 4) for use at dead low water. Owing to the steepness of the banks, intending passengers do not see the river until quite close to it, and at low water have to descend steeply to the water-level, to find that the boat trip is only a matter of a yard or two.

Since 1974 that narrow strip of water has been the county boundary of Avon and Somerset. It has also, over the years, witnessed events of drama and humour. One day after high water when the ebb, plus floodwater, was flowing strongly, Gordon was rowing some people across, as the motorboat was

Brean-Uphill: The aptly named Gordon Ferryman working the punt at low water - a tricky operation in spite of the short distance.

out of order. Headway soon became impossible, and then a rowlock gave way! Fortunately a buoy was at hand: here Gordon hung-on with his anxious passengers, until a 10 ton sloop gave them a tow. The sloop's powerful engine could only just make headway, and her log was registering 7 knots!

There is probably no ferry in the West country where it is easier to fall overboard than at Brean, at low water. This is because only a small boat can be used, the landing stages are narrow and steep, and the river flows swiftly. But humour is not always absent. In 1978 a heavy housewife fell in the water while disembarking. She was gasping and spluttering in the water as her excited daughter exclaimed: "It's a good job you've got your swimming costume on under your dress, Mummy!." The following year a 16-stone woman not only fell between boat and stage but in falling grabbed Gordon Ferryman by the hair and pulled him in also! It took three strong men to get this particular lady out of the water!

The most remarkable instance however was on a May Sunday evening in 1980. Gordon had just closed the ferry and winched up the boat when two women appeared on the Brean side, and he felt he must oblige them. "It was low water" he says. "I took the dinghy down the slip, and pushed it across, keeping hold of the painter. I told them to get in one at a time and I would pull them across. After some argument as to who should go first, the thinner one got in but didn't let go of the stage, and her feet pushing the boat out, she finished up strung full length, face down above the water". The lady was resourceful, however. She calmly pulled the boat back to the stage by her toes, against a strong tide, until she could sit on the end of the stage planking. Gordon describes it as a "super-human feat", and indeed it was.

COMBWICH PASSAGE: This once busy ferry seems not to have lasted into the present century. Mr. E. Darch, the senior resident of Combwich today, assures us that no regular, manned ferry had run since 1903 at the latest; but that in the earlier years of this century a boat was left available (usually a "Combwich flattener") and it was a case of 'Do it yourself'. In the Notes and Queries column of the 'Somerset County Herald' newspaper for 19th March 1938, a correspondent replies to a query about Combwich ferry as follows:- "The boat was always there on one side or the other, but I cannot tell exactly how the boatman was found if he was not on the spot". The last of the casual ferrymen was George Haste.

Yet the passage was extensively used in the last century both by pedestrians and for the crossing of cattle and goods. Combwich then served as an outport for Bridgwater, and loading or discharging there relieved a skipper of the rather hazardous navigation further up the Parrett, which is a very muddy river with a serpentine course. There was clearly plenty of work for the ferry when the river was lined with shipping and an average of 120 ships a month were trading into the Parrett.

On the east bank the ferry connected with the road to Pawlett Hill, and near the landing was a passage inn known as 'White House' which as a building has long disappeared, though some fragments remain. In mediaeval times the ferry doubtless carried many pilgrims to and from Glastonbury Abbey, and traces of the 'Pilgrims' Walk' can still be seen near Hill House at Combwich.

Berta Lawrence, in 'Coleridge and Wordsworth in Somerset' (pub.1970) tells us that the essayist Thomas de Quincy used Combwich Ferry on his way to see the poet Coleridge in 1796, then at Alfoxden: and that the Wordsworths advised friends they were inviting to visit them, that they would shorten their journey from Bristol by using Combwich Passage.

During the last century the ferry rights must have belonged to the Lee family, who owned the quay and waterfront and had shipping interests. Their house with its lookout tower still stands; but whether one of the row of small cottages north of the Pill once served as the ferry house, or alternatively the ferry lease was held by the publican at White House Inn, is no longer known. The river was fordable at low tide, but a causeway which existed within the memory of today's oldest residents, has since disappeared. In the Ordnance Survey large-scale map for 1904, Combwich passage is clearly marked, and footpaths shown from the Anchor Inn on the west bank and from the White House Inn on the east.

5.

Rivers

Taw &

Torridge

North Devon.

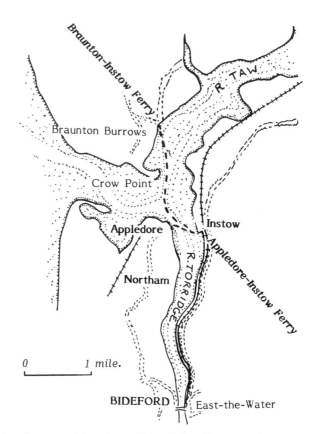

Braunton Burrows

Crow Point

Appledore

Instow

Northam

0   1 mile.

BIDEFORD   East-the-Water

BRAUNTON FERRY: This was a triangular ferry working from Crow Point, Braunton Burrows, to Instow Quay and/or Appledore. It is a passage that has not been worked for the last 40 years and possibly longer. There is little documentation, and accurate information is hard to obtain. W.G. Hoskins in his 'Devon', refers to it as being 'the only ferry of note in North Devon', but he is perhaps being less than just to the Appledore-Instow ferry with its long and interesting history.

The earliest reference we have to Braunton Passage is in 1797, when the local squire, Philip Rogers Webber J.P., in a list of local distances on routes which he habitually used, noted that the distance to the ferry from Braunton Church was "three and a half miles to the bording place". Lt.Cdr. John Gammon of Braunton Museum has pointed out that the route to the ferry was different in 1797, the roads and waterways having been modified after 1811. Ogilby's map of 1675 shows the main road from Bideford to Ilfracombe going down the east side of Braunton Burrows, between the sand hills and the marshes, to the mediaeval chapel of St. Anne's. The remains of this chapel are under sand about half a mile due west of the still-standing ferry house, and this must have been the site of the original crossing, which was no doubt much used from the sixteenth century to the nineteenth. It was then superseded by turnpike roads between Bideford and Barnstaple, and Barnstaple and Ilfracombe. Thenceforward it was no longer part of a highway, but dependent on certain traffic which was not destined to last indefinitely. There was still regular business to be had conveying passengers to the emigrant ships calling at Appledore Pool for America, and sailors of North Devon joining or leaving ships of the Royal Navy at Plymouth: but in 1860 came the closure of the Caen mills on Braunton Marsh, and in 1874 the railway reached Instow. These factors certainly sounded the death-knell of Braunton ferry.

The rights of most ancient ferries were vested in Manors, but it appears that in the case of Braunton, attempts to trace a ferry licence and thus prove ownership, have been abortive. In the tithe award of 1841 the owner of the ferry house is given as Sir Arthur Chichester, Bart. The Chichesters were lords of the manor but there is no evidence that they exerted any control over the ferry. As far as we know, boatwork was free. However, keelage was charged on landings at Page's Pill (directly opposite the ferry house) and the lord of the manor possibly made a charge for the ferry using his pill.

The diaries of Squire Webber record that the ferry toll, at the end of the eighteenth century was a shilling; and that his daughters Susan and Caroline used the ferry to reach their friends in Weare Gifford and Bideford. On one of these trips, in 1806 we learn that the friend they were to visit sent a carriage to meet the ferry at Appledore. The ferry house of those days is still standing, though modified and modernised. Sited on a small eminence known as Bench Hill, it has been known since the days of the ferry as White House, and is conspicuous from Appledore Quay. The census for 1841 shows that the occupier was then Charles Oatway (25) with his family and an 'apprentice', John Hair. The 1851 census tells us that the resident ferryman was then James Mitchell (37) and that his wife was named Maria.

In 1910 the sea bank was breached by rough seas at a high tide, and much damage was done. Mrs. Squires, the present occupant of the Marsh toll house, has told me that her father as a young man was one of a party of labourers from Appledore who repaired the breach, and that they went to and from their work by the Braunton ferry. By this time there was no resident ferryman, and the occasional would-be passenger had to stand on the shore and wave a coat or kerchief to summon the boat from Appledore. Among the last users of this passage may have been the nursing staff of the old 'fever hulk' which was moored near Crow Point in the early years of the present century.

The Braunton ferry has found at least two niches in English literature. In R.D. Blackmore's 'The Maid of Sker' (1872) we have in chapter 35 the Polite Ferryman's graphic account of starting a ferry by the Limekiln, east of Heanton Court. In J.D. Page's "The Coasts of Devon and Lundy Island" we read on page 136:- "taking one of the ferry boats that lie waiting on the beach we cross to Appledore.......you could not go very far without grounding upon a sand bank or having to pull your arms out against a current which could take you out to the bar in no time."

These references draw your attention to the fact that Braunton passage was an arduous one to work when one was dependent only on oars and a lugsail. At high water the Taw estuary is nearly a mile wide at this point, and at ebb tide a current in excess of seven knots would test both the strength and the skill of the ferryman.

APPLEDORE - INSTOW: This, the only ferry to cross the Torridge, has a multilateral history; for although the firm now running the service has been concerned with the ferry since the last quarter of the nineteenth century, they were, until World War II, just one among a number of long-established competitors.

There have never been any 'rights of ferry' and the service has always been open to any local waterman who cared to pay the peppercorn rent for landing passengers at Instow quay. The shore at Instow belonged to the Christie family of Tapley Park, and the squire's agent collected 2/6d. a year from each of the ferrymen, for the quay was the only practicable landing-place on the Instow side. The men regarded the 2/6d. as money well spent; the more so because every Christmas the squire was wont to bestow a brace of hares on every ferryman who had paid his rent!

Today the ferry runs in summertime only, and for just six hours of each tide when there is sufficient water at the landing-places: but throughout most of its history the ferry worked the year round, and at all states of the tide. The river then had not silted as it has today, and the shallow-draught ferries of lugs'l and oars could reach Instow quay via a gut (narrow channel) through the shingle. Over the years the gravel has been lifted and sold, and mud has filled the gut.

Until 1939 the ferry was kept busy by the railway at Instow station. This was the popular route to Appledore for summer visitors, and Miss D. Beara of the Maritime Museum recalls how the locals would take the ferry on Saturday afternoons at the height of the season, to see what visitors were arriving. Much the same folk came year by year and they knew for whom to look. But there was more urgent business afoot than mere curiosity. Many seaside landladies had a particular ferryman with whom they preferred to do business, and would instruct him to fetch their visitors. Before the 4pm. train from London drew in, the ferryboats were clustered at Instow Quay. The visitors, their baggage on trolleys with attendant porters, were assailed by voices shouting 'Ferry to Appledore!' If a ferryman saw his customer boarding another man's boat, he would go over and say 'Excuse me. Are you staying at Mrs. So-&-So's?' If the answer was 'yes' his reply was 'Well, I've been sent to fetch you'. The ferrymen had an 'understanding' to surrender such passengers and harmony usually prevailed, but there was the occasional flare-up! For the 'unattached' visitors the competition was keen indeed!

The ferry also conveyed parcels and light goods sent by rail the year round, and the mails. About 1848 Appledore folk had become very dissatisfied with mail service via Bideford. Many of them entered into an arrangement with Samuel Fursey, Instow shoemaker and cobbler, to have their mail delivered to his premises whence it was collected by ferryman Sam Fishley, and brought to Appledore by ferry. All such mail was addressed to 'A.N.R. Instow', and I have seen a number of these envelopes which have been preserved by Miss Beara. These letters travelled in the ferry in a large box labelled A.N.R. This had been going on for many years when one day a passenger boarded the ferry who was inquisitive about the box. When told 'Oh, that's the post for Appledore', he

Instow ferryboats at Appledore old slip c. 1914. Jack Powe is crossing the slip to make fast a painter while Jack Bailey is coming alongside with two passengers. Albert Powe, then a boy is in **Enterprise** *fending off from a moored boat (right).*

revealed that he was a G.P.O. official and had reason to suspect they were 'tampering with the Mail'. Fursey and Fishley protested that the G.P.O. had completed delivery of the mail when it reached Instow and its movement thereafter was none of their business. The inspector visited the people receiving their mail by ferry, and listened sympathetically to their complaints about Appledore-addressed mail. The outcome was that the G.P.O. agreed to regularise the position by making an agreement with an approved ferryman for official transport of the mail.

R.('Bobby') Smallridge was given the mail contract about the turn of the century. The ferry and the mail were his life's work. Daily he collected Appledore mail from the 6am. train, ferried it across and then, with another postman who met him on landing, delivered the letters. He finished by 10.30am. and returned to Instow for a late breakfast. After working the ferry in the afternoon, he would collect Appledore's outgoing mail for the 8pm. train to London. Even after other ferrymen had resorted to motorboats, Bobby Smallridge continued to work by oars and sail. His two boats were named **Royal Mail** and **Winifred**. The ferry mail came to an end when the passenger train service was withdrawn on the 30th June 1939. Thereafter Appledore mail came by mail-van from Bideford, but Bobby Smallridge continued to work the ferry till he was 81. He died in the early 'fifties at the age of 83, but his daughter is today the postmistress of Instow,

One of the best-known ferrymen was William Bailey, who died in 1955 aged 79. With his brother Jack he worked on the ferry until after World War II. Their father Philip Bailey had been a ferryman before them. William Bailey had only partially-formed ears, and always wore his hair long, and a large felt hat, to hide the deformity. He was a well-loved and much-respected character, and local people can recall how he carried children on his back through the mud, when the ferry taking them to school was working at low water. George ('Monkey') Day worked with the Baileys from 1910-1914 and then left the ferry to work in Devonport Dockyard. For years one of William Bailey's regular duties was ferrying Appledore schoolgirls who attended the Barnstaple Grammar School.

Few families contributed more to the ferry than the Fishwicks. Grandfather Ned Fishwick worked the ferry in the latter years of the nineteenth century. His son Tom succeeded him, and lost his life in the one great tragedy that occurred on the Instow ferry service. In wild weather, on 19th February, 1910, when great waves were rolling into the estuary, his boat, under lugs'l, was overwhelmed and capsized. Tom Fishwick was a strong swimmer, but handicapped by his oilskin coat and boots he exhausted his strength trying vainly to save his three passengers. He was a good man and his loss was keenly felt. Tom's younger son, John Fishwick, was only 6 years old at the time of this disaster, and understandably his mother hoped he would look for some job other than the ferry when he left school. From the age of 14 to 21 he served an apprenticeship as a shipwright, a career he had to abandon when an accident deprived him of the sight of his left eye. In 1928 he returned to the family tradition, and with successive boats named **Helena, Hilda, Petrel** and **Sally**, worked the ferry daily, winter and summer, in all weathers, from 6am. to 8pm. till he retired in 1952. Today he is still a familiar figure on Appledore Quay.

Another family whose association with the ferry began in the last century was the Vaggers. Albert Vaggers spent the greater part of his life on the ferry, and died in 1938. In the 'twenties his sons Albert and John worked with him. John invested in a motor ferry named the **Hilda**. But tragedy came to this family on 17th June, 1928. At the age of 23 John Vaggers was drowned on the bar while fishing with a 29 year old passenger named Henry Gilbert, a visitor. Their sailing boat was observed floating keel uppermost off Braunton Burrows, but there was no witness of what had happened. John Vaggers and his passenger, whose bodies were later recovered, are buried in adjoining graves in Appledore Churchyard. The Vaggers' ferry was later acquired and run by John Fishwick.

During wintertime, traffic on the ferry was insufficient to support more than a few of the men, and the remainder had to seek other employment until the next season. Among those who operated in the summer only, were the Powe family. Jack Powe started ferry work immediately after the Great War. On discharge from H.M. Forces he bought an 18ft. boat for £18. 'A pound a foot' was then the usual price for clincher-built Watermens' boats; today similar boats built of wood, cost nearer £100 a foot! Jack named his boat **Enterprise** and eventually acquired four others. His sons, as soon as they were old enough, assisted him and a good business was built up with river sailing and fishing trips in addition to the ferry. Jack Powe studied his customers. He realised that while few occasional passengers knew the name of their ferryman, they could read and remember the name of his boat. He therefore renamed his four pleasure boats **Enterprise** to match the name of his ferry, and gave his house the same name! He also reasoned that the public liked their boatman to look the part, and he and his assistants were distinctive in Appledore because they always wore seamen's caps with starched white covers. His younger son Albert, who still lives on Appledore quay, worked on the ferry till he was sixteen, and recalls that the Winterbotham family who holidayed in Appledore every summer, used to hire all their boats at £2 a week each, plus a £1 tip for the boatmen!

The Pidlers of Instow were another family long associated with the ferry. Jack Pidler was a summertime ferryman from the latter years of the last century until after the Great War. He was a member of the Appledore Regatta Committee and his name appears with others on a Regatta poster for 1900 which is displayed in the Maritime Museum. Among the events listed was the annual Ferry and Watermen's Race for 4-oar boats under 20 ft. The first prize in this event is shown as £3 - a most useful sum in those days! Jack Pidler also appears in a very fine photograph which shows a group of ferrymen awaiting train passengers at Instow quay. Jack was followed on the ferry by his son Sam, who worked the passage between the wars.

The present operators, F. Johns & Son of Instow, have been on the Ferry since the 1870s, and today they also own a chandlery and a cafe in Instow. Norman Johns, today's ferryman, took over the business after demobilisation from World War II; his father Freddy Johns, grandfather Dicky Johns and great-grandfather 'Daddy' Johns were on the ferry before him. His own son is already following in his footsteps. The regular ferry is a 32 foot motor boat **Swiftsure**, fitted with radio-telephone for ship-to-shore contact with the office at Instow. A smaller boat is available for relief work. With a crew of Cox'n and toll-collector, the ferry operates every 20 minutes for three hours either side of high-water - the nearest this passage has known to a timetable service.

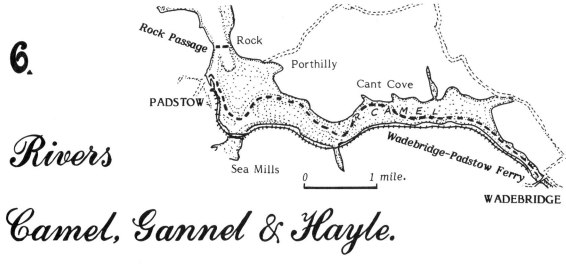

6

Rock Passage
Rock
Porthilly
Cant Cove
PADSTOW
R. CAMEL
Wadebridge-Padstow Ferry
Sea Mills
0   1 mile.
WADEBRIDGE

Rivers

Camel, Gannel & Hayle.

North Cornwall & St. Michael's Mount, South Cornwall.

PADSTOW - ROCK: The origins of the Rock Passage are lost in the mists of time. However we know that it has been a Duchy Ferry ever since the creation of the Duchy of Cornwall in 1337, and the Black Prince was therefore the original lessor. It was attached to the manor of Penmayne in St. Minver, and was originally called Black Rock Passage from an outcrop of rock near the ferry landing on the St. Minver side. Hence Rock village also derives its name. A passage-boat was rented by Penmayne Manor to the ferry tenant, who had to pay 13/- a year.

Little is known of the ferry's history through the intervening centuries, but by 1870 the rent had risen to £12, and by 1900 to £50. The latter rise clearly reflects the higher takings consequent on the new fashion of seaside holidays for the middle-classes, and the arrival of the railway at Wadebridge and Padstow. Since then the rights have been leased by the Duchy to the Padstow Harbour Commissioners. Until about 1973 the Commissioners sub-let the ferry to local boatmen, but they have since operated the passage themselves. (At one time during the 1950s it seemed that the Duchy were less than satisfied with the indirect tenancy, and proposed to offer the lease direct to tne sub-tenant, but the Commissioners somehow prevailed on them to renew the lease in their favour).

A horse-and-wagon boat operated until the later years of the nineteenth century. The last of these was eventually laid up in Dennis Creek and was not replaced. With the coming of the railway in 1899, Dennis Creek was bridged by an arch navigable only by small boats, so the old ferry was there to stay, and no trace of it exists today.

From the latter years of the last century the ferryman was Hodge Helbren, who used a row boat with lugsail, typical of the time. Crossing from Rock on one wild winter Sunday in 1906, he had unwisely made fast his sheet; a fierce gust caught the boat as she was crossing the Town Bar and capsized her, to the horror of onlookers on Padstow Quay. Hodge Helbron lost his life; the last and the only recorded fatality on the Rock ferry. Boats were hurriedly manned and rushed to the scene but they were too late, and could only retrieve the ferryman's hat from the windswept waters. Helbren's body was later recovered, and he lies buried in Porthilly churchyard.

Hodge Helbren was succeeded as ferryman by Joss Rawe and his son Will. Joss introduced a motorboat on the ferry, about 1913. When Will was called up for the Armed Forces in the Great War, Joss felt unable to maintain the service on his own, and arranged with one William ('Bluey') England to work the ferry until young Will Rawe returned from the war. Evidently there was nothing in writing: for when young Will returned from the war, 'Bluey' England refused to surrender the lease and the Rawe family's connection with the ferry which had lasted about 19 years, came to an end. A pre-1914 photo of the lugs'l ferry, with Joss Rawe and his son, can be seen in Padstow Museum.

Like the Rawes, England used an oars-and-sail ferry as well as a motorboat, and was the last Rock ferryman to do so. In the time of Joss Rawe and 'Bluey' England the ferry worked a timetable service in winter, leaving Padstow at a quarter to the hour, and Rock on the hour, with a continuous service operating in the summer. England worked the ferry for about sixteen years.

In 1932-3 the lease passed to Stephen Bate Brabyn. He used three motorboats, the **St. Enodoc** (12 passengers), **St. Saviour** (a 32ft. ex R.N. Cutter, Board of Trade licensed for 36 passengers), and the **Au Revoir** (12 passengers). Brabyn Lindsey was the first to use a semi-diesel engine in a Rock ferry, a Petter engine installed in the **St. Saviour**. The ferry toll in those days was 3d. each way. Building workers and golf course caddies were among the regular users. Stephen Brabyn worked the ferry for nearly fourteen years.

Bill Lindsey (Brabyn's nephew) was the next lessee, his 'reign' extending from 1945 to 1966. He recalls that he had to pay his ferrymen £3.5s.0d. a week, and that in winter the week's takings were often scarcely sufficient to cover this. The working hours of the ferry were now: April and October (8 - 6), May and September (8 - 7), June, July, August (8 - 8), November to March (8 - 5). This compares favourably with today, when a 12 hour service is working in August only. Bill Lindsey used four boats during his time:- **St. Enodoc (II)**, **St. Minver**, **Petrockstowe** (all of 12 passengers capacity) and **St. Saviour II**, a Board of Trade licensed boat for 28 passengers. He was a boatbuilder, and all these ferries except **St. Minver** he had built in his own yard. His **Petrockstowe** is still in use today; it was the first Rock ferry with a fully-diesel engine, a 10hp. Petter, which it still retains. This boat is now used as relief ferry and Harbourmaster's launch.

When Bill Lindsey retired from the ferry scene in 1966, the lease was taken up by John England (grandson of 'Bluey'), who was the last local operator to obtain a sub-lease from the Harbour Commissioners. His boats were noteworthy for their highly-flared bows. At least one, the **Jacqueline**, is still in use on the river. Among his ferrymen was Alfred Giddy, who had previously worked for Bill Lindsey, and today is on England's cruise boat **Tri-Star**. When John England's lease expired, the Harbour Commissioners decided to operate the ferry themselves. England's boats were offered to them, but they opted for new craft. Some of the erstwhile ferries including the 40 foot **Privateer** were sold to D.E.F. Kingsbury of Poole. The Commissioners' ferryboats are with one exception unnamed and bear numbers only. Ferry No.1 is used as a summer boat only and is hauled up on the quay for the winter. She is 42ft. in length, has a 140hp. 6-cylinder General Motors engine, and a passenger certificate for 90, with a crew of two. In addition to ferry No.2 (capacity 12) and No.3 (capacity 25) is the relief boat, **Petrockstowe** as before mentioned.

The larger ferries are fitted with a steel landing-step unit on the port side or the bow, and in good summer conditions it is common for them to cross with the steps outboard. This step-unit is needed on the St. Minver side, where successive landing-stages have succumbed to the unstable sands. At Padstow the ferry operates from the harbour-wall steps, except for the lowest half-hour or so of tide, when the boats use a landing further downstream, near Brae Hill.

During a recent season Ferry No.3 distinguished herself by stranding on Town bar on a falling tide, the passengers being taken off in small boats while in 1977 there was a near fatality when an elderly women fell between ferry and steps when trying to embark at Padstow quay. She was rescued by the prompt action of the ferrymen, but incidents such as these are occasional in the life of any ferry service. In these days when large numbers of small private craft in the hands of amateurs are proliferating in all popular estuaries such as the Camel, the need for vigilance is ever-present. On my last crossing, in Ferry No.1, Skipper Jermyn, young, friendly, and very competent, told me that only a few days previously he had had to go full astern when a private boat cut across his bows.

PADSTOW - WADEBRIDGE: One thing that has become clear in the course of our researches is that down-river ferries are much less well-documented than across-river ferries which are, in effect, parts of the highway. Down-river ferries provided an alternative highway to the road, and for the most part they flourished, defying even the turnpikes, until the railway found its way down their river-valley, and put them out of business.

On Padstow quay I questioned an elderly fish-salesman about the one-time ferry to Wadebridge. "I've heered tell ovit", he said, and that was the most informative response any of the locals were able to give me. Don Rawe, well-known Padstow resident with whom I discussed this ferry, pointed out that the River Camel is so silted up today that only a small open boat could now reach Padstow, and that only at the top hour of the tide. Almost to the end of the nineteenth century however a ferry most certainly plied the 5 miles when the tide served - a boat large enough to carry a little freight - and provided a journey 3 miles shorter than by road. Stories - possibly apocryphal - come down to us from those days, and are recorded in Claude Berry's 'Padstow 1895-1925' (Lodenek Press 1976).

In one it appears that on a day in the 'nineties, John the ferryman had reached Wadebridge when the wind rose to gale force and he realised he would be unable to return home to Padstow by the ferryboat. His brother lived in Wadebridge, but they were not close, and he did not care, he declared afterwards, 'To poke meself in there'. Overcoat over his arm, he was walking the streets disconsolately when he sighted the owner of a Padstow shipyard about to start home in his horse and trap. Old John was not one for asking favours for himself and only summoned up courage to speak after deciding on an indirect approach: "I wonder, zur, if you'd be so good as to take 'ome my overcoat?" "Certainly, John", was the reply "but how are you intending to get home yourself?" "Well, zur, oi 'ardly like to tell 'ee: but I were thinking maybe I'd get inzide the coat".

On the 27th March 1899 the North Cornwall Railway reached Padstow, its line hugging the south bank of the sandy, windswept Camel all the way, and covering the distance from Wadebridge in ten minutes. There was no way the ferry, dependent on sails and oars could compete, and if it had not already finished this was most certainly the end.

FERN PIT FERRY: This ferry is probably not more than a hundred years old. Its origins seem to have gone unrecorded, but the rights of ferry have always derived from ownership of the land, and it is thought a service was started about 1880, when Newquay was developing as a resort after the arrival of the railway in 1875. This has always been a holidaymakers' rather than a worker's ferry. The estuary is fordable for most of the tide but there is a tidal range of 14 feet.

From 1900-1912 the ferryman was "Mitch" Trethewey, who paid an annual rent to the then owner of the land on the Newquay side, a Miss Norway. He operated a summer-only ferry, from Whitsun to Mid-September, and this is still the case today. Trethewey was succeeded in 1912 by R. Hemsley Northey, who was ferryman for 33 years including both World Wars, till 1945. The fare in those days was 2d. each way.

One of Hemsley Northey's occasional customers was an Irishman, resident at Crantock. He was a big, heavily-built man and had a reputation for rather heavy drinking. On one occasion he had crossed to Newquay in his best suit for a social occasion. On his return to the ferry steps it was clear he had celebrated well, for his progress was far from steady. Disdaining assistance, he took a first step into the boat and a second out of the boat of the far side! A moment later he surfaced, and struck out strongly for the Crantock shore! He would not be picked up, and was finally seen emerging on the far side and trudging wetly uphill towards his home!

The Northey family eventually acquired the foreshore on both sides of the estuary, which gave them sole rights to operate. George Northey, the present ferry proprietor, took over from his father in 1945. Meanwhile the Gannel, with its sands washed clean by every tide, has become a popular family bathing and picnic resort, and George Northey has found that being ferryman involves also being the unofficial lifeguard.

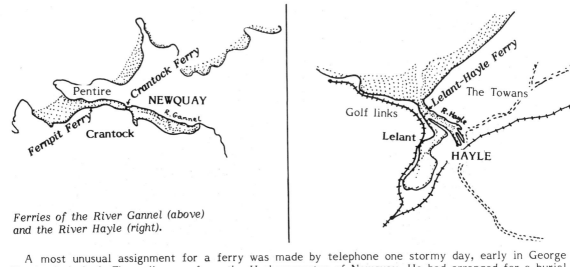

Ferries of the River Gannel (above) and the River Hayle (right).

A most unusual assignment for a ferry was made by telephone one stormy day, early in George Northey's 'reign'. The call came from the Harbourmaster of Newquay. He had arranged for a burial of ashes at sea that day, but the weather was too rough for a boat to venture out. The widow of the deceased was arriving by rail from the north with some friends, and had to return that day. Could the ceremony take place, he asked, in the sheltered waters of the Gannel, from the ferry? George Northey was somewhat surprised. The waters of the Gannel might be sheltered, but at the time of tide asked, they were also shallow. However, he felt he must help if he could.

At the appointed time a surpliced figure appeared descending the cliff path, leading the small funeral party. Parson and mourners safely aboard, George took the ferry a little way upstream, where there are some deeper pools in the channel, and the commital service proceeded. When the casket was consigned to the waters, however, it disappeared only briefly and floated on the surface! It was embarrassing to say the least, but George steered for the casket, recovered it, and weighted it with sand. A second attempt at committal was successful; the party returned to the shore and made their departure. Next day however revealed that the ebb tide had not co-operated sufficiently with their efforts: for the casket lay exposed on the sands, and George had to dispose of it sub silentis!

Fern pit ferry operates from two and a half hours before high water till two and a half hours after. Two licensed boats are employed: a rowing boat is used at the beginning and end of the period, when the crossing is short, and a motor boat takes over during the period of deep water and a longer crossing. Both boats were purpose-built for the ferry: the rowboat **Elizabeth** (1934) has a capacity of seven, while the motor-boat **Sunshine** (1952) has a capacity of twelve, and is fitted with wheel steering.

CRANTOCK FERRY: The Crantock Ferry to Newquay dates from the nineteenth century, if not earlier. From the Great War onwards it was owned by the Tozer family of Crantock, who held the land on that side. But there were no exclusive rights and eventually rivals appeared in the Morris family of Newquay. The competition was very keen during bank holidays and the height of the season. An authenticated story shows how keenly ferryman Tozer tried to assert what he felt were his prior 'rights':-

One day he had taken a large picnic party of two boatloads from Newquay to Crantock, and he fully intended to bring them back. One boatload arrived first at the landing, and he had pulled halfway across to the Newquay side when he saw the remainder of the party coming over the hill. He also saw ferryman Morris beckoning them to his waiting boat. Tozer's passengers were taken aback as he leant on the oars and increased his rate of stroke: and more so, when no sooner had the boat grounded on the sand, than he jumped up and assisted them rapidly out of the boat as though his life depended on it! As they stood proffering their fares, Tozer jumped back and grabbed the oars. "Don't matter about that" he called, as he pulled away. "I've got to fetch they other lot!" Profitability must needs be sacrificed to proprietorship! They were HIS passengers, and he meant to have them!

Today the ferry is managed by two men with a good working relationship. The ferry works for slightly less of the tide than the Fern Pit service, being farther upstream. Paul Crantock starts work from the Crantock bank and moors his boat **Endeavour** on that side; E. ('Digger') Morris starts working from the Newquay shore, with his **Girl Pat**. The Crantock ferry has never known a motor-boat. The **Endeavour** and **Girl Pat** are both 8-capacity rowboats and are smartly maintained.

LELANT - HAYLE: Local historians have been unable to discover the origins of the Lelant Ferry. Even Henderson, in his "Essays in Cornish History" says: "Of Lelant Ferry, across the Hayle estuary, I have no history,..." But there is no doubt of the antiquity of the passage. The Hayle river was a formidable barrier encountered by travellers on the north route into West Cornwall, and there must certainly have been a ferry here from at least the eleventh century. By Victorian times the crossing was popularly known as "Jack the Ferry's"; a soubriquet shrouded in mystery alike for its grammar and for the identity of the original 'Jack', but which remained in use locally till the demise of the ferry.

The earliest ferryman of whom we have any certain knowledge was Tom Gale, who held the office from about 1845 till about 1880. After the introduction of Bank Holidays in 1871 Tom had a particularly busy day every Whit Monday, when St. Ives and Lelant folk used the ferry to reach the annual regatta at Copperhouse Pool. In 1864 Hayle, previously part of the port of St. Ives, became an independent port. Virtually all the quay space was owned by the Copperhouse and Harvey's foundries. When the Copperhouse Company failed, they sold off all their harbourside premises to Harvey's, who thus gained complete control of the harbour. Harvey's controlled the harbour lights, and their operation became the responsibility of the Lelant ferryman, who paid Harvey's an annual rent for the ferry rights. In Tom Gale's time there was a fatal accident at the ferry crossing, though the ferryboat was not involved. A boatload of thirteen young people was returning from a Band of Hope gala on Phillack Towans on 10th July 1866, just as the floodgates had been opened for the periodic sluicing of the river. The boat was capsized and swept seawards over the harbour bar, all but five losing their lives.

Tom Gale was followed as ferryman by Thomas Gall Whatty (senior) about 1880, whose grand-daughter Dorothy Roach still lives in Lelant, and whom I was privileged to meet during my quest for information. Grandfather Whatty, like his predecessor, had the responsibility of tending the two harbour lights. These were in small wooden towers between the golf course and the seashore. The upper lighthouse was painted red and showed a white light: the lower was painted black and showed a red light. Both still stand but are now seldom used. Grandfather Whatty was to lose his life on the ferry, in particularly tragic circumstances. He had moored the ferry late one evening in 1889 after his day's work, when two ships' captains asked him to take them across to the Towans. It was now quite dark and a fast tide was running but Tom Whatty felt he must oblige them. An observer who saw the captains board the ferryboat said afterwards that they appeared to be quarrelling. Their agitation may well have been responsible for the disaster which followed. In midstream, in the darkness, the ferry overturned and none were saved. The cause of the disaster is not certainly known, for it was unwitnessed. The ferryman's body came ashore later at Perranporth: he was a good swimmer and it is conjectured that he died through trying to save his passengers.

His son, Tom Whatty Jnr. took over the ferry prematurely when only a boy of sixteen, but soon became greatly respected by all who knew him. He brought to his work a great love of nature and of all God's creatures, which earned him the friendship of one of his regular passengers, the American naturalist and author, W.H. Hudson. In Hudson's book 'The Land's End' (1911) Tom Whatty Jnr. has a small but secure place in English literature. On at least two occasions Tom was responsible for saving life, yet the first of these took place not on the water, but ashore. The railway line to St. Ives crosses the path to the ferry by a small bridge and then skirts the golf course on the sand dunes. One day about 1884 Tom was in his ferryman's hut when he heard an ominous sound and rushed out. The railway embankment had slipped and the subsidence had left the track unsupported. Tom knew that a passenger train was due at any moment. He ran desperately up the track for 500 yards and managed to stop the train 30 seconds before disaster.

In 1887 he went out in his ferry to save the lives of some people whose boat had capsized on the bar. For his bravery in this incident he was presented with a gold watch by the people of Hayle. Sadly, Tom Whatty enjoyed only a short life. He contracted pneumonia and died in February 1910. An article in the Western Morning News of March that year, entitled "The Passing of the Ferryman", described him thus: "a broad-shouldered figure in the prime of life, carrying not an ounce of flesh to spare, curiously garbed in corduroy and fustian, the waistcoat long-sleeved. A slouch hat suggests a noble forehead, the dark brown eyes and swarthy complexion suggest a foreign strain - for the rest a resolute mouth as far as one may judge from the dark moustache, in places turning grey, and from the chin, which nothing hides". Today his daughter Dorothy Roach recalls, of the time of his death: "Mother hoped one of my brothers might have taken on the ferry. But Tom was then completing his studies as a mining engineer - and he had just broken his leg! - while Lionel was already a golf professional". According to Cyril Noall in his 'Beloved St. Ives' (1957), 'young Tom' did take on the ferry for a short while until other arrangements could be made, but his sister does not remember this. In the event it was his uncle Joe Whatty who shouldered the responsibility.

Joe was the brother of Tom Whatty (senior) whom in earlier days he had often helped with the ferry. Looking back to that 1910 Western Morning News article, we find him described as "the patriarchal figure, almost perfect features as far as the shading sou'wester and the great beard allow one to judge them - this is Uncle!" The same article describes a visit to the ferryman's hut as it was in Joe's time. This was a quaint tarred structure, comprising an upturned seagoing barge which the sea had thrown up and wrecked there years before, and a lean-to shed which had been built on to it. "We stoop our heads and enter the narrow doorway - first a kind of porch, a lumber-room for rope and oars and grapnels; beyond and down a step the old barge proper, and the real sanctum of the ferryman - tidy and shipshape - a sandy floor, whitewashed roof and sides; a small window marks the site of the old porthole. The only furniture a small stove and a rude bench. Along the keel of the old ship are stacked rods and guns and landing-nets". Beyond this hut were a fowlhouse and pens: and Dorothy Roach recalls when there were a thousand chickens to be tended! Joe Whatty (who had been a Mevagissey fisherman) worked the ferry for about eighteen months before retiring.

He was succeeded by Tom Pomeroy, who was the nephew of Tom Whatty junior, and a cousin of 'young Tom'. He had been living in St. Austell, but moved to Lelant to carry on the family tradition on the ferry; a man with a kindly and agreeable nature, and reputedly very well-liked by his passengers. His spell as ferryman lasted 22 years and included the period of the Great War. On his retirement in 1932 the long association of the Whatty family with the ferry came to an end. Tom Pomeroy died at the age of 74, in 1957: but his widow lived for many years after.

The last of the Lelant ferrymen was Jack Couch, a fine seaman and a colourful character who is still well-remembered in the district. Jack was an ex-Merchant Service sailor. He knew his tides, and he was never worried by the rip surging out of the estuary when the sluice-gates were opened. He had an enduring fund of sea stories with which he regaled his passengers, and dramatised them with straightforward, earthy humour and the most colourful language. It has been said that it was quite an experience to travel with him, and locally he was appreciatively and affectionately nick-named 'the vulgar boatman'. Indeed, one year a holidaymaker who had taken the ferryman's photo-graph put it in the post addressed to 'The Vulgar Boatman, Lelant, Cornwall': there was no chance of mis-delivery! Even padres were not exempt from Jack Couch's expletives. On one occasion he saw a local clergyman save the ferry fare by wading across at low water. When some hours later the parson returned and hailed the ferry, Jack suggested, in over-ripe language, that his reverence should walk on the water! Jack Couch was ferryman throughout World War II and retired, after 26 years service, in 1958. He died two years later, but no one had been found to succeed him on the ferry.

It is not clear what became of the old sea-barge shack, but when Jack Couch arrived he established a little home for himself on the site. It began as a former ship's wheelhouse which he used as a cabin; but later he rebuilt the remains of a derelict stone coastguard cottage, so that Lelant passage had a ferry house for the first time. Since the ferry ceased it has been converted into a modern dwelling but unfortunately is much altered, and probably little of the original remains, though it is called 'Ferry Cottage'. The original ferryman's shack of the Whatty days stood approximately where the beach cafe is today.

For many years - certainly back to Tom Gale's time, a distinctive type of ferryboat was employed at Lelant. This was the Norwegian type praam, whose shallow draught for'ard enabled passengers to disembark on to dry sand without the use of a gangplank. The Whattys built the ferryboats themselves, copying them from examples brought to Hayle by visiting Scandinavian timber ships. Tom Pomeroy experimented briefly with a motorboat, but found it less satisfactory, and reverted to oars. Jack Couch used a clinker-built waterman's boat.

In 1975, seventeen years after closure, an attempt was made to get the ferry restarted. A complaint made to the Countryside Commission that the lack of a ferry spoiled the amenity of the north coastal footpath, was taken up by the Cornwall County Council, and referred to St. Ives Town Councillors for their views. All were agreed that the ferry was desirable but that it could not operate without subsidy, and the matter had to be shelved on financial grounds. The initiative in restarting the ferry was eventually taken by Mr. and Mrs. Tony Lake, proprietors of the Ferryman's Restaurant and Beach Cafe, at Lelant. With a purpose-built aluminium motorboat built by Truro Marine, and with bearded Allan Thomas of Hayle as ferryman, the service reopened on 1st May, 1981. Defence Minister John Nott (M.P. for St. Ives) was on board for the inaugural trip, with the Mayors and Mayoresses of St. Ives and Hayle.

The visit of a Cheltenham rambler, who was walking the coastal footpath in 1980, prompted the Lakes to contact the Countryside Commission, which agreed to subsidise the ferry. The 'Camborne-Redruth Packet' commented: "this indicates the importance which is attached to bridging this major gap in access to the coast". The service is seasonal (1st May to 31st August) and daily from 11am. to 5pm.

ST. MICHAEL'S MOUNT FERRY: Few British ferries work in a more impressive setting than those which cross the waters of Mounts Bay to the island of St. Michael's Mount. Crowned by a castle whose tower rises to 238 feet above low water the island has been owned by the St. Aubyn family since 1660, and was given to the National Trust in 1954 by the third Lord St. Levan. His son, the fourth baron, still lives in the castle. Today the Mount is open daily to the general public during the summer season, from 1st April to 31st October inclusive. A causeway half a mile long connects the island with the beach at Marazion at low water, but when the incoming tide starts to overflow it, the ferries emerge from the island's harbour and provide a shuttle service.

Until after the Great War, public ferrying, when the castle was open, was by rowing boat. John Mathews (retired Harbourmaster) recalls that when he was a boy in the first decade of the century, only one boat was an authorised ferry, and that the ferrymen were invariably retired seamen. The present Lord St. Levan recalls: "My great-uncle, the second Lord St. Leven, often had to lend his motorboat to tow the rowing boat back if there was a contrary wind". Later it became necessary to limit the number of boats allowed to land passengers on the Mount. It is said that at one time a boatman retiring from the ferry would sell his 'Lease' or 'permit' to a successor. Motorboats were first used on the ferry after the Great War, about 1921. Today there are seven motor ferries owned by local fishermen, and they have an engaging variety of names:- **Flush of Dawn, Lily Oak, Lowena, Moonbeam, Sea Mist,** and **Viking.** When the tide serves, ferries work from Top Tieb or Gwelva; at about half tide, they work from Chapel Rock, and finally from a stone jetty off the causeway. By this time the causeway is nearly clear of water, but visitors who prefer not to brave the puddles and the spray, continue to fill the last boats, which may have to be poled over a sand bar.

Prior to the 1914-1918 war a steam ferry named the **Emma** ran the three miles to the Mount from Penzance harbour. The owners were Messrs. Hendy's. After the war the **Emma** did not resume, but three motorboats appeared on this run, - the **Busy Bee, Silver Spray,** and another whose name is not recalled. During the mid-twenties they had to face competition from the steam ferry **Nora** owned by Philip Nicholls.

An all-the-year-round service for island residents is maintained by the Mount's own two ferryboats, **Elizabeth** and **Catherine.** In winter they run as required; in summer they work with the public ferries. A principal duty at term-time has always been taking to school the Mount's children at 8.30 am. and bringing them off at 4.30 pm. The Mount's own ferries are recognised by a red upper strake and a coat of arms in the bows.

Visitors landing from ferries at the Mount will see, on the east arm of the harbour, a brass replica footprint of Queen Victoria. This marks the landing-point of the Queen and Prince Albert in 1846. They were brought to the island in the St. Aubyn family barge, which can be seen, beautifully preserved, in chocks on the south wall of the harbour. Built in the last century at Peters' boatyard, Falmouth, it was working as a customs boat 150 years ago, until bought by the St. Aubyn family for use as their private ferry. It must quite certainly be the oldest serviceable ferryboat in Britain. The Mount boatmen have a ceremonial livery worn on important occasions when this family barge is used, a livery believed to have been designed in the 18th century. It consists of a helmet bearing the family crest, a long red coat, and a white fisherman's apron. Also, there is a waterman's badge (with the family crest) on the arm. In the possession of the St. Aubyn family is a coloured photograph of the boatmen wearing this livery in 1883; while displayed in the castle is a painting, sent by H.R.H. Princess of Athlone, of The Mount boatmen in their colourful finery rowing the State Barge.

7.

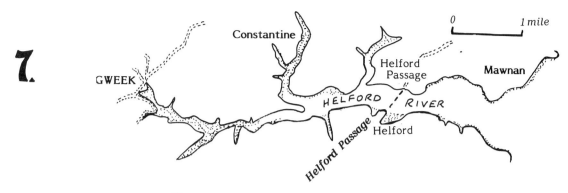

Helford River, South Cornwall

HELFORD PASSAGE: Helford Passage has always been a beautiful place. Within living memory it was also a secluded one, though the ferry was important, constituting the last water-link in the south coast road to the west. Today of course it is host to the motor-car in ever-increasing numbers, and to the boat-on-trailer. Probably the re-discovery of Helford Passage owes much to the aura of romantic adventure bestowed on the estuary by Daphne du Maurier's best-seller, 'Frenchman's Creek'.

The passage anciently belonged to the Bishops of Exeter, in right of their manors of Minster and Penryn-Foreign. Later it passed by sale to the Tyack family of Merthen, and the passage remained manorial until shortly before World War II. We know that in 1538 one John Thomas held the ferry at a rent of sixteen shillings. The passage house was apparently always on the northern side.

During the nineteenth century the boatmen to whom the Tyacks sublet the ferry had an unfortunate reputation for slackness, unreliability, and fondness for the bottle. In September 1803 'The Cornwall Gazette and Falmouth Packet' reported an exasperated Budock farmer as saying, as he waited in the Ferry Boat Inn:=

> "Of all the mortals here below
> Your drunken boatmen are the worst I know;
> I'm here detained, tho' sore against my will,
> While these sad fellows sit and drink their fill.
> Oh Jove, to my request let this be given,
> That these same brethren ne'er see hell nor heaven;
> But with old Charon ever tug the oar,
> And neither taste nor swallow one drop more".

In 1835 the Tyacks rented the ferry to the brewers W. and E.C. Carne on a ninety-nine years lease. The licence for the ferry was thereafter linked with the licence of the Ferry Boat Inn. Carne's were later taken over by the Devenish brewery. The publicans were no more successful than the Tyacks in reforming the indolent habits of the ferrymen. A Miss Fox of Penjerrick was incensed by the constant delays suffered by those going to Falmouth market. In April 1885 'The West Briton & Cornwall Advertiser' reported that she had defrayed the cost of a wooden ferry-shelter on the Manaccan side, so that intending passengers had an alternative to spending their money in the Shipwrights' Arms while they awaited the ferrymen's convenience.

Helford had handled vehicular traffic for many years. The horseboat used to run from Bar Beach on the Constantine side, which shelved less steeply. It could load carts and wagons, but the horses were then unshafted and made to swim astern of the ferry at a rope's end. The horseboat ceased to run before the Great War, about 1910, and there has been no provision for vehicular traffic since.

Reliability seems to have improved by 1914, when Ward & Baddeley's Guide reported:- "Helford ferry is certain, but rather inconvenient at low spring tides. In stormy weather it may not ply". A further improvement in the service was achieved about 1929 when Devenish's replaced the rowboat ferry by a motorboat.

In 1935 the Tyacks sold the ferry to Commander Dowding R.N. The Ferryboat Inn then became a free house and has been so ever since. Dowding demolished the old inn, and built the present one, where Mrs. Dowding presided as Mine Host. In the years immediately before World War II we find Ward Lock & Co.'s Guide to the area stating:- "from Helford a ferry (sixpence) connects several times daily with the coast-watchers' station at Helford Passage, where is the little Ferry Boat Inn, and whence it is but six miles to Falmouth". This suggests that during Commander Dowding's regime the ferry ran to timetable. If so, it was probably the only time in its history that it did. Certainly since then it has run simply as required. We may note in passing that the sixpenny pre-war fare quoted had risen from $\frac{1}{2}$d. at the beginning of the century, and in 1979 was 30 new pence.

The ferry used to ply immediately outside the Ferry Boat Inn, but now leaves from a few yards to the west. On the Manaccan side the landing is at Helford boatyard. The present owners of inn and ferry also operate a fleet of about sixteen motorboats for hire, during the summer season. The ferry boat (no name, but mysteriously numbered K 61) has a capacity of 12 persons. It is fitted with a Yan-Mar single-cylinder Japanese diesel engine which is rather noisy but gives an adequate service speed of 8 knots. "With a light load" the young ferryman told me "we can push her up to nine knots."

8.

River Fal

South Cornwall.

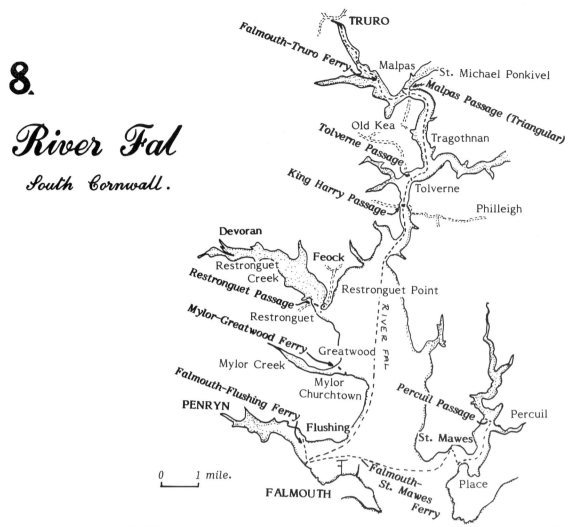

MALPAS PASSAGE: This has always been a triangular ferry, linking St.Michael Penkivel with Malpas (for Truro) and Kea. It is also remarkable for its secure place in literature, being mentioned in "Sir Tristrem", one of the earliest romances in the English language, probably dating from before 1300. Here it is related that Princess Iscult, journeying from the Forest of Morrois (now Moresk, or St.Clements) to the palace of King Mark at Blanchlands (in Kea) was ferried across the river at "Le Mal Pas." Professor Loth has shown that today's Malpas is clearly the same place: and when we recall that Tristrem and Iscult drank the love-potion which ensured their everlasting affection, we must concede that Malpas is the most romantic passage in Britain, a claim reinforced by its very beautiful situation. The name Malpas (pronounced 'Mopus' by the Cornish) seems therefore incongruous, since being derived from the French 'mal-pas' it means 'a bad passage'.

From time immemorial the ferry belonged to the manor of Fentongollan ('Spring of the hazels') on the St. Michael Penkivel side. In 1674 this manor was purchased by Hugh Boscawen, together with the passage ferry, which at the time was held by four persons at a rent of £1. The Boscawen family have lived since 1334 at Tregothnan House (overlooking the Fal, and noted for its 365 windows); the present owner being Lord Falmouth, whose brother Robert Boscawen is M.P. for Wells and Mid-Somerset.

The legendary Princess Iscult is not the only feminine character in the story of Malpas ferry. A Jane Davies, known to all as 'Jenny Mopus' was ferrywoman here for many years at the end of the 18th and beginning of the 19th centuries. A portrait of her in Tregothnan House depicts an austere character with a hawklike nose and wearing a tall hat. It is recorded that she used a large roomy boat, the **Happy-go-lucky**, with its name brightly painted above her own on the transom. An ancient stone shelter, known as 'Jenny Mopus waiting-room' survives today above the old ferry steps at Penkivel.

A horse-and-wagon boat was still in use here until the year 1925, when the delivery carts of Truro baker Mr. Blewett and Truro butcher Mr. Mutton were crossing the ferry daily. Since its abandonment there has been no provision for vehicular traffic, and today even pedestrian passengers are occasional. The remains of the old horse boat lie in the mud at the head of Lambs Creek.

Kea can only be served when the tide is not low; from here the ferry is summoned by a shout. At Malpas is a pontoon jetty (used by the Enterprise boats of the Falmouth-Truro ferry), but the Malpas ferry uses the adjacent beach, and there is a bell for calling the ferryman's attention. At St. Michael Penkivel the original steps below 'Jenny Mopus waiting-room' are no longer used, and the ferry plies from steps below the Ferry House, where the intending passenger knocks to request a crossing.

The exact age of the Ferry House is uncertain, but it cannot be later than mid-17th century, and pre-dates the Boscawen family's acquisition of the ferry. Its present roof, chimneys and facade are thought to be the result of Georgian or early Victorian workmanship on an older building. In the garden are the remains of what appears to have been a former ferryboat which was planted with flowers after its retirement from service.

Close to the Ferry House is the former Ship Inn, licensed prior to 1812 and delicensed in 1854. Now a private dwelling, and named Ferryside Cottage, it was no doubt a well patronised tavern when Malpas (as the outport for Truro) was busy with coastal shipping and the ferry was experiencing its heyday.

From the discontinuance of the horseboat until early 1937 when Sam Martin became ferryman, there seems to have been no incident of note. Malpas ferry remained in operation throughout the troubled years of World War II but there was a change of ferryman in November 1941 when Sam Martin, after nearly five years service, was succeeded by Frederick Simpson. The ferryman from 1956-1970 was named Anderson. On his death that year there was a lapse of a few months when local resident Donald Gunn and others plied the ferry if needed. In the ferryhouse shed is a 16ft. waterman's boat named **Duckweed** used before Anderson's time as an estate workboat. It is destined to be used on the ferry, and today is awaiting repair. It is a carvel-built boat with a mast-step for lug rig. Since 1971 the ferryman has been Mervyn Habgood, a former Thames Waterman of Hounslow, and the first Malpas ferryman to have a boatman's certificate. The present ferry is only a 10'6" dinghy, capacity two passengers, but equipped in accordance with present-day requirements, and well maintained. When **Duckweed** is also available, it will be possible to convey more passengers on a single crossing. No account of the present Malpas ferry would be complete without mention of Mervyn Habgood's little dog "Smee", who has learned the significance of the bell at Malpas, or a shout from Kea. On hearing the summons, "Smee" makes an immediate bee-line for the ferry steps, and races down to the boat-mooring, eager to make the crossing.

A ferryman's life has its lighter moments. One evening at dusk the ferry bell sounded at Malpas and Mervyn called through the gloom 'D'you want the ferry?' On receiving a 'Yes' he pulled across to find a lad standing on the slip with a frying-pan in his hand. It transpired that he did not wish to cross, but wanted to be rowed down-river to find some pals who had gone night-fishing and had forgotten their frying-pan. The expectations of youth are not always realistic. This young man could see nothing incongruous in a ferry (which might meanwhile have been urgently required) chasing a distant boat down King Harry Reach in the dark with a frying-pan.

On another occasion Mervyn had embarked a family at Malpas, but there remained a tall young man on the jetty, dressed rather oddly with a pointed woolly hat and his trousers tucked into his socks. As the ferry had a full load, he was asked if he wanted it to return for him, and he said he did. He was standing motionless in the same place, with his eyes closed, when the boat came back, and had to be brought back to consciousness by the call "Ferry." "I thought I had got a funny one", Mervyn recalls "On the way over I noticed he still had his eyes closed. I asked if he was on holiday and he replied that he was on a walking-and-singing holiday. When we arrived at Penkivel beach he got out, shook my hand, and thanked me for a peaceful crossing. He said he was coming back, so I told him to knock on the door when he did. I was in the sitting-room settling down to watch T.V. when I sensed there was someone about; and there was this chap, standing on the riverside of the house. He hadn't knocked on any of the doors but was just standing there. So I put my boots on and took him over - again with his eyes closed, and his face looking upwards. As he walked up the Malpas slipway he started singing hymns, and I learned afterwards he had been walking round the village singing hymns all the afternoon. Truly it takes all types to make a world.

All the ancient Cornish ferries are attached to manors. Over the years, many of these have been discontinued, while the rights of others have been acquired by local authorities or commercial operators. But not so Malpas, which has the distinction of remaining still manorial; and long may it remain so.

TOLVERNE PASSAGE: The ferry at Tolverne, now discontinued, was of ancient origin, and provided the most direct link between Roseland and Truro - which had a charter from 1135. The whole of the Roseland was then in the ecclesiastical manor of Tregear, which was regularly visited by successive Bishops of Exeter with their retinues. It seems more than probable that Tolverne passage was then in use, and was ecclesiastically owned.

By the end of the 13th century most of Tregear Manor lands had been sold to free tenants. Among the sub-manors thus established was Tolverne, held first by the Le Sor family, but in the early 15th century passing by marriage to the Arundells. Their mansion was close to, and overlooked the passage, and there can be no doubt that the ferry was much used in their time. On 25th January 1627 Tolverne was sold by the Arundells to an Exeter merchant, Mr. Thomas Walker, but in 1631 the property was conveyed to Sir Thomas Drewe and others; and before the mid-century the Tredenham family were the landowners.

There was a tragedy in 1586 when the ferry boat was capsized, though we do not know the cause. All eight passengers were drowned. Their bodies when recovered were buried in Gerrans churchyard, but the grave has no identification stone today.

It is recorded that in 1664 one Alexander Couch was granted a lease of the passage by Sir Joseph Tredenham at an annual rent of 26/8d, with the proviso that the lord was to have free passage for his family and household. The lease included the passage-boat and the passage money; the passage house and cellars; half the fish taken in Tolverne Weir; three fields and mowhay; a right to land sand and dry nets; pasture for a horse and mare in Chapel Wood; the right to draw water from the spring there, and fuel from Polgurran Wood and Lower Burlase. By the living-standards of 17th century ferrymen, the fortunate lessee of Tolverne certainly wanted for little.

Following settlement of a lawsuit between John Tredenham and one Richard Ducke in 1653, ownership of Tolverne and its ferry passage was vested in Richard Ducke and Thomas Matthews. The former died sometime after 1656, and his widow Martha and Thomas Matthews sold Tolverne to Hugh Boscawen on 28th July 1668. It has remained in the possession of the Boscawen family to the present day, and at one time a branch ferry was run to the grounds of Tregothnan.

From Tolverne Passage there is a fine view of the Boscawen's mansion. The Tolverne Inn dated from c. 1500, and successive innkeepers held the ferry lease. It ceased to be an inn after 1833. In the earlier years of the present century there were ferrymen named Gunn and Scoble.

Disaster came again to the ferry in 1933. A party of exuberant cinemagoers were returning from Truro, long after dark, when the boat overturned and sank. The ferryman, Williams, lost his life but the passengers managed to swim ashore.

Williams' successor, whose name was Jenkins, found that traffic was insufficient to provide him with a living, and obtained permission to close the ferry down. Rodney Newman, who had taken over the ferry house in 1934, restarted the ferry and ran it until after World War II broke out, but was not under obligation.At the latest the ferry perhaps ran till the arrival of the United States forces in World War II, when the Tolverne landing became inaccessible to the public. The Americans built a new road down to the old ferry landing, and assembled tank landing craft and invasion barges here until the Normandy landings in 1945. Rodney Newman's son Peter, who succeeded him at the ferry house, obliged the occasional passenger till about 1959. The ferry has not run since; but on the Kea side a sign post somehow overlooked by the highway authority, still points to 'Tolverne Passage'.

KING HARRY PASSAGE: The King Harry passage is one of Cornwall's surprises for the first-time visitor. Here, for more than a mile on both banks of the Fal, the trees come down thickly to the water's edge. From any vantage-point the scene is entirely sylvan, with scarcely a sign of dwellings or of human activity. Nowhere could a busy vehicular ferry seem less likely to be encountered. Yet the 20th century is here: a ribbon of main road, decently hidden by the forestation, emerges briefly at a slip on either shore. Between these points the ferry engulfs nearly thirty vehicles at a time, hurries them quietly across, and disgorges them into the screening of the trees on the other side. We have used King Harry Ferry a number of times, but never fail to be impressed by this astonishing juxtaposition of utter peace and frenzied activity. For the foot passenger, or motorist who deigns to leave his car, an added surprise is usually visible from the ferry's upper deck:- the sight of large ocean-going vessels laid up in King Harry Reach. For this is a deep-water anchorage, and at times of world shipping surplus there may be twenty large merchantmen moored here, unmanned and strangely silent, as though disdaining the bustle of the ferry and preferring to share the calm of the wooded banks.

The very name of King Harry passage is a surprise in itself. The casual visitor invariably assumes that it commemorates a visit to the crossing by Henry VIII. It is understandable that this belief should be generally held, for the Roseland area is full of legends concerning the Tudor monarch, and some inns (e.g.Ruan Lanihorne) bear his name: moreover he alone of our King Henrys is alternatively known to us as 'King Harry'. In fact however there is no record of Henry VIII having visited Cornwall at any time. The real origin of the name is to be found in the dedication of a little chapel which once stood at the Philleigh end of the passage, but is now only a heap of mossy stones in a field. It is mentioned in 1528 as the 'chapel of St. Mary and King Henry', and commemorates King Henry VI, the Lancastrian King murdered in 1471, whose canonisation was under consideration at the time. The chapel was erected by the Arundell family, who held the manor of Tolverne, and were Lancastrian supporters. Thereafter the name 'King Harry' was increasingly applied to the ferry, but as late as 1566 and 1586 we find the passage referred to as 'Kybyllys' or 'Kebellyan' passage, a word possibly derived from the Welsh 'ceubal' - a ferry boat.

In the latter half of the 16th century the passage belonged to William Carnsew, Esq. He held the ferry as a free tenant of the manor of Treville, in Feock, and paid his overlord 13d. rent for the privilege. His descendant Sir Richard Carnsew held the passage in 1625 on the same terms, which provided that Mr. Trefusis, the lord of the manor, was entitled to free passage, as were his servants. In 1649 John Taylor, the Gloucestershire 'water-poet' wrote: "that day I passed a ferry called King Harry's passage (but why it is so named few men know) there I lodged at the ferryman's house". The next reference we have to the ferry is in the reign of George III by which time the Trefusis family had bought in the ferry, so that once again it was attached to the manor. It was on lease to one Richard Laurence in 1767. Thenceforward it remained part of the leasehold lands of the manor until the 20th century was well advanced. It is interesting to note that in accordance with the old tithe customs of Feock, the Vicar and his family were to have free passage at all times. In January 1816 the boats and ferry were advertised to let, in the West Briton, along with the public house and gardens; Robert Watkins being the landlord.

In Laurence O'Toole's book "The Roseland" (Lodenek, 1978) is a lively description of the experiences of nineteenth century cattle drovers in getting their charges across the passage. He tells how the cattle had to be hustled along when nearing the ferry, in case they strayed into King Harry Woods; and how, once at the water's edge, the beasts had to be haltered together and persuaded to swim behind the boat. There had of course for years been a horse-and-carriage ferry, but it could not cope with whole herds on Truro market days. The boat in use prior to the introduction of a steam ferry was a broad wooden barge with a bluff bow and square transom stern. Coaches, wagons or tumbrils were side-loaded by planks and lashed athwartships after the horses had been unshafted. Two men propelled the boat, one on either quarter, with long sweeps, and in difficult conditions of wind and tide, the passengers would be obliged to help.The Punch Bowl & Ladle Inn, Feock, has a fine sepia photograph in the Lounge Bar, showing this ferry about to leave Feock beach. The crossing by horseboat could be dangerous in bad weather and was out of the question if a southerly gale was blowing. Complaints were constant from travellers that they had arrived to find no ferry running: so that they had either faced an extra day's travelling, via Tregony and Truro; or had to ask the ferryman to put them up for the night.

Conditions improved greatly when the King Harry Steam Ferry Company began operating a steam-driven chain ferry in 1889. The Company had been formed the previous year at a meeting between Captain Arthur Tremayne of Carclew and four other gentlemen, who obtained the charter and rights on a lease from the then owners, the Gilbert family of Trelissick. Some years later the Company bought the monopoly outright.

The boat which inaugurated the new service, Ferry No.1, was purpose-built by Sara & Burgess of Penryn, at a cost of £1025. She was steel-hulled, with a wooden deckhouse on one side housing a vertical boiler and the 2-cylinder compound condensing engine. This drove a large chain wheel

The second King Harry passage steam ferry approaches the Feock side.

working a single chain. The progress of the craft was steadied by a guide-wire on the upstream side. The large shed-like engine-house prompted many folk to compare No.1 ferry to Noah's Ark. Certainly it looked primitive if compared with the contemporary floating bridges on the Tamar, but this boat gave good service for twenty four years, until 1913. Although the regular use of the old oar-propelled ferry was discontinued when the steam ferry commenced running, it was retained as a stand-by for many years. Its use was last recorded as late as 1920, when the records show it underwent repairs costing £50. The first steam ferry was the scene of a mishap in 1907. A horse and cart went overboard when the ferry was in midstream. The horse had taken fright, bolted, and gone over the prow. Encumbered by the cart, the unfortunate creature was drowned. A subsequent attempt to obtain damages failed because the ferry was reckoned in law as part of the highway, and it was held that the carter should have had his horse under better control.

Ferry No.2, which replaced No.1 in 1913, was built on very similar lines by Silley Cox & Company of Falmouth for the very reasonable cost of £1620, £50 being allowed as scrap value for the old boat. Details of this second ferry do not seem to have survived, but photographs show that she carried an ornate brass lamp at either end, and that her engine-house, originally flat-roofed, was later given a corrugated-iron 'wagon' roof (49). Like her predecessor, she worked on one chain. Ferry No.2 suffered the indignity, one dark night, of being rammed by a drifting coal elevator. She sank at her moorings in deep water; but the Company acted swiftly to have her raised, repaired, and put back into service within a very short time. This was an earnest of the directors' determination to keep faith with the travelling public, despite the difficulties which beset them. From the start of the Company's operation receipts had been so low and had risen so slowly each year that in 1912 one of the directors told the Board that he was "sceptical of ever getting a dividend". Hopes for the future were based on the certainty that motor traffic would greatly increase, but the Great War of 1914-18 delayed these prospects and not until after the war was an income of £500 per annum exceeded. By 1933 increasing traffic and too-frequent repairs to Ferry No.2 decided the Company on acquiring a replacement vessel, which it was estimated would cost £4000. Ferry No.2 had run for twenty-one years when withdrawn, and she was then retained as stand-by.

Ferry No.3 was obtained second-hand from the River Tamar, where she had been made redundant after twenty-two years work on the Saltash Ferry. She had been built by Willoughby's at Plymouth in 1911 and had an upper promenade deck on both sides. Her career at King Harry however was short-lived. In service she was found heavy on coal consumption, while she required an extra crewman to work the gates. This made her running costs prohibitive, and she was withdrawn after a few months. Fortunately Ferry No.2 was still available, and after reconditioning was returned to service. Ferry No.3 was eventually sold - though at a loss - in 1937, to Scottish owners. In tow to Scotland she broke adrift from her tug in bad weather conditions, and was wrecked off St. Agnes Head. Meanwhile No. 2 carried on through the difficult days of World War II.

King Harry Ferry had an important role in the war, as the traffic then consisted principally of service transport and personnel about their necessary business; but good timekeeping proved increasingly difficult as the quality of coal supplied to the ferry steadily deteriorated and it was often impossible to maintain steam pressure. After a stoppage to regain steam one day, a senior United States Naval officer who was among the delayed, enquired the reason. When told, he evidently knew just what to do about it; for shortly after, a truckload of best steam coal was delivered to Truro for the ferry company, and this welcome supply was continued regularly till the end of hostilities!

By 1948 Ferry No.2 was thoroughly worn out and a replacement was urgent, but once again the fates seemed determined to prevent her retirement. The Company had negotiated the purchase of an ex-Government landing-craft for Ferry No.4, and entrusted the task of conversion to N. Holmes & Company of Penzance. The cost involved was £27,000 - nearly seven times greater than the estimated cost of a new craft in 1934, when Ferry No.2 should have been replaced. In expectation of No.4's delivery in the spring of 1950, No.2 was sold for £10. Her bottom plates were nearly rusted through, and at least one tender had quoted £50 for the trouble of towing her away. It was a considerable shock to the Company, therefore, to hear that No.4, while on tow to the Fal from Penzance had encountered boisterous weather, parted her tow, and met with disaster. She had drifted on to rocks in Spernic Cove, at Coverack, been holed, and had sunk in shallow water. The immediate outlook was bleak. Salvage and repair of No.4 were likely to incur almost as much cost in time and money as a new vessel. No.2 had been sold and it seemed the Company might lose a whole season's income. In the event, however, happier circumstances prevailed. No.4 was successfully salvaged and towed into Falmouth for extensive rebuilding, at a cost of £14,500; and arrangements were made for No.2 to 'soldier on' till 1951. When finally withdrawn she had completed 37 years service. **49**

Ferry No.4 was steam-driven and had a midships engine room with an enclosed conning position mounted above it. She was therefore markedly different from her predecessors, and her chain wheels were on the outside of her hull, like paddle wheels. She had run for little more than five years when it was decided to convert her to diesel propulsion. The Managing Director of the Company at this time was Mr. Jack Simmons-Hodge, a well-qualified engineer with enthusiasm for diesels. This is probably the reason that steam power did not survive longer on the King Harry passage. W.H. Argall & Sons of Truro carried out the conversion of No.4 to diesel-electric propulsion. Director Colonel John Holt has written: "It is a tribute to their ingenuity that the changeover from steam to diesel was effected with a loss of only $2\frac{1}{2}$ working hours. The conversion unit and control gear had been installed alongside the steam machinery while the boat was in service." A principal reason for the conversion had been the rising cost of coal: the 1914 coal bill had been £78, but by 1956 the cost had risen to £1,400. However by 1964 traffic requirements had overtaken the capacity of Ferry No.4, which had then been working for 13 years, and the Company found itself seeking a replacement.

It so chanced that at this time the Saltash chain-ferries had come on to the market, made redundant by the opening of the Tamar Bridge. The newer of these two steamers therefore, (Saltash No.7) was acquired for £2,500 as King Harry Ferry No.5. She had been built by Thornycroft's of Southampton in 1933 and had already seen thirty years of service at Saltash Passage. She was safely towed from Plymouth and taken up the Fal to Malpas, where she was beached at Sunny Corner. She lay there nearly $2\frac{1}{2}$ years, while Mr. Jack Simmons-Hodge, assisted by Ferry Engineer Ernie Kinley, gutted her engine and boiler rooms, and installed two 65 hp. 6-cylinder Ford diesel-electric engines and a heavy driving-shaft. Conning-positions or 'bridges' were built at either end and the engine and propulsion motor were controlled from there, as were the hydraulic loading-ramps and pneumatically worked gates. Ferry No.5 could carry more vehicles than No.4, and could load and discharge traffic more rapidly. She was to remain in service on the Fal for ten years till April 1974. Retired ferryman Fred Bowker (now Verger of St. Just-in-Roseland) recalls a remarkable accident which occurred in the early years of No.5's service. A large merchant vessel was being towed upstream for laying-up at moorings when she was caught by a cross wind. The tugs were unable to prevent their charge from careering toward the Feock bank where the ferry was loading. The runaway struck the ferry heavily, smashing the prow and driving the vessel up the hard. The service had to be suspended for several weeks while the ferry was repaired at Falmouth Docks. An extreme high tide was experienced one day in 1973, and Ferry No.5 was unable to load vehicles for the 8 am. service from Feock. When she had made the maximum possible progress on the chains, traffic was still unable to reach the prow.

No.5 was replaced by the present ferry on 2nd April 1974. Ferry No.6 was purpose-built by Dredge-Marine Ltd. of Ponsharden Shipyard, Falmouth, to the designs of R. Pearce, and inaugurated with due ceremony by Lady Falmouth. Meanwhile the ex-Saltash No.5 was bought by a Greek concern who wished to deliver her to Spain. For this purpose they acquired also a small steam tug, but the Ministry of Transport would not grant a Towing Certificate. Eventually a powerful tug was chartered to tow both the ferry and the small tug. Unfortunately the venturers did not heed the advice of the King Harry Ferry Company, to disconnect the prows from the hydraulic rams and raise them well clear of the water, and instal adequate deck combings to prevent water getting below. Only forty-eight hours out from Falmouth, at a point south of Land's End and northwest of Ushant, the ferry shipped heavy seas. The tow was hurriedly cast off and the ferry sank in a few minutes.

No.6 was designed to carry a total of 28 average-size cars between the gates, but with a proportion of Minis and other small cars, has carried several more. The prime movers are diesel engines driving a hydraulic pump and the chain wheel is driven by an independent hydraulic motor. All controls can be operated from the bridge. The steelwork of the hull was completely shot-blasted and coated with primer and first class Epoxy paints to prevent corrosion during the vessel's working life. The hull measures 70.0' x 41.0' beam x 7.0' depth, and with 37' prows the overall length is 144.0'. Loaded draught is 5.0'.

The Company own three houses on the Feock side, and these are occupied by the three full-time ferrymen. There are also two sheds: one (embellished with a painting[+] of the ferry framed by a lifebuoy) houses tools and spares; the other contains a powerful tractor, stayed in position with front axle raised, and rear wheels replaced by a drive for drawing replacement ferry chains across the river, and for raising or lowering the weights in the chain-pits. By long tradition the ferry leaves the Feock side on the hours and half-hours, and Philleigh on the quarters. Each Spring the service is suspended for a week for the annual refitting of the ferry on a river beach upstream, when the boat is scraped clean of barnacles and other growth. Every fourth year the ferry is towed to Falmouth Docks for a major overhaul. The ancient custom, already mentioned, of free passage for the Vicar of Feock has been revived, and a like privilege extended to the Rector of St. Just-in-Roseland.

All ferries have their distinguished patrons, and the King Harry is no exception. "Quite a few Television personalities come this way", Engineer Ken Ratcliffe told me; "Ken Kendall of BBC, Kenneth McLeod of Westward and Hugh Scully of HTV come to mind right away, and Claire Bloom the actress". But a very special moment in the ferry's history came on 11th May 1981 when the Queen Mother used the ferry on a visit to Cornwall. Her Majesty had called on Lord Falmouth at Tregothnan and was returning to the Royal Yacht **Britannia** lying in Falmouth Roads. The ferry was held at Philleigh while the royal cortege drove on to the car deck. The Queen Mother then boarded the Royal Barge from the ferry's prow by a gangway specially constructed for the occasion.

To stand on Feock quay and watch the ferry cross and recross the Fal is a tranquil experience. The service is punctual and reliable and the scene, in its sylvan setting, is supremely peaceful, even when the traffic is heavy. Yet on any day, at any time, hiccups can occur. Engineer Ratcliffe recalls that six years ago a large American car was stranded on the ferry with a flat battery. The crew's attempts to get the car restarted met with no success, and it completed three crossings of the river before the A.A. arrived. More recently, there was a surprise for ferry-driver Fred Bennett. He was keeping an eye on traffic approaching the ferry at Philleigh when the driver of the last car did a slow three-point turn and backed on to the prow. Fred asked the driver what he was doing.

+ painted by Ferry-Captain Ken Ratcliffe's sister-in-law, Mrs. Sheeran.

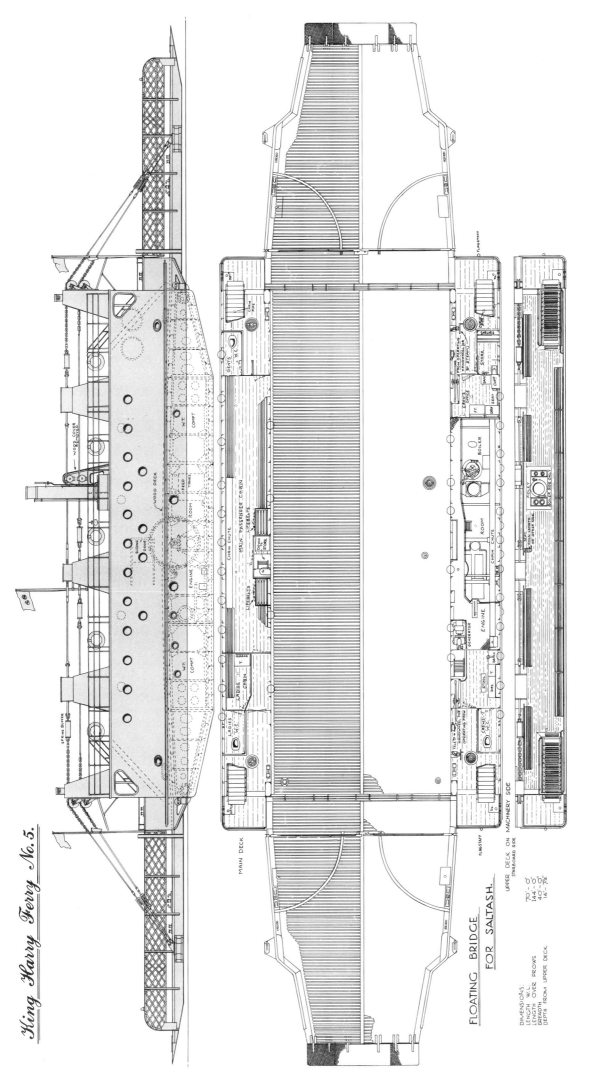

King Harry Ferry No. 5.

WOOD COVER

WOOD DECK

SPRING BUFFER

W.T. COMPT.

FEED TRANS. ROOM

ENGINE

SLIDING DOOR

W.T. COMPT.

MAIN DECK

LADIES W.C.

LADIES CABIN T. MIRROR

CHAIN CHUTE

MAIN PASSENGER CABIN

LIFEBELTS

DOWN TO STORE

LIFEBELTS

GENTS W.C.

CHAIN PIPE

TELEM'S HANDWHEEL FOR OPERATING PROW

CREW'S W.C.

CREW'S OFFICE

GENERATOR

ENGINE

STOOL DRS T DRS

ROOM

CHAIN CHUTE

BOILER

FEED

STORE

SHELVES

PROW OPERATING HANDWHEEL OR BY STEAM

SAFE COMP

SEAT GRIO

FLAGSTAFF

FLAGSTAFF

UPPER DECK ON MACHINERY SIDE

TOILET

BOILER SIDE ONLY

FLOATING BRIDGE
FOR SALTASH.

DIMENSIONS:
LENGTH W.L.   70'- 0"
LENGTH OVER PROWS   144'- 0"
BREADTH   40'- 0"
DEPTH FROM UPPER DECK   14'- 7½"

From a plan courtesy National Maritime Museum, Greenwich.

"I'm not very good at reversing", the driver meekly explained, "so I thought I'd get it over with now instead of holding everyone up when we drive off". Clearly, here was a newcomer to the world of chain-ferries! "Yes" says Fred, "we see them all here. In the drought summer of 1976 we had a lady passenger from inland somewhere who had last visited the Fal the previous year at a high tide. On this occasion the tide was very low. She said to me 'I didn't realise how bad a drought you'd had here'. And among questions about the ferry I've had put to me lately were: "Does it go on rails under the water?" and "Do the chains go right over to the other side?" One day in the late seventies Fred had brought the ferry to the Feock side when he was astonished to see a Ford Escort which had driven from the prow on to the slipway, suddenly turn abruptly to the right, bounce off the slip and over the ferry chain, and come to rest on the beach by the quay. The driver explained that he was making for Truro. "A friend told me to turn right as soon as I left the ferry" he explained. Truly, it takes all kinds to make a world.

RESTRONGUET PASSAGE: This now abandoned passage crossed the mouth of the Devoran Creek between Mylor and Feock, and belonged to the manor of Restronguet. We know that in 1468 (reign of Edward IV) it was let for an annual rent of 8/4d. But its heyday was then yet to come. The establishment of a mail service in Tudor times made Restronguet passage a part of the post-road between Truro and Falmouth. Often the ferryman as he plied his oars must have exchanged banter with the yellow-jacketed Post Boy seated in the sternsheets while his horse stood uneasily amidships. From the time of Henry VIII until they were superseded by the mail coaches, these Post Boys worked in relays between Post Houses along the mail route, where Masters of the Post paid 'postage' (original meaning of the word) to hire horses locally for their use. Carrying the mail enhanced the importance of the ferry, and the Post Boy was always welcome as the bringer of national news and a link with the 'outside' world.

Henderson, the Cornish historian reveals in his manuscripts (kept by the Royal Institute of Cornwall) that Rostronguet ferry became a cause of complaint at the manor court in 1777, when the passage boats were declared to be dangerous and inconvenient for passengers, and in need of speedy repairs. Whether the allegation was proved, and if so what remedy was undertaken, we do not know.

Notes in the Whitford Collection at the Cornwall County Record Office detail a lease of the ferry granted to a local fisherman, Thomas Harvey, in 1789:- "a cottage or dwelling house called the Passage House adjoining the beach at Restronguet Passage, together with the stable and pigs house at one end of the said dwelling house... also all that ferry or passage called Restronguet Passage together with the two Boats, Oars, Ropes, Grapples and Materials thereto belonging, and liberty of passing and repassing with the said boats... to opposite shore or beach in the parish of Feock and back again according to the ancient usage and customary right now and heretofore uninterruptedly exercised and enjoyed by former lessees of the said ferry or passage".

H.L. Douch in his book "Old Cornish Inns" (Bradford Barton, 1966) refers to a ferry disaster which occurred in September 1791, only two years after the granting of the above lease to Thomas Harvey. The ferry was heavily loaded with a number of passengers and three horses. On the crossing one of the horses became frightened and could not be stilled, the disturbance capsized the ferry and three of the passengers were drowned in midstream before help could reach them. The Exeter Flying Post reporting the tragedy warned: "This should caution boatmen against the imprudence of overcrowding their boats; a practice too frequent in Cornwall". There is a certain smugness in the final comment, coming as it did from a Devon newspaper.

At Feock the ferry worked from the beach at Restronguet Point, where between the wars a ferry-bell was mounted on a post and frame; but steps cut in the rock are the only sign left today. The bell is said to have come from the 4071 ton Falmouth tramp steamer **Penhale**; it was stolen during World War II. On the Mylor side the landing was not directly opposite, but a little to the west, below the 15th century Passage House Inn, known for a while in the eighteenth century as The Ship. Here Anne Boleyn is said to have stayed after crossing from France in 1553. Here also, in 1792, came a sailor who had had enough of the sea. He was Captain Edwards, survivor of his 24 gun frigate H.M.S. **Pandora**, which had been wrecked on the Great Barrier Reef while bringing back to justice some of the mutineers against Captain Bligh in H.M.S. **Bounty**. This officer took over the licence of The Ship Inn and renamed it "The Pandora", a name it still bears today. He must also have been responsible for the ferry, and thus ranks as one of Cornwall's most noteworthy ferrymen.

Restronguet passage foreshore, with the inn and the ferry, was eventually acquired by the Tremayne family of Carclew Estate. On the 5th April 1934 Carclew mansion was destroyed by fire. Its gaunt ruins still stand, at the end of the drive of which the gates and lodge can be seen on the road to the ferry. The estate properties were sold, and the inn and ferry rights have since been owned by successive landlords. In the early years of this century the publican/ferryman was named Rundle. In the spring of 1914 Rundle retired to a house (now named 'Whispers') behind the inn, selling The Pandora and ferry to John ('Tenzy') Ferris, who had a family of fourteen.

The Great War broke out that year, and the eldest son went to war. The rest of the family then had to help work the ferry as required, girls as well as boys. There was a lot of absenteeism from school as a result. Dick Ferris, tenth of the family, is now living in retirement in Truro. His wife reckons he was 'born with paddles in his hands', and he told me that he started working the ferry when he was only nine years old. "Father showed us how to stem the tide till we got into the lee of the point". He became the regular ferryman, and was known locally as "Dicky Ten" or "Dicky Shrimp". The fare was 1d. each way, increased to 2d. during the late 'twenties.

Dick remembers the remains of the horseboat (abandoned in Rundle's time) lying in what had been the 'timber pool' near the slip to the west of the inn. "It was falling to pieces" he says, "and an old widow named Jeannie Simmons used to hack pieces off for firewood". After sixteen years John Ferris sold the inn to George Symons, who ran the ferry during the thirties. Throughout World War II the landlord was named Dover, but he sub-let the ferry to a waterman named Peter Jacobson, who lived on the Feock side of the creek. Dover retired after the war and sold the "Pandora Inn", the new landlord, Huddlestone, ending Jacobson's lease and running the ferry himself. Huddlestone introduced a motor boat, and was the last ferryman of Restronguet. The service ended, through lack of demand, in 1952 or 1953.

MYLOR FERRY: Probably least-known among the passages of the Fal is the former ferry across the Mylor Creek. It is believed to have run from Mylor Churchtown, on the south side, to the steps of Greatwood Quay (formerly Little Quay) on the north bank. Dr. Elizabeth Bennett, in 'History around the Fal' (pub. Fal History Group, 1980) considers that the ferry must have been under the auspice of the Killigrew family, who formerly owned the land on both sides of the creek.

It is a lesser-known ferry because it did not form part of a highway, and its existence may have been confined to the period between the late eighteenth century and early twentieth century when Mylor Creek was busier than today. Before the 19th century dawned, we can reasonably conjecture that shipbuilding and repairs were carried on here. Indeed a tombstone in the churchyard, close to the east window, bears the inscription to Joseph Grapp, a shipwright who had died in a fall unconnected with the ferry accident, but Joseph and his fellows may have travelled thus to work. On the north shore Greatwood Manor was established, the home of Admiral James, and a ferry would have been needed to convey the family and their servants to and from the parish church.

From 1805 till the 1930s a small Admiralty dockyard was maintained on the south shore, employing civilian labour, some of whom must have crossed to work from the north bank. There is an implicit reference to the ferry in the Post Office records for 1811 (reference Post 48 for 28 January 1811) concerning an incident in November 1810. The packet **Princess Charlotte** had come into Falmouth after an action on 9th November with a privateer between the Scillies and Lizard Point and "the friends of the dying and wounded sent for Dr.Fox - he lives five miles off" (at Wood Cottage in Mylor) "and had two ferries to cross in the night" - i.e. Little Quay to Mylor and Flushing to Falmouth. (His fee of £5.5s. was paid by the Post Office in the summer of 1811).

A few years later ferryman and ferry were probably involved in the macabre task of recovering dead bodies from the water; for in January 1814 **The Queen**, a transport bringing home soldiers from the Peninsular War, was wrecked in a south-easterly gale at Trefusis Point. More than 200 lost their lives, many of the dead being swept on to Pencarrow Point and into Mylor Creek. When Waterloo brought the Napoleonic War to an end in 1815, Mylor Dockyard was partially shut down and was not fully reopened until the Crimean War in 1854. However comings and goings were probably sufficient to keep the ferry in business, as during that period the famous Falmouth Packets were sent here for coppering and refitting.

For thirty-three years, from 1866 to 1899, the Navy maintained a boys' training ship, H.M.S. **Ganges,** moored opposite Mylor Creek in St. Just Pool. The **Ganges** of course had her own boats, but her complement of officers, petty officer instructors and over 400 boys must have brought extra business to the ferry. After 1900 Mylor Dockyard fell into disuse, and for many years the site was utterly derelict and overgrown. (In the 1930s it was sold - leasehold - into private ownership and has since been known as Mylor Yacht Harbour).

Once the dockyard had closed, the ferry could scarcely remain economic, and it is certain that Mylor ferry has not worked within living memory. There is however, among senior residents of Mylor, a strong tradition of a ferry further upstream which would have provided a direct route between the ferries at Restronguet and Flushing: and that this was the last ferry to run at Mylor Creek. It is said to have worked from Trelew Dip in Church Road to Vatten Vane where the remains of a small quay can be seen below a hillside orchard. A sunken road, still partly traceable, ran from the now-demolished limekiln at Trelew Dip to the bend in the road from Mylor Churchtown to Flushing. From the quay at Vatten Vane another lane, part destroyed but partly discernible, leads steeply uphill to meet the Greatwood-Restronguet road. The existence of these lanes is all but proof of the ferry that once linked them.

World War II saw an increase of activity at Mylor Harbour, but no civilian ferry was restarted. In 1941 Free French Resistance fighters arrived in small batches for spells of training, and were accommodated in the storeshed on the old Admiralty pier. In 1943 men of the U.S. Navy came to Mylor to fit out Seebees, the landing craft used in June 1944 for the invasion of Normandy. But both French and Americans provided for themselves such ferrying as they required. Since 1962 maritime life in Mylor Creek has centred around the Restronguet Sailing Club, and they are scarcely in need of a boat.

PERCUIL FERRY: The story of Percuil Ferry goes back into the mists of local history. It would have started as an adjunct to the ford, which was probably only negotiable at low water. Laurence O'Toole in his book 'The Roseland' states that there is today a submerged causeway crossing the channel which is still fordable at low spring tides.

The rights of ferry belonged to the manor of Tregear, which included the land on both sides of the river. Tregear manor was held from the middle of the 9th century by the Bishops of Sherborne but it passed to the Bishops of Crediton (later, Exeter) during the 10th century. Reorganisation of ecclesiastical properties in 1835 brought the passage under the control of the Church Commissioners. For the greater part of its history, therefore, Percuil was an ecclesiastical ferry. Giving Gerrans and Portscatho folk a direct passage to the St. Just peninsular, it connected on that side with ancient footpaths to St. Mawes and Bosloggas. It shortened the journey to the former by six miles.

In Victorian and Edwardian times the Percuil ferryman conveyed the occasional passengers from Trewince to the St. Mawes steam ferries **Jane** or **Roseland**: but the majority of passengers to and from the St. Mawes boats were not his concern. The steamers usually had a boat for a tender moored off Percuil, or arrived with one in tow astern. The Gerrans donkey-trap however brought him some passengers, while on fine summer evenings he would be hailed by intending visitors to the long-vanished tea gardens. The last of the Victorian ferrymen was Edwin Pascoe (1878-1900).

There will be those who still remember the ex-Navy Petty Officer Thomas Medlyn, who was the Ferryman of Percuil from before the Great War until the early nineteen twenties. He was regarded as a 'hard case', a man not to be trifled with, and the loss of an eye had lent him a piratical aspect.

Percuil Ferry: Ferryman about to land passengers at Percuil boat-stage (of which the remains still exist!). St. Mawes Ferry **Roseland** *at mooring. Sketch - Terry Duggan.*

Accompanied by his rather fierce dog, he worked the ferry in all weathers and at any hour: and for the 1d. toll he often had to carry passengers on his back over yards of mud when the tide was very low. His wife (locally renowned for her large rabbit pies) ran a sweet shop in the front room of the ferry cottage; for in later years passengers were few, and the ferry alone did not constitute a living. Their son Charles, who had followed his father into the Navy, assisted with the ferry when home on leave.

Medlyn's successor, in 1922, was Cecil Raspision. Married, and with two sons, he also was ex-Navy, and as a reservist was called up in 1939 to serve in Plymouth R.N. Barracks. He and his family vacated the ferry house to live in Plymouth for the duration, and the cottage began to fall into disrepair. The caretaker of Wetherell House was persuaded to keep the ferry working in addition to his own duties, but in the meantime the Church Commissioners secured freedom from obligation to maintain the service. When hostilities were over, Raspision opted to remain in Plymouth and did not return to the ferry.

Voices were raised locally to insist that the Commissioners should put the ferry-house in repair and reinstate the ferry. Many were then surprised to learn that there was no longer any legal necessity for the ferry. A new ferryman was found, however - Johnny Sayce of St. Mawes. The ferry house being now semi-derelict, he had to come over from St. Mawes daily to work the ferry. He was the last full-time ferryman at Percuil. On his retirement, Arthur Perry, proprietor of Percuil Tea Gardens since 1920, stepped into the breach, as an act of service to the community. There was no longer the need for a ferryman in constant attendance, and intending passengers applied at the Tea Gardens.

The last person to work Percuil ferry was Jack Webb, proprietor of the boatyard, who now lives at Trewithian. "The service really ended about 1970", he says "but the ferry house had gone long before. At the end of the war the roof was falling in and the chimney breast was giving way, so we took it down: the site is now occupied by a small car park".

On our visit, we found no long-standing residents with tales to tell of the past; but on the beach were the remains of the wheeled gangway which served the ferries years ago. Today the foreshore is dominated by the modern boatyard and chandlery, and Percuil beach - so busy in the heyday of the ferry - is now deserted in Winter and the preserve of the small yacht fraternity in summer. The Passage Inn was the earliest casualty. The last Mine Host was Mrs. Jane Cragoe, and the licence was given up in August 1878. Today only the steps and footpaths on either side of the river remain as evidence of the crossing.

FLUSHING - FALMOUTH: This is one of Cornwall's older ferries, chartered in the Restoration days of 1666 to the Trefusis family, who were the landowners at Flushing. But the story of Flushing ferry has hitherto gone unrecorded and today conjecture has to play some part in reconstructing history.

The original service was to Greenbank, directly across the Penryn River, for the service to the Prince of Wales Pier, Falmouth does not predate the steam era. In the 1870s and 1880s the ferry was worked by John Mead of Greenbank, who used two rowboats and charged a toll of ½ d. each way. The boats hoisted yawl rig when the wind made it worth their while, and an old colour-postcard displayed in the Watermen's Shelter on Flushing Quay shows both Mead's boats under sail off Greenbank pier. About the turn of the century there was a fatal accident when a ferry under sail capsized in midstream, and a butcher's errand boy from Dunning's of Falmouth who was crossing to deliver orders, lost his life.

When the first steam ferry was introduced, passengers were landed at Market Strand, Falmouth, and the importance of the Greenbank service dwindled. Eventually the Flushing ferry company allowed local watermen to take over the service, provided no power-boats were used. It is said that a Mr. Harley Mead kept a regular ferry going between the wars, from 6 am. to 8 pm. daily, using two rowboats with lugs'ls. World War II brought the Greenbank service to a close, but there was a brief revival in the summer of 1974 when a Miss Trembarth put a boat on the crossing with herself at the oars.

It seems, although this is disputed, that the first steamboat used on the Flushing ferry was the **Greyhound**; and that John Meade was her owner - though this also is a matter of dispute. The **Greyhound** - 16 tons, and undecked - was a wooden screw steamer built by Darton at Turnchapel, Plymouth, and had a simple 2-cylinder non-condensing engine by Sara of Penryn. Vaguely remembered by the eldest residents as having a very tall, thin funnel, the **Greyhound** ran on the Flushing ferry for 15 years from May 1889 till broken up in 1904. The fare charged between Flushing and Falmouth quay (Market Strand) was 6d. return.

By 1894 business apparently justified the provision of another boat, for in that year the **Greyhound** was joined by the **Armine**, an open steam launch of only 7 tons gross. She had been built by White of Cowes, probably as a yacht, and had a 2-cylinder simple engine by Plenty of Newbury. It is thought she had another name before she was bought in 1894 by Charles Rusden (who two years later put the steamer **Truro Belle** on to the Falmouth-Truro run). It is not clear whether Charles Rusden took over the Flushing service from John Mead, or went into partnership with him, or hired the **Armine** to him. We know however that the **Armine** was on the Flushing run for only three years, from 1894-1897, when she was sold to Weymouth. There she was employed by the Great Western Railway as a tug and tender to the packet steamers. She appears in the frontispiece of J.H. Lucking's "The Great Western at Weymouth" (David & Charles 1971) having brought a coal barge alongside the S.S. **Reindeer**.

When the 20th century dawned, ferry traffic was considerable and the Flushing boat transported a large number of dockers every morning and evening. Falmouth Quay was extended by a steel, wood-decked jetty in 1905 and the enlarged landing-stage named Prince of Wales Pier. It was opened by the future King George V on 5th May that year.

Jack Blight, longest-serving of all Flushing ferrymen (and whose father rowed the Greenbank boats) recalls that in the early years of this century the Flushing ferry was being run by a character named Jack Angel. He was very deaf, frequently in liquor, and always black and oily because his ferry's engine gave constant trouble. This was a small undecked steam-boat whose name Jack Blight does not remember; but it may well have been the **Lily** which was running about this time. Before the service changed ownership a more reliable steam ferry, the **Express**, had replaced the worn-out **Lily**. The **Express** had an upper deck over the engine-room amidships, was about 60 ft. to 65 ft. long, with a helm-wheel in the bows, and probably had a 2-cylinder compound surface-condensing engine (55).

The next operator on the scene was Charlie Hughes, in the years following the Great War. He disposed of the **Express** within a few years, and replaced her with the motor ferry **Miranda** (1). This boat (alleged to be still afloat on the Dart) originally had a Kelvin engine, later replaced by a Britt. Jack Blight recalls that it was very difficult to disengage from forward gear - and that this had to be borne well in mind when approaching a jetty.

After Hughes, the ferry was taken over by Horace Reece, whose son lives beside Flushing Pier today. Jack Reece told me that his father charged dockers $1\frac{1}{2}$ d. each way, and that in the World slump year of 1929 he ferried the unemployed without charge. About 1933 Horace Reece sold Flushing ferry to Arthur Kessell. In 1934 Kessell acquired another motor ferry, **Miranda II** (16 tons), built at Flushing of pitchpine on oak, and with a 78 passenger capacity. **Miranda** (1) is said to have been offered for the Dunkirk evacuation in 1941 but apparently was not accepted, so was still on the ferry during World War II.

The Flushing Ferry Company Ltd. was formed in 1946 with Harry Johns as manager. Harry Johns later bought up the company and ran the ferry for more than 25 years. He and his son Alistair Johns also operated the Truro boats, so both services were for awhile under the same ownership. In 1951 the motor ferry **Nankersey** (23 tons) was acquired, built at Falmouth. Presumably at this time, if not earlier, the **Miranda** (1) was sold, as three boats would not have been required.

Next on the scene was a London company of entrepreneurs who bought up both the St. Mawes and Flushing ferries. They later began to sell off their new acquisitions in separate lots. The **Nankersey** was sold to an owner who used her for sea trips. Following storm-damage and rebuilding of her port side she was purchased by the St. Mawes Ferry Company and now runs on that service. The London venturers eventually sold the Flushing Ferry Company, together with **Miranda II** and Flushing Quay, to Colin Parker.

Skipper of the ferry then for some years was Micky Oliver, succeeded in 1973 by Paul Dash, who is still in command of **Miranda II** today. Meanwhile the winter service was proving uneconomic, but a clause in the charter provides that exclusive rights are lost if there is no service for 14 days. This difficulty was overcome when an arrangement was made by Parker with the St. Mawes Ferry Company for the latter to take over the winter service on his behalf. A reduced winter timetable for both services has since been run by one boat working St.Mawes-Falmouth-Flushing and return, from October to May. The usual 'Winter boat' is the twin-screw **New Princess Maud**, but when I last crossed from Flushing, at Easter 1980, the **Princess Maria** was deputising.

*The **Express** about to leave Falmouth Old Quay at the turn of the Century.*

Photo: Glasney Press

Probably the most interesting incidents in the recent history of Flushing ferry occurred a few years ago when "Beaky" the friendly dolphin was haunting the Fal estuary. He would playfully push away their buoy when they were trying to come to moorings, says Paul Dash, and this could be amusing, if frustrating: but when the 10ft. creature took to leaping over the moving ferry's bows it could create fear and was potentially dangerous. "Beaky" eventually left the Fal and has not been heard of since.

Colin ('Tangle') Parker quite suddenly sold the Flushing ferry on 25th March 1980 to the present owner, Dr. Clynick of Hertfordshire: thereby fulfilling a long-treasured ambition to give up the water and become a farmer.

ST. MAWES - FALMOUTH: There was no recognised ferry between Falmouth and the Percuil River until the advent of the steamer **Wotton** in 1869. The only predecessor to the steam ferries was the 'Market Boat', which ran on market days only from Percuil, Place, and St. Mawes, to Falmouth Market Strand. The Market Boat was an open thirty-foot sailing cutter, built on the lines of a working boat, and carrying the odd calf or sheep in addition to passengers and baskets of produce. If the wind was favourable, the Market Boat would cross the harbour in under an hour; in a calm it took a long time and the ferrymen would expect the passengers to lend a hand at the sweeps. In rough weather one was thrown about, perhaps amongst wet and frightened sheep, and baskets of fish, and the boat would certainly ship some water. In the worst conditions the skipper might decide against completing the return journey, and make a run for St. Just, in which case his passengers had a long walk home.

When the steamers took over, the Market Boat was continued as a rowing-boat and was towed, loaded, to Falmouth. An old Portscatho man kept this service going into the 1920s, by which time it had become more of a shopping boat. He undertook purchases, collection of laundry, parcels from the railway station, and so on, and for this personal service - charged at 2d. - delivered in Percuil at the end of the day. In 1867 there arrived in the Fal the steamer which was destined to revolutionise the St. Mawes-Falmouth traffic. This was the 28 ton iron screw steamer **Wotton**, which had been built the previous year at Neath Abbey, and had a simple diagonal 2-cylinder engine. The **Wotton** had been bought by the Fox brothers and what work she did remains a mystery but two years later they sold her to a partnership of three St. Mawes mariners, Ezekiel Tucker, William Jenking and Frederick Andrew, who put her on as a ferry between Falmouth and St. Mawes. The **Wotton** was an undoubted success: as tide served and business required, she called also at Percuil - where a rowboat was used to transfer passengers and similarly at Place. In the summer she ran excursions in addition to her ferry work. She had shown the way, and fresh development soon followed.

In 1878 the St. Mawes Steam Tug & Passenger Company Limited was formed, and put on to the ferry the 16 ton, Newquay-built wooden screw steamer **Jane**, which had a single-cylinder vertical engine of 10 hp. The original syndicate were still running the **Wotton** and in 1882 they had her engines converted to compound. In 1886 the **Jane** was also fitted with a compound engine, but she was proving small and slow for the increasing traffic, and that same year the Company took delivery of a new steamer. This was the 41-ton steel screw **Roseland**, with triple-expansion engines, built by Cox of Falmouth (57). The **Jane** was now relegated to relief boat, and sent trawling when not on the ferry. It was while thus engaged that in May 1889 she ran aground in Port Eynon Bay in a sou'westerly gale. Two men waded out into the surf with a rope and rescued her crew of two. The **Jane** was later refloated but her hull had suffered extensive damage and she was not retained for the ferry. Offered for sale, she was bought by John Rowlands, a Swansea publican.

The **Roseland** proved a good investment: strongly built and well-designed, she was a typical Fal river steamer, equipped for towing but with sufficient deck space for excursion work. She appears anonymously in countless photographs of the Percuil River, and served on the ferry nearly 60 years. She was then sold to the Falmouth Docks & Engineering Company and used as a work-boat. In April 1894 the St. Mawes Company took delivery of a similar but larger vessel, also from Cox's, the 66 ton **Princess May**, nearly 77 feet long. She worked eight years on the ferry and was then sold, quite abruptly, to the Port Elizabeth Harbour Board in South Africa in 1902. They had offered a good price for just such a maid-of-all-work as the **Princess May**, and the Company decided to take advantage of the offer and part with their principal ferry. A replacement was immediately ordered from Cox's yard.

Meanwhile the Company had in 1896 bought up the veteran ferry **Wotton** but after only a few months they sold her to a Falmouth Shipbroker, W.H. Lean. Within a year Lean had resold her to J. Watkins, London tug owner. Later she was sold to Irish owners, and was finally broken up in 1930 at Belfast, after a working life of 63 years. The replacement for the **Princess May** was the even larger **Alexandra** (73 tons gross). She had a draught of 7'7" aft, and this must have inhibited her service to Percuil. (When the steam ferries could not reach Percuil at spring tides, passengers had to cross by the rowboat ferry, and follow the footpath to St. Mawes, boarding the ferry there).

The **Alexandra** was delivered by Cox's in December 1902 and her appearance made no concessions to her status as a ferry and excursion boat. The **Alexandra** was unashamedly a tug, and it was as a tug that she earned her living when after 17 years on the ferry, she was sold to Reynolds' of Torpoint in 1919. There she became one of the best-known tugs of the Port of Plymouth, and her duties included the relief of Eddystone lighthouse keepers - a task to which few ferryboats could aspire.

The last steamer built for the St. Mawes Company was the 80 tons steam tug **St. Mawes** which was delivered in 1917 during the Great War, when both towage and ferry work in the harbour had much increased. The **St. Mawes** gave 31 years service before being sold to Inverness in 1948, and broken up three years later. Throughout all these years, from the inception of the ferry, the steamers were met at Percuil by a two-horse waggonette which ran every day in the summer, twice a week in the winter, till the outbreak of World War II. The fare was 4d. but a $1\frac{1}{2}$ mile journey was saved, walking to or from the creek.

The first diesel-engined ferry was the **St. Gerrans**, 73 tons gross, and completed in 1927. She

Scene c.1903 at Falmouth Old Pier before its extension to form Prince of Wales Pier. Truro ferry **Queen of the Fal** *(1) is on the left, and St.Mawes ferry* **Roseland** *in the centre.*

Photo: Glasney Press

was joined, temporarily, in the early 1930s, by the wooden screw motor-vessel **Berry Castle** (38 tons] which had been chartered from the River Dart Steamboat Company. The **Berry Castle** eventually returned to the Dart. The next acquisition in 1938 was the **Royal Jubilee**, a 3-year old diesel vessel of 59 tons. She was promptly renamed **New Roseland.** Ten years later, in 1948 came, the 75 tons **St. Mawes Castle**, also diesel; and that same year the steamer **St. Mawes** was sold out of service, bringing the steam era of the ferry to a close. The ferry fleet was brought up to four in 1950 by the addition of the 20 tons **New Princess Maud**, built that year.

The St. Mawes SteamTug & Passenger Company was taken over in December 1967 by the consortium of Smith Bros., who later sold the purpose-built **St. Gerrans** (although she was the best boat on the service) to an operator on the Thames, where she was to remain for 9 years. The career of the St. Mawes ferry now became somewhat chequered and uncertain, and local opinion considered the new owners were less interested in running the ferry service than in the development of the former company's properties in St. Mawes, which they had acquired with it.

In April 1968 - only 4 months after takeover - all four ferryboats came under the hammer at a surprise auction sale at Mylor. Two long-serving ferry skippers, Jack Andrew and John Bulpin, made a bid for one of the boats, in an attempt to keep the service going: but in the event none of the vessels reached the reserve price. The auctioneer was Mr.Tom Treloar, who had been Assistant Secretary of the old company, and was the only local director of the new concern. The auction went as follows:- M/V **St. Gerrans** (310 passengers) withdrawn at £6,750. M/V **New Roseland** (260 passengers) - no bid. M/V **St. Mawes Castle** (171 passengers) withdrawn at £6,000. M/V **Princess Maud** (113 passengers) withdrawn at £3,250 bid by skippers Andrew and Bulpin. The directors declared they had been considering replacing the boats with a hovercraft, but if so this project was soon abandoned. Finally Smith Bros. sold the business to a Mr. M. Miller, but the large boats were disposed of separately to a firm working from Westminster Pier in London River. The **New Roseland** later returned to the West Country and is now at Dartmouth: the **St. Mawes Castle** was sold at scrap value (£300) after gale damage at Mylor, but was refitted after purchase and followed the **New Roseland** to London. In 1975 Mr. Miller put the ferry business on the market again: this time it was taken by a Major Ancliffe who maintained the service for three years. In 1976 the former ferry **St. Gerrans** returned to Falmouth, having been purchased for excursion work by the partners Pill, Son and Jenkins, trading as the Falmouth Passenger Boat Company.

Major Ancliffe sold out in 1978 to Mr.T.E. Mattocks of St. Just, who within a year found that he had a war on his hands! Pill and Jenkins began to operate a rival ferry service in the summer, which was legally in order, since the original Company - despite 100 years of operation, official recognition as a public service, and an annual subsidy from the County Council - have never had exclusive rights. Local fishermen, however, determined to assist the ferry company against the interloper. On Saturday 21st April 1979 they converged with their trawlers on the 'pirate' ferry the **Devon Belle** (ex-Millbrook Company) and hemmed her in at St. Mawes Pier. Tempers became frayed and the local policeman had to pour oil on troubled waters. The 'Western Morning News' reported that Mr. George Pill (Jnr.), Managing Director of the rival company was unrepentant, declaring "Now we are going to put two boats on the Prince of Wales Pier-St. Mawes service, and during the winter we will run our big vessel, the **St. Gerrans**, on the route. On this, passengers will be able to have coffee and hot drinks and will be able to shelter in a warm and comfortable saloon". This was fighting talk and roused further the ire of the local boatmen. At St. Mawes a petition against the rival service was organised at the Ship and Castle Inn. Mr. Eric Mattocks of the Ferry Company, commented, with more restraint: "The St. Mawes Ferry Company is part of the port's heritage...we are keeping to our scheduled service, summer and winter. We have never let anyone down, and even in bad weather the service has been run". On the following Monday however, it seemed further trouble was brewing. The Pills anticipated another threat from the local fishermen, and replaced **Devon Belle** by the **St. Gerrans,** sending her to St. Mawes with an augmented crew; 'ready', said George Pill Snr. 'to sort out anyone if they attempted any more monkey business'. This time the St. Mawes Piermaster intervened as conciliator, and a compromise agreement was reached. Mr. Mattocks sold the ferry to the present owner, Peter Sparkes, in March 1980.

Truro-Falmouth

The St. Mawes ferry has certainly seen difficult times since the original company was wound up, but it has a record of service to the public of which its present owner is justifiably proud. This has been possible, in spite of the vicissitudes, because of the outstanding service rendered by experienced and long serving skippers. They provided continuity of a high standard during the difficult years from 1967-78 when successive managements were engaged. Deserving of special mention are Fred Ferris (50 years service, retired 1973), John Bulpin (36 years), Jack Andrews (35 years) and J. Ferris (son of Fred Ferris; 15 years).

The boats currently running the service are: **New Princess Maud** (20 tons, built London 1948); **Nankersey** (former Flushing ferry rebuilt in 1977 after gale damage); **Princess Maria** (100 passengers); and **Princess Marina** (a smaller but fast launch, 80 passengers). One boat is sufficient for the winter service; two or three, when required, are used in summer, while one is generally refitting.

Your authors were crossing from St. Mawes to Falmouth in July 1979 in the **Princess Marina** and chatting with the present Senior Skipper. He told us that he could remember skipper Jenking (who pioneered the service with the steamer **Wotton** in the 1870s) and that he had lived to be a grand old man of 101.

TRURO - FALMOUTH: The purist will maintain that this was a packet service rather than a ferry. The realist will argue that it fulfilled the dictionary definition of a ferry, and that even the Western Ocean mail steamers were dubbed 'The Atlantic Ferry'. But though sailing packets and market boats had worked up and down the Fal for many years, there was neither the availability nor frequency of service that one associates with a ferry until 1872. It was in 1872 that Philip Thomas of Falmouth inaugurated a Truro-Falmouth timetable service with the 60 ton passenger steamer **Rapid**. The **Rapid** had been purpose-built that year at Charlestown, and was a wooden screw-driven vessel with a single-cylinder engine. She maintained the up-and-down river service for seven years, five of them without competition. In 1879 she was sold to a Medway Company.

A competitor appeared in the summer of 1877 when the Truro pilot Richard Benney introduced the 32 ton **Resolute**, a wood screw-driven tug built on the Fal at Malpas. Five years later, with a temporary monopoly of the traffic, Benney had another steam tug built, the **New Resolute,** also of wood, from the same builders at Malpas. She was of 40 tons gross and had a compound engine. The original **Resolute** was fitted with a new compound engine by Cox's in 1886, but it is not clear whether she was still in Benney's ownership at that time. She was eventually lost in the English Channel in 1920. The **New Resolute** worked the Truro ferry for 45 years and old-timers remember her as a familiar sight on the river. She had a single mast with a gaff-rigged derrick, a raised wheelhouse on the main deck and carried a lifeboat in radial davits on the starboard side abreast the funnel. In the tradition of the Fal river steamers for years to come, the **New Resolute** was a tug in design, with few concessions to passengers, and was able and intended to earn revenue from towage when offered. In practice the roles of tug and ferry were often combined, and a photograph of 1910 shows her passing Trennick Row with about 60 passengers on deck and a sailing barge in tow. This practice was unpopular with passengers seated in the stern of the ferry, but their objections did not weigh heavily against the extra revenue and were invariably ignored. Richard Benney died about 1890 but his widow, Sarah Benney, continued the business. For her, Cox's of Falmouth built - and engined - the first **Queen of the Fal**, in 1893. Of 70 tons gross, she was a steel screw vessel, 10 feet longer than the **New Resolute**, more powerful, and carried two boats abreast of the funnel.

Benney's monopoly of the Truro ferry was challenged briefly in 1896 when Charles Rusden, a Falmouth engineer who had been principal operator of the Flushing ferry for two years, introduced the 45 ton steamer **Truro Belle** to the service. She was a white-hulled vessel with a promenade deck and spacious cabin, and a varnished boat carried in stern davits. The **Truro Belle** offered more passenger comfort than the **Queen of the Fal** and clearly could have posed a threat: but it is thought that she ran in the summer only. In any case she was withdrawn two years later and sold to a Captain Douglas of Sunderland, who used her as a ferry on the Tyne.

A longer period of competition followed, from 1900 to 1905, when Messrs. Thomas & Chard, Falmouth engineers, put the **Victoria**, a fine steel twin-screw steamer, on to the Falmouth-Truro service. Six months later a good offer was made for her by a Walter Cox, who wanted her for work at Port Louis, Mauritius. The offer was accepted, and Thomas & Chard immediately placed an order with Cox's yard for a second **Victoria**, very similar to the first. They were thus out of the ferry business for eight months till August 1901 when the new steamer arrived and began running. She had two masts, a promenade deck, awning stanchions on the open decks for'ard and aft, and carried a single lifeboat abaft the funnel on the starboard side. She took part in the opening of the Prince of Wales Pier, Falmouth, on 5th May 1905. Later that year however she was sold to the Portuguese Government.

In 1906 Mr. Benney's **New Resolute** and **Queen of the Fal** were acquired by Gerald Nalder of Falmouth, who then founded the River Fal Steamship Company Limited with a capital of £8,000. This company enjoyed nearly 40 years of virtual monopoly of the Truro ferry, and engaged also in sea and river excursion work. Although based on Falmouth the company maintained the Benney tradition of registering its steamers at Truro. Flaunting distinctive black, red and white funnels and splendidly maintained, they were until World War II an integral part of the life of the river. Almost the first move of the new company was to order from Cox's the 67-ton **Princess Victoria** which appeared on the ferry in 1907. She was a twin-screw steamer with a promenade deck and carried two lifeboats abaft the funnel: although basically a tug it was clear from the layout of her upperworks that she had been fitted out primarily for passenger work. Even so, traditons die hard, and mackerel fishermen from the Roseland harbours would, if prices were low in Falmouth, invoke the assistance of the ferry to get their catch to Truro. For a basket of mackerel, the skipper would probably agree to tow their loaded boat the $9\frac{1}{2}$ miles to Worth's quay.

In November 1911 the first **Queen of the Fal** was sold to Morgan's of London, and thereafter worked on the Thames under the management of Messrs. Watkins. An immediate replacement was

*In the salad days of the Truro Ferry before road transport reduced its importance, **Queen of the Fal** (2) was pride of the fleet. She did not return to duty after requisitioning in the Second World War.*

Photo: E.A.Deacon.

ordered from Cox's, of the same name and approximately the same measurements. The second **Queen of the Fal,** of 71 tons gross, had a wider beam like the **Princess Victoria** and a similar passenger capacity, but she was single-screw (59). She appeared on the Truro ferry in the mid-summer of 1912, but was also regularly used on sea excursions. In 1927 the **New Resolute** was sold out of service to Albert Benney, a director of the River Fal Steamship Company, and a member of the family which had originally owned her. She reverted to the role of a tug, and after periods of ownership by Harveys of Hayle and Roberts & Burt of Tresillian, she was scrapped at Truro in 1946 after a remarkable 64 years of continuous service.

The **Queen of the Fal** suffered a mishap on 3rd June 1931 which might have had serious consequences. With about 30 passengers on board she was on a sea excursion bound for Fowey and Looe when she encountered thick fog off the Dodman. With her crew peering anxiously ahead for Cadythew Rock, and unaware that the current had set them to the west of their course, she stranded at Vault Beach where the coast is largely rock-bound. By extraordinary good fortune she touched on the sandy bottom of a gutter between two reefs, and here she settled as the tide receded. The Fowey lifeboat **C.D.E.C.** was alerted, and with masterly seamanship managed to find the stricken ferry in the fog, while the sea remained calm. A towline was passed, and the lifeboat lay off to await the rising tide. Two hours later with her own engines assisting the tow, the **Queen of the Fal** was refloated, none the worse for her misadventure.

In 1939 the Second World War broke out, and the Truro ferry service was soon after suspended for the duration. The **Princess Victoria** and **Queen of the Fal** were requisitioned for war work in 1942 and never returned to civilian use. Their demise spelt the end of the river Fal Steamship Company. There followed four years during which there appears to have been no Falmouth-Truro service regular enough to deserve the designation of 'ferry', but in 1946 Peter Newman of Tolverne ran two small boats on the service. One of these was the 45-foot **Skylark,** which had a passenger capacity of about eighty. Newman was later joined by Harry Johns of Flushing, who contributed two further boats to the venture, the **Enterprise** and the **Kingsley. Enterprise** was a flush-decked vessel with a 44 hp. Kelvin engine, and could carry a hundred passengers. **Kingsley** was a long, narrow-beamed boat engined with a Kelvin Riccardo and licensed to carry about fifty: she was later sold to the Scilly Isles, where it is believed she is still in use.

About two years later, competition appeared in the form of a company entitled "Victory Pleasures" which ran three boats - **Lily of Laguna, Gondolier,** and **Worcester Castle.** Of these the first two were 40-footers and had passenger licences for about forty within the river limits. The **Worcester Castle** however was a more formidable competitor. Built at Appledore in 1926, she was a twin-screw 40-tonner with a length of 63'9", powerful Dorman engines, and carried 250 passengers, a capacity akin to the former steam ferries.

In 1950 Harry Johns bought the goodwill of the Victory Pleasures Company, and one of their smaller boats. Peter Newman bought the **Worcester Castle,** but largely rebuilt her and changed her name to **Skylark of Tolverne.** In 1951 Harry Johns acquired a new vessel built that year by Fraser's at Mevagissey: of 50'6" length by 14'9" beam, and with a passenger capacity of 115, she was the third vessel on the service to bear the time-honoured name **Queen of the Fal.** Newman and Johns had been running the Truro ferry with these three vessels for some years when misadventure befell them. Peter Newman's son lost his life when he fell from the **Skylark of Tolverne** while mooring up after an evening passage. His tragic death caused his grief-stricken father to withdraw altogether from the operation of the ferry; while the former **Worcester Castle** was sold, going first to Paignton and later to Tenby.

This tragedy left Johns as sole operator, but he later formed the company Fal Pleasure Cruises Limited, with three boats each named **Enterprise** after his original vessel, and numbered 1, 2, and 3. The **Queen of the Fal** was sold in 1963 to A. & J. Paynter, St. Ives, who renamed her **Cornish Belle.** The Enterprise boats were built at Bideford and are still in service on the ferry and excursion work. They carry approximately 165 passengers each, and are 60 ft. in length by 16 ft. beam: numbers 1 and 2 have Ford diesel engines and number 3 a Gardner.

Since the death of Harry Johns the business has been carried on by Alistair Johns, his son. One of the skippers is Frank Anthony, who has had over 20 years experience on the Truro ferry, and whose reminiscences were a substantial help in compiling this record. Mervyn Habgood, ferryman at Malpas, told us: "Those Enterprise boats run a good timetable service. Some days it's wet and miserable on the river and the boat hasn't had a worthwhile pay-load. But look across to Malpas pier at the time the ferry's due, and she'll be there". Few would argue that the romantic days of the Truro ferry were when the handsome steamers were cleaving the water of the Fal, but the old spirit of service, reliability and pride in the job is very much alive today.

9.

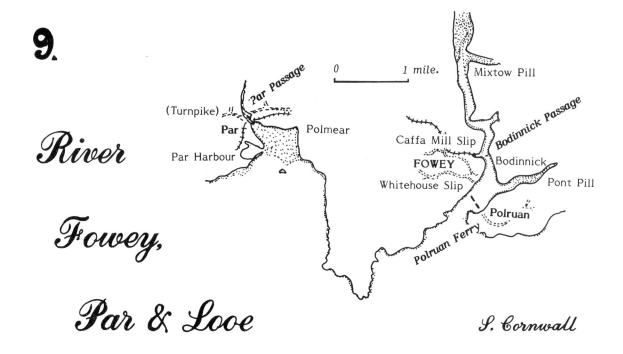

River

Fowey,

Par & Looe

S. Cornwall

Map labels: Par Passage, (Turnpike), Par, Polmear, Par Harbour, Mixtow Pill, Caffa Mill Slip, Bodinnick Passage, FOWEY, Bodinnick, Whitehouse Slip, Pont Pill, Polruan, Polruan Ferry, 0 1 mile.

PAR PAR PASSAGE: The mediaeval traveller via the south coast road through Cornwall, having negotiated the Tamar and the Fowey, encountered a third ferry across the Par estuary. Records show that in 1732 the ownership of the passage and the ferryboat was a matter of fierce dispute between a Mr. Scobell of Roselyon and the lords of Tywardreath. It was probably the shortest and smoothest crossing on this route, and its importance would have necessitated a horse and waggon float. Strangely, however, the passage exists no more. In what Henderson, the Cornish historian, describes as "a most surprising manner", the Par estuary began to silt up after the 1780s and has long ago disappeared. Indeed by about 1770 a wooden bridge spanned the estuary and had made the ferry superfluous. Your authors visited Par, intent on locating the site of the one-time ferry, but in vain, for the area is completely built over.

RIVER FOWEY BODINNICK PASSAGE: Bodinnick Passage is the second of the four water-links in the mediaeval road through the south of Cornwall, already referred to. It belonged to the manor of Bodinnick, and the earliest mention we have of the ferry is in 1344, when Edward III was king. In the Yorkist days of 1478 it is recorded that custody of the Bodinnick ferry was granted to one John Davey, 'Yeoman of the king's Chambers and valet to the King's Crown'.

The passage is set amid great natural beauty. In August 1644 Charles I, during his pursuit of the Parliamentary army under Essex, came to see Lord Mohun of Bodinnick (owner of the ferry) and enthused with him on the glorious panorama from his grounds, before broaching the sterner business afoot. A detachment of Royalist infantry and guns were then positioned to guard Bodinnick passage, as Charles threw a cordon round Essex's army and forced it to surrender at Lostwithiel. Without doubt the ferry transported supplies from Fowey for this detachment, and messengers to and from Lord Goring, whose cavalry were tightening the net round Essex from the west: and probably carried the two deserters from the Parliamentary army, who crossed the river on 30th August to betray their General's escape plans. The Fowey estuary is rich in political and commercial history, and Bodinnick passage has played a full part through succeeding centuries. A drawing of c.1660 by Schellinks, of which the original is in Venice, shows the Bodinnick ferry of restoration times. It was a primitive craft - a rectangular wooden deck carried on two parallel hulls and rowing it must have been arduous work. Certainly there was always a small boat for pedestrian passengers.

The fortunes of the Mohun family declined, Bodinnick Hall became a ruin, and early in the reign of George I (about 1720) the ferry and all its rights were purchased by Governor Pitt. The ferry rights were eventually assigned to the Passage House (later, Old Ferry) Inn, at the foot of Bodinnick hill. Within living memory successive landlords named Butson, Jackson and Green, hired local boatmen to run the ferries. The animal/waggon floats, known as cow-boats, needed two men to row them with heavy sweeps, and were in use until the later 1920s. The passenger fare in those days was $\frac{1}{2}$ d. return for local residents. When Mr. Green retired he managed to separate the ferry rights from the inn licence, and bequeathed them to his step-daughter, Miss Clapham.

Miss Clapham was an enterprising but demanding employer. Once every year she had the gates at Bodinnick slip closed, to claim rights of the slipway. She experimented with installing an engine in one of the passenger rowboats, and used it as a tug to propel the cow-boat. But it did not have the power to steer the float effectively in the tideway, and the two men on her were obliged to steer with one of the sweeps, which was hard labour. Retired ferryman Fred Bunt recalls that in Miss Clapham's earlier days the pay of the ferryman was £2.2s. a week, and that when off-duty they were expected to work in her gardens or kitchen.

Hours of duty on the ferry were arranged in alternate weeks of 7 am. to 5 pm., and 9 am. to 9 pm. (10 pm. on Saturdays). Besides animals (principally horses, cattle, sheep and pigs) to be coerced aboard, there were frequent heavy consignments of beer to manhandle, so the ferrymen's money was well earned. Following the unsatisfactory performance of the improvised tugboat, Miss Clapham introduced purpose-built powerful motor tugs, and replaced the cow-boats with modern car ferries. The present 6-car float came into service in 1963, and was the first Bodinnick ferry to have wheel-controlled prows. An 8-car float, to cost £20,000 was under construction at Toms and Sons yard when Miss Clapham died in 1976.

On the death of Miss Clapham the ferry rights came on to the market. Toms & Sons tendered successfully and acquired the rights and properties - reputedly for £60,000 plus the cost of the uncompleted car float, on which they were still working. This new float, with a capacity of 8 cars, was brought into use the same year. It is 80 ft. long and is readily distinguishable by having gates instead of chains between the prows and main deck. The other float in current use is Miss Clapham's 6-car ferry of 1963. The motor tugs employed today are double-transom boats with propellor and rudder at either end, and central controls. They do not require to turn at the end of a crossing and the cox'n has only to 'face-about' himself (61). On service they are lashed fore and aft to the car floats, which their twin 43hp. engines handle with ease.

On the Fowey side, Passage Slip in North Street had been the landing-place from time immemorial till 1976. The adjoining boat basin was then filled in to make a commodious car and boat-trailer park, and a new ferry landing, Caffa Mill Slip, was constructed on the north side. This has given the ferries a more direct route and improved the approach for vehicular traffic. At Bodinnick however room is restricted, and landing is not possible when very high tides coincide with high winds. The car ferry then has to be temporarily suspended, and a motorboat is put on to carry the pedestrian traffic.

Every crossing is operated by a crew of three:- one 'driver' (i.e. cox'n of the tug) and two deck-hands on the float, one of whom must be a qualified 'driver'. The service operates from dawn to dusk, and in the summer season cars ferried average 1,200 a day. The $\frac{1}{2}$ d. toll of the days when the publicans ran the ferry is now of course but a cherished dream, and pedestrians today pay 10p.

Prior to decimalisation on 15th February 1971 the toll for a private car was 2/6d. But 22 $\frac{1}{2}$ p. proved inconvenient for giving change and gave rise to delays, so the fare was increased to 25p. The present car toll is 45p. Even so, this compares favourably with some similar crossings elsewhere.

Apart from the old Passage Slip, some other relics of earlier days remain to be seen. The last-withdrawn ferry, replaced by Toms' 8-car float, is today in use as a jetty in Mixtow Pill, owned by a Mr. Tomlin. It had spring-loaded prows instead of the wheel control afterwards adopted. A villager of Lanteglos tells us that an old Bodinnick ferry built in 1917 by Slades is lying derelict at Pont Pill. The original two-vehicle car ferry was, until 1975, still in use as a barge for conveying scrap at J. Toms & Sons shipyard.

Bodinnick Ferry has its place in English literature: the late Sir Arthur Quiller-Couch brings it into his romantic novel 'Shining Ferry' (1905), in which Nicholas Vro the ferryman is a principal character. Perhaps Sir Arthur, who was in love with Fowey, was making amends for an incident in the past. His father, when a General Practitioner at Bodmin, had been summoned urgently one night to a patient at Bodinnick. He had saddled his horse and ridden to the Passage Slip, Fowey, only to be told the ferryman had refused to turn out, as 'the ferry closed at 10 pm.' Rowed across, after some delay, by a private boat owner, Dr. Quiller-Couch had afterwards successfully taken the ferry lessee to court, on the grounds that the ferry was part of the King's Highway and as such must operate on request at any hour of day or night.

Incidents of drama, humour or tragedy occur from time to time in the operation of any ferry service. Ferryman Len Slade has told me that in 1943 an Indian cavalry regiment stationed nearby sent a detachment to be crossed by ferry. The horses were led safely aboard but then decided they preferred to swim. They made a rush for the outboard prow and plunged overboard. The sergeant's comments were colourful but unrecorded. There was a fatal accident in 1971 when a car being embarked at Bodinnick failed to stop. It plunged through the safety-chains of the 6-car ferry and over the prow into the river. The driver and his lady passenger, a middle-aged couple, lost their lives. The failure to stop remained unexplained, but a verdict of accidental death was recorded. In 1972 two Spanish seamen whose ship was loading in Fowey were enjoying a 'busman's holiday' in the estuary. At Passage Slip their hired self-drive motorboat drove under the ferry's prow, knocking them into the water. They were rescued by prompt action of the ferry crew, and revived at the Riverside Hotel.

Bodinnick Passage with the **No.5** *(1963) car float leaving Caffa Mill Slip at Fowey in March 1980. Photo: Western Morning News.*

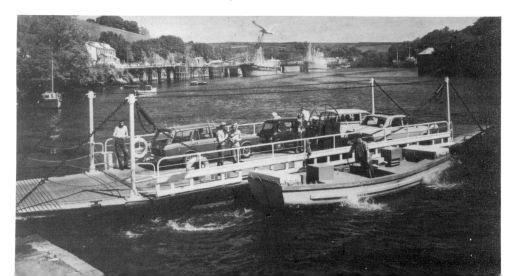

Some ferries, such as Tolverne, have closed because their passage does not, in terms of the motor-car age, save sufficient mileage to make them viable. Some, like Antony or Lelant, have gone because the population or industry which they served has so declined that they are no longer relevant. Others, on trunk routes, have given place to bridges, as at Saltash. None of these circumstances threatens Bodinnick ferry which seems destined, like Tennyson's Brook, to 'go on for ever'. And this is no bad thing, for not only does it ply in a beautiful setting, but it is, in many ways, a model ferry.

POLRUAN - FOWEY: A 1772 deed in the Cornwall County Record Office mentions Polruan Ferry as being within the manor of Bodinnick. In 'Lanteglos by Fowey with Polruan and Bodinnick' (authors Ackland and Druce) it is stated that the Fitzwilliams owned this manor in the 13th century and resided there for several generations. The Fowey River was then already a busy port and the ferry certainly was in being at this time. Early in the 14th century Reginald Mohun courted the Fitzwilliams' only daughter and married her, but in 1333 she sued for divorce. About three years later the manor passed to her heir by Reginald Mohun. The Mohuns continued to live at Bodinnick Hall, and flourished there for 300 years. In 1347 Fowey assembled 47 ships manned by 770 men for Edward III's siege of Calais, and this activity in the port must have kept the ferry busy.

In 1534 John Leland crossed the river here from Fowey by 'the Trajectus' (i.e. ferry). About 1580 the Mohuns bought Boconnoc near Lostwithiel, and lived there afterwards. During the latter years of their ownership we have a reference to the ferry by W.G. Maten in his 'Early Tours of Devon and Cornwall' (1704-6) where he describes taking the ferry from Polruan and mentions inhaling the stench of pilchards long before landing at Fowey. In 1717 Lady Mohun sold Boconnoc to Thomas Pitt (Kinsman of the Georgian Prime Ministers) but he died without issue and it passed to his only sister, Lady Anne Grenville.

Up to 1793 the Fowey landing-place of the ferry had been in natural rock; local residents then raised subscriptions and built a slip, Lady Grenville contributing two guineas. By 1820 the Fowey slip was breaking up, and the ferry owner was advised to agree with the local inhabitants to contribute to its repair. The repairs, if made, were not long-lasting, as fifty years later the want of a slip was to cause a minor accident. An estate account book dated 1845-9 shows Captain Richard Pill as lessee of Polruan ferry, for which he paid Lady Grenville £5 rent a year. Pedestrian passengers at Polruan paid 1d. for the return trip. In 1860 there was a conveyance for the Prince of Wales to Anne, Baroness Grenville of several portions of foreshore and bed of water of Fowey River between low and high water for £150. By 1863 Mrs. Pill (presumably the Captain's widow) was paying the rent to run the ferry under Lady Grenville. That year there was a court case.

The monopoly rights of the manor were challenged when a Polruan longshoreman began to use his own boat as a ferry in competition. There were complaints from the village as there clearly was insufficient business for two services. The offending boatman was sent to prison for some months. During this time an unemployed seaman started a rival ferry but desisted when threatened with prosecution. The original offender was then released from prison on compassionate grounds on a promise to behave, but within a month was using his boat as a ferry once more. This time the law seems to have failed to assert itself, as the 'pirate' service continued to threaten the viability of the official ferry, until the hour brought forth the man. This was a Polruan resident who undertook to manage the ferry for Lady Grenville for twelve months, or until things settled down. If the situation was unresolved by the end of the year he agreed to surrender his lease so that Lady Grenville could dispose of the ferry. A man was hired as ferryman for 14s. a week, and the rescue operation was evidently successful for no more is recorded of 'the opposition' and the manorial ferry did not cease to run.

When Lady Grenville died, the ferry passed by her will to her husband's nephew, the younger son of the first Earl Fortescue, whose descendants live at Boconnoc today. In 1874 a resident named Richard Martyn suggested building a sea wall and jetty to make a small inner harbour with ferry steps, on the Fowey side. This proposal followed a mishap. A well-known architect, Sylvanus Trevail, had fallen overboard when the ferry arrived at Fowey. The ferryman still had his oars in the water and was giving change to a passenger; he told Mr. Trevail to wait until he could hold the boat against the rock landing. The architect however had jumped ashore, missed his footing, and suffered a soaking and some bruising. It was agreed that a better landing-place was needed: the existing one being ledges of rock with a cleft between through which the boat was brought. The unfortunate Mr. Trevail claimed that the rocks rose at a 60 degree angle at half-tide. It seems that Richard Martyn's proposal was deemed too ambitious, but a slip was constructed on a ridge of rocks out from the shore, at a cost of about £100. Mr. Fortescue donated three years ferry rent (£36), and the remainder was met by grants from Fowey and Polruan councils and public subscriptions. This slip is probably the one in use at Whitehouse today.

There are still a few older local inhabitants who can remember the 'penny-return' rowboat ferry as it was at the beginning of this century. At Polruan, landings were at the quay if the tide served; at the rocks below Polruan Castle if the tide was too low. The ferryboat held 12 people and in rough weather at least two men rowed. Passengers could row across and travel free, and girls often enjoyed doing this as much as the men, sometimes rowing two to an oar. It was unremunerative for the ferryman when the passengers rowed, but at least he could sit back and enjoy his pipe. Commercial directories of Polruan for 1902, 1906, and 1910 list George Ede as ferryman. Jim Barnes is listed in 1913, and a number of local folk can still remember him, as he was associated with the ferry for many years, and was the first to put a motorboat on the service - in 1912. He ran the ferry from 1912 for the Fortescue Estate until Captain "Taffy" Waters bought the ferry and the ferry rights from the Manor, about 1920.

Captain Waters lived in Looe and commuted the 10 miles or so in pony and trap. Business was increasing and Jim Burns was retained on the ferry, while his brother Douglas and son Alphonse also helped as required. In 1924 Captain Waters decided to replace the motor-ferry and had a new boat purpose-built, with a Kelvin engine, by Mitchell's of Mevagissey. In view of the quicker service and the running costs, the ferry toll was raised to 1d. each way. This led to a court case and the increase was refused. It was usual for Jim Burns to run the motor ferry till noon, when he went home to dinner. His son Alphonse would then work the rowboat ferry for the lunch hour: but as its capacity was limited to 12 passengers some had trouble getting to and from home for their meals without returning late for work. Vital though the Polruan ferry was to the community, its operation seems to have been somewhat casual in those days. Captain Waters would sometimes take the local shop-girls for a short trip to the castle or around the moored ships, even if others were waiting for the ferry. But it seems no-one complained. It is said that if you wanted to catch a train it was best to be philosophical about it and leave an hour early to make certain. However for a 2/- tip the ferryman would carry your cases up to the station. On May Day each year Captain Waters would take the shop-girls up-river at 6 am. so that they could gather flowers to take home before work.

The lease of the ferry was for 24 hours daily, and for many years what was known as the 'night ferry' had taken over after dusk until about 11 pm., and was available, at least in theory, on request during the night. This was in the nature of a sub-lease, different men and boats taking over. The brothers Bill and Ernie Hanson, who had run this service for years, gave up in 1925 and the night ferry was taken over by William Tomlin and his sons, who were destined to run it for over thirty years. These years were the heyday of the night ferry. The Tomlins ran till midnight seven days a week, and at any night-hour with due notice. Their boats' hulls were painted white with blue water-line, and were built by Slade's.

In 1926 a second motor-ferry, similar to its predecessor, was built at Mevagissey and put into service. These two motor ferries, which have always been well maintained are still in regular use today. When Captain Waters retired, Jim Burns took over the ferry in partnership with his son Thomas and grandsons Douglas and Jim (junior). A new (third) motor-ferry was built by Slade's in 1928, and application was made to the court for an increased toll of 1d. each way. In these days of rampant inflation it seems incredible that the $\frac{1}{2}$ d. fare charged from time immemorial had persisted well into the 20th century. Isaac Foot was the magistrate and he decided to compromise, sanctioning $1\frac{1}{2}$ d. as the return fare, which is shown in Wark Lock & Co's Guide published later that year. Perhaps Jim Burns permitted himself a wry smile. He was aware that Polruan was strongly Liberal and that Isaac Foot was preparing to contest the Bodmin seat he had lost in 1924.

The new motor ferry (which was painted blue whereas its predecessors were black) had a short life. Within about twelve months she broke loose from her moorings one night in a south-easterly gale, suffered damage, and sank. A dredger later - by chance - brought up her engine, but the hull was never recovered.

Jim Burns died in 1931 and by 1935 the name 'Polruan Ferry Company' appears for the first time in commercial directories. Wyatt and Mitchell were the partners. They repainted the boats' hulls dark green with red boot-topping. In 1957 the Tomlin family gave up the night ferry, which was taken over by Claude Richards, and run by him for the next twenty years. Wyatt and Mitchell meanwhile had sold out to a newly-constituted company formed by Henry Charman, William Stone, Fred Ricketts and others, but still trading as the Polruan Ferry Company.

A London-based company acquired the ferry in 1977, and there is undoubtedly a local feeling of loss, that the service is no longer Polruan-owned. The new owner, trading as the Polruan Ferry Company Limited, repainted the boats with orange hulls and the word FERRY prominently displayed on the bows. They also took over the night ferry themselves, reducing the winter service to three nights weekly. Lack of sufficient demand brought the night ferry to an end after 1978. Today the boats - which have a passenger capacity of thirty - are fitted with powerful diesel engines, and carry three 'buoyant apparatus' rafts for 27 persons, and four lifebuoys. A third boat (capacity 12 persons) is moored off Polruan quay as a relief ferry when required. There are occasional memorable interludes in the life of any ferry service. In 1913 Polruan ferry was hi-jacked when Alphonse Burns, then a teenager, camouflaged the boat with the help of another local boy, and put to sea to go and join the army! A Dutch coaster picked them up in the Channel and brought them home.

EAST LOOE - WEST LOOE: The twin villages which nestle one on either side of Looe River are **LOOE RIVER** ancient, but until they developed to the south, the many-arched bridge provided adequate communication. Thus there has never been an established ferry with rights belonging to a local manor, or the Duchy. The need for a ferry began at the end of the nineteenth century, when Joseph Thomas, a retired civil engineer, cut the road from West Looe to Hannafore, opened with much local rejoicing in July 1895. Thereafter the Hannafore estate grew rapidly, where once there had been a solitary cottage, and ferryboats have plied ever since from the East Looe lower slipway to Pennyland - a name no doubt deriving from the 1d. toll charged for the crossing.

There have never been sole rights, and today any boatman licensed by the Caradon District Council can work the ferry, on a full-time or part-time basis. The pioneer of a regular service seems to have been a disabled boatman of West Looe named Luther Marshall who worked all the year round, in every kind of weather, but had to face unlimited competition in the summer. To combat this, in the early nineteen-thirties, Luther marked his boat 'The Official Ferry': but this caused great resentment on the part of the summer-only ferrymen, and the Looe Harbour Commissioners intervened to make Luther remove the sign. Some time later he provided his boat with a notice-board proclaiming 'The Recognised Ferry', and this time was not challenged. Luther was also a pioneer of the 'season ticket' principle. As business folk and shopkeepers in East Looe came to live at Hannafore, he would charge them half-a-crown a week for any number of crossings, and such a passenger became known as a 'weekly'.

An amusing incident is recalled of a day when a solitary gentleman awaited the ferry at Pennyland slip. A ferryman resting on his oars awaiting trade wanted to make sure that this was not one of Luther's 'season ticket holders', and called out "Are you weekly, sir?" "No, my good man" came the reply "I'm very well, thank you." It is unrecorded who was the more surprised, the visitor by the question, or the ferryman by the answer.

Retired fisherman A.J. Pengelly, author of 'Oh for a Fisherman's Life', can remember how Luther in his latter years sometimes saved himself undue exertions by an ingenious way of using the tide. In the latter half of an ebb tide he would let go a small anchor in midstream and make fast the anchor rope to a thole pin. By positioning the thole pin foreside of midships, and using a paddle on the boat's quarter, he could sheer the boat across the stream from east to west or vice-versa, according to the pegging of the thole pin on the starboard or port bow.

About 1933 some of the watermen began an additional service upstream from Granite Steps, by the Fishmarket, to West Looe Quay. This service also has prospered during the summer, but today the same boats and men work either crossing as the need arises, or the tide dictates. Looe began to develop as a resort when the railway from Liskeard was opened to passenger traffic in 1879. In the years between the wars the hotels and guest houses would fill with visitors in July and August. Mr. Austin Toms, (author of "About Looe" 1978) and once on the ferry himself, recalls that there were then often fifteen to eighteen boats on the ferry. The boats were expected to take their turn and work a shuttle service. "One boat might have to leave with just one or two passengers whilst the next might have ten. No waiting was allowed, but I have seen some old tricks to hang on until more people arrived."

During the 'twenties and 'thirties the Great Western Railway steamers from Plymouth, **Sir John Hawkins** and **Sir Richard Grenville** ran regular excursions to Looe, often bringing upwards of 800 people. The ferrymen with the larger, 18ft. boats would go out to meet the steamer, bring the passengers ashore in relays, and later carry them back. The men with smaller boats remained on the ferry and benefitted from the reduced competition.

About 1935 some of the ferrymen installed engines in their boats and today all the boats are motorised; one wonders why, when the distance to be covered is so short. The answer appears to be twofold; none of the boats is exclusively a ferry, and the engine is advantageous for fishing; also there are strong tidal currents of up to five knots in the estuary, and an engine enables a service to be maintained in conditions unsuitable for oars and sail. At low water the motor-boats have too much draught to ply; but some of the ferrymen then don waders and push rowboats across and back.

Today a service operates throughout the summer from 8 am. to 11 pm: and during the six or so busiest weeks of the season it is common for about twelve men to be working boats on the ferry. On weekend evenings men employed elsewhere during the day will augment the 'regulars', a practice which is not always welcomed by the latter if their own boats are sufficient to handle the numbers offered. There is no service from Christmas to Easter, but at weekends in autumn and spring, if the weather is good, one or other ferryman will sometimes find it worthwhile to ply for a few hours.

A view postcard of the ferry on sale in some Looe shops shows the late Stan Tamlin, a regular ferryman, clambering aboard after pushing off from Pennyland slip, and Jack Hosking, a still-operating part-timer, about to land three passengers from West Looe. Some old-timers who have been well-known on the ferry for many years have recently retired, and Bob Sargent is probably the longest-serving of the ferrymen working today.

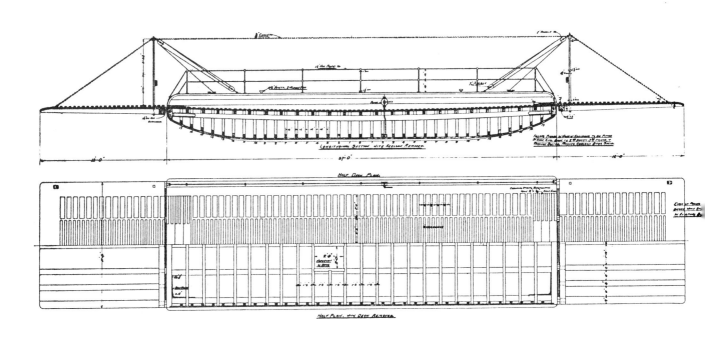

Horse Ferry Boat of 1907. Service: Lower Dart Ferry (1907-c.1926).
Plan courtesy National Maritime Museum, Greenwich.

10.

Port of Plymouth.

Upper Tamar & River Tavy

Netstakes-
Morwell
Morwellham-
Harewood
Rumleigh-
Calstock

Netstakes-Morwell

Morwellham-Harewood

CALSTOCK

Calstock Passage

Rumleigh-Calstock

Cotehele-Ward

0   1 mile

Halton Quay-Bere Alston

Lopwell Dam

Lopwell Ferry

Bere Ferrers

Cargreen-Thorn Point

Bere Ferrers-Blaxton

Cargreen

Blaxton

Warleigh House

Warleigh-Yellowstones

Tamerton Crossing

Budshead Passage

UPPER TAMAR

NETSTAKES - MORWELL: This was a private ferry in the sense that there were no public crossing rights and it operated at a point between Netstakes Quay and the Tamar Manure Canal gates. The ferry "rights" belonged to the Duke of Bedford who owned the east bank of the river, and the landing on the Devon side, at Russell House Steps, gave access to "The Duke's Drive", which linked Morwellham with the Duke's residence 'Endsleigh' at Milton Abbot.

The ferry must have been quite busy in the days of the mining boom. It was the route taken by Gunnislake men who worked at Morwellham Quay, and of barge or coaster skippers arranging repairs or refitting at Crocker's shipbuilding yard, which had opened at Netstakes in the 1830s and was in business till about 1868. The ferry was operated by the lock-keeper of the Manure Canal, whose house was on the island between canal and river, and the fare was 1d. each way, the 'perks' of the lock-keeper. This Ferry House is still there, in use as a private dwelling, and is reached by a small wooden bridge from the Cornish side. The decline of mining and closure of Morwellham as a port meant that the usefulness of the ferry was much diminished after about 1900. From being a vital link in industry it became a convenience for the leisured making their way to the once-popular beauty spot of Morwell Rocks.

The last ferryman at Netstakes was Albert Teague, who is still remembered by the older generation in the district. He took over after the Great War and maintained a service for a few years, by which time demand for the ferry had dwindled to the occasional pedestrians. Retired water-bailiff Herbert Symons recalls that Teague continued to work his boat when needed, often conveying only a single person in a day, till 1948; his son deputising if he was not himself available. Chris Cockram of Gunnislake remembers using the ferry between 1946 and 1948 and even then the fare was still 1d. Albert Teague died about 1950, but by then the boat had been laid up, and the ferry had not run since.

MORWELLHAM - HAREWOOD: The history of this ferry must certainly go back at least to the beginning of the 12th century, when Morwellham had become established as the port for Tavistock. Certainly its usefulness increased and declined with the fortunes of this river port, which had nearly 1000 years of active life. Morwellham's trade and importance increased greatly after the opening of the Tavistock Canal in 1817, when manganese, lead, and copper ores were exported in great quantities for more than 60 years. Many miners and quay workers crossed the river daily from Calstock. The crossing was between the dock beside Devon Great Consols quay to a muddy slip still visible below Ferry Farm.

The competition of the railway and resultant redundancy of the canal at last brought Morwellham's heyday to an end: and though the export of arsenic from Devon Great Consols Mine occupied the port till the late 1880s, by 1890 or soon after, all trade had ceased. The demise of the port however did not bring about the closure of the ferry. Morwellham Wesleyan Chapel (enlarged 1861) was served principally by ministers and local preachers who had to use the ferry, and the conveyance of the preacher was a regular Sunday duty for the ferryman. Clearly the congregation were aware of their indebtedness, for it is known that at least one of the boats used between the wars was provided at their expense. When the London & South Western Railway linked Calstock to Bere Alston in 1908, Morwellham folk were provided, via the ferry, with an alternative route to Plymouth, being undaunted by the uphill walk from the ferry landing at Harewood to Calstock Station.

For many years prior to World War II, the ferryman was "Jopey" Nicolls, whom older residents well remember. Captain Jack Adams took over the ferry when he became Water Bailiff in the nineteen-forties. Mrs. Clarice Adams, his widow, recalls that he used an 18ft. boat which he sculled on the crossing. In the nineteen-fifties the traffic dwindled to a few school-children and the occasional traveller. The last regular passenger was schoolboy, Peter Stone of Ferry Farm, Harewood, who crossed the river to attend the Grammar School at Tavistock. The end came in the severe winter of 1963, when the swollen river swept the ferry boat from its moorings and carried it a mile and a half downstream, to be wrecked near Danescombe Quay.

RUMLEIGH - CALSTOCK: Information about this ferry is hard to come by. Certainly it was not one of the long-established public passages: it was probably an industrial ferry which was born with the mining boom and died with it. As far as I can discover the boat worked between a hard near Rumleigh brick works on the Devon side to Okel Tor mine quay, Calstock on the Cornish bank. There seems little doubt that it was for miners, and other workers coinciding with the shifts: but the public were welcome to use it, and it provided a link between Tuckermarsh and East Calstock or - by using also the Morwellham ferry - between Tuckermarsh and the quays of Morwellham.

Mr. W. King of Botherick, near Cotehele, has told me: "My father and uncles were coopers at Rumleigh Mine, and they used this ferry daily to get to work from Calstock". Mr. E.M. Fry remembers a Calstock Baker named Hickman who regularly crossed by the ferry with bread for delivery to the farms around Tuckermarsh and the resident mine officials at Rumleigh and Gawton. Ferries such as Rumleigh seldom get a mention in books on the Tamar Valley, and their only memorial is in the memories of those of the older generation who still live by the banks of the Tamar.

CALSTOCK - CALSTOCK PASSAGE: The Calstock Ferry was one of the oldest on the Tamar, and probably dates back to Saxon times. The ferry rights anciently belonged to the Valletort family, who owned Calstock Manor, but in 1270 the Valletorts sold out at Calstock to Richard Earl of Cornwall and King of the Romans. Thence the estate and ferry passed to the earldom and duchy of Cornwall. This was an obvious crossing-place, and the quays of Calstock became historically important in their own right long before the industrial boom of the 19th century: while as long ago as the early Middle ages the mines of the Bere Peninsular were being worked by the Crown for silver. Thus for generations, merchants, seamen and miners must have been among the principal users.

The importance of the passage increased greatly in the heyday of the Tamar Valley's industrial activity. On the Devon bank Browning's (later Goss's) shipyard was working from the early 1840s to 1923, and the Bere Peninsular mines were producing lead till the 1860s; while from 1890 to 1908 Calstock folk needed the ferry to reach the L. & S.W. Railway at Bere Alston. On the Cornish side Calstock boasted a paper mill, brick and tile works, a tannery, a brewery, quarries, and iron foundry, and the terminus of the East Cornwall Mineral Railway, while surrounding mines were disgorging tin, copper, lead and mispickel.

By the 19th century the ferry rights had passed to the Passage Inn, on the Devon shore, well-known for its rose trees and cherry orchards, and which still stands as "Ferry Farm". Frank James was the landlord in the latter years of the century, and he employed an assistant ferryman to deputise when the bars claimed his undivided attention. The Devon and Cornwall County Councils took over when the slump came and the service was becoming uneconomic. When trade declined in the Shipyard, James Goss's sons Lewis and Tom worked the ferry, each crossing it on alternate days. Mud was a chief enemy, and until the end of the service the ferryman had the responsibility of keeping the 'hards' washed down at each ebb tide.

The building of the viaduct in 1908, and the link-up of the railway with the old mineral line to Kelly Bray dealt a severe blow to the Calstock ferry and the loss of the licence for the Passage Inn hastened its decline. However, there was a 30 minute service in 1915 and probably later. Ward and Baddeleys Thorough Guide to Devon and Cornwall" advises the traveller from Bere Alston: "Hence to Calstock by path and ferry (1d; at half hours: returning at quarters). Go under the line S. of station, and take at once a field-path, left. This soon becomes enclosed, and, after a rise, bends to the left and descends through wood to the ferry, with the neat "Passage Inn" on the Devon side."

In the early 'forties the ferryman was "Nemo" Larsen, who retired in 1945. The last ferryman was Douglas Langford, who worked the service from 1945 till its closure in 1949 (66). "The wages at first were only £3.10s. a week" he told me, while the hours were 7 am. - 9 pm. The rate rose only slowly with the years: to £4 (winter) and £4.10s. (summer); to £5.10s. (winter) and £5 (summer): until the job was combined with other Council work, when the wages reached £13. A new ferryboat was acquired in 1947 at a cost of £70 - which was less than the cost of its overhaul about fifteen years later. In the 'fifties and early 'sixties the ferry was still busy at weekends. "Often on a Saturday" Douglas Langford says, "I've taken two or three hundred across to watch the football on the pitch which used to be on the lower side of the viaduct on the Devon side". The end however was in sight. The last regular users were schoolchildren from Calstock, and though the passage is still shown on Ordnance Survey maps, the ferry has not run since 1969.

COTEHELE - WARD: Among the Tamar Ferries which have disappeared within living memory was that between Cotehele and Ward. On the Cotehele side the ferry worked from the strip of foreshore between the quays - quays which in the heyday of the river traffic were a hive of activity, with sailing barges loading and discharging, and excursion steamers making their regular calls. The hard on the Devon Bank at Ward can still be seen, though much muddied, and it gave access to a footpath which branched to Bere Alston and Calstock Passage.

It is doubtful if there was any public ferry here before the 18th century, when the quay was busy handling copper ore and arsenic. By the middle of the 19th century till the early years of

Calstock Passage. Sculling oar at the ready, Doug Langford awaits passengers on the Devon side, about 1950.

Photo: Camel Cards.

the twentieth the soft fruit traffic was considerable. Between 1900 and 1905, 500 tons of fruit crossed the river here for transport by rail to Plymouth, and more than 2000 tons for London, the North, and Scotland. Although local growers transported most of this in their own boats, there can be no doubt that the ferry did its share; and also brought the workers from Calstock and the Bere peninsular.

The Ferry provided Cotehele and St. Dominick folk with their most convenient route to Calstock: they took the lefthand path after landing at Ward, and used the upstream ferry from Calstock Passage to complete the journey. The railway, which reached Bere Alston in 1890, and Calstock in 1908, probably increased ferry traffic for a while, by providing an inducement to travel to Plymouth or beyond; but in the end it was the executioner, destroying the trade of the river and quays and consequently the ferries.

Twice yearly the ferry was in demand by the Earl of Mt. Edgcumbe's tenants arriving to pay their rents. Mr. E. Paige in his book 'The Tamar Valley at Work' tells how it was the custom for tenant-farmers and others to pay their rents in person at the Tudor Hall of Cotehele House to the Earl's agent.

Here tankards of ale were provided so that the creditors could regale themselves before departing. Many availed themselves fully of this privilege, and the ferry was sometimes crowded with late-returning tipsy farmers, so that some had to stand for the crossing. On one occasion one of them fell overboard into the river, and was not missed till, late at night, an unavailing search was organised.

At the time of the Great War and after, the Ferry was owned by a Mr. P. Simmonds, who ran a store near the quay. Throughout the twenties John Hoskin took over the service. He had previously assisted Simmonds with the ferry, but was a market-gardener. He had an assistant ferryman, Fred Braund, in the early 'twenties. Latterly Mr. E. Fry, now living at Botherick, used to deputise for Hoskin when needed. He recalls that the fare was 2d. each way, and that the ferry was a 17ft. waterman's boat, which Hoskin and Braund always sculled on the crossing. "But I didn't consider myself a great sculler" he explains today "and I always rowed across with both oars". Mr. W. King, an octogenarian also living at Botherick, remembers being called on late one evening to ferry a family across when John Hoskin was otherwise engaged: "I was an apprentice at the blacksmiths at the time" he says "but I can well remember that one occasion when I worked the Ferry". Within living memory it was never a full-time job, and a loud cry of 'Boat!' was necessary to summon the ferryman. Regular passengers for some time were a Mr. Maunder (water diviner of Callington) and his son, who crossed daily while engaged on digging wells near Bere Alston. It seems that the Ferry ceased altogether about 1930.

HALTON QUAY - BERE ALSTON: This was a very ancient ferry which originally belonged to the baronial family of the Valletorts, the ferry rights being attached to their manor of Halton and West on the Cornish bank of the river. For long this was a busy and important mid-Tamar passage, from Greenbanks or Halton Quay (outlets for the St.Dominick hinterland, long famed for flowers and soft fruit) to North Hooe on the Devon bank, the nearest beach for Bere Alston. At an unknown and distant date, the ferry rights changed hands and the passage became one of the very few on the Tamar operated from the Devon side.

From the later Middle Ages it had been incumbent on the Mountbatten family, who then owned North Hooe, to maintain a ferry to either Greenbanks (a creek just opposite) or, dependent on tides and weather conditions, to Halton Quay. On the Devon side the ferry used a hard below North Hooe farm. The service was once known locally as Chapel ferry, originally because of the Halton Wayside chapel with a holy well on the site now occupied by Chapel Farm; but latterly perhaps because of the so-called chapel on Halton quay. This building, now Church property, still stands: it served as a quay trading office within living memory, but may once have been a ferry house. Pilgrims, fruit-growers, and miners on the Bere peninsular were doubtless the most regular users,

In the 19th century miners crossed at this point to work in the mines at Lockeridge, Furzehill and Whitsam, the bell at Whitsam Count-House calling to the ferry the men working the next 'core' or shift. Bags of lime from Halton's Kilns, or baskets of Halton cherries for market, were likely freight. There is a reference to the ferry in G.P. Hearder's "Guide to the Tamar Valley", published in 1841. The author records seeing the Halton ferry at work, while he was being rowed upstream. He noted that the ferryboat was half full of water, and that the unfortunate passengers were having to sit with their legs up on the thwarts. The London & South Western Railway reached Bere Alston in June 1890 and no doubt benefitted the ferry awhile with its direct route to Plymouth; until in 1908 it crossed the Tamar and linked with the Plymouth, Devonport & S.W. Junction railway, which sounded the death-knell of this and most other Tamar ferries.

When the 20th century dawned, Halton Quay was still busy with imports of timber, coal, limestone and manure, but the end was in sight. The mines had closed, rail and road-motor transport were killing the barge traffic, and difficulty was experienced in renewing the lease. The quay closed in 1926 and by then the ferry had ceased running. About the turn of the century a Mr. Down was the tenant farmer of North Hooe, and he maintained the ferry till he bought the farm outright about 1920, when the ancient requirement lapsed. His son Horace Down, who still lives on the Bere Peninsular, says that when his father took over the ferry, conditions had not much altered from G.P. Hearder's description of sixty years earlier. No doubt conditions then took a turn for the better, however; for as children, Horace Down and his sister and brother crossed daily to attend school at St. Dominick. Almost certainly they were the last regular passengers. A footpath led down from Bere Alston station to the ferry landing, and can still be traced. It is perhaps the last visible reminder of a crossing which once played an important part in the economy of the Tamar Valley.

CARGREEN - BERE FERRERS: This was an ancient passage, and an important link in Mediaeval times in the much used pilgrim route to and from the Continent. The churches at Bere Ferrers and Landulph were 'staging-posts' on this route. The pilgrims crossed from Bere Ferrers to Cargreen for Landulph and then took ship for the Continent. Nor was the traffic one-way, for pilgrims from overseas came this way for Glastonbury.

Lopwell
Ferry
Bere
Ferrers-
Blaxton Quay
Warleigh
Ferry
Tamerton
Crossing
Budshead
Passage

The Cargreen ferry assumed increased importance when the railway came to Bere Ferrers. On the Devon side, the footpath from the station to the ferry landing at Thorn Point can still be traced. A hard was built out through the mud, and a flagpole erected on which intending passengers could hoist a red flag to summon the boat. On the Cornish side the ferry worked from still-existing steps at Cargreen Quay, just below the Royal Oak (now, Spaniards) Inn.

The ferry rights were held by the publican, and the last ferrymen to work the passage were Tom Spry, landlord of the inn, and his assistant J. Best, a shoemaker. Local fruit and flower growers used the ferry extensively to take their produce across to the railway or to Devonport Market. Strawberries, gooseberries, black cherries and other soft fruits, with hundreds of bunches of local violets and primroses in springtime, were carted down the hill to Cargreen Quay, stacked on the ferry, and offloaded on to carts at Thorn Point. In 1906 the Cargreen Parish Council petitioned the London & South Western Railway for a properly-surfaced road on the west side of Bere Ferrers station to connect with the ferry, but to no avail.

Clergy also travelled via the railway, footpath and ferry. Joan and Terry Doyle in their book 'Tamar Valley Traveller' record how, in wild and wet weather, a considerate stationmaster at Bere Ferrers used to keep a set of dry clothes and a lantern to help the minister on his way. Octogenarian Mrs. G. Braund, who still lives in Cargreen, remembers that her late husband, when serving in the army in the Great War, used to return and leave via Bere Ferrers station and the ferry.

Today, at Thorn Point the footpath is overgrown, the flagpole has gone, only the hard has endured. Cargreen is a much-changed place from the days of the ferry. Its life is centred on yachting, most of the houses have been acquired by non-Cornish folk, and those who remember and used the ferry can be counted on the fingers of one hand. The service ceased to operate in the early 1920s.

RIVER TAVY LOPWELL FERRY: An old ferry which ceased running about 1930 crossed the higher reaches of the Tavy just up-river from the present Lopwell Dam. The ferry was necessary when the ford, where the causeway has since been built, was not passable due to rising tides. The remains of the ferryman's cottage can still be seen on the west bank; but the ferry inn, which was close by, has long disappeared. For many years, up to the end of the Great War, the ferry was worked by two brothers, Joe and Silas Vivian, whose sister was the local midwife. The last ferryman was a retired Commissioned Shipwright of the Royal Navy, named McLeod, but the use of the passage had much declined in the post-war years. Two senior residents of Bere Ferrers, Mr. and Mrs. Pedlar, can remember the ferry at work in the days of the Vivian brothers. The ferry rights must have belonged to the Lopes family of Maristow, who were the landowners on both sides of the river.

BERE FERRERS - BLAXTON QUAY: A ferry much used by woodmen going to and from their work was that between Bere Ferrers quay and the quay below Blaxton village on the east side. The service was dependent on tide, and the nearest alternative was the stone-paved ford at Chucksford. Both ferry and ford were used to take goods to Plymouth Market. In the years immediately preceding the Great War a regular ferry passenger was Miss Davey, a schoolmistress who lived in Bere Ferrers but worked in Plymouth. Early every Monday she would take the ferry to Blaxton, and walk from there, in all weathers, to her school in Plymouth, a distance of six miles! She lodged in Plymouth until the Friday, when the ferry brought her home to Bere Ferrers.

The last ferryman was William Doidge; and his death, soon after the Great War, brought this ferry service to a close. His grand-daughter Mary Spurr still lives in Bere Ferrers. Prior to the building in 1890 of the L. & S.W. Railway line through Bere Ferrers, the Blaxton ferry provided a link with the G.W.R. Plymouth-Launceston line at Bickleigh. When the mines of the Bere peninsular began to close in the 1870s, many local miners, their livelihood gone, crossed by this ferry to reach the railway and try their fortune in America.

WARLEIGH FERRY: For many years a ferry plied across the mouth of the River Tavy, from Yellowstones quay on the Bere Peninsular to Warleigh Point. At Warleigh the ferry steps, and an old boathouse, can still be seen, and a right of way existed through the grounds of Warleigh House. This ferry was effectively killed off when the L. & S.W. Railway line was constructed in 1890, the present bridge over the Tavy being at the site of the ferry. Together with the ferry at Budshead across Tamerton Creek, it provided a direct pedestrian link between Plymouth and the Bere Peninsular, and was probably used daily by workers on the Warleigh Estate. The rights of ferry would have belonged to the Copplestone family of Warleigh House.

TAMERTON CROSSING: At the head of Tamerton Creek lies the former village of Tamerton Foliot, now a part of Plymouth but having a history of its own going back to the 12th century. A ferry which once plied a quarter of a mile downstream from here did not survive into the twentieth century. However there was a ford for horses and vehicles until about 1922, which was passable up to about two hours either side of high water. The site is just below the two now-dilapidated quays near Salts Cottage. With tidal delays to wheeled traffic not more than four hours, it is very unlikely that there there was a horse-and-waggon boat here: but a rowboat ferry for pedestrians was necessary for most of the tide. The rights of ferry would have belonged anciently to the Copplestone family, landowners of Tamerton from 1470; and then to their successors, the Bamfields and Radcliffes.

BUDSHEAD PASSAGE: Near the mouth of Tamerton Creek, but to the east of the railway bridge, is the site of a ferry which has not run for sixty years. In the last century however it was busy enough, and it is said that the ferryman's cottage was standing within living memory, on the Warleigh side. The ferry plied from there to the now-demolished tidal mill at Budshead, which was being worked by Harold Doney until the early 1920s. Doney carried out his own deliveries and had his own boat, but while his mill worked there was some need for a ferry. In conjunction with the Warleigh ferry across the Tavy, Budshead Passage provided a direct route between Plymouth and the mines and market gardens of the Bere peninsular. The Radcliffe family were lords of the manor of Warleigh, and would have owned any ferry rights. In the early years of this century the ferryman was William Colwill, but it is unlikely that by then it was a full-time occupation. Colwill was followed by still-remembered Fred Kitts, who was not a resident ferryman, but was always willing to oblige those who wished to cross.

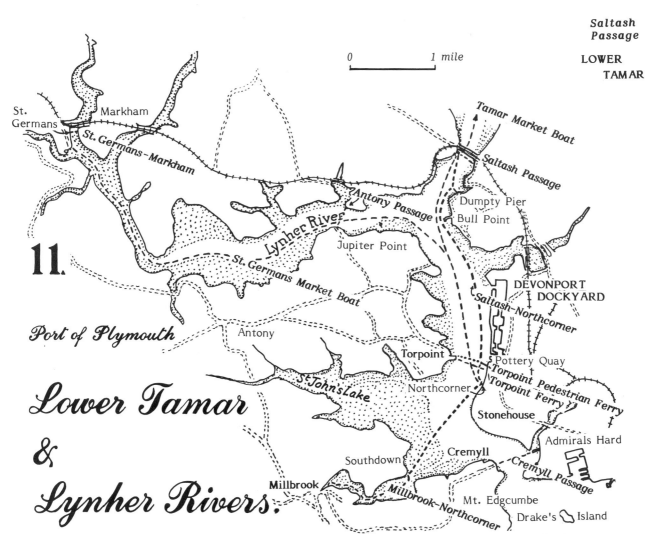

0   1 mile

St. Germans · Markham

St. Germans-Markham

Tamar Market Boat

Saltash Passage

Antony Passage

Dumpty Pier

Bull Point

Lynher River

Jupiter Point

St. Germans Market Boat

11.

Port of Plymouth

DEVONPORT
DOCKYARD

Saltash-Northcorner

Antony

Pottery Quay

Torpoint Pedestrian Ferry

Torpoint Ferry

Torpoint

St. John's Lake

Northcorner

Stonehouse

Lower Tamar

&

Lynher Rivers:

Admirals Hard

Cremyll

Southdown

Cremyll Passage

Millbrook

Millbrook-Northcorner

Mt. Edgcumbe

Drake's Island

SALTASH PASSAGE: Between the piers of the Royal Albert and Tamar bridges at Saltash, a plaque on a roadside wall proclaims: "BOROUGH OF SALTASH: This plaque commemorates the closing of the ferry across the River Tamar at Saltash on the 23rd day of October 1961, after more than 700 years of service." For the greater part of that time this ferry was the most important in the west, and the prosperity of the Borough of Saltash greatly depended upon it. There is no doubt that Saltash has been adversely affected by the ferry's closure: and certainly the £35,000 compensation paid to the Borough by the Government was less than generous. Today the new Tamar Bridge is already taxed by its traffic; and the reinstatement of the chainferry (at least as a summer alternative) although unlikely to be considered, has much to commend it.

Saltash Passage is documented as early as the 13th century; and Douglas C. Vosper in his 'The Ancient ferry at Saltash' declares there is evidence that it was an important crossing at the time of the Norman Conquest. It was anciently known as "Ash-Torre Passage", from a rock on the shore which has not been visible since the engineer Brunel used it as a foundation for one of the piers of the railway bridge. Richard Carew in his "Survey of Cornwall" (1602) says that this rock was invested with the jurisdiction of a manor "and claymeth the suites of many Gentlemen, as his free-holders in Knight's service".

The rights of ferry at Saltash belonged to the great baronial family of Valletort from the years following the Norman Conquest until 1270, when Roger de Valletort sold Trematon Castle and estate to Richard Earl of Cornwall. Thereafter, the Earl's bailiff received the rents which fell due to the manor for Saltash passage: in the 1290s they amounted to £6.18s. a year. An inquisition taken at Launceston in 1276 contains a complaint of the Earl of Cornwall that when the Earl's men of Esse (Saltash) tried to charge some servants of the Bishop of Exeter for their ferry crossing, the Bishop excommunicated them and placed an interdict on the chapel of Saltash for seven years! The Earl's complaint against the Bishop, it is good to record, was upheld.

From 1337 the burgesses of Saltash leased the ferry from the Duchy of Cornwall for £10 a year, the Duchy providing the boat. They continued to hold the ferry on lease except for one year (1356-57) when the Black Prince granted it to his military porter, William Lenche, in consideration of his services and his disfigurement by the loss of an eye at the battle of Poitiers. In 1355 the Black Prince received a complaint from the master of a foreign trader - a Hamburgher - that his boat had been commandeered for the Cremyll ferry; the Cremyll ferryboat having been seized to replace the Saltash boat, which was under repair.

In 1385 the ferry rights were bestowed for 200 years upon the Mayor and Burgesses of Saltash by a Royal Grant. It was not an easy passage to work: wind and tide could make the crossing prolonged and dangerous; yet it appears that many of the rowers were women. Amazons they must certainly have been. Horse-boats to convey animals as well as pedestrians were probably introduced at an early date. Queen Elizabeth's charter to Saltash in 1585 specifically grants the passage, and this is confirmed by charters of 1678, 1683 and 1774; but Richard Carew explains that this was no more

69

than 'benefit of the passage': and that a rent always remained payable by Saltash to the Duchy of Cornwall because of the manorial origin of the ferry. By 1618 the rent of the ferry had increased to £20 a year. The passage rose to considerable importance in the later years of the 17th century, and was the coach crossing for Cornwall, and the mail route. In 1724 Daniel Defoe wrote of his crossing from Plymouth to the "little, poor, shattered town" of Saltash: "The Tamae here is very wide and the ferry boats bad, so that I thought myself well escaped when I got safe on shore in Cornwall". On 29th May 1733, the ferry overturned and sank with the loss of twenty lives, nine of whom were Plymothians.

Anxiety on the part of passengers can be readily understood in the light of a letter written by a Mrs. Russell of Bedfordshire to her brother on 11th October 1760. She was travelling with her husband, a retired naval captain, to visit Captain (later Sir) William Trelawney of Coldrenick. From Butshey, she wrote, they "mounted on horses double and single, with cloak bags, bandbox, dog, etc. in our laps, for no carriages can go, and away we went for Saltash, about two miles, in order to ferry over. When we came there we stayed..... near three hours for the boat: but by the time it came there, the market people came so fast upon us that we were quite jockeyed, for it holds but nine horses, and sixteen wanted to get in. We stayed a little while, but both men and women were so brutish and dexterous at it that, though they each had panniers, they leapt in like dogs, on their horses; sometimes their panniers went over the other side, and their horses down. It became quite a battle which would get in first, either by fair means or foul. This deterred Mr. Russell from venturing ourselves among such West country brutes, and luckily a man-of-war's boat with eight oars happened to come ashore with the Lieutenant, when Mr.Russell begged the favour of him to let it carry us over, which he readily agreed to. So we left our horses for the two men (ferry crew) to get over as they could the next turn, which they did with the same difficulty as before, which obliged us to dine at Saltash".

Probably the Russells dined at the Passage House Inn, which has outlived the ferry. In September 1764 we find Mr. Tucker, the landlord there, stating in the 'Sherborne Mercury' that he "has lately fitted up his house, made a large stall-stable, and is provided with everything good for the reception of travellers... due attendance is given at the ferry, and carriages safely and expeditiously put in and out of the ferry-boat, the passage of which, for the encouragement of travellers, the Corporation have fixed at the following low rates, viz. for a coach and six 7s.6d., a carriage and four 5s, a carriage and pair 2s.6d. and a one-horse chair 1s.3d."

Leases of the ferry in the latter half of the 18th century provide for Saltash residents to cross free with horses and carriages. Clearly wheeled vehicles were regularly conveyed by this time, in spite of Mrs. Russell's comment in her letter. At Michaelmas 1772, the highest bidder for the ferry tolls had to pay a rent of £223, to work the boat himself: and the lease was to be void if complaint was laid before a J.P. that any person had been kept waiting for the boat for more than half an hour. The Saltash route into Cornwall was improved by the construction of a new road in 1761 from Trerulefoot to Saltash, and on the Devon side to Weston Mill. In 1791 however came the opening of the Torpoint "New Passage" two miles downstream and this caused ferry traffic at Saltash to decline, though gradually. The competition probably made the Saltash operators look to their laurels. No more is heard of the disorder and overcrowding which had discouraged the Russells in 1760. By the turn of the century, conditions seem to have improved, for about 1795 we find Dr. Maton, a visitor to Plymouth, recording that opposite Saltash "we found a commodious ferry boat, which wafted us and our horses across the Tamar". In 1804 the right of working the old horse ferryboats was let for £360 a year.

Saltash Corporation continued to let the tolls until 1832, when the Earl of Morley, Mr. A. Edgcumbe, Sir William Molesworth and other prominent local gentry secured an Act of Parliament authorising them to purchase the ferry rights from Saltash Corporation and establish a steam-powered floating bridge.

Tolls were increased to provide better accommodation, and Pope's shipyard at Turnchapel started work on the new steam ferry under the direction of J.M. Rendel, the Devon-born engineer who had pioneered his chain-system ferry at Dartmouth and at Gosport. This first Saltash chain-ferry was 80 feet long overall, with a midships engine and vehicle decks on either side with 15 foot prows. Beam measurement was 30 feet. A new landing-slip, downstream, below the Devonport Inn, and an approach road were constructed on the St. Budeaux side. The steam bridge, as it was first known, was ready by the end of 1832, and according to the newspaper "Western Luminary", did its trial run in $4\frac{1}{2}$ minutes. After barely two year's service however the new ferry was withdrawn for repairs and taken to Stonehouse. In fact it was not used again. It was an untimely failure, for this was the heyday of the coach, and the 'Quicksilver' Devonport Mail was putting up very good times between London and Falmouth. According to its 1837 timetable, it left London at 8 pm. reached Exeter about noon the next day, and expected to cross by the Saltash ferry at about 5 pm.

Oar-propelled horse boats were put on again, but the higher steam ferry tolls continued to be charged and there were loud complaints. Saltash Corporation then tried to reclaim possession of the ferry. They ran horseboats at the old rates in competition with the company, and claimed that the rights sold to the promoters of the 'Floating Bridge Act' had lapsed by default. Rival ferries continued to run for some years, until Saltash Corporation won an action at the Cornwall Spring Assizes of 1839, by which the ferry rights reverted to the town. The occasion was celebrated by civic festivities and the ringing of church bells on Boxing Day, 1839. In February 1840 the 'Royal Cornwall Gazette' announced an auction that month at Weakley's Hotel, Devonport, to dispose of 'the floating Steam bridge across the Tamar at Saltash, with engines, machinery and appurtenances thereto, now lying at Messrs. Hocking's Yard, Stonehouse'. Horseboats continued to operate until 31 May 1850, when a lease of the ferry for 21 years at £195 a year was granted to a new company, who were prepared to re-introduce steam power to the crossing.

The new steam ferry commenced running on 1st July, 1851. She was built of wood by Ratcliffes' of Mount Batten, and engined by Mara, Plymouth foundry. The vehicle deck was amidships. Length over prows was 86 feet; the centre deck measured 50 ft. x 11 ft; and draught was 18 inches. On one side were two 6hp. compound engines: on the other side, the boiler and two cabins. Her capacity was about 90 passengers, and three carriages and pairs. In 1865 this ferry met with disaster. After the day's work it was moored too close to the slipway on the Plymouth side. When the tide ebbed, the vessel grounded and slid down the muddy, weedstrewn slip, flooding her compartments, and sinking in the channel. When the ferry crew came on duty in the morning, no ferry was visible, and there was much consternation. Divers were sent down, and soon located the wreck. Chains were passed around her amidships, but were not well enough positioned to distribute the weight of the ship's engines, and the ferry broke her back. However her compound engines were salvaged and later installed in her successor built 1865-6. The new ferry,was built at a cost of £1,300. She was in service 35 years.

Meanwhile in 1854 Saltash Corporation had received £1,700 advance compensation for depreciation of ferry tolls when the railway bridged the river in 1859: but even so, ferry traffic increased quite steadily and the lessees - who had been granted a new lease for 25 years at a reduced rental of £127, made handsome profits, as evidenced by dividends of 25 to 33 per cent and occasionally even higher. At the end of the lease Saltash Corporation, spurning eager bids by Devonport, repossessed the ferry, and with the help of the Earl of Mount Edgcumbe had a new steel vessel built by Willoughby's of Plymouth,   which came into service in December 1891, and new chains were laid for her. There was great public rejoicing in Saltash, and well there may have been! For at the time dividends were running at nearly 50% and considerable benefits were to be reaped in town improvements.

The new steel ferry had cost £2,200. She was 10ft. wider in the carriageway, and 4ft. longer from gate to gate, than her predecessor. Engines and boilers were housed on one side of the carriageway, the deckhouse on the other side being a long passengers cabin with entrances each end and stairs to a promenade deck above, the first Saltash ferry so provided. She was driven by a pair of compound surface condensing engines of 12nhp, with a powerful marine boiler. Her designer was Mr. A.M.Brumage, C.E., R.N. The euphoria which greeted her arrival was followed by anti-climax when she broke down after only a few weeks. While she was under repair the old ferry had to be brought back into use although by this time she had been sold for scrap! It is rare indeed for a ship to return to service from the "Knacker's Yard" if she is time-expired! In 1895 the new Willoughby ferry was temporarily withdrawn again - for reboilering, by Biddles of the G.W. Docks. This time the service was maintained by a barge obtained from Reynolds, the Torpoint towage firm, fitted with prows and lashed to one of Reynolds' tugs. A set of rules for the ferry crew was drawn up in 1899 when it transpired that the entire ship's company of three was going ashore between trips every half hour for a quick tipple! In future it was forbidden for the ferry whilst on service to be left without a crew member on board.

By 1911 a larger ferry was built, costing £3,500 - again by Willoughby's of Plymouth. Evidently their reputation had survived the breakdown of their previous vessel. The designer was Mr.Tobias Bickle. She carried two rows of four vehicles each, with their horses; and had a top deck on each side for foot passengers. To accommodate the new vessel, the chain-pipes and moorings were re-sited at $33\frac{1}{2}$ feet apart, with wells containing three ton weights which acted as springs. The 1891 ferry was retained as reserve boat, moored on the St. Budeaux side. This situation obtained throughout the Great War years and after. Traffic continued to increase, but no action was ever taken to lay a second pair of chains, nor did the ferry run after 11 pm. except by special arrangement. A 2d. rowboat ferry was operated however by Saltash licensed watermen, including Bill Powell-Thomas, and three generations of the Bazeley family. This service was available at night, for a fare of 10/-; but there were occasions when a young reveller, missing the last ferry from Plymouth, would prefer the risk of crossing illegally via the Royal Albert Bridge! The last horse-boat was sold in 1913 - for the sum of £2.10s. The reserve steam-ferry, moored on the Plymouth side, was sometimes used as a bandstand for the St. Budeaux Regatta. Cattle continued to be a regular freight. When the car deck was full they were usually herded on to the prow. They would often jostle one another and it was not unusual for one or more to fall overboard.

In September 1927 a new ferry, larger than the 1911 boat, was purchased from Philip and Sons of Dartmouth, and the 1891 ferry was then sold to Messrs. Vick Brothers, Plymouth shipbreakers, for £75. The new ferry cost £8,950. It had mechanically-operated prows and accommodated 15 average-size cars in three rows. This vessel was widened in 1938 - cut from end to end and six foot added to the car-deck.

The last of the Saltash chain ferries was built by Messrs. Thornycroft of Southampton, and came into service in December 1933. The 1911 boat was then sold to King Harry Ferry for £750, where she was found too large for their requirements. Sold again, to breakers in Wales, she sank while under tow, off Pentreath. The Thornycroft ferry cost £10,750, and was designed by S.H. Hambling. She measured 72ft. length x 42ft. beam, had 28ft. prows and could accommodate 24 cars in four rows of six. In 1935 there was a somewhat comic mishap when Engineman W. Gill went "astern" instead of ahead, stranding the ferry on the Saltash side. Thornycroft ferry plan; page 51.

The Philip and Thornycroft ferries between them, maintained the service throughout World War II and until closure in 1961. They were painted a reddish brown from the waterline up to about three feet, and above that a buff colour, with black funnel. Both before and after the Second World War, "Royal Blue" coaches used. the Saltash ferry - one route to Penzance, another to Delabole. When the war ended the ferries were running from 6.30am. to 10.30pm: but by 1950 the service had been extended. Thereafter it started at 6am, and ran to timetable - from Saltash on the hours and half hours, and from Plymouth on the quarters. The last boat left Saltash at 11pm. and Plymouth at 11-15pm. Occasional late ferries were run by request. The Committee appointed by the Minister of Transport to investigate ferry service recommended in 1948 that the "service should be operated at intervals of 20 minutes, as was done before the war", but this suggestion was not implemented. Saltash residents travelled free, if on foot; thus it was that when the ticket man came round the passengers, all those in the know, were heard to murmur "Saltash". When occasionally the ferry failed, Saltash motorists were faced with a 19 mile journey to the Torpoint ferry.

Apart from some sudden encounters with small naval craft, without serious consequences, there were no collisions such as the Torpoint ferries suffered. River traffic at Saltash was comparatively light. Nevertheless life for the ferry crews had its moments. During the '50s a heavily-laden baulk-timber lorry had left the ferry on the Plymouth side when it stalled while ascending the hard, and ran backward on to the ferry, shedding part of its load, and badly damaging the ferry's prow.

A regular customer in those days was Percy, who drove a heavy Plymouth Breweries lorry. The ferry deckhand, knowing that Percy's lorry and load was a considerable weight, endeavoured to place it amidships, to trim the vessel. Percy however was averse to being held back, when necessary, to allow cars to pass him on the hard. He would edge determinedly forward, forcing back the unfortunate deckhand who was signalling him to stop! One day Percy arrived, with a massive load of beer, and was first in the queue. 'First come, first on, first off' was Percy's motto, and despite the frantic signals of the deckhand, he drove straight up to the gates. In a strong tide and contrary wind the ferry started across, well down by the head. By the time they reached the Saltash side, the lorry's wheels were awash, and a white-faced Percy was very relieved to drive off. Thereafter he would always stop on the hard and call to the deckhand "Where do you want me, mate?"

In 1956 the ferry grounded a number of times due to silting of the river near the slips, and dredging had to be carried out. On Saturday, 2nd March 1957 she stranded again, for a different reason. The mechanical prow gear failed when landing at Saltash on an ebb tide, and before the ferry crew could complete the changeover to manual operation the ferry was firmly aground. Service could not be resumed till 3.30 pm, and hundreds of Cornish supporters trying to reach a Plymouth Argyle home match had to switch to the railway or make a long detour via Torpoint or Gunnislake. In August 1958 the Thornycroft ferry was aground for four hours at Saltash and nearly broke her back. One third of the hull had been on the slip: the rest hung over a dam, without enough water to give buoyancy. The ferry's structure moved, but sealed again when she refloated. It had been a near thing.

During the 'sixties the ferry was crossing to the Plymouth side when tension was lost on one of the chains. The crew thought the chain had parted, but it was discovered that the vertical pin holding the weights on shore had rusted through, shedding the weights into the weight-pit. Moreover there had been sewer-leakage into the pits so that the task of recovering and re-pinning the weights, a night-time job, proved unforgettably unpleasant.

Gerald Truscott, who was a ferry engineman for 15 years (72), says that the wages were only £4.18s. when he began in 1949, and the work could be arduous. On a falling tide it was necessary to be continually working the ferry back as the load increased, to avoid stranding. "It was very easy to get caught", he says, "and you had to be alert. If you made a misjudgement, you would be aground, and the service would stop for six hours. When the tide returned, you would ship some water before she lifted, but she always did lift". A steam engineer to his finger-tips, Gerald Truscott left the ferry for awhile to superintend the steam compressors working on the caissons for the piers of the Tamar Bridge. But he returned to 'see out' the last days of the ferry, and then was appointed a bridge tollkeeper, having the honour of admitting the first vehicle to cross. "But that job was not for me" he says; "sitting cooped up there like a budgerigar in a cage was very different from the freedom of the ferry's engine-room."

Once the end of the ferry service was in sight, there is no doubt that there was reluctance to spend money on the vessels and they were run to the limit of their endurance. Mr. Harold C. Jewell, ferry superintendent from 1949 till 1961 had an anxious time, as the ferries had been neglected and were in urgent need of complete replating below the water-line. The Thornycroft boat ran for 22 years before a dry-docking, and many of her bottom-plates were then found to be only 1/16th of an inch thick. Reporting this, the "Western Morning News" went on to quote Saltash Councillor Mr. T.H. Stanhope who said he thought it most irregular that the insurance company had not demanded a more frequent examination. Repairs on this occasion cost £7,000.

Saltash Passage: Engineman Gerald Truscott at the controls of the Thornycroft chain ferry with crewman Arthur Dale beside him. Photo: Jack Tofts.

The ferries were being required to take overloads when traffic built up, and it was not unusual for them to make a crossing with portholes submerged 18 inches! When the Philip ferry was dry-docked for a survey at Willoughby's, the marine surveyor was aghast! As the water level dropped below the keel blocks, water gushed out from the ferry's bilges where cement-filling had been insufficient to plug holes in the wafer-thin plates. Bottom plates which should have been 5/8" thick were in places found by drilling test to have been 1/32". The surveyor ordered the cement removed, new bottom-plates rivetted in, and airtight compartments installed. The cost put the Borough's ferry account well and truly 'in the red'!

The Tamar road bridge was scheduled to open on the 24th October 1961, and the 23rd was the last day of ferry operation. A carnival atmosphere surrounded the final ferry crossings. The Waterside Handbell Ringers played on the last trips, and three policemen travelled to and fro to keep a watchful eye on boisterous behaviour. The final ferry, 11 pm. from Saltash, 11-15 pm. from Plymouth, carried the Mayor and Town Clerk of Saltash and the Chairman of the Ferry Committee. It was also joined by students of Plymouth Technical College - some in funeral attire - carrying a coffin. Five rockets roared up into the night sky as the ferry left Saltash: one traveller tried to seize the Borough flag for a souvenir and another tried unsuccessfully to let go the anchor. The honour of driving the very last car on to the ferry was won by Mr. P. Joblin of Quethiock. "I have caught this 11.15 pm. ferry by the skin of my teeth for many years" he said "and if I don't know how to do it, no one does".

When the ferry reached Saltash again the passengers gave three rousing cheers and sang "Auld Lang Syne". Then followed the 'race' to drive the last car off. This lasted about five minutes with dozens of passengers pushing cars which had mysteriously broken down: Mr. Joblin again triumphed. Meanwhile in the Passage House and Union Inns there had been revelry all the evening. Ferry superintendent Mr. Jewell, who was retiring with the ferry, told the press "Certainly I feel very sorry about the ferry passing away. Everybody does - including the crew. They are celebrating over in Saltash tonight. They didn't ought to be. Saltash is going to catch a cold".

Within a month of closure both ferries had been sold. The "Western Morning News" for the 29th Novwember 1961 reported that the Thornycroft ferry had been purchased by the King Harry Ferry Company, on the Fal, for £2,500: while the Philip ferry had been bought by Haulbowline Industries Ltd. for £1,750, and was to be towed to breakers in Southern Ireland. The Thornycroft ferry was towed safely to the Fal, and for a long time lay on the foreshore at Sunny Corner, Malpas, where her new owners converted her from steam to diesel. The Philip ferry destined for Ireland, eventually left in charge of the Dutch motor tug **Loire**, but was swamped and sank 10 miles off Falmouth.

Although the ferries have gone and the chains long been lifted, the ferry hards on either side still remain, disused and slimy with weed. At Saltash the upstream chain-pipe and well survive: both pipes and wells can be seen on the St. Budeaux side, where also, the wooden grid on which the ferries were placed for bottom-cleaning and minor repair, is still in position though dilapidated. On the St. Budeaux side the grandiose waiting-room bearing the Duchy Arms and the legend 'SALTASH FERRY' in stone capitals, is now owned by the Plymouth Sea Scouts, together with the adjacent store-cum-workshop. The Passage House Inn, Saltash (1595) and the Ferry House Inn, Plymouth are still in business with names unchanged. The former displays a framed photograph of the fifth steam ferry: the latter a fine colour print showing the second steam ferry. Each ferry had two brass bells which were originally used to give one minute's warning of departure. After closure, one was found to have been stolen, two were sold as souvenirs (one to Saltash Sailing Club): and one, fittingly, was taken into the Saltash Borough Regalia.

SALTASH - NORTHCORNER: This service, which had a life of about 45 years, was started by William Gilbert of Saltash, sometime between 1870 and 1882. Gilbert's steamer services began in 1870 with his purchase of the 73-ton **Eleanor**, an iron-hulled paddler built on the Thames in 1866. The **Eleanor** was lengthened some years later and fitted out for excursion rather than ferry work: indeed she became one of the most popular pleasure steamers on the river. It seems unlikely that she was confined to ferry work where her potential could not be realised. However, about 1880 Gilbert acquired the smaller 59 ton wooden paddler **Fairy**, which had been operated for many years by the Saltash and St. Germans Steam Boat Company.

With two vessels Gilbert would have been much better placed to commit himself to the running of a ferry, and the probability is that the Northcorner service started in 1881 with the **Fairy**, or the year following when Gilbert had a new and purpose-built vessel available. This was the **Victoria**, an iron screw-driven tug of 41 tons, built by Allsop & Sons of Preston, and fitted for passenger work. She arrived on the Tamar from her builders in November 1881 and worked on the Northcorner ferry for 30 years. The next year Gilbert provided the **Victoria** with a consort, the larger 60 ton **Albert**, Plymouth-built by Willoughby's of Millbay. The **Albert** was also primarily a tug(74), and earned revenue as such when not ferrying.

The service operated half-hourly from the public landing-jetty at Saltash, crossing the river to Dumpty Pier at the mouth of Kiln Bay to pick up passengers from St. Budeaux. The ferry then hauled out to clear Bull Point, and after passing the mouth of the river Lynher to starboard, turned south-east to make her way downstream between the ranks of warships and hulks lying at buoys on one hand, and the panorama of Devonport Dockyard on the other. After calling at Pottery Quay jetty, the steamer crossed the track of New Passage (Torpoint) Ferry, and passing Morice Yard and the Gun Wharf, made fast at Northcorner Pontoon, $2\frac{1}{2}$ miles by the ferry route from Saltash.

In 1885 the service was enjoying its peak: there was as yet no serious competition from the Great Western Railway's suburban trains from Saltash, as there were only two a day, and they ran into Millbay. Gilbert ordered a third steamer, the 45 ton **Prince**, similar in size to the **Victoria**, but with compound engines. The service was now frequently extended, when the tide suited, into Millbrook, an extra 2.2/3 miles. This was by way of an invasion into the territory of John Parson, whose red-funnelled steam ferries worked an intensive Millbrook-Devonport service. It also roughly doubled the distance covered by the ferry, and required the use of extra craft. The shallow-draught

*A Victorian scene at Saltash. The Ferry **Albert** has just landed passengers from Northcorner at the public jetty. **Chain ferry No.4** (Willoughby's) is discharging horse traffic at the beach.*

paddler **Lady Ernestine** was introduced for working into St. John's Lake, backed up if required by the **Prince Edward**. Competition with Parsons' ferries reached cut-throat proportions, the Millbrook-Northcorner fare coming down to an absurd ½d. at one time!

In 1892 Gilbert founded the Saltash, Three Towns & District Steamboat Company, to which the ferry was transferred. The day-to-day management was taken over two years later by William Dusting of Saltash, who in 1897-8 had the engines of the **Victoria** and **Albert** modernised by compounding. When not on the ferry, the three steamers were a familiar sight on the Tamar, towing schooners or barges; but when Millbrook was being served, three boats were necessary on the ferry, and the Company's larger paddlers often deputised between Saltash and Northcorner. Gilbert's vessels had to be versatile.

At this time the Saltash Company's excursion steamers worked from West Hoe Pier, and Dusting would have preferred to use the Promenade Pier from which Parson's excursions were run. An agreement was entered into by which the Saltash Company shared the use of the Promenade Pier but ended the incursion of their ferry service into Millbrook. For the Saltash Company the arrangement was perhaps premature: on 27th April 1910 they were taken over by the Plymouth Promenade Pier & Pavilion Company Limited, and thereafter used the pier by right. The new company sold the **Victoria** the same year to a marine store dealer, who resold her soon after to a firm in Hull.

The threat of things to come appeared in 1901 when Plymouth trams linked up with the Saltash chain ferry. The Devonport & District Tramway Company had opened a new route between Morice Town and Saltash Passage. It was not immediately attractive as an alternative route to the ferry, because the wooden bridge at Camel's Head was unable to take tramcars, and passengers had to alight and change cars, crossing the bridge on foot. By 1903 however the present Camel's Head Embankment had been built, and through trams provided a more tempting alternative to the ferry.

It is likely that the ferry was cheaper, and probably as quick, as its route was more direct, but the chain-ferry and tramcar offered protection from the weather, whereas conditions on the tug-style ferries were decidedly spartan. A Plymouth Guide Book for 1913 shows the departure times from Northcorner as:- 6.30,7.00,7.30,8.30,9.30, then half-hourly to 7.30 pm. This would imply two steamers on the service, and - the **Victoria** having gone - the excursion paddlers being called on more often to deputise. In 1923 the 38 year old **Prince** was withdrawn and sent to the breakers, the older **Albert** being retained for three more years before suffering the same fate. Neither was replaced, and thus the down-river ferry came to an end. Northcorner pontoon still remains, but no ferries call today where once queues formed for four different services. Saltash public jetty has been rebuilt since then, and Dumpty Pier and Pottery Quay jetty are no more.

THE TAMAR MARKET BOAT: Older residents of Plymouth and the Tamar Valley remember nostalgically the days of the 'Market Boat', which three times a week brought the fruit and vegetable growers of Tamarside with their produce to Devonport Market. It seems that this service began in the early 1820s, when according to J.B. Rowe's 'Panorama of Plymouth' the first paddle steamer to appear on the Tamar inaugurated a market boat service between Calstock and Devonport. There must certainly have been a continuity of this service by one operator or another, for the Tamar valley was the established market garden of Plymouth, and in 'The Plymouth & Devonport Guide' (1830) H.E. Carrington reports that the Devonport market was known to be the cheapest in the kingdom for provisions. But documentary evidence appears to be lacking until the emergence on the scene of William Gilbert of Saltash in 1870. A licensed victualler turned shipowner, he quickly established himself as the principal steamboat operator on the river. He first put into service the four year old iron paddler **Eleanor**, had increased his fleet to six (including three screw tug/ferries) by 1886, and went on to absorb the Devonport & Cornwall Tamar Steam Packet Company and the Tamar & Tavy Steamship Company, in 1891. The following year he formed the Saltash, Three Towns & District Steamboat Company, operating sea and river excursions, an intensive ferry service between Saltash and Devonport, and the Tamar Market Boat.

The paddlers were invariably used on the market runs, having the necessary deck-space for the scores of chips, hampers and baskets. The service operated on Tuesdays, Thursdays and Saturdays, and, subject to tides, started from Calstock about 6 am, reaching Northcorner pontoon three hours

later. The market gardeners were charged 1/- return, and 6d. per two hundredweight of goods. *The Tamar Market Boat*
Calls were made at Cotehele, Halton Quay, Hole's Hole, Cargreen and New Quay, loading, according to season, flowers, soft fruits, eggs, butter, vegetables and poultry. There was a licensed bar on board and meals were served in the steamer's main saloon.

Although the calls and constant manhandling of deck cargo meant a rather tight schedule, there was ample opportunity for social intercourse, and the market run became a ritual in the lives of the growers, combining necessity with pleasure. The crew's wages varied from 14/- to 28/- a week, but the Company organised a crews' benefit excursion each year, and the ship's company, who came to know their regular passengers well, were allowed to canvass support and sell tickets long in advance of the date. The masters of the river steamers enjoyed a position of respect, even awe, which has no parallel in public transport today, and there was no lack of applicants when a command was advertised. For many years carriers named Whitfield (a father and his two sons) awaited the steamer's arrival and conveyed the produce by horse and cart to Devonport Market. This was an imposing building erected in 1852 and dignified by a clocktower 124 feet high. The day's business over, the return trip up-river usually began at 4 pm. Two steamers successively became principally associated with the Market run, the **Aerial** for about thirty years till the turn of the century, and the **Empress** thereafter until the Great War.

The **Aerial** (built at Govan in 1865) was acquired by the absorption of the Tamar & Tavy Steamship Company. She was a 43 ton iron paddler, 115 feet in length, with 2-cylinder oscillating engines and a speed of ten knots. Advertised as having "two spacious saloons 7 ft. high handsomely fitted up for accommodation of passengers", - they had plush velvet upholstered seating and mahogany tables - she introduced a new standard of comfort to travel on the Tamar. Nicknamed 'the glasshouse' on account of her long glass-topped saloon, and having graceful lines, she was a firm favourite with regular passengers: and rhymes were composed locally to extol her excellence, one of these effusions proclaiming "the prettiest little vessel that ever was afloat". After the turn of the century she was relegated to relief boat, but when she was scrapped, about 1905, many of her fittings were eagerly bought by erstwhile passengers as souvenirs. Her original master, Captain Whitburn, transferred with her from the Tamar & Tavy Company. He later took command of the new **Empress**. and was succeeded on the **Aerial** by Captain Jim Trenance, and later by Captain William Worth.

The **Empress** (built at Preston, Lancs. in 1880) had the same 115 ft. length as the **Aerial**, but was wider in the beam and her tonnage was 101 gross. She carried two lifeboats on account of her greater passenger capacity. Her engines, at 40 hp., were more powerful, but she proved unable to match the **Aerial** in speed. She made the market run her own, but when not available **Aerial** (till 1904), **Eleanor**, **Alexandra** or **Prince Edward** would take her place. Captain Whitburn was succeeded by Captain Hawken. The Plymouth Promenade Pier & Pavilion Company Ltd, which had taken over the Saltash Company's fleet in 1910, surrendered the market boat service to private operators in 1918, but the **Empress** was retained for excursion work. In 1927 she was swinging at a buoy, in reserve; and by 1931 she was on the Yealm, converted to a houseboat. From there she was later towed to serve a new owner at Salcombe. When, through dilapidation, she threatened to sink at her moorings, she was run ashore at the head of Waterhead Creek, and abandoned. The remains of her iron hull are still to be seen there.

After the Great War, the Tamar Market Boat service was taken over by William Worth (ex-captain of the **Aerial**) and Sam Vosper of St. Dominick. Using a Kelvin-engined motorboat with a 10-ton capacity, they continued the service till 1928 when they formed, with others, the River Tamar Transport Company. Their fleet now expanded to five boats, as follows:- **Tamar Belle** (steel, now on the Thames), **Princess** (42 ft, later sold to Exmouth), **Tamar Queen** (of teak, and double-skinned: took part in Dunkirk evacuation and later sold to Southampton), **Prince** (later sold to a Mr. Taylor) and **Tamar Belle II** (ex-Kitley Belle, from the Yealm). The River Tamar Transport Company continued the market boats till the mid-1930s, when road competition was being severely felt. William Worth then bought out the company, and operated a more competitive service with his son Ken Worth, who is now living in retirement in Calstock.

W. Worth and Son purchased the paddler **Kenwith Castle** from the G.W.R. when they closed down the Kingsbridge-Salcombe ferry. Renamed **Whitsand Castle** she was to be the last market boat on the Tamar. They acquired motor lorries and thereby collected produce from the farms and fruit-growers, and brought it to the quays. But when World War II intervened, and the **Whitsand Castle** was requisitioned, the Worths found it necessary to abandon their riverborne transport and

*Tamar Market Boat **Aerial** at Weir Head in 1895. A favourite ship with passengers, her smaller fittings were sold as sentimental keepsakes when she was scrapped.*

Photo: Jack Kingston

Torpoint Ferry

handle all the produce by road motors. Thus the Tamar Market Ferry passed into local history.

THE TORPOINT FERRY: Beyond any doubt the most important river passage in the south-west of England today is the Torpoint Ferry across the Tamar. Yet it is not one of the ancient crossings, its history going back only to 1790. In January of that year, in the reign of George III, the Pole-Carew and St. Aubyn Families obtained an Act of Parliament for a Ferry between Torpoint and Morice Town, as a commercial venture. The service began operating the next year on 4th July, and became known as the New Passage.

It was advertised that "proper and convenient boats, manned by able and careful seamen, will be constantly ready to accommodate all travellers desirous of passing to and from the adjacent parts of the counties of Devon and Cornwall". An early lessee was Walter Cross who became mine host of the Ferry House Inn, Torpoint, in 1793, advertising that "a sufficient number of convenient boats and able men are kept in readiness for to carry over coaches and other carriages". Competition from the Ferry-operators at Cremyll and Saltash was keen and not too scrupulous. The rumour was circulated and then reported in the press that three passengers had lost their lives when Cross's Ferryboat had capsized in a gale; the passage was subject to storms until the late 1830s when Rennie's breakwater across the Sound was nearing completion. Cross immediately denied the story and attributed it to the malice of one of his rivals. He was certainly still in business in September 1802 when from The London Inn, Torpoint, he advertised in The Sherborne Mercury that he had two horseboats each manned by three men and two footboats constantly plying during the usual hours of the day. From 1800 New Passage became the post route, the mail being brought across the Torpoint Ferry and loaded into the waiting coach for Truro.

Whitaker, in his "Plymouth, Devonport and Stonehouse in times of peace and war" quotes from the original tenancy agreements: "the Ferry man is bound to keep in constant use a certain number of boats and able men..." but explains that notwithstanding penalties such conditions were not easy to enforce. During the Napoleonic Wars, 1803-1815, "in consequence of the great increase of wages and the difficulty of procuring fit men", the service became more and more inefficient. In 1809 the proprietors, to finance an improved service "insisted, for the first time, upon exacting the full toll allowed by their Act from all persons travelling with horses and other animals: twopence for every horse, etc. and one penny for each person accompanying the same, whether going or returning".

Until 1872 the service was maintained by two horse-boats propelled by sweeps and two oars-and-sail pedestrian boats, plying from 6 am. to 9 pm. in summer and 7 am. to 8 pm. in winter. Delays were frequent when wind and tide carried the boats off course and prolonged the crossing time.

It seemed that a great advance would be made when a private company was formed in 1829, secured a lease of the Ferry and placed an order for a steam Ferry with shipbuilders at Neath Abbey, South Wales. This was the **Jemima**, launched on 29th September that year and named after the Countess of St. Germans. The **Jemima** was constructed at a cost of £3,500 in the form of twin hulls connected by a traffic deck. The booklet "Tamar Bridge" (pub. Tamar Bridge and Torpoint Ferry Joint Committee, 1961) records the vessel's measurements as 70 ft. long by 25 ft. beam and states "The Devonport Telegraph and Plymouth Chronicle for 3rd October 1829 records that 'the novelty of the construction of the vessel attracted a vast concourse of spectators'." Sources of information disagree as to how long the **Jemima** was running from 'six months' to 'some years' but she was not the success that had been hoped. Her twin 12 hp. engines were inadequate to stem the spring tides when crossing, or to hold her square to the beach in these conditions or in strong winds: there were no chains. There may have been a brief return to oars-and-sail before the appearance of the first steam chain-ferry or 'floating bridge' in 1834.

Built to the order of the same company, the new Ferry was the invention of J.M. Rendel, a marine engineer who had already experimented twice with his design - on the Higher Ferry of the River Dart in 1831, and at Saltash Passage from 1832-1834. Rendel's powers of persuasion must have been good, for neither of his earlier vessels had been successful. Clearly he had also learned from experience, for at Torpoint he made no mistake. His first craft came up to expectations and was soon followed by another.

Torpoint Ferry: Steam Ferry No.4. of 1871 landing school children and other pedestrians at Devonport c.1890.

The first Rendel Ferry was 55 ft. long by 45 ft. beam and its construction was trimaran, with the machinery amidships and the traffic decks (11ft. wide) on either side, so that there were two ramps at each end of the vessel. This was the opposite arrangement to that of the **Jemima** and of the present-day ferries but was repeated in all ferries built prior to 1925. The midships structure included a passenger cabin at either end, and provided an upper promenade deck for pedestrians in the vicinity of the single funnel. 'The Penny Magazine' for 1st April, 1843 reported that "Mr. Rendel says that he has seen at one time on the bridge three 4-horse carriages, one with two horses, seven saddle-horses and sixty foot passengers. The chains of the bridge are sufficiently loose to dip deeply in the water, as a means of allowing the ships of war, many of which are kept on either side of the line of passage, to pass safely over them." In 1835, a few months after the first Ferry began running, a second similar vessel was delivered and a second set of chains was laid. The company then started a 15 minute service with both ferries, but this had to be abandoned when it was found that the chains were too close together and the craft drifted across each other's course in midstream. The company then reverted to a half-hour schedule and it was not until 1932 that two chain ferries were able to be worked simultaneously. The cost of the two Ferries and the laying and springing of the chains, came to approximately £9,000. Actual crossing time was about $7\frac{1}{2}$ minutes, achieved by an engine speed (reckoned in progress over the chain) of 320 ft. per minute. Both ferries had been built by Hocking's of Stonehouse Pool, and had 8 ft. diameter chain wheels. From 1836 the Cornwall Mail started from Fore Street, Devonport and was driven on to the Ferry, instead of awaiting the transfer of mailbags from the Ferry at Torpoint.

At one time it seemed that the Torpoint Ferry would provide a vital link in the growing railway system. David St. J. Thomas in his "Railways of the West County" (David and Charles, 1960) points out that "The South Devon Railway's Act of 1844 had envisaged... a terminus at Devonport New Passage, where it was planned to transfer traffic by Ferry to the Cornwall Railway". In the event, however, the Cornwall Railway decided against the Ferry link, and Torpoint was never to have a railway station. On the Plymouth side, an inland site for Devonport Station was chosen at Albert Road. This was the same route of course for which Brunel's bridge at Saltash was built in 1859. Its opening adversely affected passenger receipts at Torpoint, and the mail coach to Cornwall ceased to run, as the Post Office transferred its custom to the railway.

After thirty-seven years service, the first Ferry was replaced in 1871. The new Ferry, also built by Hocking's was 58 feet in length by 46 ft. beam, and was driven by two 10 hp. high-pressure engines. Design was generally similar to the earlier boats, with engine and boilers amidships, side traffic decks, and a single, tall funnel (76). The second Ferry was retained as relief boat for seven years, a twin-funnelled Ferry with a higher superstructure being delivered in 1878, when No.2 was disposed of, presumably for scrap.

The 1871 and 1878 steam Ferries were destined to give fifty years service to the passage, and in fact outlasted the private ownership of the Pole-Carew and St. Aubyn families. There were of course the occasional breakdowns, such as that reported by the Western Morning News on 26th July 1879: "The new Ferry bridge to Torpoint stopped running yesterday for 5 or 6 hours, owing to a difficulty with the machinery. The passengers had to be taken over in shore boats as the other bridge is undergoing refit". Since these earlier Ferries had side car-decks, the skippers endeavoured to balance the weight of vehicles to keep an even keel; and this could occasion delay. For instance, when circus or fairground vehicles were using the Ferry, a steam traction engine and its trailer might be seen in isolation on one side, while the maximum number of light vehicles were crowded on to the other.

During the 1890s the Royal Navy kept several 'Training Brigs' at Devonport to give young officers sail-handling experience. Tacking down the Hamoaze one day was one of these brigs under the command of a young officer who was engaged to the daughter of the C. in C., Plymouth. The Torpoint Ferry was in midstream when the brig came heavily into collision with her, and for a while the two vessels were locked together. There followed some caustic exchanges between the Ferry skipper and the captain of the brig, who gave full vent to his naval vocabulary. Unfortunately for his matrimonial prospects as well as his chances of promotion, his prospective father-in-law, the C. in C., was a passenger on the Ferry and was not amused by what he had seen and heard. Our hero on the brig received a curt notice a few days later that the engagement was terminated!

Harry Downing, a Torpoint carrier who used the Ferry a great deal in the early years of this century, reminisced at the age of 72, in the Western Evening Herald of 1st December 1960: "I began to work with my father at the age of 12. I can remember waiting fourteen hours for the Ferry to pick me up at Devonport, and long waits on either side of the river were nothing unusual". Mr. Downing went on to describe a memorable crossing on a quiet Sunday afternoon at the start of the 1914 war. A hundred horses had been requisitioned from Cornish farms and the whole herd was loaded aboard the Torpoint ferry with Mr. Downing and his father in charge of them. "Some of those horses had never seen the light of a candle" he said "so you can imagine what their reaction was to a puffing steaming old ferry. We just could not keep them still and were mighty thankful when we got them to Devonport".

About 1910 the Ferry was in collision with a Naval destroyer and suffered damage to a prow. The Commanding Officer of the destroyer stated that the Ferry's progress was so slow that the direction in which it was proceeding was not immediately evident. The naval enquiry can hardly have been impressed with this defence, but the authorities decided thereafter that the Ferries should always fly a red flag at the 'fore' end in the direction of steaming, and this has been done ever since. In 1920 the Torpoint Ferry Company, about to wind up, gave first offer of the service to the Torpoint Council, who declined. On 21st July 1922 Cornwall County Council acquired the Ferry undertaking by purchase and inherited the 1871 and 1878 Ferries, both overdue for replacement and the two elderly steam launches (see 'Torpoint Pedestrian Ferry') which had been providing a 15 minute service for foot passengers. The most urgent need was for new Ferry bridges, and an order for these was placed with Philip & Son, Dartmouth, to the designs of Mr. T.P. Endean, the then Ferry Manager.

The first of the new steam ferries cost £14,650 and was launched at Philip's yard on 27th January 1925 by Mr. G. Harris, Vice-Chairman of the Cornwall C.C. Ferry Committee, who declared as he swung the inevitable bottle of champagne, "I christen you **Ivy** - a compliment to Mrs. Ivy Endean, wife of the Ferry Manager. Although the name was never exhibited on the vessel, and has since been declared to be 'unofficial', there is no doubt that the ship had been well and truly named. After fitting out, she was towed to Plymouth on 17th April, and was 'linked up' with a new and heavier chain than previously used, on 18th April. There was a minor set-back three days later when she grounded on a falling tide at Torpoint and was photographed as a stranded whale by the local press; but matters passed happily from the ridiculous to the sublime when an official inauguration ceremony was held on 24th April, conducted by the Chairman of the Ferry Committee, Mr. A.S. Liddicoat, at which the new Ferry was dedicated by the Rev. Montague May, Vicar of Torpoint. A celebration trip was run, across and back, free for all Torpoint schoolchildren. Schools marched their children down in processions to the Ferry, and on board each child was given an orange and a bun.

Two 'sister' Ferries followed, in 1926 (cost £20,000) and 1931, and were dubbed locally **Ivy 2** and **Ivy 3**. One of these nearly came to grief on delivery passage from Dartmouth, as she stranded temporarily and lost both her prows in the process! In Torpoint there were ribald jokes about 'Ivy clinging to the rock,' etc. The three new ferries each had a capacity of 800 passengers and 26 average-size cars. They had a single wide car deck amidships, with deck structures housing the machinery and cabins, on either side. On one side were twin black funnels from the boiler room, which supplied steam to the engine on the other side. This drove a large chain-wheel shaft which spanned almost the width of the vessel. The height of this shaft necessitated making the traffic deck arched from end to end to clear it: and the whole Ferry superstructure and top passenger decks were given the same arched shape. This was a marked difference to the earlier ferries, which were flat-decked. Retired Ferry engineer Harvey, of Torpoint, recalls: "The **Ivy** ferries all had the same pattern compound engines, but No.3 had the best engines. No.2 was a bit of a bitch. Her engines tended to race, and you had to watch her carefully when nearing the slips". Their refits were originally carried out at Willoughby's in Millbay Docks; when they closed down, in H.M. Dockyard. One of the last of the Plymouth watermen, Joe Saxon, provided an alternative rowboat Ferry service for pedestrians who missed a Ferry, or wished to cross after midnight (night trips to be booked in advance). On occasion, Joe would hitch his boat to the Ferry and get an unauthorised tow!

Despite the increase in motor traffic between the wars, cattle and horses were still being regularly transported, up to 60 head of cattle "on the hoof" being not uncommon. Cart horses were daily carried on the 8 am. boat from Torpoint. They belonged to W.J. Reynolds Ltd., the tug-owners, and were going to work hauling refuse carts in H.M. Dockyard. They would be led or ridden down the hard, each by his own groom, and placidly take their places behind the vehicles. Although heavy animals, they proved nimble on the Ferry; they had good sealegs and gave no trouble.

Mr. Bernard Williams (a retired senior officer of the G.W.R. and later British Railways) recalls that from 1925-29 he was Delivery Clerk at Devonport Goods Station, and says: "The Torpoint carrier Mr. Downing called at our station with a horse and van every day, and took charge of packages for Torpoint. We allowed him "cartage rebate" to compensate us for not having to cart the packages to Devonport".

On 1st July 1932 the then Parliamentary Secretary to the Minister of Transport came to Torpoint to inaugurate the long-awaited service of two ferries working simultaneously. The pedestrian Ferry steamer was now withdrawn, as the chain Ferries were providing a 15-minute service. Mr. S.J. Holloway of Saltash, a one-time regular Torpoint Ferry passenger, recalls: "Imminent departure was announced by a loud melancholy bell sounding twice, which was the signal for the gates to be closed at the top of the Ferry beach to stop further traffic, and also for those coming down the beach to hasten aboard - last-minute pedestrians sprinting down the slip and leaping on to the rising prow to the remonstrations of the Ferry crew. For those living in Devonport, the doleful sound of this bell could often be heard late at night".

The most exciting incident involved an elephant. It was a Saturday afternoon, and a travelling circus which had performed the previous evening in Torpoint, was being conveyed to Devonport. Each circus wagon was hauled by six horses but these animals often had difficulty negotiating the steep shingle slipways and Julia had been taken from her cage to use her weight and push from behind. Mr. Downing, the carrier, was standing near her on the Ferry crossing, and he said afterward: "All at once this elephant began to rock. She swayed from side to side as though the ferry was in a heavy swell. Her trainer realised what was going on and whipped some chains round her legs - but she just lifted a foot and snapped them... then pounded in her tracks and charged. Ferry Manager Endean was nearly swept overboard by her waving trunk. She breasted the gates, they went away like cobwebs, and landed out on the prow. The prow gear would not hold her weight, and the prow just dropped - and down went the elephant into the water. What a commotion!" When 'Julia' surfaced, a passing dockyard pinnace got a line around her and she was towed to the Devonport shore, to walk unconcernedly up the slipway! The bull elephant who was her mate had already landed, and bellowed a welcome - which scattered the watching crowds. Her circus owners capitalised on her adventure, advertising, "Come and see Julia - the elephant who swam the Tamar!"

"Various stories have been told" says Mr. Holloway "about cars inadvertently starting and running off the Ferry into the depths of the Tamar; but at least one must have been true, as demonstrated when in the late 1930s a catenary wire from a tug towing HMS **Norfolk** up harbour, dropped to the bottom at the Ferry passage and came up twirling the sad remains of an Austin 7!"

In 1939 came World War II, and throughout the hostilities the Ferries each carried a convoy-type barrage balloon and R.A.F. personnel to tend it. Retired engineer Harvey reminisces: "During the war special trips had sometimes to be run (day or night) with ammunition for the port defence guns at Tregantle, etc. These trips were not much enjoyed by the crews! During the blitz on Plymouth one Ferry was ordered to cease working one evening and wait at the Devonport side for a fire-engine urgently needed at Torpoint. The crew waited and waited as the bombs rained down, but the fire-engine never arrived. It had become a casualty! In 1941 Ferry personnel suffered tragic casualties when three men lost their lives while on duty. A bomb dropped on the Ferry hard at Torpoint, its blast killing Toll Collectors Ernie Everingham and Bernard Gorman as they stood at the turnstile, and the aircraftman in charge of the Ferry's barrage balloon, who was talking to them. The Ferry **Ivy 3** suffered 48 shrapnel holes in one raid, and though these were all above the water-line, "one piece of shrapnel only missed the main steam pipe by three inches!"

In those, and immediate post-war years, a state of 'cold war' is alleged to have existed between the dockyardees and the Ferry crews (80). Men who missed the Ferry always averred it had deliberately sailed on sighting them! "Of course these were the habitual late arrivals", says Engineer Harvey, "but I kept my watch accurate by radio time-signals, and whenever possible always left on the stroke". However, an 'us and them' attitude was sometimes apparent, for instances are related of groups of dockyardees dashing on board past the toll-collector and dispersing on board before their fares could be collected!

On Friday 5th October 1956 H.M.S. **Keppel**, a Captain class frigate of 1,300 tons, came into collision with the 8.15 am. north Ferry from Devonport to Torpoint. The Ferry was stationery at the time, having given way to a vessel passing upstream. Pedestrian passengers were transferred to a river steamer but vehicle drivers were much delayed. The **Keppel** badly damaged her own stern, and dislodged the Ferry's anchor, which plunged to the river-bed and firmly anchored the Ferry in near-midstream. The Ferries could recover their anchor by steam-power, but it was a laborious business.

Engineer Harvey recalls one occasion when the engineroom telegraph was rung just too late, and the Ferry hit the end of the hard, nearly exposed at low water springs. There was an enquiry, and the skipper was perhaps fortunate to retain his job. On another occasion a heavy baulk of timber drifted on the hard, half-submerged. Skipper Albert Knott had little chance of seeing it, and the Ferry grounded until the tide returned.

In 1934 shore improvements were carried out when new offices (designed by S. Pool, County Architect), waiting rooms and control gates were built on the Torpoint side. Mr. John Mather succeeded Mr. Thomas Endean as Ferry manager in 1954. By the next year the County Council were considering enlargement and modernisation of the three Ferries but were advised that the age of the hulls precluded this. The decision was taken in January 1959 to order two new diesel-electric Ferries from Thornycroft's of Southampton, at a cost of £315,000. Thus a new era began in the Torpoint Ferry service.

The first new Ferry left Southampton for Plymouth in October 1960 but suffered serious storm damage on passage and could not be put to work until January 1961. Meanwhile the second Ferry arrived safely and commenced running on 13th December 1960. On a test run, a crossing of the river was made in 2 $\frac{1}{2}$ minutes. The new ferries were 182' overall length, including the 40' prows, and had a beam of 54' giving a traffic deck 32' wide. Diesel-electric engines of 172 bhp. gave a speed of 630 ft. per minute. Steam ferry **Ivy No.3** was retained as reserve boat: the other two were sold to Davis & Cann Ltd., and broken up at Laira Bridge.

In 1964 the Ferry Manager asked for a radio-telephone link between Ferries and shore after an incident when a brawl led to a young woman being thrown off a ferry at night. The newly-formed Tamar Bridge and Torpoint Ferry Joint Committee however seemed alarmed by the £100 per ferry cost of installation, and turned the request down. Some years later they had to change their mind. The same meeting deferred for a year a decision on whether to recondition the remaining steam ferry of order a third diesel-electric. The latter alternative was eventually chosen.

It was late in 1966 before the new Ferry arrived. Built by Charles Hill & Son Ltd. of Bristol, it was a slightly-enlarged version of the Thornycroft boats. Its overall length was 6 ft. greater at 188' and a 3 ft. greater beam gave a 35' traffic deck. This Ferry completed the trio of diesel boats which are still working today. A third set of chains was laid in 1972, and the new Ferry has since occupied the centre position. It is distinguished by narrower funnels and the fading marks of five traffic lanes on its decks. In fact all the Ferries had been carrying five rows of vehicles until 1970, when a complaint was made to the insurance company that there was not room to open car doors in an emergency, and the Ferry Committee had felt obliged to restrict loading to four lanes. The immediate consequence was, of course, longer queues on either shore. The arrival of the new Ferry meant the departure of **Ivy 3** which was sold to Belgium, and there used as a floating platform for welding and drilling equipment.

The fourth collision to be recorded between Torpoint Ferries and vessels of the Royal Navy occurred on 21st January 1973 when H.M.S. **Scylla** (Leander class frigate) struck the north ferry during a fog. The 9 am. ferry from Torpoint was heavily loaded toward the end of the morning rush-hour from Cornwall into the City, when the accident occurred about 200 yards from the Plymouth side. The Devonport-built **Scylla** (2,900 tons) was proceeding to sea after a long dockyard refit. No one was hurt, but the Ferry's side was gashed, leaving broken windows and tangled metal, while the frigate sustained damage to her bow. The damaged ferry was the new, Bristol-built boat. At that time the third set of chains had not been laid, and as one boat was refitting, several days with only a single ferry running followed the withdrawal of the damaged craft. The resultant Court Martial found Captain Sutton of the **Scylla** guilty of negligence for proceeding too fast in fog conditions, and he was reprimanded.

There was excitement of a different kind on 24th March the next year when a woman's screams were heard on board. She was the centre of a 'love triangle', and her companion, an able seaman, had been stabbed by her erstwhile boyfriend, who had followed them on to the Ferry in a frenzy of jealousy. Fortunately the victim was not seriously hurt. In July that year (1974) there was an un-avoidable tragedy at the Torpoint slipway. A retired Royal Marine Officer, Major Hedley, accom-panied by his wife, had driven his car on to the slip to await the Ferry when he had a heart attack. Out of control, the car plunged into the Tamar. Recovery of the bodies was rapid but the Major was already dead and his wife died before reaching hospital.

1977 was a year of tensions. The Ferry Committee were shocked by an inexplicably high price demanded by H.M. Dockyard for repairs to Ferry No.3, a price bearing no relation to private tenders. The suspicion was expressed that the Dockyard was taking advantage of the fact that towing the ferries to Falmouth or other parts was a hazardous operation. Later in the year the ferry service was halted for 90 minutes one August afternoon while the Ferry maintenance staff met to discuss their latest move in a long-running pay dispute.

On 18th October 1977 the north ferry (one of the Thornycroft boats) sustained an unusual accident. The vessel was carrying 24 cars from Torpoint and was two-thirds of the way across when part of a chain wheel fractured, flew off, and sheared a 6-inch square hole through the bottom of the hull. Water flooded into the engine-room, and on reaching the Plymouth side five fire engines met the ferry, and used their pumps on her. A fireman said "We were pumping out about 1,000 gallons a minute at the worst point". Temporary repairs were carried out by Admiralty divers. On a late evening trip on 7th July 1978 rival gangs of "yobboes" clashed in a fight which took place both among the cars and on the upper decks. Police were summoned to meet the ferry and fifteen of the brawling morons were afterwards fined a total of £1,400 at Plymouth Crown Court for what Judge Lavington described as "a wholly disgraceful episode".

In a bid to reduce the number of local cars using the ferry, and to help pedestrian passengers who had to change buses, a Ferry Bus service was inaugurated in 1979. Bearing a signboard displaying the Plymouth and Cornwall arms, buses on this route cross the Ferry with their passengers and are given priority over other traffic. Many critical letters appeared in the local press however. Drivers alleged their cars were sometimes in a queue for two hours, that the Ferry timetable was disrupted by waiting for the Ferry Bus when it was delayed in traffic, and that only the provision of a fourth Ferry would solve the problems. The Ferry Committee issued a statement in December 1979, answering their critics. The principal points they made were that the cost of a fourth Ferry would necessitate unacceptable rises in bridge and ferry tolls; and that an increased ferry capacity would be likely to increase the demand for it.

The shore arrangements for the Torpoint Ferry have developed from the modest wooden - and draughty - waiting sheds on either side to the present-day stone shelters and toilets but the improvement has been largely negatived by constant vandalism. The wooden hut turnstile at Torpoint where once pedestrians paid 1d. has given place to the seven-lane car park with signal gantries (1973) seen today. Indeed the Ferry has transformed Torpoint. According to Symons' Gazeteer of Cornwall (1884) Torpoint had only four or five houses in 1790, whereas thirty years later there were 200 or more. Its population today is ten thousand. Torpoint owes its rise entirely to the existence of the Ferry.

The Ferry itself is no longer a paying concern. In the days of its infancy, when costs were negligible, it was a different story. The proprietors were gratified when toll receipts rose steadily from £1,980 in 1837 to £3,100 in 1854. Today there is an annual loss well in excess of half a million pounds. This loss is currently covered by the profits on the Tamar Bridge, bridge and ferry being now one undertaking, and the tolls on each being kept at the same figure. Torpoint is one of the most important river crossings in the United Kingdom, and the traffic demands upon it can only increase.

TORPOINT PEDESTRIAN FERRY: Many of today's regular passengers on the Torpoint Ferry, accustomed to a ten minute service by three large floating bridges, might be surprised to know that until 1932 the service had long been augmented by small passenger steamers. In the nineteenth century complaints had been many that the single chain-ferry stopped running at 9 pm. daily, as this imposed a considerable restriction on the social life of those who perforce must cross the river.

In 1897 this situation was rectified when Messrs. Reynolds (tug-owners of Torpoint) provided a late evening service from 9 pm. till 12.30 am. using small steam tugs. The three steamers used on this run were the **Link**, the **Lorna**, and the **Dainty**. They worked between a wooden jetty at Torpoint and Pottery Quay, Devonport, and had little comfort to offer their patrons as their decks were entirely unsheltered. A surviving photograph of **Lorna** shows that she was a broad-beamed vessel, with no wheelhouse for the helmsman, and that she had guard-rails rigged up aft when passenger carrying.

To the dismay of the public, in 1902 Reynolds abandoned the late-evening ferries on account of higher landing-dues imposed by the Carew-Edgcumbe Torpoint Ferry Company. There was considerable public outcry, and the ferry company yielded to pressure. They acquired a small steamer from Portsmouth named the **Volta**, which took over the late service, Reynolds' steamers reverting to tug work. The **Volta** had a sister-ship the **Vesta**, owned and captained by a Mr. Edward Stephens who used her to supply bread to ships lying in the Sound: but the **Vesta** was never on the ferry service.

Collectors Jim Broad (left) and Bill Higman conversing by the Torpoint tollbox. Photo: J. Broad.

In 1904 the Ferry Company had a new steamer built for the service by Rogers of Cremyll. This was the 51½ ton **Lady Beatrice**, named after Lady Beatrice Pole-Carew, licensed to carry 191 passengers, and destined to have a career of 44 years, 28 on the Torpoint ferry. What had been only a late-evening service was now operated throughout the day. **Volta** and **Lady Beatrice** worked a triangular route, Torpoint - Northcorner - Pottery Quay carrying motorbikes and bicycles as well as foot-passengers. Some senior citizens may remember the three skippers who for many years worked these ferries between them: Tommy Toms, Robert Deveaux, and Tommy Williams. In 1920 the Torpoint Ferry was taken over by the Cornwall County Council, who thereby inherited the two pedestrian ferry steamers. The **Volta** was withdrawn in 1921 as worn out, and **Lady Beatrice** then operated alone, being relieved by the Oreston & Turnchapel Company's **Dart** or **May Queen** when absent for periodic overhaul.

In 1923 two soldiers of the South Staffordshire Regiment were drowned when they were lost over-board from the **Lady Beatrice**. Deckhand Donald Hacker - then only sixteen - went over the side and made heroic but vain efforts to save them. The regiment did not overlook his courage, and presented him with a silver cigarette case, while from the Royal Humane Society he received a Recognition on vellum signed by Edward Prince of Wales. Nor was this his only lifesaving venture, and he later was given a gold watch inscribed: "Presented to Donald Hacker, aged 16 years, by the inhabitants of Torpoint in recognition of several acts of bravery in saving life, 1923."

The **Lady Beatrice** continued in service until July 1932, when a second chain ferry was introduced and the improved timetable made the separate pedestrian ferry unnecessary. The **Lady Beatrice** was then sold to the Oreston and Turnchapel Steamboat Company.

The jetty used by the pedestrian ferries at Torpoint was demolished when the third ferry chains were installed in 1972, and Pottery Quay was obliterated at the same time.

THE MILLBROOK FERRY: In the spacious days before World War II there were some institutions which seemed endowed with permanence and invulnerability. The British railway system was a prime example. To pre-war Plymothians this air of permanence was equally associated with the Millbrook ferry service. As the little red-funnelled, blue-cabinned steamers shuttled back and forth ferrying the workers of the world's largest naval dockyard, there was no reason to assume that they would ever not be required. Today the boats are gone and the piers of Millbrook lake are ruinous, yet the company who ran this ferry have proved the most enduring and successful of all Plymouth passenger boat operators.

The civilian workforce of Devonport Dockyard - which rose from about 4,000 in 1880 to over 12,000 by 1912 - included a strong contingent from the Cornish shore, and John Parson of Millbrook set out to transport them. In the last decade of the 19th century he began running the small steamer **Old Millbrook** to Mutton Cove from Millbrook, Southdown or Anderton (as the tide served) and later added the **Lady of the Lake**, **Iolanthe** and the **Despatch**. Old guide books describe the service as "frequently during the day according to the tide". All four steam ferries were small, unregistered boats of which no measurements nor engine details have survived, and all except the **Despatch** had gone by 1900. The **Despatch**, which closely resembled the later Turnchapel steam ferries, was painfully slow. When her skipper was making his last trip of the shift, his wife at Millbrook did not start cooking his dinner till she knew he was due to be leaving Northcorner or Mutton Cove!

In the early years of the present century the Fleet was brought up-to-date with the introduction of new, purpose-built steamers. The paddlers **Britannia** (64 tons, built 1900) and **Hibernia** (94 tons, built 1904) now joined the screw steamers **Devonia** and **Cornubia** which had replaced the oldest boats in the 1890s. W.T. Crawford, later to become Managing Director of the Company, was at this time the youngest passenger boat skipper on the Tamar. He started on the Millbrook ferries in 1906, and obtaining his certificate in 1910 at the age of 18, was given command of the **Cornubia** (83).

During the Great War the **Hibernia, Devonia** and **Cornubia** were requisitioned for Admiralty work. **Hibernia** served glamorously as a tender to the fleet in Scapa Flow. On return south she was sent to Cork as a ferry for the Southern Railway of Ireland after a bridge had been blown up in 'the troubles'. She got back to Millbrook eventually, but being a larger vessel with a passenger capacity of 360, was more used for excursions than ferrying. **Devonia** and **Cornubia** were returned from war service in poor condition and were disposed of.

Bernard Williams (formerly of the GWR General Manager's Office, Paddington) recalls the post-1918 years nostalgically: "There were two paddlers on the service, **Hibernia** and **Britannia**: at low tide they sailed only to Southdown, where they were met by some horse brakes which took one to the top of Whitsands Cliff for 6d. - Father always made us walk! One day, on a paddler approaching Southdown, the other paddler was just leaving and in manoeuvring to pass we ran hard on to the mud: fortunately the tide was on the turn and eventually, which much pushing on the pole and use of the engines, we got off as the tide made: this incident clear in my mind shows that the two paddlers were in service at the same time. The 'King-size' boathook-pole was always carried on the paddle boats and was used in turning them in restricted waters, such as at Weir Head". Mr. Williams then adds "There was also a screw boat laid up then at Southdown: it reminded me of an elongated Turnchapel boat, with red funnel and blue saloon, black hull; but I never got close enough to establish its identity". This was almost certainly the **Cornubia**, which was later sold for scrap value to the Oreston Company, who wanted her boiler.

Northcorner had now replaced Mutton Cove as the landing on the Plymouth side. Here were encountered **Lady Ernestine** (83), **Prince Edward** and other steamers of the Plymouth Promenade Pier Company, which under their previous Saltash ownership had for awhile challenged Parson for the Millbrook passenger traffic. In those days of direct competition with the Saltash Company, each firm had its specific landing-places in Millbrook Lake, and all boats ran to published timetables. Even so, the tide compelled the rival ferries to arrive and depart at almost the same times and in close proximity. It was commonplace for a skipper to try to nudge or jockey his opposite number on to a mudbank! The passengers apparently entered into the spirit of the thing, and if there were complaints the passing of the years has obliterated the record. An intensive passenger and parcels service was worked in the years between the wars from Northcorner. Again Bernard Williams re-miniscies: "From 1925 to 1929 I was delivery clerk at Devonport Goods Station, G.W.R. We used to get packages for Millbrook and Torpoint: the Millbrook packages were taken by our Fore Street area carman down to Northcorner to meet the Millbrook steamer: he handed the packages over to the steamer men who signed for them. The Steamer people then delivered the packages to the consignees at Millbrook and presumably raised and collected their own charges".

In Millbrook Lake there were five landing places which the steamers used according to the tides. At Millbrook were Limekiln Pier (of stone, replacing 'Twin Piers'), Higher Pier (a two-berth wooden jetty), and Lower Pier, a small wooden staging. At Anderton there was a pontoon (replacing an earlier stone quay which had decayed) and at Southdown the still existing commodious stone quay was used. Prior to the Great War, Parson had a small floating dock for his steamers, moored between the millhouse and mill quay. Later a slip for maintenance of the vessels was improvised by grounding the gutted shell of an old Admiralty barge near the tide mill. In later years a modern covered slip was erected alongside this. Until some years after the Great War the Company had a fitters' shop nearby where they carried out repair work. The building still stands, but was long ago sold by the Company and is now a store.

In 1929 John Parson formed the Millbrook Steamboat and Trading Company Limited, with W.T. Crawford and others, and transferred his boats to the new company. They were later joined by the Worth Brothers, whose father Jack Worth had been a well-established excursion boat prop-rietor. His undecked petrol-engined motor boats - mostly built at Mitchell's yard, had also been ferrying dockyard workers to and from Tamarside villages. On his death his sons merged the business with Parson's company. The motor cabin-launch **Lady Elizabeth** came on to the ferry about this time; 53 ft. in length, she had accommodation for 113 passengers and was re-fitted with a Gardner diesel engine. She was later hired to the Drake's Island ferry.

Compared with the heyday of the ferry, Millbrook is today a forlorn village, while Southdown is a depopulated, ruinous area threatened with becoming the site of a nuclear power station. It requires a powerful imagination to recapture the scene of busier days. The ferries then started at 6 am. and made 13 return trips a day till 9 pm. Hundreds of 'dockyard mateys' formed the backbone of this weekday traffic. In the years prior to, and after, the Great War, weekends and bank holidays saw large numbers of Plymothians coming to Millbrook - mostly for Whitsands - and these had to be got back to Plymouth at the end of the day. The larger boats of the Company which had been running sea and river excursions had to join the ferries in Millbrook Lake at the end of the day to deal with the huge queues which built up. Mr. W.J. Dunstone of Millbrook remembers how the Company's 'crack' steamer, the **Brunel**, would steam majestically in to pick up her quota. "She would embark her permitted 600 and the queue seemed no smaller when she left". The waiting throng good-humouredly amused themselves with concertine-playing and impromptu singing. Between Millbrook and Whitsands ran a considerable number of Wagonettes and brakes. The wagonette was an open carriage with transverse seats in front and side benches at the rear, pulled by a single horse. The brake was a larger vehicle requiring two horses. At weekends and bank-holidays these little carriages did a roaring trade. "Even so" Mr. Dunstone recalls "ninety per cent of the ferry passengers walked to the beach and walked back".

The parcel and package service provided by the ferries also prospered. A dumb barge was even-tually acquired as cargo vessel, so that the packages and crates conveyed would not clutter the decks of the passenger ferries. This barge was towed by a motorboat. Deliveries in the Millbrook area were made by the ferry company's carrier, Jack Pawley. There was a store-shed on Higher Pier where goods could be kept pending delivery. When the tide was well down the ferries had to leave from Southdown. Returning "Whitsanders", seeing the ferry on the other side would take a short cut to reach her by hurrying along the wall of the millpond. A late-night ferry leaving North-corner at 11 pm. was run on Saturday evenings to bring back Millbrook and Southdown folk who had gone to Plymouth theatres, cinemas, or dance-halls.

Buses were introduced at Millbrook in 1922 to meet the ferries. The first bus, a 'Napier', was involved in a fatal accident near Cremyll but after this inauspicious beginning thousands of passen-gers were conveyed without loss of life till the ferries ceased to ply. The steamboat company owned a fleet of Crossley charabancs, coloured the same pale blue as the cabins of their steamers, and advertised as 'the Whitsand Belles'. In competition were Skinner's motor buses, mostly Chevrolets and on account of their buff livery known locally as 'the yellow peril'. Skinner's service linked the ferries with Cremyll, Cawsand and Whitsand, and the same company also ran Model T Ford taxis. Former ferry passenger Mr. S.J. Holloway recalls: "When the ferry could get no higher than Anderton Quay, Skinner's would meet it there, hastening round the many bends in the country lanes leading there to the accompaniment of a raucous hand-operated Klaxon". The last wagonette driver to face all this competition was Jack Warren. Mr. Dunstone recalls that old Jack was unabashed by the array of taxis and buses with which he was lined up. "Ere ye are, m'dears" he would address the passengers, with a sweep of his arm toward Whitsands, "Rush ye up for sixpence!"

Two steam ferries from other concerns were acquired during the 'thirties'. The **Kitley Belle**, Hodge & Sons' ferry on the Yealm, was fitted with a diesel engine by the Millbrook Company and renamed **Tamar Belle**. Although used also on excursions, she did a great deal of work on the ferry. The other acquisition was the 53 ton paddler **Kenwith Castle**, which had been working the Kingsbridge-Salcombe ferry for the Great Western Railway until purchased by Mr. Kenneth Worth of Calstock. Now renamed **Whitsand Belle**, she was sold by Mr. Worth to the Millbrook Company, who put her to work on Weir Head and Morwellham excursions. However she proved unable to maintain steam on the long runs, and thus came on to the Millbrook ferry as consort to the ageing **Britannia**. Ac-quired in April 1933, she was sold in May 1935 to Wm. S. Murphy of Edinburgh. She safely crossed the Irish Sea to Belfast Lough, where she was employed on summer cruises from Bangor; but the following January she broke adrift from her moorings and was wrecked.

Meanwhile the fleet had acquired its first sizeable motor-vessel, the 38 ton **Manna**. Built in 1922 by Albert Hang of Berlin as the **Marie**, this vessel had worked in Belgium, and from 1925 at

Yarmouth. The Millbrook Company replaced the original Kamper 4-cylinder engine with a Parsons' paraffin, and later with an Atlantic diesel. Until repainted in company colours, she ran with a white hull and varnished cabin woodwork. In her last years with the company she had yet a fourth engine installed, a Gleniffer-Gardner diesel. Renamed the **Devon Belle**, she proved a very satisfactory vessel, and did her share of work on the Millbrook ferry after the departure of **Whitsand Castle**.

The diesel 56 ton **Western Belle**, built by Fellows of Great Yarmouth, joined the Millbrook fleet in 1935. During World War II the service again reached a peak, with queues hundreds of yards long awaiting the steamers. **Western Belle** and **Devon Belle** were mainly responsible for the ferry during the war years. Skipper Arthur Grylls recalls the **Western Belle** being chased by a low-flying German aircraft on one occasion bombs dropped in her wake but did not detonate!

The **Britannia** now had the distinction of being the last paddle passenger steamer on the Tamar. The distinctive smack! smack! of her six-float paddles was familiar to all regular passengers with whom she had become a firm favourite. She had served more than half a century on the river when she failed her Board of Trade inspection in 1953, and was sent to Vick's, the shipbreakers at Stonehouse Bridge, for cutting up.

By the mid-fifties it was clear that the Plymothians of the new, re-building, post-war Plymouth did not use the ferries for their weekend excursions: they took to their cars and went farther afield. Even the 'bread and butter' weekday traffic was disappearing. The dockyard traffic dwindled rapidly as the men began to go to work in groups, in private cars which they drove to the Torpoint Ferry and parked, pending their return as pedestrian passengers when the day's work was over. Meanwhile the situation at either end of the ferry route had completely changed. The industries around Millbrook Lake had died: the last survivor, the Southdown Brick Company closed in 1956. In Plymouth, the Abercrombie Plan had developed the city centre at the expense of Devonport, which could no longer attract weekday shoppers or weekend entertainment seekers from across the Tamar.

These were the factors which brought the Millbrook ferry to an end in 1964. Meanwhile the Company has continued to be successful in the river excursion business. Were John Parson able to see today the business he had pioneered in 1900, he would no doubt permit himself a contented smile. He devoted his life single-mindedly to his steamers. He remained a bachelor and employed a housekeeper. It was said in jest that when she got married, his wedding-present was a seven-day season ticket on his vessels!

STOKE PASSAGE: The rebuilt Stonehouse Bridge in Plymouth is today a bridge in little more than name. Water flows under its steep arch no more, and the creek whose tides once washed nearly a mile inland to Pennycomequick is now reclaimed land. Stonehouse Creek was always an unwanted barrier and until the sixteenth century the Wise family, lords of the manor of Stoke Damerel, maintained a ferry at what is now Millbridge. It was probably a well-used passage but the crossing was short and capable of being bridged.

In 1525 Sir Piers Edgcumbe, lord of the neighbouring manor of East Stonehouse, acquired the rights in the ferry and its approach road from the Wises, and erected Millbridge, whereupon the ferry was withdrawn. The tolls were waived until Sir Piers' descendants re-imposed them, despite public outcry, nearly three hundred years later, when they remained until redeemed by Plymouth Corporation in 1924! If one stands on the site of the bridge today it is scarcely possible to visualise the old ferry crossing, as due to land reclamation the water is now almost a mile away to the south-west.

STONEHOUSE PASSAGE: Until the late eighteenth century the direct route between East Stonehouse and the Mount Wise estate which eventually became Devonport was the ferry across Stonehouse Pool. The area was sparsely populated, and the passage - attached to the manor of Mount Wise and owned by the Morice family, was of minor importance until the founding of the Dockyard by William III in 1691. The rapid growth in population of the new town of 'Plymouth Dock', and increasing wheeled traffic in connection with the extensive building works as the dockyard was developed, began to place on the ferry a burden it was unfitted to bear. When Sir Nicholas Morice died in 1749 the manor and ferry passed to the St. Aubyn family who quickly set about increasing their manorial revenues. In partnership with Lord Edgcumbe, lord of the manor of Stonehouse, Sir George St. Aubyn commenced the building of Stonehouse Bridge and its approaches in 1768. It was completed in 1773, when the ferry ceased to run. Tolls however were retained until 1924, pedestrians being charged $\frac{1}{2}$ d. return, and the bridge being known thereafter as 'ha'penny gate'. Remains of the picturesque old

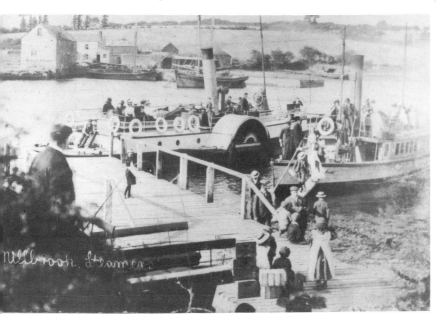

A Millbrook wagonette driver in the foreground watches possible customers landing from Cornubia whose deadly rival Lady Ernestine is about to depart from lower pier. The Cornubia has beached herself and rigged her own 'gang plank'.

83

Cremyll Passage ferry house could be seen on the Devonport side of the bridge until 1830, and in Whitaker's "Plymouth, Stonehouse & Devonport in Times of Peace and War" is reproduced a copy of an old sketch of this half-timbered ferryhouse, with the original 'Ha'penny Gate' in the background.

CREMYLL PASSAGE: The Cremyll ferry passage is of great antiquity. It was the main link from Devon with the mediaeval road through south Cornwall which led via the Bodinnick, Par, and King Harry ferries to Land's End. Its history can be traced back to the 11th century and it must certainly be older than that, though its exact course and landing places have changed during the centuries. It is possible that a ferry was working here as early A.D. 705, when Maker was granted to the Bishop of Sherborne by King Geraint of Cornwall.

When William the Conqueror rewarded his barons after the victory at Hastings, the former West Saxon Kings' estates in Devon and East Cornwall went to Count Robert of Mortain. Among Count Robert's sub-tenants was Reginald de Valletort, in whose control the ferry first appears in written records. In 1204, in the reign of John, Roger de Valletort granted Cremyll and the ferry to Ralph, an ancestor of the de Stonehouse family. For a period in the mid-fourteenth century Thomas de Stonehouse granted the ferry rights to one John of Maker, who in 1350 leased the ferry to William Smale of Dartmouth, a relation of the de Stonehouses by marriage.

The Duchy of Cornwall had been created in 1337, and the Duke of Cornwall therefore exercised overlordship of the manors. So it was that in 1355 we find William Smale complaining to the Black Prince "that the prince's farmers of the ferry of Saltessh, whenever the Saltessh boat needs repair, claim the use of his boat with which he serves the ferry of Crimele, and half a mark of rent, whereas this never used to be done save by suffreance of the said ferry of Crimele". The Black Prince obliged with an order to his steward on 5th September that year "to make inquisition by those who are most worthy and have most knowledge of the matter, and to do right to the Prince and to the said William".

Early in the fifteenth century the ferry passed, probably through marriage, from the de Stonehouses to Sir William Bigbury. In 1488 (reign of Henry VII) Joan, a descendant of Sir William, married Sir Piers Edgcumbe and thus the Mount Edgcumbe family acquired part control, and in 1511 full control, of the Cremyll ferry. It was to remain in their possession for more than four hundred years. The rent for the ferry lease at the time of takeover was £5.6s.8d.

William Lawrens, Walter Lawrens and William Doswell are among sixteenth century ferrymen recorded in the account rolls for West Stonehouse manor. By 1588, the year of the Spanish Armada, when Macaulay tells us "the beacon blazed upon the roof of Edgcumbe's lofty hall", the passage was let at a rent of £6.10s. to one Henry Blake. From 1591 the lease was held by Henry's son Peter Blake, with his wife and their son. With the ferry went the use of "the great passinge boate" and the fees and profits, except that the Mount Edgcumbe family were to enjoy free passage. The lease remained with the Blake family almost until the Civil War. The ferry service probably suffered some interruptions during the hostilities, as Plymouth was under siege and there were Royalist batteries at Mount Edgcumbe.

In 1682 Sir Richard Edgcumbe leased the ferry to John Collings of Maker, sailor. The document shows that the rent of the ferry was then £4 a year plus £8.10s. monthly for the fares. Two ferries and a smaller boat were used for the passage and the lessee's responsibilities were to maintain these boats in good order and provide crews for working the ferry and transporting mails. By the end of the century Cremyll passage was carrying the mail for most of Cornwall, and did so until the Torpoint ferry secured the contract in 1791.

A 1643 map of Plymouth shows that the original passage was from the northern side of the tip of Devil's Point to Barn Pool near Mount Edgcumbe house, a slightly shorter but more exposed crossing than that used today. The great breakwater in the Sound was not completed until 1841, so in bad weather the crossing was not to be undertaken lightly. It was in such conditions that the famed Celia Fiennes used the Cremyll ferry in 1685. In 'Through England on a side-saddle in the Time of William and Mary' (published 1888 and again, re-edited, in 1947) she describes her crossing at Cremyll as "a very hazardous passage by reason of three tides meeting. Had I known the danger, I should not have been very willing to have gone it... I was at least an hour going over: it was about a mile, but indeed in some places, notwithstanding there were five men rowed and I set my own men to row also, I do believe we made not a step of way for almost a quarter of an hour, but blessed be God, I came safely over...". The dangers were real enough: from Rame Church registers it appears there was a ferry disaster in 1701 when seven lives were lost.

The establishment of the naval dockyard in 1691 and its enlargement in 1728 created a demand for a service between Cremyll and Mutton Cove, and from about 1742 an additional ferryboat supplied this need. The Mutton Cove ferries ran for over a hundred years, ceasing about 1845. The route of the main ferry was changed in 1730 to run between Stonehouse Pool Steps and Cremyll beach. It is recorded that the move from Barn Pool was made because of annoyance to the Mount Edgcumbe family by the proximity of the traffic. On the Stonehouse side the Royal William Victualling Yard was built in 1835 on land purchased from the Mount Edgcumbes, and as part of the agreement the Admiralty built Admirals' Hard to provide a new berth for the ferries. Thus the present route became established. The old road cut through the cliffs to the Devil's Point landing, and this road and the Passage Inn which stood at the back of the beach were both obliterated when the Victualling Yard was built.

The years 1690-1790 were undoubtedly the heyday of the Cremyll ferry. By the end of this period there were two passenger boats and one horseboat plying throughout each day, with a second horseboat in reserve. Most of the ferrymen were accommodated in passage houses built by the Mount Edgcumbes. But when the Torpoint ferry opened in 1790, offering a shorter and more convenient communication between Plymouth and Cornwall, Cremyll traffic began to decline. The discrepancy between the services was accentuated when the Torpoint ferry went over to steam in 1879.

Steam came to the Cremyll passage in 1885 when the ferry **Dodo**, built the previous year at a cost of £600, began to ply, providing a fifteen minute service where the two pulling-boats had operated half-hourly. A second steamer, the **Ferryboat**, built at Yarmouth 1883, was later purchased to augment the service. She ran until sold in 1907 but little else is known about her. In spite of the higher running costs, tolls continued at 1d. per foot passenger. The rowboat ferries continued to run for awhile, and the date of their withdrawal is not recorded. The horseboats were propelled as and when required, by the steamers.

Before the turn of the century two other steamers appeared on the ferry:- the **Armadillo** (1) believed built by Waterman's of Cremyll, and the **Shuttlecock** (1) older and smaller, bought second-hand and believed built in the 1870s. Neither were decked in, and they were liable to ship a lot of water on stormy crossings. In "The History of the Cremyll Ferry" by P.L. Hull, the following statement is quoted from a Mr. T. Willcocks of Cawsand:- "On one occasion... the **Shuttlecock** only just reached Cremyll in time to prevent her being in a sinking condition. The Superintendent of the ferry at that time, a Mr. Marchant, was a very distressed and worried man as he watched the ferry crossing and shipping heavy seas". The same book recounts how a Mr. E. Porter of Millbrook recalled a pre-Great War crossing he made with Captain Jim Lugger of the **Armadillo**:- "During one very severe gale I was the only passenger crossing from Stonehouse to Cremyll on a late evening trip when the Captain said to me, handing me a lifebelt, "You had better put this on - I doubt if we will reach the other side". We did, although we had a severe drenching".

In 1910 the **Shuttlecock** (1) broke from her moorings in a gale, drifted across the mouth of Stonehouse creek, stranded by the old bathing pool at Mount Wise, and became a total loss. She is still remembered by a few older Plymothians, who have told me that she had no condenser, and exhausted up the funnel. Consequently she always sported a black-painted funnel, as the standard Cremyll livery of 'cream' did not stand up to the heat. William Bright was usually her engineer. Information is lacking about the end of the **Dodo**, which also became a casualty about this time. As for the **Armadillo** (1), a scale model was made of her by a Mr. Robert Cook in 1932. It can be seen at Buckland Abbey in the collection of model ships.

Toward the end of the nineteenth century the Earl of Mount Edgcumbe took delivery of the steamer **Carrier** from Messrs. Waterman's yard. She was used for family excursions up the Tamar, but also did duty on the ferry. Larger than the other boats, she had difficulty berthing at Admiral's Hard at high water. The **Carrier** had a single funnel and two masts, with powerful engines and a speed of 10 knots. All the ferries had an inner cabin for the use of the Mount Edgcumbe family and their guests, but the **Carrier's** private cabin was roomier and better appointed, and she was generally entrusted with the conveyance of King Edward VII on his occasional visits to Mount Edgcumbe Hall. She had a crew of three and a passenger capacity of 150. With the loss of **Shuttlecock** (1) and **Dodo**, the **Carrier** appeared regularly on the ferry with the **Armadillo** (1) until two new steamers were purpose-built by Rogers of Cremyll (successors to Waterman's).

The new steamers perpetuated the names of two of their predecessors, **Shuttlecock** (1924) and **Armadillo** (1926). They ran the service throughout the inter-war years and until the Mount Edgcumbes sold the ferry rights in 1946, and earned the affection of hundreds of regular passengers. **Armadillo** (1) was scrapped after the introduction of the new **Shuttlecock**, and the **Carrier** went to the breakers late in 1927. I have seen the original specification for the **Shuttlecock**, as given to Rogers & Co. Ltd. The two vessels were sister-ships, and the principal details almost certainly apply to both:- Built of pitchpine on oak, and bottom sheathed with muntz metal. Length 69'0" x beam 13'6" x depth 4'6". Compound surface condensing steam engine working at a steam pressure of 120 lb. p.s.i. Capacity 128 passengers.

In the meantime Mr. Marchant had been succeeded as ferry Superintendent by a Mr. Wonnacott, and he in turn by Mr. S.B. Wilcox, who held the office from 1910 to 1946. The Marine Engineer was Mr. Butler, who carried out routine maintenance on the compound engines, and acted as relief engineer on the boats when required. Skippers A. Tucker, Jim Lugger and Sam Wilcox, and Engineers Wm. Bright, S. Crowther and Sam Simmonds are among the best remembered crewmen who maintained the service during these years between the wars.

In those days the horseboat was fully employed bringing Co-operative bread-delivery vans, coal carts, and Plymouth Breweries wagons, with supplies for village inns, from Admiral's Hard and taking the livestock of East Cornwall farmers to market. The horseboat was not easy to handle in a stiff breeze or strong tide. An extra crewman was required to man it and bring it alongside when cast loose from the steamer. Nice judgement was required in the use of the rudder which could be lifted clear of the water after use and in poling the craft alongside. The horseboat lowered its ramp on the beach at Cremyll or the hard at Stonehouse to load and offload, but did not always make fast on a flood tide. There were occasions when horses and carts slipped off into two or three feet of water and had to be recovered, with consequent delay to the ferry! At Cremyll can still be seen a handwinch which was used to drag the barge on to the shingle. In a strong wind it was not uncommon for the horseboat to go adrift and have to be 'chased' by the steamer. Once in 1934 the horseboat, then coming to be known as the 'car ferry', broke adrift from the steamer while returning light to Cremyll from Admiral's Hard. Sam Wilcox was on board her, and he has told me that they drifted past Barnpool before the steamer could secure her again!

On a later occasion, when Sam was skipper of the ferry, the horseboat grounded on Admirals' Hard on a falling tide after landing a single horse. She was there all day before refloating. When Sam reported the mishap to his father, the Superintendent, he got scant sympathy. "Too much wind" said Wilcox senior. "You shouldn't have taken her over". Passenger traffic remained adequate and was often heavy on Saturdays. Both steamers were kept very busy when the Scout Jamboree was held in Mount Edgcumbe Park in 1935. Among distinguished passengers in the inter-war years were the Duke (later King George VI) and Duchess of York in 1932, and on other occasions H.R.H. Princess Mary, Prince Henry Duke of Gloucester, and Lord Baden-Powell, the Chief Scout.

In 1936 **Armadillo** broke loose from her moorings during high winds and a flood tide, and was picked up by a Dockyard craft, adrift off the Victualling Yard. Sam Wilcox recalls that it fell to him to fetch her back, but misadventures were the exception. Former passenger Sydney Holloway

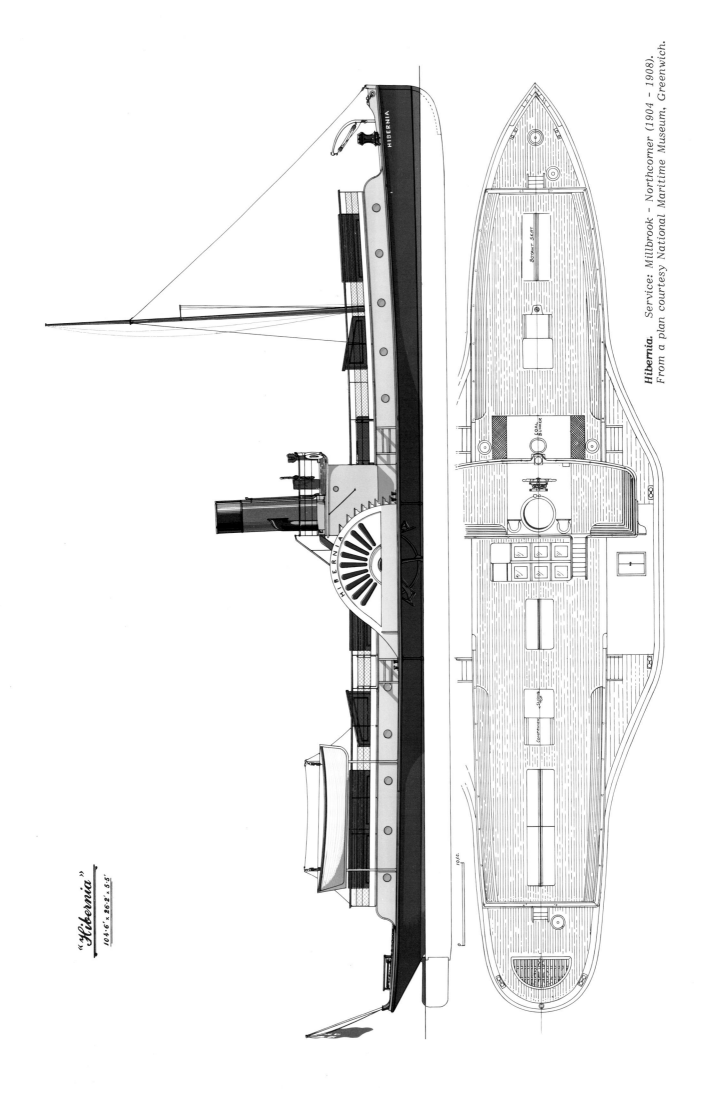

"*Hibernia*"

104·6' × 26·2' × 5·5'

HIBERNIA

HIBERNIA

HIBERNIA

BOYANT SEAT

COAL BUNKER

SLIDING TOP

COMPANION

10 ft.

0

Hibernia. *Service: Millbrook - Northcorner (1904 - 1908).*
From a plan courtesy National Maritime Museum, Greenwich.

Armadillo (2) off Admiral's
Hard, c.1912. Railway carriages can be seen at
the L.S.W.R. Ocean Terminal
and Plymouth watermen in
the foreground.

recalls: "Arriving at Admirals' Hard near dusk one would be treated to the grand spectacle of 'Sunset' played by the buglers at the Royal Marine Barracks just above the ferry landing".

The horseboat/car ferry continued in use until the year that war broke out. Taken out of service, it was loaned some months later to a local longshoreman, on his request, and became a casualty. Sydney Holloway reminisces again: "Once the horseboat had gone, no vehicular traffic was normally carried, except that on holiday weekends an ice-cream cart was taken over to Cremyll in the morning and back in the evening. This was loaded with much muscle-straining up a wide gang-plank on to the steamer's prow, where it remained for the crossing like a bizarre figurehead".

Tragedy came to Cremyll Passage during World War II when skipper Tucker and engineer Crowther were killed in an air raid. They had finished duty for the day, and were caught by blast whilst standing in the entrance of a shelter. This increased the difficulties of wartime manning, and from 1943 the Millbrook Steamboat Company assisted in the operation of the ferry. Mount Edgcumbe House had been bombed and burnt out in 1941, and the Earl was minded to sell the ferry rights which his family had now held for well over four hundred years. On various occasions the ferryboats had stranded on a tide at Admirals' Hard, usually with no ill-effects. However in 1944 the **Armadillo** was less fortunate. She stranded awkwardly on the Hard itself, and broke her back. She was out of commission for some months, while Mashfords of Cremyll (successors to Rogers) took her in hand and rebuilt her.

In 1945 the Millbrook Steamboat Company tendered successfully for the ferry, and took over the running on 1st June 1946. Their first move was to convert the steamers to diesel, to reduce running costs. The **Armadillo** which had been at Mashford's yard under repair was fitted with a Kelvin diesel engine, and renamed **Northern Belle** to conform to the nomenclature of their fleet. She is still in service on the ferry today, with a wheelhouse in place of the open-bow steering, her mast removed, and a new squat funnel. In March 1954 **Northern Belle** showed that she had not forgotten that she was **Armadillo**, by stranding again at Admirals' Hard, on a spring tide! This time she was refloated unscathed. The **Shuttlecock** however was extensively altered, and a passenger deck built over her cabin. She was given a Glennifer diesel engine, and renamed **Southern Belle**. Used principally for summer river excursions, she makes only occasional appearances on the Cremyll ferry, where her place has been taken by the **Eastern Belle**.

The **Eastern Belle** was acquired in 1955 from the Oreston & Turnchapel Steamboat Company, who had built her in 1946 as the **May Queen. Eastern Belle** has a Thornycroft engine and a passenger capacity of 196. The Oreston company had used her almost exclusively on excursion work, and the Millbrook company had employed her in the same way until 1957, when she began to appear on the Cremyll ferry. In the Western Morning News for the 1st December 1972 it is recorded that the 8 pm. and 9.20 pm. ferries had been withdrawn by the Millbrook Steamboat Company pending the result of an application to Cornwall County Council for a subsidy. Company director William Crawford was quoted as saying: "The Cremyll ferry is not a viable proposition at the moment". The subsidy was later granted.

All ancient ferry crossings had their inns, and Cremyll was no exception. The former Passage House, later Ferry Inn, was praised by a Mrs. Topsham, who stayed there in August 1796 and recorded in her diary: "...got to the Cremmel Ferry House opposite to Plymouth at 12 o'clock. Phillips is the name of the man that keeps it....an excellent house, good beds, good victuals of all sorts, fish in the greatest perfection, very pleasant rooms..... everything was so comfortable...." The inn has since been renamed The Edgcumbe Arms. There is also a Ferry Inn at Admirals' Hard. For many years the ferry toll was paid on the boat, but in the nineteenth century the Mount Edgcumbe family erected a picturesque tollgate at Cremyll, and today this also houses the registered office of the Millbrook Steamboat Company. There is a clock on the tollgate, presented by Colonel Edgcumbe in 1885, and it bears the inscription: "Dost thou love life, then do not squander time. Time and tide tarry for none".

ST. GERMANS - MARKHAM: An almost forgotten ferry which disappeared at the beginning of the present century used to ply between St. Germans (Old Quay) across the Lynher to Markham, whence a footpath led to Markwell, for St. Erney. After the modification of the Eliot Estate foreshore, the ferry ran from the beach beside what is now known as Higher Quay. The G.W.R. main line viaduct crosses the river between these earlier and later landing places. The last St. Germans resident to remember the ferry working was Mr. D. Lang who passed away, an octogenarian, in 1977. The first cottage on Higher Quay (opposite the present-day Sailing Club Headquarters) was the ferry house; and later stonework clearly visible around a ground-floor window shows the position of the former ferry-passengers' waiting-room. The present owner, Mr. Spiller, has renamed his home Ferry Cottage to preserve the link with the past.

*St. Germans
Market Boat
Antony
Passage-
Jupiter
Point*

Up to the Dissolution, the ferry was no doubt largely used by the monks at St. Germans Priory, and visiting pilgrims. In the eighteenth and nineteenth centuries the ferry probably derived most of its then slender traffic from workers on St. Germans once-busy quays. Here tin, copper and lead were taken away in coasting ketches, and coal, culm, and machinery parts for mine engines were unloaded. The working quay throughout the centuries was 'Old' Quay, Port Eliot, upstream from the present railway viaduct. The present quay, where the former ferry house stands, was a commercial venture of the Eliot family. The lower quay dealt chiefly with limestone, and rusting stone-shutes against the old limekilns are still to be seen. Goards' (Millwrights) whose surviving building housed a machine-room over a blacksmith's shop and stables, employed fourteen including apprentices, within living memory. A proportion of these quay and mill workers certainly came by ferry; and when the quays declined, the mines shut down and the mill closed, the need for a regular ferry had gone. As far as is known, there was no horseboat, and the service was for pedestrians only. The rights of ferry must have been obtained from the Earl of St. Germans, whose family acquired the foreshore from the Duchy of Cornwall about 1840.

ST. GERMANS MARKET BOAT: Few of the near-130 services recorded in this book gave such trouble in research as the Market Boat on the River Lynher. That there was a regular ferry to Devonport on market days from St. Germans for most of the period from the mid-nineteenth century until the 1930s is beyond doubt. For the greater part of this period there was no other acceptable route to market for the soft-fruit and vegetable produce of the area than by water. But today there are very few long-established residents living by the Lynher who have any memories of the service, and local libraries have been combed in vain for written references. Possibly a diligent search of the Port Eliot Estate records would produce a few references of interest. What is certain is the advent of paddle steamers at St. Germans in 1855.

In that year the partners Gilbert and Wilcocks of Saltash began operating steamers on the River Lynher and it is a fairly safe assumption that they then provided the market ferry service which had formerly been worked by sailing barge. The first Gilbert & Wilcocks steamship was the **Gipsy**, an iron paddler of 46 gross tons which had been built on the Torridge and was ten years old when brought to the Lynher. She was joined the following year by the wooden paddler **Lord Yarborough**, 30 years old, and hailing from the Isle of Wight. This vessel had been lengthened and substantially altered in 1835, and grossed 79 tons. She lasted barely a year on the service before being sold to John Hyde of Turnchapel. Subsequent owners worked her until 1868 when she was scrapped. In 1857 she was replaced by a new purpose-built wooden paddler, the **Fairy**, registering 59 tons and built at Stonehouse, Plymouth.

A year later, with these two steamers, Gilbert and Wilcocks promoted the Saltash and St. Germans Steamboat Company, financed by gentlemen, farmers, and residents of Devonport, Saltash and St. Germans. This Company continued in being until 1876, although in 1870 Gilbert branched out on his own as an independent shipowner, starting the Saltash-Northcorner ferry and later founding the Saltash, Three Towns and District Steamboat Company. It is reasonably certain that during the twenty-one years that these two steamers covered between them on the Lynher, one or other worked the ferry to Devonport Market. The **Gipsy** was withdrawn and broken up in 1870. The **Fairy** was sold in 1876: but by 1881 Gilbert had repurchased her for his new and expanding fleet. She survived until 1890.

From the demise of the company in 1876 the story of the Lynher Market boat has yet to be brought to light. It may be that the run was taken over for a while by the **Volunteer** and **Aerial** of the Tamar and Tavy S.S. Company of Devonport; or that the gardeners and their produce made their way by horse-drawn carts to the Tamar market boat at Saltash, or to the nearer horse-boat at Cremyll passage.

A more attractive alternative was by rail. The railway had bridged the Tamar in 1859, causing rapid decline of river traffic, and had given St. Germans a station on the main line. The journey by rail however was nine miles and Devonport G.W. station was less convenient for the market than Northcorner Jetty. The distance run by the Market Boat from St. Germans Quay to Northcorner was $6\frac{1}{2}$ miles. With the advent of the marine petrol engine, however, the St. Germans market traffic returned to the River Lynher. The last operator was a Harry Dayman, who used an un-named and reputedly not very seaworthy motorised barge until the mid-1930s.

ANTONY PASSAGE - JUPITER POINT: Antony passage was a ferry by prescriptive right, i.e. a ferry run since 'time immemorial'. It is mentioned as early as 1324 as 'the passage across the waters of Lynher'. In those days the Daunay family owned the manor of East Antony, to which the ferry belonged throughout its known history.

In 1450 the manor passed, with the ferry rights, to the Carew family, who built the present Antony House in 1721. This mansion stands on the right of the carriage drive leading from the ferry landing. Disaster overtook the ferry in April 1768. At that time a ring of six bells was being installed at Landulph Church, supplied by Fitz Antony Pennington, a bellfounder of Lezant. One of these bells was being conveyed by the ferry to Antony passage on a stormy day, when the ferry capsized and sank. Fitz Antony, who was accompanying the bell, was drowned, as was the ferryman, and the bell was lost in the mud of the river bed. Fitz Antony's body however was recovered, and laid to rest in Landulph Church. A plaque in the south wall of the tower bears the inscription:-
30 April 1768: "The boistrous Wind & Billows sore Hath toss'd me To and Fro By God's decree in spite of both I rest now here below".

Little else is known of the history of the ferry until its working was undertaken, before the end of the eighteenth century, by the Crosley family. The Crosleys operated the ferry for several generations, until its gradual 'phasing out' in the early 1950s. During the present century the ferry operated from 8am. till 8.45pm. (summer) or 7.45pm. (winter), and was well patronised until after World War II. There has never been a road following the west bank of the Tamar, as the estuary of the Lynher and numerous creeks to the north, would have entailed a succession of long and costly bridges which could never have been justified by traffic requirements. Thus the Antony Ferry provided a valuable link by crossing the widest barrier (the Lynher) and saving the long detour via St. Germans.

It was not however a ferry used by many to get to and from their work, though it was well used by the Carew family and the large staff of the Antony estate. The principal users were Plymothians who in days when people had to make their own pleasures, liked to use it in the course of a 'round tour' which for a long time was very popular. One caught the ferry to Torpoint, walked the two miles through the Antony Estate to Antony Quay, and took the ferry to Antony Passage, where in nearby Forder village the Secombe family ran a Tea Garden at Apple Tree Cottage, with a small stores-cum-sweet shop. From here there was another 2-mile walk to Saltash, where the chain ferry to Saltash Passage connected with the terminus of a Plymouth tram-route. Alternatively the journey could be made in the opposite direction, depending on what time one wished to be at the Tea Gardens.

The Antony Estate provided a 16 foot rowboat, and until the early years of this century a horseboat, which conveyed animals but not wagons. The passenger fare was 2d. return. The ferryman was also licensee of the Ferry House Inn, Antony Passage, where he lived. The river is over 700 yards wide at this point, and in a two or sometimes three knot tide the ferryman's money was hard-earned. The last operators of the horseboat were Abram Crosley and his eldest son Stewart, who propelled it with long sweeps. The craft had a cut-away portion in the gunwale to allow the horses, cattle or sheep to board or disembark from the side. The last horseboat was taken out of service about 1910, and lay for many years derelict on the beach between Antony Passage and the railway viaduct. Jack Crosley, last of the ferrymen, tells today how a few calves or sheep were often rowed across in the passenger ferry to save unnecessary hard work with the horse-boat; but the difficulty was in preventing them from jumping over the side. "The trick" he explains "was in splashing them with the oars as one rowed, to keep their heads down. It only wanted one to go over the side and the rest would follow".

During the Great War of 1914-18, when the Crosley menfolk were on active service, Doris Crosley ran the ferry virtually single-handed. She was well able to do so, being an accomplished rower, and she regularly won all the women's events at Watermen's regattas. In the years between the wars the ferry continued to be busy, but was fighting a losing battle against the encroachment of the motor car. Sir Reginald Pole wanted to close the ferry in 1921, but this did not come to pass. A new route was suggested, if the ferry was to continue. Instead of running from Antony to Trematon, the route was to be from Wilcove Head to Wearde Quay. The new route was not adopted, but the ferry continued to run. On bank holidays it was not unusual to take between £15 and £20 in 2d. fares. To expedite the service when there were queues of waiting passengers, the Crosleys from about 1925 used a motorboat of their own, often towing a loaded ferry and other boats astern of it! In pre-motorboat times these large crowds had been shared with Plymouth watermen, who however were obliged to collect tolls for the ferry in addition to their own fares, and so had to charge 4d. instead of 2d! Passengers not in a desperate hurry preferred to wait for the official ferry! With a wind up or down stream, the ferry was often sailed across, and a mast and sprits'l were carried for this purpose, but the boat was not fitted with a centre-board. The ferryman was recalled from the opposite side by waving a flag provided.

After World War II, the proliferation of the motor car and of ready-made amusements, caused a collapse in the ferry's passenger traffic. Jack Crosley, who returned from war service to take over the ferry again, found that it was no longer a full time employment. His father had arranged with the Antony Estate before the war to give up the licence of the Passage House Inn; now Jack arranged gradually to phase out the ferry service. The last two rowboats used on the ferry, purpose-built by Mashfords for about £20, can still be seen, grey-painted, on the Passage beach, but they have made no ferry crossings since about 1952. If one of these cannot be preserved, there will be no lasting reminder of more than 600 years of ferry history except the Passage House, of which the future is uncertain. The Carew family sold their properties on the Forder side (including the Passage House) in 1951. Antony House itself has since been acquired by the National Trust. The Passage House (former Inn) was sold to a Mr. Coombes. The Antony foreshore which included the ferry landing has been leased by the Royal Navy, who have small craft moored there, used for sail-training. The land steps used by the ferry have been demolished, and what was always known as 'Antony Quay' to the locals, is now known by its geographical name of Jupiter Point.

Within living memory the ferry crossing has a record free of fatalities or serious accidents. However, many years ago Abram Crosley found himself in a very anxious situation. He had embarked 15 children from an orphanage, who were accompanied by two convent nuns. When nearing midstream, he was aghast to see water rising over the bottom boards. A disaster seemed imminent, but he quietly asked the nuns to keep the children calm and in their places. Any panic would have been fatal. He leant on the oars with all his strength and hustled the boat across despite the incoming water which was soon up to the children's knees. When the boat's bow touched the shore at Antony Passage, it settled on the bottom and filled. As the famed Duke of Wellington said after Waterloo, "It was a damn close-run thing". Subsequent examination of the boat showed that the cause of the trouble was no worse than a displaced bung!

In lighter vein is the story of a grumpy old woman resident on the Antony side who was scared of sailing, as it caused the boat to list. Abram Crosley arrived under sail at Antony Quay when she was waiting. "I'm not getting in that boat with the sail up," she declared "so you can take it down." "Very good ma'am" said Abram and lowered the sail. After pulling clear of the quay a few strokes, Abram hoisted the sail and took the tiller. The woman's complaints were loud and long, but Abram sailed across. On her next crossing the ferryman was Abram's son Jack, and he too was under sail. "You can get that sail down", she shouted "I want to be rowed over and don't get up to your father's tricks and put it up again, I'm telling you". Jack obliged her by rowing across, and was astonished to receive a one penny tip for being co-operative!

It seems that officially the Antony ferry is still in existence, since as a public ferry an Act of Parliament would be necessary to terminate it, and it still appears on Ordnance Survey maps. The ferry rights, however, no longer exist, nor are they retained.

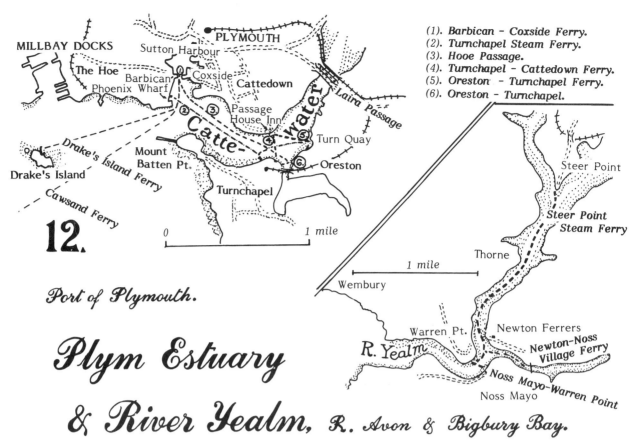

(1). *Barbican - Coxside Ferry.*
(2). *Turnchapel Steam Ferry.*
(3). *Hooe Passage.*
(4). *Turnchapel - Cattedown Ferry.*
(5). *Oreston - Turnchapel Ferry.*
(6). *Oreston - Turnchapel.*

Port of Plymouth.

Plym Estuary
& River Yealm, R. Avon & Bigbury Bay.

LAIRA PASSAGE: The Committee appointed by the Minister of Transport in 1948 to report on ferry services linking major roads recommended: "the inconvenience and delay associated with a ferry....compared with the uninterrupted progress possible where there is a permanent crossing, lead us to the opinion that a ferry should be regarded as a substitute for a bridge...until such time as the provision of a permanent crossing may be justified". Exactly the same conclusion had been reached in 1807 by the lord of Boringdon manor, whose family - later the Earls of Morley, maintained a ferry across the Plym at Laira. This ancient passage, which was possibly originated by Plympton Priory, had only a side-loading 'horse-boat' to handle the increasing volume of vehicular traffic. In 1807 therefore a reputable engineer named Alexander was engaged to survey the possibility of erecting a bridge at the crossing-point between Prince Rock and Pomphlett. He reported that because of the unfavourable nature of the river-bed, the erection of such a structure, if at all practicable, would be attended with enormous expense.

His Lordship therefore abandoned the idea of a bridge, and concentrated his attention on the improvement of the ferry. He provided a larger ferryboat which became known as the 'flying bridge', and was a forerunner of the so-called 'floating bridge' ferries which were later to appear at Saltash and Torpoint. The new Laira ferry was "open at both ends for the purpose of admitting wagons, carts, carriages and other vehicles with their horses attached, as well as cattle of all descriptions, and passengers". This boat "was propelled by means of a strong iron chain, stretched across the channel and passing over trucks in the boat which were made to revolve by means of two winches". Although the service was liable to interruptions through bad weather and spring tides, this ferry ran successfully for 20 years. It was withdrawn, and Laira Passage passed into history in 1827, when the Earl of Morley built the Iron Bridge - designed by J.M. Rendel, and the first iron bridge in the south of England. It was replaced by the new Laira Bridge in 1961. A picture of Laira's 'Flying Bridge' ferry, painted by artist P.H. Rogers (1794-1853) can be seen in the Plymouth Room of the Plymouth Museum.

ORESTON PASSAGE: A ferry with origins which must lie deep in history used to operate between Turn Quay, Oreston, and Passage House Inn, Cattedown. Certainly it was in existence in the sixteenth century, when we know there was a road to the ferry from Martyn's Gate (demolished 1789). The ferry beach at Cattedown is believed to have been the landing-place of the French raiders in 1403, when they ravaged the area since known as Breton side. It is believed the service ended in the nineteen-twenties. In the early years of this century and during the Great War the ferryman was Tom Couch. Among his regular passengers are said to have been dockyard 'mateys' who lived in Oreston and district. They arrived before daybreak at Turn Quay, paid the $\frac{1}{2}$d. toll for the crossing, and on landing at Cattedown walked the whole way to Devonport!

Tom Couch was succeeded by Edward Harper, known to all as 'Uncle Ned'. There can have been no exclusive rights at this time, for Harper is known to have had some competitors, one of whom was a waterman named Perce Williams whose boat was named **My Bond**. Ned also served the coal hulks of Turnchapel. Of the last ferrymen, undoubtedly the best-known was old Tom Landers. In addition to running the crossing and taking crewmen to ships at moorings, Tom used to collect the drinks for Passage House Inn from Sutton Harbour, loading his boat at Custom House Steps. He was a cripple, and lived on his own, but he was something of a character, and when in liquor often sang lustily as he rowed. Speak to anyone who remembers him and they will invariably say

Laira
Passage
Oreston
Passage
Oreston-
Turnchapel
Hooe
Passage
Plymouth,
Turnchapel
and Oreston

'Tom had a good Voice'. On the run from Sutton Harbour he would often bring back a basket of fish, giving most of them away to children when he beached at Oreston. It was his habit to go down on the end of the ebb tide, if the time served, so as to return, if need be drifting! - on the flood. Some years ago an Oreston resident wrote to the South Devon Times: "When I was a girl of eight or nine years of age my mother used to send me up to Oreston Quay with hot soup and something cooked, for Tom. At times we could see his boat drifting upstream. Tom, who had often had one extra before leaving the Barbican, would be in the bottom of the boat singing 'Polly Wolly Doodle All the Day'."

For as long as anyone can remember, this ferry commenced daily at 6 am. to fetch the postman. From time to time it performed a more solemn duty and conveyed the coffins of deceased Cattedown residents for internment in Oreston Methodist Churchyard. Today the men and the boats of the Cattedown ferry have gone. Only the name of the Passage House Inn still bears witness to their service to the community.

ORESTON - TURNCHAPEL: Until the early years of World War II, a rowboat ferry operated across the mouth of Hooelake from Pickleyard Steps at Oreston to Point Beach on the Turnchapel side. It originated as a Government-sponsored ferry in connection with the Breakwater Works at Pomphlett Quarry, and provided a direct route to and from work for employees living in Turnchapel. The waterman to whom the ferry was leased lived rent-free in a tied-cottage at Oreston. The ferry was available to the public at 1d. each way and became popular with Oreston folk as a short cut to Jennycliffe beach.

For many years the ferryman was Dick Frost, who used a 16ft. Waterman's boat, and could be summoned from the opposite bank by a shout of "Over!" At one time Dick was plagued by young practical jokers who shouted for him but disappeared before he had completed the crossing. Thereupon this resourceful character rove an endless rope across the passage, so that intending passengers could haul the boat over and then pull themselves across! A notice requested that the fare money be left on the stern seat. Should the passengers prove forgetful in this respect, and Dick not be at hand, his father-in-law, Mr. Calloway kept a lookout and came forward to collect the toll!

Dick Frost was succeeded between the wars by the disabled Sam ('Peg-leg') Wright, who it is believed was still plying till 1941. Sam had lost his leg in action in the Great War. With his retirement the ferry closed down, and in 1967 the site of the Breakwater Quarry which had given it birth was re-developed as a gasworks. Although this ferry dated only from the last century, it was plying over a route which has its place in history. When Sir Walter Raleigh returned in 1618 from his ill-fated El Dorado expedition, he lodged at nearby Radford House. Here his wife advised him that his life would be forfeit and he must flee. His friends rowed him across Hooe Lake at dead of night, to reach his ship. But Raleigh then determined he would not go. Sadly they rowed him back, and after arrest and detention at Radford, he went to the Tower of London and his execution.

HOOE PASSAGE: The long-discontinued passage between Sutton Harbour and Hooelake must anciently have belonged to the Priory of Plympton. The earliest reference we have is in 1274, when King Edward I received a complaint from the townsfolk of Plympton that the Earl of Cornwall's bailiff for the Trematon estate had appropriated the ferry from Sutton Pool to Hooe and deprived them of the tolls. The complaint was probably made without much hope of redress, for Edmond, Earl of Cornwall was a cousin of the King. Moreover, as lord of Trematon, he had rights over the waters of the Plym which were difficult to dispute.

R.N. Worth, in his "History of Plymouth" (1890) quotes an un-named document as recording "There was a ferry in the water of Plimmoth, between Sutton and 'hole' so far back as 1281, worked by a barge belonging to John Baupre, the toll being a halfpenny for horse or man!! Little more is known, but by the sixteenth century it may well have been falling into disuse: for Plymouth was spreading to the east of Sutton Pool, and the Oreston passage from Cattedown had already been established, with an access road from Martyn's Gate. The likelihood seems to be that the old ferry from Sutton Pool was superseded by the ferry from Cattedown, and Hooe passage was a forerunner of Oreston Passage.

PLYMOUTH, TURNCHAPEL AND ORESTON: I have always maintained that in pre-war Plymouth there was no better three pennyworth to be had than that offered by the "P. & O. liners", - to give the Turnchapel ferries their local nickname. For a pre-decimal 3d. one could spend 40-45 minutes on the interesting waters of Cattewater harbour, with calls at Turnchapel pier and Oreston jetty, and often a visit to R.A.F. Mt. Batten thrown in for good measure.

The poet, Wordsworth, writing in the early nineteenth century on the view from Westminster Bridge, declared: "Dull would he be of soul who could pass by a sight so touching in its majesty". We won't dispute his claim: but certainly the same was true of the view from the decks of the little red-funnelled Turnchapel steamers as they hustled across the Plym estuary. There was the panorama of south-east Plymouth, its towers, spires, and waterfront, with vessels discharging cargoes at Cattedown wharves; the majestic Staddon heights overshadowing Mt. Batten and its castle; the 'Mackay' cable steamers at their moorings, dwarfing the air-sea rescue launches and even the Short Sunderland flying boats. Yes, there was much to see. The service moreover was as good as the view: the ferries were well-appointed, and they ran to time, from early morning to late evening, in all weathers. Nor was there any serious accident in nearly 100 years of operation.

The ferry rights across the Plym between Sutton Harbour and Hooe date back to 1281 in the reign of Edward I, but information as to the operators or the service in the days of oar and sail appears to be totally lacking prior to th 1860s, when a ferryman named Dickie Pearn worked a service from Hooe Quay charging it is said, a 6d. fare. In 1869 two companies began operating in competition, with steam ferries, so it would seem that the rights had lapsed. The rival concerns were the Oreston Steamboat Company with the steamers **Little Pet** and **Favourite**, both new that year, and the Turnchapel Steamboat Company with the **Greyhound** and **Eclipse**. **Greyhound** was also employed in towing sailing ships in and out of Cattewater Harbour.

Turnchapel Steam Ferry:
Lively *off Phoenix Wharf,*
Elphinstone about 1947,
after provision of a
foredeck wheelhouse.

A joint committee of these companies was formed in 1871 by Henry E. Elford, who founded the Oreston & Turnchapel Steamboat Company later that year. To encourage punctuality, a directors' meeting in 1872 resolved to fine crews 1s.6d. if a boat started more than five minutes late! Four boats were then running - the **Greyhound, Eclipse, Beagle** and **Lightning,** but the former two were sold the following year. There was considerable buying and selling of boats during the early years, and with no records extant it is impossible now to compile an accurate record. Though about 1874 the fleet included two 22 ton steam ferries named **Wideawake** and **Nick o' Time.** However by 1880 all the original boats had gone except the **Lightning,** which was joined shortly by the **Lily,** purchased secondhand that year from a Mr. Greaney, who had been running her in opposition to the Company. Six years later the **Lily** was largely rebuilt and renamed **Swift.** There is some uncertainty as to whether this was the same **Swift** which remained in service - several times rebuilt - until 1962. If so, the vessel had an active life of over 80 years. In 1885 Greaney had another boat running in competition - the **Teaser.** This time the Company dealt with him by obtaining a superior vessel, the **Express,** but her subsequent history is unknown. A surviving minute-book of the Company for 1887 notes: "Police Constable Fleming to be reminded about keeping the Turnchapel waiting room free from interlopers......The manager was instructed to pay the constable two shillings and sixpence".

The boats ran between Oreston (which also had a waiting room), and Mayflower Steps at the Barbican, calling at Turnchapel in both directions. The fare was 1d. between any two of the places served, later increased to 2d. or 3d. return, children half price. The Company advertised the beauty of Radford woods and duckponds, which became a favourite excursion for Plymothians on summer evenings and at weekends. The ferry skippers were paid 23s. a week with an extra 3s. for working the Sunday half-day service. Company rules strictly forbade smoking or bad language by the crews, who were also required to pay for any damage caused by the steamers they were working. There was a stipulation that on Sundays the steamers' sirens were not to be used except in emergency. The accounts show that coal was then costing the Company 16s. a ton.

In 1881 a lease was signed for landing at Mount Batten, which became a new mecca for pleasure-seekers. So great were the numbers embarking for Mount Batten during fine weekends and holidays prior to the Great War, that extra services were run from Plymouth for Mount Batten only. Here there was everything for the family, or for organised parties:- a pub, (The Castle), a Cafe run by the Andrews family, beaches, country walks, swings, hoop-la, coconut shies and, for the energetic, a scramble up the crag to Batten Castle. Return journeys on the ferries were enlivened by lusty singing to the accompaniment of mandolin, concertina, or mouth-organ. Amid the merrymaking the occasional minor mishap was inevitable: in 1898 a Mrs. Edwards fell off the gangplank on return to Gutter landing and asked for compensation. She was paid £2. In 1905 the ferries carried over 10,000 passengers to and from Mount Batten and Turnchapel on the August Bank Holiday!

Oreston jetty, always known as 'The Dummy', was erected in 1884. Its site, outside the 'King's Arms' was built over, when the waterfront was developed in recent years. At low water the steamers used a pontoon landing a few yards upstream, known as Gutter Landing. Turnchapel Pier (now ruinous) was opened by Mrs. Elford in August 1889. It was built by Lapthorne & Good of Plymouth for £1,200, and measured 182ft. x 8½ ft. The opening ceremony was enlivened by the music of the Kitto Institute fife and drum band, and followed by a celebration tea. Steamers for Plymouth used the east side of the pier, and for Oreston the west side. The superior facilities offered by this pier caused the collapse of a rival ferry concern started by some of the Company's former employees from the public landing-stage. However, the victory had been hard won, for all that generation of Elford wives and daughters went without new dresses for a year while the pier was being paid for! Plymouth Corporation opened Phoenix Wharf pier in 1895 to ease the congestion at Mayflower steps, and the directors of the Oreston & Turnchapel Steamboat Company were guests at the opening ceremony. The ferries thenceforward had free use and priority rights on the north side. A lasting disadvantage however was the greater walking distance for passengers from the nearest bus stop or city shops. In 1902 Plymouth Corporation requested that watermen should be allowed to land passengers on the quay leased by the Company at Batten, since the Company was allowed free use of Phoenix Wharf. The directors replied that the watermen were becoming so violent and aggressive that it had been necessary to place a man at Batten to maintain the Company's rights and collect their tolls.

The improved facilities had been accompanied by the acquisition of new and improved vessels. The **Dart, Rapid, Lively, Swift** and the **May Queen** now formed the fleet which was to serve the Company for the rest of its existence. In 1894 river excursions were begun in addition to the ferry service, for which an iron steamer, the **Countess of Morley** was sailed to Plymouth from Liverpool by the brothers C. and B. Elford, and ran till 1903. The ferry **May Queen** (designed by Sidney Elford) also did excursion work from 1902. Much later the motor-vessel **City of Plymouth** (new 1929), and the ex-Torpoint passenger steam ferry **Lady Beatrice** (bought 1932) were added to the excursion fleet.

In 1914 came the Great War. The ferry service was maintained throughout, but the **Lively** was chartered to the Royal Navy as a Liberty boat. She returned the following year so damaged that the Company would not accept her until full repair had been carried out by the Dockyard. In 1916 Henry Elford retired, and was succeeded as managing director by his son, William Elford, who held the office till 1940. The Royal Flying Corps took over Mount Batten in 1917, and the public have since been excluded. Plymouth lost a holiday resort and the ferry company lost valuable revenue, although the boats still called at Mount Batten to transport service personnel as required. Among these, from 1930-35 was none other than Lawrence of Arabia, who in the guise of 'Aircraftman Shaw' was engaged on the design of R.A.F. air/sea rescue launches. He was often on board when I was making a crossing, but always appeared aloof and clearly took no pleasure in being recognised. Nevertheless it still further enhanced the value of the 3d. fare to be in the presence of one of the most remarkable and influential Englishmen of the century. Meanwhile, during the 'twenties and early thirties, business remained brisk, and it was common for large queues to await the ferries. On one Good Friday (about 1920) after a thunderstorm, the Turnchapel pier queue extended back to Stamford Fort!

The ferry company made probably the biggest mistake in its history in 1932 when the chance came to buy up a struggling concern named the Tamar Trading Company, which operated the Millbrook ferry. The directors of the Oreston and Turnchapel Company decided to turn the offer down, but it was a fateful decision. The business they might have acquired expanded and prospered, and today the Millbrook Steamboat Company have proved the most enduring and successful of all the local ferry and pleasure-boat operators.

Soon after the outbreak of war in 1939 the **May Queen. Lady Beatrice** and **City of Plymouth** were requisitioned by the Admiralty. None of the three ever returned to service. In 1940 the ferries ceased running after 9pm. because of the intensive air-raids and that same year William Elford was succeeded as Managing Director by his brother Clare. In 1941 the **Swift** was badly damaged by an incendiary bomb, and the following year the **May Queen** was sunk near Saltash after collision with an armed trawler. During an invasion scare, the ferries **Swift, Rapid** and **Lively** were kept on standby for 24 hours for troop movements, and on a test run the **Swift** carried over 120 soldiers and some stretcher cases from Turnchapel to Phoenix Wharf in eight minutes.

After the war a new diesel **May Queen** was built for excursion work, but occasionally appeared on the ferry in emergency. The beginning of the end for the Turnchapel ferries came in 1948 when the Western National Omnibus Company extended its Oreston bus service to Turnchapel and Mount Batten. The buses on their roundabout route took longer than the ferries, but had the great advantage of being accessible from the City centre. Even so, another (motor) ferry was added to the fleet in 1949 when the **Sweet Marie** (45ft. x 12ft.6ins., capacity 85 passengers) was bought at auction for £1,270. Her ultimate fate is unknown, but she was not in service for long. The threat posed by bus competition was slightly offset in 1951 when the Southern Railway closed their Turnchapel line, but this brought only a temporary reprieve. Harry Elford (grandson of Henry Elford) had become the Managing Dirctor in 1950, and he was destined to preside over the last years of the Company.

The ferry **Lively** (92) was sold in 1951, but the **Swift**, after being again gutted by a fire, was rebuilt with a diesel engine, wheelhouse and squat funnel, in 1954. In 1956 the **Rapid**, after removal of her engine and boiler, was sold for conversion to a houseboat. By 1955 Harry Elford was not enjoyng good health and his doctors advised him to give up the business. The ferry was put up for auction as a going concern, together with the excursion boat **May Queen**, the pier and workshops at Turnchapel, and Calstock Quay, but there were no bids. Fares were increased to 4d. that year and to 5d. the year following. In 1957 the business was sold in separate lots, the **May Queen** (2) being bought - ironically - by the Millbrook Steamboat Company, and renamed **Eastern Belle**, while the ferry service was taken over by C.A. Partridge of Plymouth and renamed the Plymouth & Oreston Steamboat Company. Oreston, in fact, was now only served in Summer or by special arrangement. Attempts to reconcile ferry and bus arrival times at Phoenix Wharf were unsuccessful. The more economic motor boat **Tiger** had been introduced on the service, but was no real substitute for the saloon steamers.

The last boats acquired for the service were the **Ivie** and **Noela**, but their performance was disparate. The **Ivie** could do the Phoenix Wharf to Turnchapel run in 8 minutes, but the **Noela** needed 13 minutes! Mr. Partridge was fortunate to obtain the services as a skipper of Stan Daymond, a very experienced former master of tugs and dredgers; upon him the maintenance of the service largely depended in the last years. The end drew nearer when the **Swift** was sunk at her moorings in a hurricane and became a total loss. In 1965 the Plymouth & Oreston Company abandoned the ferry as uneconomic and a century of steam ferry service on the Cattewater came to an end. Plymouth is the poorer for its passing.

The Turnchapel steam ferries were mostly built of oak and elm. None had copper fastenings; all were iron-bolted. Maintenance was carried out at the Company's store next to Turnchapel pier, where 'Jakie' Phillips, Elford's 'right-hand man', ran the machine shop on the ground floor, while Harry Tucker, regarded as 'Senior Skipper' did the necessary carpentry on the first floor. It was almost unknown for outside labour to be employed. When a ferry was refitting, her crew were expected to work on the job under 'Jakie's' supervision. The same building also housed the office. The crews worked in shifts recurring every three days, as follows: Day 1 (1pm. to 10pm.), Day 2 (6.30am. to 2.30pm.), Day 3 (6.30am. to 1pm.). But a 15 hour day was quite usual during the peak of the summer season. Before a day's ferrying, crews had to replenish fresh water, and berth at a coal hulk to coal ship: and after the last trip of the day the Plymouth-Oreston takings, collected on board, had to be delivered to the home of Mrs. Turpitt (nee Elford). Fares to or from Turnchapel were collected at the pier toll-huts; and on duty here one might find Gwen Phillips (Jakie's daughter),

Turnchapel-
Cattedown
Barbican -
Coxside
Drake's
Island Ferry

Edie Townsend (his daughter-in-law), Edie and Bessie Dungey (skipper Sam's sisters), or Ivy Tucker (daughter of skipper Harry). The Oreston and Turnchapel Steamboat Co. was very much a family affair. A crew of three worked the boats:- Skipper, Engineer and Mate (deckhand/purser). Most of the skippers had served as third hand before promotion.

The local historian or industrial archaeologist will find few remains of the Turnchapel ferry today. Phoenix Wharf of course still stands, but the north steps are now used - ironically - by the boats of the Millbrook Company which Elfords had spurned to buy. The name "Oreston & Turnchapel Steamboat Company", and the rights of landing at Phoenix Wharf, are held by Mrs. Jean Curtin, owner of the Drake's Island ferry.

At Oreston the site of the jetty is now an esplanade, and the pontoon has been towed away. Turnchapel pier and works site are now the property of the West of England Fishing & Ship Co. Ltd. The Works where Jakie Phillips and Harry Tucker once toiled were destroyed by fire, and new buildings cover the site. The pier is being gradually demolished and replaced by a stone quay. Models of the steamers are however, possessed by the Elford family.

TURNCHAPEL - CATTEDOWN: This Watermen's ferry ran between Turnchapel New Pier and Cattedown Steps. It came into being as a result of industrial development on both sides of the Cattewater in the latter half of the nineteenth century. As stone was quarried from Cattedown cliffs to meet the requirements of building enterprises in Plymouth, there was created beside the Cattewater a levelled area which became an industrial site. Here sprang up the rival fertiliser works of Norrington, Gibbs, and Burnard & Algar; while Cattedown Wharves were constructed for trading vessels in 1888. On the Turnchapel side, Pope's shipyard was flourishing, and from 1897 the new Turnchapel Wharf gave employment to dockers.

Best-remembered of the ferrymen was Jack Oates, who operated between the wars. He was renowned locally for his great physical strength. About 6.30am. every weekday Jack ferried across the workers at the fertiliser factories, and ferried them back at 5.30pm. The fare was 1d. each way for the general public, but dockers paid a weekly fare of 8d. for one return trip daily or 1/6 for two return trips daily. Jack also ferried barrels of beer to the inns at Turnchapel, Hooe and Oreston from Sutton Harbour, which was arduous work.

There was no exclusive rights on this ferry, and at weekends up to seven other boats might be operating: Fred Thomas, John Dungey, Vic Salmon, Will Dungey, Alf Burridge and Bill Cowell were among the locals who earned some extra beer money this way. Jack Oates was succeeded by Fred Thomas, who used an 18ft. waterman's boat named **Try Again**, which was licensed for nine passengers. The service survived World War II by a few years.

BARBICAN-COXSIDE: Few ferries can have had a shorter distance to ply than the Barbican-Coxside boat which worked between the piers of Sutton Harbour, Plymouth, but the service saved several miles of walking for crews leaving and returning to their ships berthed at Victoria Wharves, Coxside, or Cattedown. Today the ferry is no more and the demand would never make it economic. Yet the need for it is in a sense greater: for the once ubiquitous watermen are no more.

The service ceased after World War II, but the last Ferrymen to work the crossing, the brothers Frank and Tom Marshall, still live in Plymouth and Millbrook respectively. Tom Marshall has told me that they took over the service at the end of the Great War from two then-elderly men. "One was very tall" says Tom "and I know his sons still live in the Barbican area".

Frank Marshall used a 12 foot boat named **Farmer's Boy**, and Tom a 16 foot boat, the name of which he cannot recall! Although the fare remained 1d. till the service ended, it could be a profitable occupation in the summer, when, says Tom, he sometimes collected up to £11 a day, as most passengers paid "over the odds". He has kindly memories of the steamers **Corberry Queen** and **The Sultan**, two regular callers whose crews saw him well tipped and provided with paint.

The last trips of the day often meant conveying inebriated seamen back to their ships and it was by no means uncommon for some to fall overboard in the dark, and get a ducking. Tom recalls one skipper who was expecting his girlfriend to visit the ship, and instructed Tom to watch out for her and see her safely across, adding that she was a 'very smart girl'. "And she was," says Tom, "the real McCoy, I can tell you." The gratified skipper crossed Tom's palm with three half-crowns when the beauty was safely delivered to the Coxside pier!

On another occasion Tom moved an entire household of furniture for a Coxside man who was moving house to the Barbican side. Kitchen stove, wardrobes, double-bed and a three-piece suite all came over via the 16 feet boat! To-day Sutton harbour lacks much of its old colour and variety. And not least of those things now gone for ever was the Coxside Ferry.

DRAKE'S ISLAND FERRY: Drake's Island, formerly a fortress and a state prison, and now an adventure centre for young people, lies in Plymouth Sound and is reached by ferry from Mayflower Steps in Sutton Harbour. Extending over six acres in area, rising to a height of 96 feet, and formed of volcanic rock, the island is strewn with military remains, honeycombed by casemates, and rich in historical associations. Until recent years the island has been closed to the public, a place of mystery; so the Drake's Island Ferry offers its patrons a unique experience.

When the island was returned by the War Department to Plymouth ownership, no regular boat service was established until Mr. C.A. Partridge of the Plymouth & Oreston Steamboat Company experimented with motor boat excursions during the summer of 1972. Three boats were variously used on the service: the **Ivie** (now Dartmouth), the **Noela** (since renamed **Our Queen** and working at Torquay), and the **Mayflower** which is still at Plymouth. Perhaps because the island was then less-prepared for visitors, and the advertised survice failed financially before it became a regular ferry.

The credit for establishing the present May-to-October timetable ferry service belongs to Mrs. Jean Curtin, who had in the meantime acquired the name and rights of the former Plymouth & Oreston Steamboat Company. In 1975 a regular service was started with the M/V **Lady Elizabeth**, hired from the Millbrook Steamboat & Trading Company. This was a 53ft. boat, engined with a Gardner diesel, and licensed for 113 passengers. Each season till 1979 the **Lady Elizabeth** was chartered for the ferry and the same crew re-engaged annually. Six return trips were made daily, the 1¼ mile crossing taking about 10 minutes. The ferry is now well-established and the years have passed without major incident.

In October 1979 the **Lady Elizabeth** was sold by the Millbrook Company to Peter Moule, proprietor of the Kingsbridge-Salcombe ferry. Her replacement was the **Edgcumbe Belle** (ex. Humphrey Gilbert), which arrived at Mashford's Yard, Cremyll, before the end of the year, having come from the Thames. The **Humphrey Gilbert**, with her sister **Adrian Gilbert** was built at Bideford in 1957 for the railway ferry at Dartmouth. Her tonnage figures are 35 gross, 22 net, and her length is 57'9".

The passage from Mayflower Steps to the island takes the ferry past Plymouth's waterfront, the Hoe; and there is more to see than the principal features which are described in local guidebooks. As the ferry steers out into the estuary of the Plym, with Skipper Ben Curtin at the helm, passengers should notice, to starboard, the ruined tower of the Castle Quadrate which once guarded the Sutton Harbour entrance. Begun in the reign of Richard II and completed in the time of Henry VI, its four towers are depicted in the City's coat-of-arms.

The peninsular of Mount Batten, with its 910ft. breakwater, is conspicuous on the port side. As Fishers Nose is cleared and course is altered about 65 degrees to starboard, passengers can see, crowning the rocks below Madeira Road, old walls and bulwarks which once carried gun platforms and are remains of fortifications ordered by Henry VIII in 1539.

Between the Hoe foreshore and Drake's Island the ferry is crossing the 28 fathom main channel used by warships to and from Devonport Dockyard. Here on the 20th June, 1798 took place what is claimed as the first-ever dive by a submarine. The invention of a Suffolk designer named Day, the little vessel submerged in view of a large crowd, but failed to surface again. Day lost his life, and the remains of the wreck, never located, must lie below the ferry route today.

Drake's Island pier, where the ferry makes fast, dates from 1939, when the island's fortifications were being modernised under the threat of impending war. From here the Mayflower Trust who now administer the island run a non-public year-round ferry with a 24ft. fibreglass motor-boat named **Sir John Cadbury**.

CAWSAND FERRY: Cawsand beach has been popular with tourists and Plymothians at leisure for a good many years, and at one time was a regular venue of excursion steamers from Northcorner. Since then, motor-boat services from the Barbican and the Hoe beach have operated as occasion demanded. But not until 1979 was a regular timetable service offered to Plymouth, and this came about through the visit of two men to Cawsand village in 1978. Ian Watts, 32, self-employed civil engineer in Weston-super-Mare, and Martin Finlay, also 32, a Devonport Dockyard fork-lift truck operator, paid a weekend visit to Cawsand and were delighted with its unspoiled beauty. They were also surprised that no one was operating a boat service from Plymouth and determined they would make good this deficiency.

Ian Watts brought to Cawsand the 36ft. passenger launch **Weston Lady** which he had built himself. Throughout the 1979 season this boat offered a regular timed ferry service which was to have included an early-morning "commuter run" into Plymouth, though this latter intention did not prove possible. The weather was not very co-operative, but their verdict at the end of the season was "surprisingly successful". Accordingly, during the winter, Ian returned to Weston-super-Mare and built a second boat - **Weston Maid** - at a cost of about £20,000. The 1980 season started optimistically with two boats, and two crewmen were added to the venture - Peter Reynolds and Bernard Watts (6). The weather however proved even worse than in 1979, and it became clear that there was insufficient business to support two boats and crews, except when conditions were ideal. However, the service was advertised as a ferry, and the operators kept faith with their customers, running to time irrespective of pay-load. Both boats, with fibreglass hulls and built to the same basic measurements, are licensed for over 60 passengers, and engined with Perkins 6-cylinder diesels. But consideration is already being given to replacing them with a larger and faster vessel.

The half-hour trip, reasonably priced in 1980 at 60 pence, takes the passenger diagonally across Plymouth Sound, passing Drake's Island, Picklecombe Fort, and Mount Edgcumbe Park. The service operates from Mayflower Steps in Sutton Harbour, with five runs a day at the height of the season. Small yacht racing between Batten Breakwater and Fishers Nose is a hazard of the run, and a keen lookout has to be maintained. The ferry has operated as an unofficial lifeboat on occasions when small boats and surf-sailers have been found in difficulties and towed in.

Landing arrangements at Cawsand are still rather primitive. Journalist Jean Campbell, writing in the "Plymouth Extra" commented "Walking the plank on to the beach is one of the highlights of the trip with locals watching with amusement as tourists slither down on to the shifting shingle". Martin Finlay intends to provide a railed gangway for future seasons, but a DUKW such as used at South Sands in the Kingsbridge Estuary might be the perfect answer. When extreme low spring tides occur it is sometimes necessary to cancel the 12 noon and/or 14.30 services, as the outer shelving of Cawsand beach is very gradual and there is insufficient water for the boat to work with an ordinary gangplank. But whatever the outcome as to size of boats and methods of landing, and in spite of starting with two seasons of adverse weather, this summer ferry seems to have established itself on the Plymouth scene.

RIVER YEALM

STEER POINT FERRY: Until the Great Western Railway opened its Yealmpton Branch in January 1898, the people of Newton Ferrers and Noss Mayo had no form of public transport to Plymouth other than the weekly carrier's cart and the occasional summertime excursion steamer from Plymouth promenade pier. Soon after the opening of the railway however, a Mr. Hartnell began to operate a ferry from Newton and Noss, with a paraffin-engined motor-boat, to meet the railway trains at Steer Point. About a year later this ferry service was taken over by a Mr. Jim Ford (builder of the Yealm Hotel), using a small steam launch with the engaging name of **Yam-Yam**.

Steer Point Ferry: **Kitley Girl** *under way about 1900. Her origins are unknown, but she enjoyed a long and hard-working 'Indian summer' on the Steer Point run.*

In 1900 Jim Ford was bought out by George Hodge of Noss Mayo, who, with a partner, provided an all-the-year-round steamer service which was destined to last nearly 30 years. The partner's name is thought to have been Hartnell, the pioneer of the ferry. The new service was inaugurated by the small vessel **Puffing Billy**, but after a few months, Hodge's partner retired owing to ill-health, and the **Puffing Billy** was replaced by the steam ferry **Kitley Belle**, purpose-built for George Hodge, which had a Board of Trade licence for 78 passengers within the river Yealm. The **Kitley Belle** was open-decked fore and aft, with an upper deck over the cabin. She was steered from the customary unsheltered position in the bows, where passenger space was partly encumbered by the need to carry a long gangplank. Rested only for annual overhauls, the **Kitley Belle** operated continuously for the whole 29 years of the service. The longer, but older twin-screw **Kitley Girl** was acquired secondhand about 1902 as relief boat. On peak days at the height of summer both steamers would be running.

There was a brief threat to the ferry service in 1906 when work commenced on the Devon & South Hams Light Railway, but the project was soon abandoned though some of the earthworks can still be seen. Meanwhile the ferry continued to prosper; there was a regular service of six trips a day, Sundays included in the summer and George Hodge now had the assistance of three of his sons, George, Ernest and Elliot, and a nephew, Lionel Baker. Hodge (senior) was principal skipper until he semi-retired during the Great War. George was deckhand and relief skipper, who eventually took over from his father: Ernest and Lionel were engineer/stokers: while Elliot was a shipwright who refitted the ferries when required in his own boatyard at Noss, and was available for the crew when required. Mr. Edgar Foster of Newton Ferrers recalls: "All the staffing was done by members of the family. Mind you, they were a large family!"

During the 1914-18 war when George Hodge's sons were away in the Services, he had to turn to his grandsons for help to keep the ferry running, and at times the young women of the family were also required. The Government had taken over Membland Hall (a mile from Bridgend, but now demolished) as an officer training centre with an intake of 300 men for each course; and the wives and families of some of the trainees came to stay in Newton and Noss. The requisitioning of Membland Hall increased the need for direct contact with Plymouth, and made the ferry busier than ever. After the war, Hodge senior retired, and the business was carried on by his sons, with George as senior partner. The service started from Pope's Quay, Noss Mayo, or from the Pool at low water, the ferry then calling as required at Kiln Quay, Newton Ferrers; Wide Slip, Noss; Yealm Hotel jetty; Warren Point, Wembury; and Thorn Quay, before reaching Steer Point. Numbers of Newton and Noss children, who attended schools in Plymouth, used the ferry daily.

At Steer Point, although it appears that Kitley Quay was sometimes used, embarkation was generally from a small slipway: but at low water the steamer had to lie off and a rowing-boat tender was used. Mr. Bernard Williams of London, recalling boyhood days, says: "The service was not confined to daylight hours - I remember one dark night when my cousin's husband was arriving on the last train and I was kept up to see him: we stood down on the foreshore, and following arrangements made, he signalled to us with a torch to show he was on board". Train passengers had a mile walk between Steer Point station and the steamer slip: and that was not the only trial, for at low spring tides the steamers could not get nearer to Steer Point than about 550 yards. The passengers were then put in the rowing-boat which had been towed astern, and the ferry crew rowed them as near to the slip as possible. This might be 50 yards short, and ladies and others unsuitably shod for traversing the mud were carried pick-a-back by the ferryman. This duty, it seems, usually fell to George, Junior.

It was common for the ferries to tow a boat astern, so that passengers could be embarked or disembarked at points en route irrespective of the tide. This towing however was taken a considerable stage further when the Hodges acquired two mercantile ship's lifeboats, one wooden-hulled, one steel. When the queue awaiting the ferry exceeded the number for which she was licensed, the remaining passengers would be embarked in one of these lifeboats and towed astern! This practice would not be countenanced by the authorities today.

Although the ferries did not operate a regular parcels service, there was the luggage of summer visitors and other train passengers to be handled, for which a small charge was made. A handcart was kept at Steer Point for moving trunks and cases between station and steamer. At Newton and Noss all luggage was manhandled, usually by George junior, who seems to have been the official strongman! Coaling ship was another strenuous chore. Most services could get this done before embarking passengers, but it was different on the Yealm. Coal for the steamers arrived by rail at Steer Point Station, whence it was carted the mile to the waterside and tipped into a rock crevice which the steamers could reach when the tide was up.

By 1920 passenger traffic on the Yealmpton railway was probably at its peak, and the service of the 'Kitley' ferry steamers made Steer Point the busiest of the intermediate stations, for all trains were met by ferry. Toward the end of the 'twenties however, motor bus services were becoming well established and private cars more numerous. Passenger traffic on the Yealmpton line was declining sharply, and it was clear that the end was in sight. During the last year or so of the service, the **Kitley Girl** was only occasionally needed, and the more economic motorboat **Pioneer**, purchased from St. Mawes, Cornwall, and powered by a semi-diesel Gardner engine was used. The **Kitley Belle** was converted from steam to paraffin motor, though her funnel was retained.

In 1929, a year before the passenger trains ceased on the railway, the Hodge brothers brought the ferry service to an end. This may have been because the G.W.R. had withdrawn the 'Through' tickets (rail and ferry), or because it was now clear that the steamer route (with the mile walk at Steer Point) could be bettered by a motorbus to Yealmpton, and the Hodges wished to forestall such competition. Whatever the reason, the ferries never ran again. The **Kitley Belle** was sold to the Millbrook Steamboat and Trading Co. **Kitley Girl** was still at her moorings when the **Kitley Belle** was sold, in poor condition. One night in a gale she broke adrift, was swept up to Bridgend and was badly damaged. She was then sold to Mr. George Revel who broke her up at Bridgend Quay.

Mr. Bernard Williams made an entry in his diary that he saw her there on the 26th April. As for the **Pioneer**, she was put ashore at Noss beach, where she quietly rotted away. Ernest and Elliot Hodge immediately started a bus service from Newton to Yealmpton to meet the trains; but George, who did not drive, went to Saltash and started market-gardening. After the 7th July 1930 the passenger service on the railway was withdrawn; and a Plymouth-Yealmpton bus service was operated by the Railway-owned Devon Motor Transport Co. - who then bought out the Hodge brothers, and took on Ernest Hodge as a driver.

Little evidence remains today of the Steer Point Ferry and the Yealmpton Railway line was finally closed in 1960. By following the road along which George Hodge once trundled the handcart, one can find the steamer slipway at the beach. At Newton Ferrers the Yealm Hotel jetty has been shortened since the ferry days, while Kiln Quay has now become a private garden. Popes Quay at Noss decayed and has been rebuilt. The Swan Inn used to have a small bar known as the Cabin, fitted up as a replica of the cabin of the **Kitley Belle**. This was dismantled about 1970. The Ship Inn (formerly The Globe) still displays one of **Kitley Belle's** lifebuoys.

NEWTON & NOSS: Some kind of ferry service must have operated here since the twin villages became sufficiently populous for parish churches to have been built. Noss's original church is early 14th century, and Newton Church has a 13th century chancel. Local fishermen were on call to ferry passengers as occasion arose. The Yealm estuary became a resort for Plymouth small yacht owners, steamer excursions from Plymouth and the railway steam ferry service via Steer Point, combined to increase village ferry traffic by the mid-1920s. It was then that W.Roach, ex-landlord of the Dolphin Inn began a permanent ferry, which ran as required for about 20 years.

In the 1930s the local council took control, and when Roach retired about 1946 a licence to ply for hire was required. J. Northcott (operator of the Warren Point ferry) took over the village ferry for 2 or 3 years before retiring. The Carter family (Northcott's successors), worked the ferry till its closure, about 1970. Its demise was due to the motor car.

It was always a rowboat ferry until Roach's withdrawal, but motor boats were regularly used from 1947. Mr. Edgar Foster of Newton Ferrers, can recall the days before Bill Roach, when there was usually someone available with a boat to act as ferryman if needed. "When I was young", he says "anybody would put people across when the tide was in; and we never thought of making any charge".

NOSS MAYO TO WARREN POINT: A ferry still shown on Ordnance Survey maps operated from Yealm Steps in Passage Road, Noss Mayo, for many years. It provided the most direct, if not the quickest, route to Plymouth. The ferry rights, originally owned by the Kitley Estate, were granted in the nineteenth century to the residents of Ferry Cottage, Noss Mayo. They employed a ferryman who was housed in a smaller cottage nearby. In the 1890s Mrs. Algate, a widow, was the proprietor and a young man named Foster worked the boat. When Mrs. Algate left, the cottage and ferry were taken over by a Mr. Williams. Boats of 16ft. and under were used for the crossing. During the Great War a Mr. Hockaday became owner, and his daughters ran the ferry in the 1920s. After the Hockaday sisters, a Mr. J. Northcott operated the service for 16 years, but did not acquire the rights, which remained with Ferry Cottage, and still do.

Northcott initiated two changes: he employed a motorboat instead of a rowboat, and he worked to Wide Slip (below the Yealm Hotel) as well as to Warren Point. This additional service, to the Yealm Hotel, probably reflected the increase in visitors to the villages in post-war years. I have been unable to discover when the service to Warren Point ceased, but there is some evidence from maps to suggest it was working till 1968, if only in summer. Northcott retired in 1934, when the Carter family of Newton Ferrars began working the ferry as a summer-service, with the assistance of others.

The service, which today operates as needed, and not to timetable, is maintained by a 16-foot outboard motorboat which was specially built for the ferry. Mr. Len H. Carter, the present ferry proprietor, tells me: "I have operated motor launches up to 32ft. long when business warranted it; but I do not believe it practical to operate on a regular basis, successfully, anything longer than 20 feet". From 1935-52 the service was worked by the 18ft. **Jason**, which for 50 years had been plying from Plymouth to Bovisand and Cawsand under oars and sail. The blue-hulled **Marie** replaced her in 1952.

BANTHAM - COCKLERIDGE: The river Avon in South Devon which meets the sea at Bigbury, where its estuary is dominated by Burgh Island, has only one ferry passage. From the beginning of the present century this ferry was operated by the Elliot family of Bantham, the lady members taking their turn at working the boat as occasion required.

**The Sea
Tram**

The last Elliot to run the ferry gave up in 1974 - although his brother-in-law still serves as Bantham Harbourmaster. It was the end of an era which spanned six reigns. Since 1974 the ferryman has been Hugh Cater, who has motorised the service by using a Seagull outboard motor on the cream-hulled waterman's boat. The council pay a retainer as the ferry does not provide a living. It is a summer-only service providing hikers with a necessary link and much used by the residents of Youth Hostels on either side of the estuary.

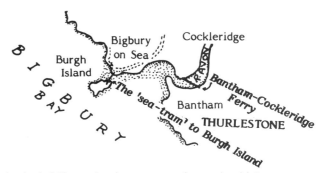

On the Cockleridge side passengers are embarked 150 yards downstream from the high-water landing when the tide is low. The estuary is strewn with banks and there is a six-knot tide. Until the use of the "Seagull" motor, the ferry fares were indeed hard-earned. The service operates from 10am. to 11am. and from 3pm. to 4pm. weekdays from April to September and on Sundays in July and August.

THE SEA TRAM: Burgh Island, 250 yards seaward of Bigbury-on-Sea, has a ferry that is different. This is a Sea Tram, which is believed to be the only one of its kind in the world. The island has a fourteenth century inn, but may not have been continuously populated since then. In the early days of this century all provisions were taken across at low water by horse transport. Visitors were brought over by fishermen's boats 'on the tide'. When the original Burgh Island Hotel was built (now used as staff quarters) it was determined to provide transport in the summer season which was independent of the tides.

So it was, that in the early 'thirties, when the island was owned by Lady Anderson, a half-track vehicle was designed and built for the service by Messrs. Nettlefold. A passenger deck, on which the engine was mounted, was set on a frame about nine feet above a track drive, with small leading wheels. Even at high water spring tides, the deck would be at least two feet clear of the water. It had a petrol engine, was distinguished by large guards over its fore wheels, and had a passenger capacity of about thirty. A photograph of the first Sea Tram (or bus?) survives on the island, but it was scrapped after World War II.

About 1946 an experiment was made with an ex-army Terrapin, an amphibious twin-engined personnel carrier. A second Terrapin was later acquired. They were engined by two Ford V8 motors and had a passenger capacity of twelve, to which they were limited by the bye-laws. It was found that breakdown of one of the engines made the craft virtually unsteerable and breakdowns were unacceptably frequent. On these occasions Raglan Vine, now Hope Cove Harbourmaster but then Burgh Island fisherman, worked a boat ferry between island and mainland. Today he recalls "It was a somewhat tricky job, particularly in bad weather and several of the well-dressed and very wealthy guests at the hotel often got a 'dowsing' on the crossing." The Terrapins were withdrawn in less than two years.

A second Sea Tram was built by Oak Brothers of Kingsbridge. It had a petrol engine till 1956, when, after a swamping incident, a change was made to a Perkins diesel. the motion comprised half-track and leading wheels, as with No.1, and the passenger deck had a canvas awning. Affectionately known as **Puff** by the local fraternity, Sea Tram No.2 rendered yeoman service for more than twenty years. In 1961 small brick-and-concrete landing piers were built on either side of the crossing, so that passengers could cross to the vehicle's raised deck by a short gangway, and not have to mount the steps from beach level. Within a few seasons these piers had been destroyed by winter seas and have not been repaired.

By 1969 it was clear that the sea had taken its toll of **Puff**, which was in a rusting condition and a new machine was designed - by a R.N. Submarine designer who had visited Burgh Island. This could well have meant the demise of No.2, had not salvation been at hand in the person of transport enthusiast Colin Shears. He despatched a low-loader to Bigbury sands, and No.2 was taken away to a secret place of retirement in North Devon. She is still there today, in somewhat forlorn condition, awaiting the hand of a restorer. Photograph page 125.

The third Sea Tram, which is still in use, was constructed in 1970 by Beare's of Newton Abbot at a cost of £14,000. It is basically a tractor, with large tyred wheels, and is officially described as the "Sea Tractor", although its function makes this a misnomer. The deck is twelve feet above beach level, and the retractable steps, although an improvement on those of its predecessors, take up part of the deck space, so that the passenger capacity (30) is a little less than that of No.2.

Your authors recall that on a visit to Bigbury-on-Sea in June 1975 they saw the sea tram abandoned in the water with a broken axle: the passengers had been taken off by boat. Later, from Bantham beach, we saw the tram being towed to Burgh Island, silhouetted by the setting sun. Mishaps however are few and far between. In 1980 the present vehicle was overhauled at a cost of £2,500, and given a new perspex roof. A re-launching ceremony was held, when Mrs. Susan Waugh, now owner of Burgh Island, smashed a bottle of champagne on the steps and three musicians played sea shanties on the first crossing. The Sea Tram operates, weather permitting, for three hours either side of high water. It does not normally have to traverse water more than five feet deep, but can cope with twice this depth in calm conditions. In heavy weather the service has to be suspended.

Meanwhile **Puff No.2**, languishes in its North Devon hideout. It is greatly to be hoped that someone with the necessary resources will undertake the restoration of this unique vehicle. Ideally it should be on public display somewhere in South Devon where its working life was spent: somewhere where transport enthusiasts foregather, and visitors throng, such as Buckfastleigh Station or Exeter Maritime Museum. It would not be expensive to acquire and Colin Shears tells us that he can supply originals or alternatives for most of the parts which are missing or require renewal.

13.

Kingsbridge

Estuary

South

Devon.

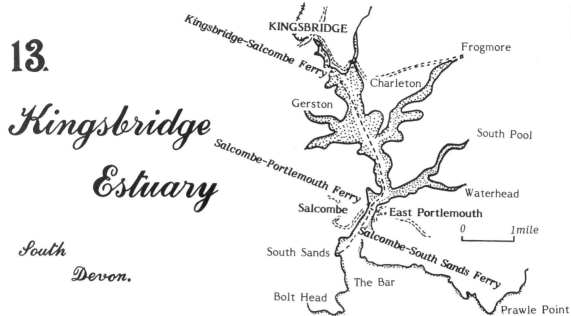

KINGSBRIDGE

Frogmore

Charleton

Gerston

South Pool

Waterhead

Salcombe · East Portlemouth

0   1mile

South Sands

The Bar

Bolt Head

Prawle Point

Kingsbridge-Salcombe Ferry

Salcombe-Portlemouth Ferry

Salcombe-South Sands Ferry

KINGSBRIDGE - SALCOMBE: In the past, there must always have been a need for a down-river ferry from Kingsbridge. The inlets on the western side of the estuary caused the road to Salcombe to meander over six and half miles and, not being turnpiked, it was poorly surfaced, so that travel was slow and uncomfortable. The 4 mile water route was infinitely preferable. As far as can be ascertained, the first regular ferry service between Kingsbridge and Salcombe was provided by the wooden paddle steamer **Queen**, built in 1860, and broken up in 1876. She was not registered at Salcombe and little is known of her. During the year before she was scrapped, she was supplanted on the ferry by the paddle steamer **Reindeer**, a 71 foot, $44\frac{1}{2}$ tons wooden vessel built by Date of Kingsbridge.

We have been unable to discover her original owners, but it seems that latterly she was run by Captain Nicholas March. **Reindeer** was a single-decked saloon steamer with large paddle wheels, a single mast stepped well for'ard, and steered from an open platform between the paddle-boxes. She seems to have been withdrawn in 1902 and was derelict by 1906 after rather a short life. During her last four years she was joined by a second steamer, ordered by Nicholas March in expectation of increased traffic.

This was the **Salcombe Castle** (100), built in 1898 at the yard of Philip & Son, Dartmouth, with a tall stovepipe funnel but having more elegant paddle-boxes than the **Reindeer**. The castle after which the vessel was named is now an insignificant ruin, but achieved renown for its stubborn four-month resistance to siege in 1645. The vessel's appearance was improved when the height of her funnel was reduced about 1910. After withdrawal of the **Reindeer**, **Salcombe Castle** had the ferry to herself for over three years. Dependent on tide, she ran four times daily from Kingsbridge to Salcombe and back. Fares were 6d. single and 10d. return. In addition to running the ferry she was in demand for party outings and made sea excursions to Dartmouth. Older residents can still remember her crew of the post-war years:- Charlie Hutchings (skipper), Tom Adams (engineer) and Messrs. Stumbles and Hannaford (deckhands).

Soon after acquisition of the **Salcombe Castle** March took into partnership Captain Nick Southward, a younger man, who took command of the third steamer to run on the ferry - the steel paddler **Ilton Castle**. Built to order by Willoughby's of Plymouth, she came into service in 1906 and was named after a ruin of which little remains today, on the hill between Lincombe and Batson Creek. **Ilton Castle** had two cylinder compound diagonal engines and was a larger and improved version of her predecessors. Nat Sheppard was her engineer and a naval pensioner named Pepperell is remembered as one of her deckhands. Her design included a small refinement which must have been welcome to the helmsman - a windbreak at the steering position.

In 1909 competition appeared in the form of a Kingsbridge-Salcombe bus service started by the Great Western Railway, meeting all passenger trains at Kingsbridge terminus. Ferry traffic was little affected at first. The early buses were none too reliable, the roads were poor and the route circuitous. The ferry, with its direct route, took little longer and offered an infinitely more pleasant journey. Nevertheless, for those with eyes to see, the writing was on the wall. Meanwhile Captain March's only daughter had married Captain Southwood; and when March died in 1912, Nick Southwood and his wife took over the business, which was still prospering. Two years later they took delivery of a third steamer, the **Kenwith Castle** mysteriously named after an early mediaeval earthwork near Appledore in North Devon. **Kenwith Castle** was built in the same yard at Plymouth as **Ilton Castle** and to virtually the same design. The Mercantile Navy List however records a minute difference in the vessels' lengths:- **Ilton Castle** 80.5ft., **Kenwith Castle** 80.2ft.; while the new steamer was recognisable by having a proper wheelhouse.

The Great War now intervened and it seems probable that the **Salcombe Castle** was requisitioned for Admiralty work and perhaps did not return to her owners. As far as we can ascertain, she did not work on the Kingsbridge-Salcombe ferry again after the war. The post-war years soon revealed the seriousness of road competition. Reliable motor buses running to a faster schedule over improved roads were a formidable threat, and river traffic began to decline rapidly. In 1927 the Southwoods sold out to the Great Western Railway, but that company had no plans for developing the service and had bought the steamers to eliminate competition.

*Kingsbridge Ferry. The crew of the **Salcombe Castle** relax on deck between runs about 1920, after shortening of her former 'Woodbine' funnel. Photo: L.Fairweather.*

In 1929 they sold the **Ilton Castle** to two members of the Salcombe Sailing Club, Sir Raymond Beck and Mr. Alfred Pasolt, after her engines had been removed. She was used as a floating head-quarters to enable the Sailing Club to be separated from the Yacht Club. Alderman W.E.Burner J.P., Hon. Sec. of the Sailing Club, recalls that members removed bulkheads to provide a large saloon below deck and erected a deck house between the sponsons for the use of the Officer of the Day. When World War II broke out the **Ilton Castle** was commandeered by the Ministry of Sea Transport and used as a mooring pontoon for oiling American landing craft from a supply position at Snapes Point. Her hull was already in poor condition when a landing craft rammed and sank her, toward the end of the war. She was later raised, beached in The Bag, and cut up in situ for scrap. After **Ilton Castle**'s withdrawal, **Kenwith Castle** maintained the ferry service alone for five years. The G.W.R. then decided to suspend the service, and put the **Kenwith Castle** on the market. Soon after she was acquired by Kenneth Worth of Calstock, who renamed her **Whitsand Castle** and within a year resold her to the Millbrook Steamboat and Trading Company, Plymouth.

As the G.W.R. had been preparing to bow out from the Kingsbridge ferry scene, competitors had been moving in. In 1931 three motorboats appeared on the service - the **Mermaid** (owner, M. Overy), the **Moulton** (G. Gidley) and the **Ayaha** (J. Middleton). **Mermaid** and **Ayaha** were fitted with Britt petrol engines, while the **Moulton** had a Kelvin engine. All were non-Board of Trade boats and their passenger capacity was limited to twelve. They could not compete with the **Kenwith Castle** for passenger amenities, but they could easily undercut her fares. Overy and Gidley however with-drew after the 1931 summer season and it was left to Middleton's **Ayaha** to outlast the **Kenwith Castle** and continue a summer-only ferry until World War II intervened and caused the service to close down. In 1946 Overy and Gidley re-appeared on the scene. Overy used his **Mermaid** as before, but Gidley introduced a much larger and superior vessel, the **Rivermaid I**, re-engined in 1957 with a 27 hp Lister diesel, and licensed for 62 passengers. She was joined in 1958 by a smaller launch, **Rivermaid II** (owner, L. Gidley: capacity 52 passengers) which had a Kelvin engine since replaced by a Lister diesel.

In 1974 the Gidleys retired and sold the **Rivermaid I** to Mr. Peter Moule, the present operator, who runs the ferry under the name of the Rivermaid Motor Launch Service, from May to September, Sundays excepted. The **Rivermaid I**, 36 feet long, and built at Mevagissey, is now a popular institution on the river. Her thirty-odd years of service on the ferry eclipse the records of the more glamorous paddle-steamers, of which the longest-serving, the **Reindeer**, managed only 27 years. In the autumn of 1979 a yet larger ferry was acquired, to commence operating in the 1980 season. This was the **Lady Elizabeth**, purchased from the Millbrook Steamboat Company of Plymouth, and formerly on the Drake's Island ferry. Fifty feet in length, she is fitted with a Gardner diesel engine: her passenger capacity is 113, and she has a large cabin abaft the wheelhouse.

At Kingsbridge the quay from which the steamers used to run has now been filled in by the land reclaimed for the car-park. Today the ferry operates from the Quay Promenade or the Ferry Boatyard Pontoon, according to tide. At Salcombe the steamers berthed at Custom House Quay, but the present-day landing is at Salcombe Pier, near the Ferry Inn. For most of the season four trips are made daily in each direction, and sometimes five, according as tides permit. As the ferry route is four miles, this is a good service by any standards. Since the steam ferries gave place to motor ferries perhaps the best-known personality among ferry skippers has been the late George Gidley. As a Salcombe pilot and skipper of the ferry **Rivermaid I** for many years, he was a well-loved local character, and this history of the ferry would be incomplete without paying a tribute to his long service.

Ilton Castle at Salcombe Regatta in 1925. Photo: P.N.Thomas.

EAST PORTLEMOUTH: This ferry is officially recognised as 'from time immemorial'
and is a statutory passage whose operators have monopoly rights. It is certainly much older than the
reign of Queen Anne to which period it is sometimes locally ascribed. For a great many years
it was the property of the Holdsworth family and the earliest extant reference is in a lease of
the ferry dated 23rd July 1784 from Arthur Holdsworth to Arthur Masters. ".....the said Arthur
Holdsworth......doth demise lease grant to and farm let unto the said Arthur Masters All That
the passage and ferry of the Harbour of Salcombe aforesaid And also the boat commonly called
or known by the name of Salcombe Passage Boat and also the small boat thereto belonging or
commonly used therewith which boats are now.....(indecipherable).....and being at Salcombe aforesaid and also all sails oars tackle apparel furniture profits commodities advantages and appurtenances
whatsoever to the said passage and boats or either of them belonging or in any wise appertaining
together with free liberty to carry and re-carry all passengers goods and other things whatsoever
to and from Salcombe aforesaid and elsewhere within the limits of the said passage.......".".

Other existing documents include a lease of the ferry from Arthur Howe Holdsworth to Mary
Dawe, dated 2nd November 1836: and a memorandum for lease of ferry rights dated 28th December
1897 between Arthur Frederick Holdsworth and William Distin. A blown-up photograph of this
William Distin, on duty with the ferry, forms a striking mural in the foyer of the Salcombe Hotel
today. The long association with the Holdsworth family ended in 1909 when the ferry was acquired
on 19th November by Captain Samuel Wills Ryder, a former master mariner in sail. The conveyance
from Holdsworth to Ryder contains interesting phrasing:- ".....whereas there has existed from time
immemorial a certain ferry between the town of Salcombe in the Parish of Salcombe in the said
County of Devon and the village of Portlemouth or East Portlemouth in the Parish of Portlemouth
or East Portlemouth in the same county for carrying and conveying in boats within the limits of
the said ferry all passengers and other persons having occasion for the same......." Captain Ryder
became a well-known figure in Salcombe, and built the York ('Salcombe') Hotel. The ferries left
(and still do) from the Jubilee Steps (102), just below the Hotel and the Ferry Inn. In the summer
of 1911, Captain Ryder introduced motor boats to the service. The 'Salcombe Times' noted on
26th June that year:- "On Saturday, for the first time on record, a smart little motor launch took
the place of the well-known 'man and pair of paddles' ferry which has hitherto done duty between
Salcombe and Portlemouth. The new boat, christened **King George V** is of about 20 ft. and beamy
with accommodation for about twelve people. She is fitted with a two-cylinder motor and runs
across and back under the five minutes as compared with about fifteen, which was the average
record under favourable conditions of the old rowboat. Mr. S.W. Ryder has recently acquired the
Ferry and has added considerably to the comfort of those using it by erecting a shelter on the
Portlemouth side and improving the hard. With the advent of the **King George V** the trip across the
harbour and back for a penny, which has formerly been made only on necessity, may now be looked
upon as a pleasure and must do not a little to facilitate business between Salcombe and Portlemouth".

This pioneer motor ferry lasted well into the 'twenties. It formed the pattern of four or five
successive boats, all clinker built, all around 20 ft. in length, and powered with Kelvin petrol engines.
As traffic increased, three boats were in service at any one time; only one of course being needed
in winter, when a relief boat was on the moorings and the third under repair and maintenance in
the boat house. In the 'sixties, first one and then two boats were converted to Lister diesel marine
engines. When the Salcombe Hotel's present car park was constructed, two of the older ferryboats
which had been for sometime disused, were buried amid the rubble and are still under the car
park today! Part of the ferry 'set-up' when Captain Ryder took over was the horseboat - always
known as the 'scow' - which remained in use up to about 1929.

A succession of very competent and loyal ferrymen served Captain Ryder over the years and
no record would be complete without reference to some who gave long service. In the post-Great
War period were Ned Cook (throughout the 'twenties and 'thirties); Victor Ford, who served virtually
his whole working life on the ferry from about 1920 into the late 'sixties: and Willing ('Willen')
Jarvis, who, joining as a young boatman in the early 'twenties, made the ferry his life's work until
retirement age. During the 'forties and 'fifties Fred Spry worked on the ferry - brother of the
South Sands ferryman; and Eddie ('Bubbles') Distin - son of Lifeboat Cox'n Eddie Distin who survived
the terrible 1916 disaster - was a Salcombe ferryman during the 'fifties and early 'sixties. 'Bubbles'
himself became cox'n of the lifeboat, but sadly he died prematurely in 1972 when only 53 years
of age. To approximately the same period on the ferry belonged Arthur Distin, a dour character
perhaps less loved by passengers but a very loyal individual and a first-rate seaman. During the
'sixties there was ferryman George Clements; he was also the shipwright/mechanic who serviced
the boats and their engines during the winter.

When Captain Ryder passed away the service was carried on by his sons, S.W. and W.E. (Peter)
Ryder, to both of whom we are indebted for assistance in recording the ferry's story. The Ryder
brothers sold the ferry to the Ollivers (present owners of the Salcombe Hotel) in 1971, and the
ferry remained re-associated with the hotel for the next five years. In 1976 the Ollivers resold the
ferry to Limhart Ltd. of 8 Currer Street, Bradford, West Yorkshire and thus it passed, to some
local dismay, out of local ownership. But the ferry is still statutory, requiring an all-the-year-round
service to be maintained and the boats are still manned by local men. The longest-serving of the
present ferrymen is Bill Honey, with about nine years service.

Normally one boat is adequate for the traffic, but three stoutly-built motorboats are maintained
for summer crowds. Two are carvel-built wooden boats, by Cove of Salcombe; and the third has a
fibreglass 'Cygnus' hull, fitted out by Cove's. All are powered by two cylinder Lister engines,
and their hulls are painted royal blue and are not named or numbered. The fibreglass boat is regarded
as reserve boat. None have B. of T. certificates, so passenger capacity is limited to twelve.

A strong sou'westerly gale can make conditions in the estuary very unpleasant. In bad weather,
landings on the Portlemouth side are made further upstream at Ditch End; but occasionally conditions
are such that the service has to be suspended. The Limhart ownership has recently adopted the
new name of The Salcombe Ferry Company.

*East Portlemouth: Shuttle service in operation as Salcombe ferrymen clear the queue
from Jubilee Steps.   Photo: E.T.W.Dennis, Scarborough.*

SALCOMBE - SOUTH SANDS: This is a summer-only service, but provides a direct route to
Bolt Head, below which lies the submerged wreck of the **Herzogin Cecile** in Starehole Bay, while
beyond are the cliff walks of Bolberry Down. The service was pioneered by Captain Samuel Ryder,
owner of the Portlemouth ferry and a Mr. Albert Stumbles in about 1910, and staked a place in
Salcombe's marine history by operating the first commercial motorboat in the harbour. The purpose
at the time was to carry people to tea gardens that Albert Stumbles had opened just previously.
The service was suspended during the First World War.

After the war, Theo Dickinson bought the original boat, acquired also a second boat and employed
various longshoremen to run the service. After about ten years, Theo Dickinson sold the boats
and gear to the ferrymen he was employing, William Spry and Fred Kendall. They maintained the
service in partnership until the outbreak of World War II in September 1939. The ferry was restarted
in 1946 by Jack Field, who had bought the boat **Jubilee** formerly operated by Spry. Field was joined
a few weeks later by Henry Putt, with the **Grace**, which enabled a two-boat service to be restored.

Field retired three years later and sold his interest and the **Jubilee** to Cyril Baskerville. Henry
Putt and Cyril Baskerville then ran the ferry from 1949 to 1959 when ill-health compelled the
former to retire. His son Gilbert Putt, the present proprietor, then took over his boat as from
the 1960 season but in 1964 replaced it with the **Theodora** which is still on the run today.She is
a 30 ft. carvel-built launch with a wheelhouse, fitted with a Perkins 4-cylinder diesel engine and is
licensed for 26 passengers. Cyril Baskerville then sold the **Jubilee** and worked with Gilbert Putt
in the **Theodora** until 1971, when he retired. He had served a total of 24 years full-time and 3
years part-time on the South Sands ferry, was regarded as one of the characters of the port and
had become well-known to countless visitors. The distance from Jubilee Steps to South Sands is
rather more than a mile and the service is maintained at half-hour intervals. Until 1976 landings at
South Sands at high water were at various points on the beach; while at low water all landings
were on the rock steps at Splatt Cove. An ex-army DUKW (amphibian military landing-craft) was
acquired in 1977 and provides an all-tides landing at South Sands.

Not only is the ferry route the most direct to Bolt Head, it is also the most scenic and interesting. Two-thirds of a mile from Jubilee Steps, passengers can see, on the starb'd side, the remains
of Salcombe Castle, at the water's edge. it was defended so resolutely by Sir Edmund Fortescue
in 1645 that when after four months the defenders had to surrender to the Parliamentary forces,
they were allowed to march out with the honours of war. A moment later the ferry passes North
Sands, whence a submarine cable was formerly laid to France.

The low cliff between North and South Sands is crowned by The Moult, the picturesque residence
in the last century of J.A. Froude, the historian. Here the poet Tennyson sometimes came to stay
and here he was inspired by the sound of the harbour bar in wild weather to write the immortal
poem with the lines "And may there be no moaning of the bar when I put out to sea".

1 mile

TOTNES

The Totnes Boats

Fleet Mill

Stoke Gabriel

Sharpham

Duncannon

Ashprington

Bow Creek

River Dart

Duncannon-Bow Creek Ferry

Dittisham

Greenway

Dittisham-Greenway Ferry

Old Mill Creek

Higher Ferry, Dartmouth

R.N. College

Dart Railway Ferry

DARTMOUTH

Kingswear

Lower Ferry, Dartmouth

Castle Ferry

14.

River Dart

South Devon.

THE 'TOTNES BOATS': For more than fifty years an all-the-year-round, up-and-down river ferry operated on the River Dart between Dartmouth, Dittisham and Totnes. The story begins in 1877 when most of the fleet of the Dartmouth Steam Packet Company - which had gone into liquidation - was acquired by a partnership led by a Dartmouth businessman, James Read Tolman. The four vessels which changed hands were the **Pilot, Dartmouth, Newcomin** and **Hauley.** Of these the first three had been previously employed by the D.S.P. Co. on the Railway Ferry, and river excursions: the **Hauley** ordered by the old Company for the same work, was not delivered until the fleet had passed to Tolman and partners. Two other vessels, acquired elsewhere by Tolman, were the **Kite** and the **Dart.** All except **Newcomin** were basically tugs, but adapted for passenger work also. These steamers were put to work, in addition to excursion and towage duties, on a Dartmouth-Totnes Ferry service, timetabled for the tides; and they carried passengers, parcels, market garden produce and the mails. They came to be known throughout the valley of the Dart as 'the Totnes boats'. At Dartmouth they berthed at the South end of the Quay; at Dittisham they used a long-since demolished jetty when the tide served, or were tended by the Greenway Ferry when it did not; and at Totnes they embarked and discharged passengers at the Steamer Quay on the east bank.

None of these vessels which pioneered the ferry were still there at the turn of the century. The **Pilot,** a wooden paddler with a single-cylinder engine, was sold to G.P. Ward of Teignmouth in 1879, only to be scrapped two years later. The **Dartmouth,** an iron paddler with 2-cylinder oscillating engines, went to the breakers in 1881. The **Newcomin,** a 47 ton iron river steamer, was sold to France in 1884; and the **Hauley** was bought in 1898 by a Liverpool Company, who renamed her **Greenfinch.** We have been unable to discover the fate of the **Kite** and the **Dart.**

Tolman and partners took a considerable step forward in 1880, when they took delivery from the Pollyblank Co., Kingswear, of the 73 ton, 108 ft. long iron paddle steamer **Berry Castle** (104). Offering more passenger amenities than her predecessors, **Berry Castle** was purpose-built for the Totnes-Dartmouth service and set the precedent for the 'Castle' nomenclature to which the owners adhered thereafter. With her tall 'Woodbine' funnel and large paddle-boxes, she can be readily identified in old photographs depicting scenes on the river. She gave 38 years service on the ferry and excursion work, not being broken up till the end of the Great War. Five years later, when all the original fleet except the **Hauley** had gone, Tolman and partners put into service the **Dartmouth Castle,** a paddle steamer of 59 tons built by Harvey's of Hayle. The **Dartmouth Castle** was sold in 1907 to the Youghal and Blackwater Tourist Steamship Company in the south of Ireland where she worked for six years before being scrapped.

In 1888 the **Berry Castle,** with 200 passengers aboard, went aground on a bank near Dittisham in fog at 10pm. on the 8th August. The **Dartmouth Castle,** in going to her assistance, also went ashore, but both vessels were refloated the following day without having suffered serious damage. The third steamer to be built for the service was the **Totnes Castle,** launched in Philips yard at Sandquay in 1894. She was much smaller (8), than her predecessor and the reason is difficult to understand, since trade was booming, unless it was intended she would operate the ferry in winter, when the payloads were smaller. After 18 years service she was sold to a Mrs. Mabel Biss, of Poole, Dorset. Renamed **Wareham Queen,** she plied in Poole Harbour till purchased by a Preston firm eight years later, being withdrawn in 1923 for conversion to a houseboat.

A fourth purpose-built steamer, the **Kingswear Castle,** arrived from the yard of Cox & Co., Falmouth in 1904. A steel paddler with 2-cylinder compound engines, her measurements approximated to those of the **Berry Castle,** and she set the pattern for future construction. Arguably the most handsome paddler to work the Totnes Ferry, she ran for 20 years and when she retired in 1924 was used for a while as a fever hulk before being put ashore in Fleet Mill Creek, where her remains can still be seen. A second **Dartmouth Castle,** ordered from Cox of Falmouth to replace the 1885 steamer of the same name, commenced running in 1907, the year that her namesake was sold. She was the first of that last quartet of steam paddlers which operated between the wars, and are still remembered with affection by thousands of erstwhile passengers. She was always distinguishable from her later consorts by her narrower deck, not carried out over the sponsons, and by her less substantial wheelhouse. She was probably the fastest boat of the four, though by a small margin. At the end of World War II, after 40 years service, she was withdrawn: and after her engines and upperworks had been dismantled, she was grounded in Old Mill Creek for a landing stage, a duty she still performs today.

Tolman and his partners formed the River Dart Steamboat Company Ltd. in 1906, with offices in an elegant terraced building on Dartmouth quay. The steamers were transferred to the new flag in June that year. In 1914 a replacement for the **Totnes Castle** came into service. This was the **Compton Castle**, a 97 ton steamer by Cox of Falmouth, and destined to serve on the river for 48 years. After withdrawal in 1962 she became a floating restaurant at Kingsbridge and her engine room featured in one or two T.V. films. In 1979 she was bought by Cornish Publican, Ernest Clayton, and towed to Looe, where she is now being restored to passenger carrying standards. It is hoped she may then return to the Dart. The Totnes Ferry was maintained throughout the Great War, but some of the Company's vessels were employed locally on war work.

Motor vessels made their first appearance on the ferry in 1922, when the 38 ton **Berry Castle** and 13 ton **Dittisham Castle** were completed by Philips of Dartmouth, who also supplied the 67 ton **Clifton Castle** in 1926. With their advent it became the practice to employ one of them as 'Winter boat' on the ferry, in the interests of economy. At this time the fare was 1/6 for the ten mile single passage, and 2/6 return. Meanwhile the last two paddle-steamers joined the fleet, both built at Noss by Philip's. The second **Totnes Castle** - a belated replacement for **Berry Castle,** appeared in 1923. She gave the Company 40 years hard service, but tended to 'wallow' in disturbed water and her ports had always to be screwed tight when she was well loaded. When sold in 1963 she became a floating hostel at Kingswear for amateur yachtsmen, until 1967. Disposed of for scrapping that year, she was on tow to a Plymouth shipbreakers when she foundered on 9th November off Hope Cove in Bigbury Bay, after rounding Bolt Tail in a choppy sea. **Totnes Castle** plans page 132.

The **Kingswear Castle** replaced her namesake and came into service in 1924. She ran for 41 years and was acquired on withdrawal by the Paddle Steamer Preservation Society, who are currently renovating her on the River Medway. But for only five of her 41 years on the Dart was she taking her share in working 'the Totnes boats': for this latter quartet of vessels long outlived the ferry.

In 1929 the Company lost the Post Office Contract for mails, and the withdrawal of this subsidy rendered a year-round service uneconomic. This brought the Dartmouth-Totnes Ferry to an end. The last boat to operate the run was the M/V **Berry Castle.** The service between Dartmouth and Dittisham however was continued till World War II, the final ferry run being made by the M/V **Greenway Castle**, which had been acquired in 1937. The River Dart Steamboat Co. was primarily in the excursion business and none of the vessels was exclusively employed on the ferry. Nevertheless the Dartmouth-Totnes ferry was an important venture of the Company for more than half a century and played a vital part in the economy of the Dart Valley. Beside the passenger and mail traffic, the steamer brought the produce of the valley to Totnes, for local sale or for the London Trains. At Dittisham (when the tide was too low for the jetty), and at Duncannon, the 'Totnes boat' was met by the local ferryman, who brought out baskets of salmon, and cockles, and hampers of Victoria plums and other soft fruits from riverside orchards.

Certainly few ferries worked a more enchanting passage than the 'Totnes boats', or one more rich in maritime history. On leaving Dartmouth Quay the steamer passed the 'Britannia Royal Naval College' to port and Philip's shipbuilding yard (1858) to starb'd. After $2\frac{1}{2}$ miles she was off Dittisham, with Greenway House (birthplace of Sir Humphrey Gilbert, the Elizabethan navigator) dominating a steep, finely wooded bank to the East. In midstream could be seen the Anchor Stone, reputedly a favourite smoking haunt of Sir Walter Raleigh, whose boathouse still nestles under the trees of the Eastern Shore. Then after negotiating the broad sweep of Galmpton Bay, came a

*First of the purpose built Totnes ferries **Berry Castle** is seen here at the turn of the century with a full load. Photo: Roy Barnes Collection.*

view of Sandridge House (birthplace of John Davis, discoverer of the N.W. Passage and the Davis
Straits); and a mile further upstream, a momentary glimpse of Stoke Gabriel Church, with the
oldest and largest Yew Tree in England in its churchyard. After rounding Stoke Point the steamer
was likely to be met by the ferry from the picturesque hamlet of Duncannon, before entering the
serpentine windings of Sharpham, 7 miles from Dartmouth. From the water's edge upwards the
banks here were richly wooded with lichen-clad oak; and passengers could see, on the left, the
mansion of Sharpham, white and square, cresting the hillside. Beyond lay another bend, with islets
in midstream, and the long straight reach to Totnes. Today, in the summer months, the excursion
launches of Dart Pleasure Craft Ltd. traverse the waters of what has been called, in doubtful
compliment, 'the English Rhine'; but the 'Totnes boats' with their churning paddles are no more.

DUNCANNON - BOW CREEK: Duncannon, a sheltered, picturesque hamlet on a bend of the
Dart, had a ferry to Bow Creek from time immemorial. The rights of the small quay, and a tied
house, went with the ferry, and the service was maintained by a single rowboat until its closure
in 1964. There was never a timetable, the ferry simply running as required; intending passengers
at Duncannon called the ferryman from his house, and those across the water whistled lustily and
shouted 'over!' to draw his attention.

The service was to Ashprington Point or Cornworthy Weir. Ashprington point was latterly not
accessible at low water, when passengers were embarked or landed about 80 yards downstream. By
the twentieth century however, the ferry's most important function was meeting the Dartmouth-
Totnes steamers, which hove-to in midstream to embark or discharge passengers from Cornworthy
and neighbouring villages. Until World War II, the River Dart Steamboat Company maintained an
all-the-year service to Totnes, and the ferry was in regular demand, especially on market days,
as the link with the steamer. If the paddler had passengers to land, it arrived with a flag hoisted
to warn the ferryman. A two-step platform was put down from the sponson and a deckhand assisted
the passengers while the ferryman held his boat alongside with a boathook. The operation had to
be carried out smartly as the Channel was narrow and the steamer could not afford to drift.

During World War II, the few regular ferry passengers included a Belgian seaman who was caretaker of eight interned Belgian trawlers lying in Bow Creek. The name of the ferryman during
and after the last War was Hammock. In his time the ferry left Duncannon on the lower side of
the quay. An extra service was the landing of Cafe customers at a floating tearoom run by the
Baker family on a hulk at Stoke Gabriel. In the late 'forties and throughout the 'fifties, the ferryman
was Captain Rowe, still well-remembered in the district. During his time the Stoke Gabriel tea-
hulk closed down and, then due to silting of the river, the ferry landing at Duncannon was moved
to the higher side of the quay. Here there was a waiting shed for passengers known as the
Fishermen's Shelter. Captain Rowe was succeeded as ferryman by S.J. Collins, who maintained
the service, at a 2d. fare, until its closure. He used a 17ft. rowboat, un-named, and built locally,
as his predecessors had done. His daughter and son-in-law still live in the village.

The demise of Duncannon ferry was directly due to the proliferation of the motor car. Use
of the ferry involved considerable walking on both sides of the river: today's generation prefers
the expense of driving to the floating bridge at Noss Point or Sand Quay.

DITTISHAM - GREENWAY: The origins of the Dittisham - Greenway passage are shrouded in
the mists of history but for several hundred years until the Great War, the ferry rights were vested
in the owners of Greenway House. Greenway was a manor within the parish of Churston Ferrers,
and for many generations it was held by the Gilbert family, which included the famous navigator
Sir Humphrey Gilbert (1539-1583), who was born there. The ferry must certainly pre-date the
sixteenth century and no doubt Sir Humphrey, drowned in the sinking of the **Squirrel** whilst seeking
the North West Passage, and his half-brother Sir Walter Raleigh, whose boathouse was close by,
often used the passage and must be reckoned its most distinguished passengers.

Before the motor-age, Greenway Quay was surely one of the most picturesque ferry-landings in
the country. Old photographs show the ferry bell-cote which stood within living memory, in the
centre of the quay. Today, alas, the little quay is a car park, and although the bell is retained
in a boathouse, its rustic housing has long been demolished. The quay has a slipway on the north
side, nowadays often cluttered with dinghies on car trailers, but formerly the access to the ferry
for horseriders, cattle, and wagons. In the years prior to the Great War there was a horseboat with
a ramp at one end only, and a rowboat for pedestrian traffic. The float was rowed by a crew of
two using thirty-foot sweeps. In a strong wind or tide the float could be difficult to control, but
a tug was seldom requested as a tow could cost £5! Galmpton shipyard built the floats for the
ferry, and the remains of an early one, partly burnt, can be seen on the north side of Galmpton
Creek.

The passenger fare was then $\frac{1}{2}$ d., while telegrams for Greenway House had to be carried free.
A regular passenger was Mary Ellis of Dittisham, 'the cockle-woman', with her donkey and cart.
Huntsmen often used the ferry when riding to a meet. Cattle and sheep were carried regularly to
Churston market. Hay was loaded in bales and off-loaded on to a cart after the crossing, the ferryman having to shift it! Bill Rendle, now living in retirement at Dittisham, ran the ferry for most
of his working life until 1958. He started as a youngster before the Great War, in which he served
in the Forces. Of those early years he recalls an occasion when the float fouled a large anchor,
which burst through the bottom and deck. It was an anxious moment, but the crossing was completed
safely.

Shortly before the Great War, the ferry rights were acquired by a man named Rice, who was
also Mine Host at the Ferry Hotel, Dittisham (now the Ferryboat Inn). Rice applied to get the
fare raised to 1d, for even then 6d. was not a high reward for rowing a load of 12 people across
a tideway! The case went to the Crown Court, who refused to grant the increase and awarded
costs against Rice. Shortly afterwards, Rice refused a crossing to a lone passenger (on what grounds,
nobody remembers), who was eventually rowed across by a local boatman, Sam Coombes. The
passenger sued Rice for breach of his obligation; but the case was never finished, as Rice collapsed

and died meantime in the bar of his inn. Rice's assistant was a likeable and worthy fellow named George Sage. He was on duty at Dittisham one day when the Greenway bell rang, and he dutifully rowed across. The waiting passenger was Mrs. Williams from the 'big house'. As George got out and pulled up the boat, the lanyard securing his trousers gave way, with disastrous results. Mrs. Williams was not amused, and had the unfortunate George sacked!

Bill Rendle returned to the ferry after the war, to find there was now a more convenient two-prow float in use. One evening he was on duty alone with the rowboat. A respected local resident arrived, leading his horse and was dismayed to find he was too late for the float, whose crew had finished for the day. Bill decided he could cope with the situation. Putting his coat over the horse's head, he coaxed the animal with the owner's help into the rowboat and pulled across strongly, the horse fortunately not panicking, and disembarking, head still covered, without incident. Today Bill Rendle lives in a charming Dittisham cottage, its front garden filled with fuchsias, rhododendrons and clianthus, and its orchard reaching down to the bight of the creek. He enjoys reminiscing over his days as a ferryman.

For some years Bill Harris, a rustic character and part-time barber, worked on the ferry. The service operated till 10pm. daily but it was customary to wait up to a quarter of an hour for last-drinkers at the inn. One night as Bill Harris was securing the boat before going home he thought he heard a cry of 'Boat, ahoy!' But no one appeared "oo is it? I can't own yer voice!" shouted Bill. When the call was repeated he realised it was an owl! In those bygone times the first vehicle daily would be the 'fish trap' from Brixham, arriving at Greenway Quay. This was a pony and trap which brought fish landed by Brixham trawlers for sale in Cornworthy and other villages of the area. Life for the ferrymen however had its livelier moments. Bill Rendle remembers when a bull, enraged at being urged toward the float, plunged into the water and swam across, Bill and the farmer giving chase in the motor ferry which had now replaced the rowboat. The farmer expressed his confidence that the swim would exhaust the bull and they would easily secure him when they landed. It was an error of judgement. The bull emerged from the water as wild as before, went on the rampage and had to be shot soon after. Before World War II the horseboat, coming to be known as the car ferry, was propelled from abeam by a motorboat, and the fare had gone up to 3d. 1d. was charged for 'market baskets'. These were a regular cargo, being filled with the once-famed Dittisham plums, Victorias, grown in local orchards and put aboard the Dart steamers for Totnes. Baskets of Dart Salmon were also loaded for the Totnes Boats, which hove-to off Dittisham for the ferry to come alongside.

During World War II the River Dart Steamboat Co., took over the running of Dittisham ferry, but steamers were never employed on the service. After the war two partners, Herbert Fletcher and George Passmore acquired the ferry rights for £600. The service of passengers and market baskets to the steamers was not resumed however, as the year-round Totnes ferry had ceased and no calls were made at Dittisham on the summer excursions. But the ferry was kept busy serving the buses to and from Paignton and carrying Churston and Torquay schoolchildren during term-time. Among regular passengers were the gardeners at Agatha Christie's. Cattle were still conveyed and Percy Andrews remembers a cow ferried to Greenway which promptly entered the water and swam back!

Fletcher and Passmore were succeeded in 1964 by a man named Richardson, who brought to the passage a jet-propelled pontoon built by Rowhedge Ironworks Company Ltd. Two Lister air-cooled diesel engines drove Rowhedge Gill Hydraulic Jet-propulsion units, and the float was thus able to operate in very shallow waters. It could load six cars. The motor tugs were sold off and the horseboat/car ferry lay disused on the beach for some months before being towed to Stoke Gabriel for use as a boat pontoon. The Jet Ferry however was not a success. It broke down constant-ly, usually through sucking up weed: and its suction disturbed the beach at Dittisham, scouring out pits deep enough to endanger young bathers. One disillusioned local resident told me "It was no good arranging to meet anyone the other side at any particular time, nor reckoning on catching a bus. You just didn't know when you'd get there". Two years of this decided Richardson that enough was enough. The jet ferry was towed off to a new sphere of work at Portsmouth, and Richardson surrendered the ferry rights to his very capable assistant. This was Roy Andrews, who still runs the ferry today. The vehicular traffic has been abandoned, but two smart motor boats (a small winter ferry, **Arrow**, and a larger summer ferry, now **Mary D.**) maintain a timetable service. A Government grant of £500 p.a. is made to ensure the ferry's viability.

HIGHER FERRY, DARTMOUTH: Although this is the 'youngest' of the principal ferries on the Dart, its story is not without interest and it can claim distinction on several counts: it was almost the first ferry in England to be run by steam, second only to the **Jemima** at Torpoint, 1826: it was the first diesel-electric ferry in the West country, and it operates the only paddle-driven vessel in the south-west today. The original statute which authorised this vehicular ferry was the Floating Bridge Act of 17th June 1830. It was under this Act that Sir John Seale, Bart., and his son Sir Henry Paul Seale (owner of the Sandquay Shipyard) built the new road from Noss to Hillhead and the first floating bridge ferry, in 1831. Chains were laid between new slipways at Sandquay and Noss; from Sandquay slip a road was laid to meet the Modbury Turnpike at the Ship-in-Dock: and from Noss slip the ferry road climbed steeply to meet the Kingswear-Paignton turnpike at Hillhead, half a mile beyond the Nethway tollhouse. The Seales engaged J.M.Rendel, a rising marine engineer, to instal a 'steam-bridge' chain ferry of his own design. No picture seems to have survived, but Rendel's craft, which inaugurated the service in 1831, was not a success. A few years later however Rendel successfully designed a steam ferry for Torpoint, and left a record that 'by the mistake he made and the experience he gained in Dartmouth, he was able to assure the directors of the Torpoint ferry that steam would work'.

Meanwhile the ferry at Dartmouth had gone over to horse-propulsion. An 1848 picture of this ferry shows it to have been a pontoon with some covered deck-space and a wagon-roofed shelter where the horse worked a winch which wound the vessel across the river by rope. Business was far from brisk in those early days; the road and floating-bridge were never a real success until the

Higher Ferry: An 1866 photograph. The horse can just be made out in the winch-house.

advent of the motor car. A photograph of 1866 shows a later horse-driven ferry, beam-loading, with a lifting prow and deck space for possibly two wagons (107). The horse can be seen looking disconsolately from the wooden hut where he paces round turning a winch reminiscent of the old cider-presses. In May 1861 there had been a complaint about the ill-treatment and overworking of the 'pony' which appears from another account to have been blind.

By this time however the ferry was under new ownership. The arrival of the railway (Totnes 1847, Torquay 1848) had made the turnpike - and therefore the ferry - uneconomic. An 1850 newspaper notice shows the ferry bankrupt and up for sale. John Williams of Plymouth became the new owner. In 1867 a steam ferry was built for Williams by Philip & Son in which the steam engine wound and unwound chains after the same principle as the horse and rope. No photographs seem to have survived. In those days there was an inn, the 'Britannia', on the Kingswear side; and prior to the enforcing of statutory closing hours, Dartmouth workers in Philip's shipyard used to congregate here on landing, and once in, were loathe to leave. They had 6d. "workman's weekly" tickets for the ferry.

A new steam ferry took over the service in 1896, with machinery and boiler by Lees Anderson & co. The 90hp. compound engine wound wires over external sheaves. This iron-hulled vessel could accommodate four vehicles, and lasted till 1920. A passage time of three minutes was advertised. In November 1896 the old floating bridge with its engine, boiler and chains, was up for sale, but it is reported to have been in a dilapidated condition. Financially the ferry continued to languish and by the end of the Great War, during which it was doubtless overworked and under-repaired, it came on to the market and into new ownership. According to company records the Floating Bridge ferry was conveyed to Philip & Son Ltd. - the present operators - on 28 July 1920, by "John Williams and Mortgagee". The cost to Philip of buying up the shares was £2,000, and for this they now owned also the turnpike from Hillhead to Ship-in-Dock.

The new owners meant business and constructed a new steam ferry, Yard No. 584, but incorporating the 1896 steam engine. There was an eighteen-month suspension of service while this work was carried out. The new craft was paddle-driven, but using wires and guides, the system which has been employed since. No.584 measured 55ft. in length x 32ft. beam and had deck-space for eight cars. With her tall buff-and-black funnel she was to be a familiar feature of the Dart scene for the next 40 years.

Among the many distinguished passengers she carried were the Princesses Elizabeth and Margaret in 1938. Their Royal Highnesses crossed in a Grey Cars coach when Sea-Rangers at a local camp, in a party visiting the Royal Naval College. It was a fateful visit, for there, Princess Elizabeth first met her future husband, Prince Philip. Distinguished passengers on the ferry were usually either V.I.P.s going to the college, or 'show-biz' personalities on summer tours at Torbay theatres. Cary Grant, Sid James and Kenneth More are among film stars whom the crews can remember making the crossing. The new ferry had not long been in operation when a bizarre mishap occured on board. A herd of cattle were being crossed from Noss to Sandquay when a nervous bullock squeezed through the engine-room door and plunged head-first nearly 8 feet into the stokehold, in the confined space before the boiler. This was a major crisis as there was no way the live beast could be removed, and without stoking, the ferry was immobilised. A vet was hurriedly secured at Dartmouth to put the creature out of its misery and enable the carcase to be hauled clear.

The only fatality on this passage occurred in the late 'twenties with the death of 'Peg-leg' Ferris. He was a fish-salesman who crossed daily from Brixham, and after selling in Strete and other South Ham villages, returned in the evening. In those days it was not customary to close the prow gates of the ferry if conditions were calm. On this occasion Ferris drove his van on to the ferry, and is believed to have suffered a fit or stroke at that moment, as he drove right over the car deck and into the river. Disabled as he was, he drowned before help could reach him.

At about this time Totnes Rural District Council agreed to accept responsibility for the Noss-Hillhead ferry road, which must have been a matter of considerable relief to Philip and Son. Some years later the Company's managing director, Mr. Sauter persuaded Dartmouth Borough Council to take over the road from Sandquay to Ship-in-Dock! Thus after a hundred years the roads built by the Seales were separated from the ferry undertaking.

During World War II, a Torquay lorry which crossed by the Higher Ferry every day on general haulage work, was lost overboard. The driver had parked on the car-deck, and left the cab. The lorry apparently had a defective handbrake. It broke through the gates and went over the prow into the river. About eighteen months later the ferry wire chanced to pick up the lorry's chassis, and skipper Fred Mills steered the wreckage to the slip. Of the cab and truckwork there was no sign. All chain and wire ferries face the possibility of cable parting, and the consequences of going adrift and needing a tug. The Higher Dart ferry uses ex-colliery pithead cables (the finest wire ropes obtainable), but a breakage occurred shortly after the last war which left the ferry to its own devices. In a north easterly wind and tide, Steam ferry No.584 parted a wire and the consequent strain on the other caused that to part also. The ferry, now completely adrift, was swept downstream to off the gasworks, with Skipper Mills signalling for Philip's tug. The tug however was not immediately available, and the ferry had to let go its $\frac{1}{2}$-ton anchor. This was an emergency anchor with no means for winching up again; so when a tug finally collected the ferry the anchor had to be cut loose and left on the river-bed.

Among well-remembered skippers of steam-ferry days who have now passed on, were Albert Widdicombe, who was a skipper of the pre-1920 ferry, Jimmy Ellis, Wilf Hayter, and Alf May; an ex-Falkland Islands tug engineer. They were followed by the skippers who were destined to see the change-over from steam to diesel-electric:- Fred Mills, whose 40 years of service constitute a record for the ferry (1930-1970) and Vic Anderson from 1956, who is the senior skipper today. The steam ferry crews' duty hours were 5am. - 12 noon, or 12 noon to 10pm. Bunkering, fire-lighting and steam-raising occupied the early hours of the first shift. The deckhand joined the skipper and engineer at 7am. when the service started. The introduction of the diesel-electric ferry meant a welcome later-rising for crews on the first shift, but it meant also that the ferry could be run by two men, a third hand being employed in the summer only.

The changeover was announced on 6th July 1960 by the 'South Devon Journal' as follows:- "The old paddle-driven ferry at Dartmouth with its 1896 steam engine, is to be replaced". The new floating bridge, like its predecessors, was purpose-built at Noss Yard by Philip & Son, and is still in service. Measurements are 84ft. x 32ft. x 6ft.10ins: the prows, at 28ft. are longer than those of the steam ferry. This is an advantage when embarking vehicles on a falling tide. The car deck is 24ft. wide and accommodates 15 average-size cars with ease, in three rows. All controls are worked from the skipper's elevated bridge. A simple handwheel controls the direction in which the paddles rotate. By means of another handwheel one paddle can be increased in speed and the other reduced within limits: this assists the ferry to combat strong tides. Each paddle is driven by a 45hp. engine working at 40rpm. The crossing, subject to rise and fall of tides, is about 440 yards and the present ferry can cross in three minutes without putting the diesel-electric motors under full load. After withdrawal, the steam ferry had its engine and boiler removed and was then towed to Kingsbridge for scrapping. Her boiler was in use till recently at Noss shipyard, for steaming wood.

The new ferry - bearing the name **Philip**, had been at work little more than a year when it was in the news over 'the disappearing Bentley'. It was nine o'clock one Sunday morning when a Bentley automatic saloon was driven on to the ferry, the driver getting out to visit the toilet. Before he returned, and when the ferry was in midstream, the Bentley started; and to the astonishment of crew and passengers, crashed through the gates and disappeared over the prow. Skipper Vic Anderson had the ferry's boat lowered very smartly, and an attempt was made to secure the still floating car and tow it to shore. It was not to be, however. The car filled and disappeared into 25ft. of water. A few hours later it was located by a diver from the R.N. College, raised by the Harbourmasters' lifting craft and landed on Moore's quay.

The service operates daily from 7am. to 10.50pm., the last boat leaving Sandquay at 10.45pm. Apart from the first and last trips, a shuttle, not timetable, service is worked. Crossings sometimes have to be suspended when very strong sou'westerly or nor'easterly winds prevail, particularly when these coincide with spring tides. When the ferry is under lateral pressure from combined wind and tide, the guide-wires are pulled out in a bight, and may snag on the fore and aft sheaves. To prevent this it is often necessary for the skipper to put the deckhand ashore on the slip, and back the ferry off while his mate lashes the guide wires to a greater tension. The annual overhaul of the ferry normally occupies about two weeks in the early Spring. As there is no relief car-ferry, this closure of the service is always advertised to traffic well in advance. Pedestrian traffic, which is very light, is then catered for by a motorboat ferry (capacity 3 passengers) - a works boat provided from Noss Shipyard.

Business at Higher Ferry has changed much over the years. At one time the ferry waited for cars to appear; today cars are invariably queued up, awaiting the ferry. Equestrian passengers were once common, as there was a busy blacksmith's forge at Sandquay: today horse-riders are rare, as the smith now operates from a van as a mobile farrier. Herds of cattle and sheep used to be a familiar sight on the car-deck: today animal traffic is mostly conveyed in cattle-vans. Naval personnel once strode the deck, to or from Britannia Railway Halt: today the halt is little used and officers and men off duty wear civilian clothes. Truly, "the times change, and we change with them".

DART RAILWAY FERRY: Latest on the scene of all the Dart ferries is that which has plied for over 100 years between Kingswear railway pier and Dartmouth's 'Station without trains or rails'. Today, when we have become accustomed to a decimated railway system, a 'station without trains or rails' evokes no comment; but in 1864, when this service commenced, Dartmouth Station with its floating platform was a novelty and a talking point and undoubtedly gave this ferry service its major distinction.

The act incorporating the Dartmouth and Torbay Railway was passed in 1857, and by 1861 the line had reached from Torre on the South Devon Railway to Churston (known till 1868 as Brixham Road). Plans were then considered for taking the line across the river to Dartmouth itself. The House of Lords rejected this proposal however and the initial scheme was revived for a terminus at Kingswear and a steam ferry across to Dartmouth. Eventually the line opened on the 16th August

1864. The act invested rights of ferry in the Railway Company, but it was to be 37 years before their successors, the Great Western Railway assumed responsibility for its operation, and the service was worked from its inception by lessees - the Dartmouth Steam Packet Company. For the first four weeks the Company used their 101-ton wooden paddle tug **Pilot**, which met all trains at Kingswear; times of arrival at Dartmouth being included in the railway timetable. The **Pilot** was then succeeded by the purpose-built ferry **Newcomin**, and reverted to packet and excursion work, serving as relief ferry when required. The **Newcomin** was a 47 ton iron paddler built at Blackwall. She was destined to give twenty years service on the ferry. Within 12 months the Company had taken delivery of a smart cross-channel paddle steamer, the **Eclair**, and endeavoured to establish a service to St. Malo and the Channel Islands. In this venture however the ferry proved a liability rather than an asset, as it involved train passengers in a double change, and the Cross-Channel service was soon abandoned.

In 1869 the **Newcomin** was joined on the ferry by the **Dolphin**, a 61 ton iron paddler purpose-built by Harveys of Hayle. This vessel had some unusual design features. She was a double-ender, with an ingenious arrangement of two drop-rudders which enabled her to steam ahead in either direction and very slightly reduced the crossing time, as she could berth more quickly than a conventional vessel. She was skippered, in shifts, by Captains Thorn and Gurney and her engineers were Fred and Edwin Roper. On 7th March 1902 King Edward VII and Queen Alexandra crossed from Kingswear by the **Dolphin** when the King was going to lay the foundation stone of the Royal Naval College. Mrs. Kathleen Davies of Kingswear has a photo of the **Dolphin** on that crossing, dressed overall with bunting, and showing the King wearing his Admiral's uniform, on the open bridge with the skipper. Other steamers of the Company which appeared on the ferry from time to time either to double-up when traffic was heavy, or relieve the regular ferries when refitting, were the **Guide**, (104 ton wooden paddle tug) and the **Dartmouth** (42 ton river excursion paddler).

In 1877 the Dartmouth Steam Packet Company was wound up and its vessels (except the **Guide**, sold to Milford Haven) were acquired by J.R. Tolman and partners, who also took over the lease of the railway ferry. By the 1880s **Dolphin** was the sole regular ferry, with the **Hauley** as relief boat.

In 1901 the Great Western Railway, deciding not to renew Tolman's lease, took over the running of the ferry themselves, and bought the **Dolphin** from their former lessees. She continued to run until sold for scrap in 1908, after nearly 40 years continuous service. The unidentifiable remains of a very old paddler can still be seen on the north bank of the entrance to Old Mill Creek, and it is possible that we have here all that remains of the ferry **Dolphin**.

Her successor was the immortal **The Mew**, which was to become an institution in the life of the river (111). Although broken up in 1955, she is remembered with great affection by thousands of her former passengers, local folk and visitors alike: for in days when everyone travelled by rail, **The Mew** was the beginning or end of everyone's journey. Purpose-built by Cox of Falmouth, **The Mew** was a 117 ton twin screw steel vessel with a passenger capacity of about 520, and a maximum speed of 10 knots. She was 14ft. shorter than the **Dolphin** but 7ft. wider in the beam, and a reversion to orthodox construction, with a counter stern.

During the Great War she conveyed countless British soldiers from Kingswear troop trains, and a photograph of 1914 shows her decks packed with men of the 7th Battalion London Regiment on their way to the front (110). After the war **The Mew** was altered to permit the carriages of two commercial vans of up to 2 tons unladen weight, or 4 private cars. Her saloon was cut back to provide a vehicle space at the stern, where the deck was strengthened: and the opportunity was taken to replace her open bridge by a covered wheelhouse. This meant of course that the G.W.R. were now, to a small extent, in competition with their lessees on the Lower Ferry for vehicular traffic. The pontoon and gangway roofs were raised at the same time, to give headroom for G.W.R. vans to use the ferry, and hinged flaps were fitted to the landing edge of the pontoons where **The Mew** side-loaded the vehicles.

Public consternation was caused when in 1925 the Railway refused to renew the Lower Ferry lease to Casey and Heal, presented the rights to the Dartmouth Borough Council, and withdrew the Lower Ferry car floats. **The Mew** was now the only alternative to the Higher Ferry for vehicular traffic, and was obliged also to take herds of cattle, pigs and sheep. The pontoons and their bridges were those which are still in use, and one has only to walk on them today to realise the congestion that must have constantly occurred, and the discomfort, if not risk, to passengers. Complaints were loud and long, and (see under Lower Ferry) were voiced in the press. Conditions did not return to normal until the new lessees of the Lower Ferry re-introduced the car Floats.

The Mew's greatest adventure came in World War II when she was over thirty years old. On 30th May 1940 she was abruptly requisitioned by the Admiralty to take part in the evacuation of our army at Dunkirk. Her crew, under Captain Palmer, volunteered to a man to go with her, and were ordered to proceed to Dover, and thence to Dunkirk. Notwithstanding **The Mew**'s business-like appearance and her record of reliability, this was a tall order. The ship had been designed for short river crossings and not for continuous steaming. The boiler room temperature rose to 120° and the firemen had to wear jackets in those conditions to protect their arms from the heat of the white-hot furnaces. The engine-room staff worked two hours watch and watch-about, and the firemen's feet suffered from the hot deck plates of the stokehold, as **The Mew** ran the gauntlet of German U-boats and kept her engines at 'full ahead' till Dover was safely reached after 28 hours steaming. Then came anti-climax. The senior naval officer at Dover decided that **The Mew** was unsuitable for the work required at Dunkirk beach; too large for beach embarkations, and too slow for towing duties. On 2nd June, Captain Palmer was given permission to return to Dartmouth as soon as new firebars could be fitted to replace those warped and clinkered from the ship's dash up-channel. The return passage was made safely, **The Mew** resumed her ferry crossing and though German bombers periodically raided the Dart estuary, she came through the war unscathed.

At her first refit after the war **The Mew**'s appearance was modernised when her original stove-pipe funnel was replaced at Philips' yard by a shorter stack of wider diameter and her for'ard

*Dart Railway Ferry: Troops of the 7th Batallion, London Regiment throng the decks of **The Mew** in 1914*

cabins were enlarged. Her ownership changed when the Great Western Railway ceased to exist at midnight on 31st December 1947, and British Railways became the new operators of the Dart ferry.

Internationally famous author Derek Lambert, then a junior reporter on a West country paper, was a regular passenger on **The Mew** in those early post-war years, and in his recent book "Don't Quote Me But...." he tells how he met his first love on the decks of **The Mew**. "My only distraction from learning my trade" he confesses "was the girl on the ferry". Every day she crossed from Kingswear at the same time as he, and for weeks he gazed at her across the decks. On a day when he had been fortuitously given two theatre tickets he plucked up the courage to introduce himself...... learning her name was Maureen.......took her out that evening, and experienced his first kiss! One wonders how many romantic encounters **The Mew** must have known in her 46 years of crossing the Dart fifty times a day!

The ship was normally worked with a crew of four:- skipper, engineer, a deckhand and a fireman. The fireman had to act as additional deckhand when berthing. Two crews worked in shifts. The first shift came on at 5.45am. and worked the ferry from 6am. to 2pm. The next shift worked from 2 - 10.55pm., but one of the crewmen was replaced at 10pm. by a nightwatchman who had the job of preparing the fire for the next day's steaming. In foggy weather a Dartmouth station porter was stationed on the pontoon with a handbell (!) to guide the ferry to her berth, but no such provision was made on the Kingswear side. One Christmas Eve in the later 'thirties **The Mew** which had a locomotive, not marine boiler, required the immediate attention of a boilersmith. The G.W.R. called out Robert Girling (Newton Abbot loco-shed boilersmith) to go to the ship and effect repairs by night. His wife had perforce to carry the role of Father Christmas for their daughters. **The Mew** was thus the inadvertent cause of destroying the girls' cherished myth of Santa Claus.

At length the economics of coal fuel and a wages bill for 8 crew told against this grand old ship: but she was far from worn out when British Railways decided to withdraw her in 1954. She made her last trip on the 8th October that year and the people of Dartmouth and Kingswear made it a nostalgic occasion. As Captain Bob Legg took her across the river for the last time, a chorus of sirens sounded from ships in the harbour, and rockets soared into the sky. The Dartmouth Borough Band played the National Anthem and Auld Lang Syne. There were valedictory speeches by the Mayor of Dartmouth and the Chairman of Kingswear Parish Council. Thousands of local people lined the banks of the river. Few humble ferry-steamers can have had a more memorable swan-song.

Finally, she was towed to Plymouth for breaking-up and today the only reminders of her long reign on the ferry are the raised roofs of the pontoon gangways and the remains of the hinged flaps by which vehicles were driven aboard. Eight skippers had commanded her during the 46 years:- Captains Boxall, Brown, Palmer, Harris, Leggs, Coombes, Chase and Legg. In her last years senior deckhand George Clements was Relief Skipper. Her first engineers were Edwin and Fred Roper, who had previously served in the **Dolphin**. In August 1978 the 'Western Morning News' reported that a 24 inch scale model of **The Mew** had just been completed by Felicity Vallance of Ilfracombe, as a nostalgic tribute to the ship that had ferried her daily from Kingswear to school in Dartmouth in pre-war years.

The replacement for **The Mew** eventually took the form of two 35-ton sister diesel ferries, the **Humphrey Gilbert** and the **Adrian Gilbert**, built by M.W. Blackmore & Sons of Bideford in 1955. Just under 60ft. in length, wooden-hulled and sporting dummy funnels, they were handy vessels for manoeuvring in a busy estuary and able to make a quicker crossing. However, they were unable to carry vehicular traffic and the railway had to surrender this to the Lower Ferry.

When British Rail abandoned the line south of Goodrington on 30th December 1972, the ferry rights and both vessels and the landing pontoons were put up for sale. Since the service had been making a loss for some years, there were bids only for the two boats: but Dartmouth Borough Council, anxious to preserve a valuable public amenity, purchased the service after very lengthy negotiations. The council considered that by building a workshop at Old Mill Creek for the maintenance of boats for this and the Lower Ferry, already in their possession, their Ferry Department as a whole would save sufficient money to offset the losses and achieve viability. This in fact

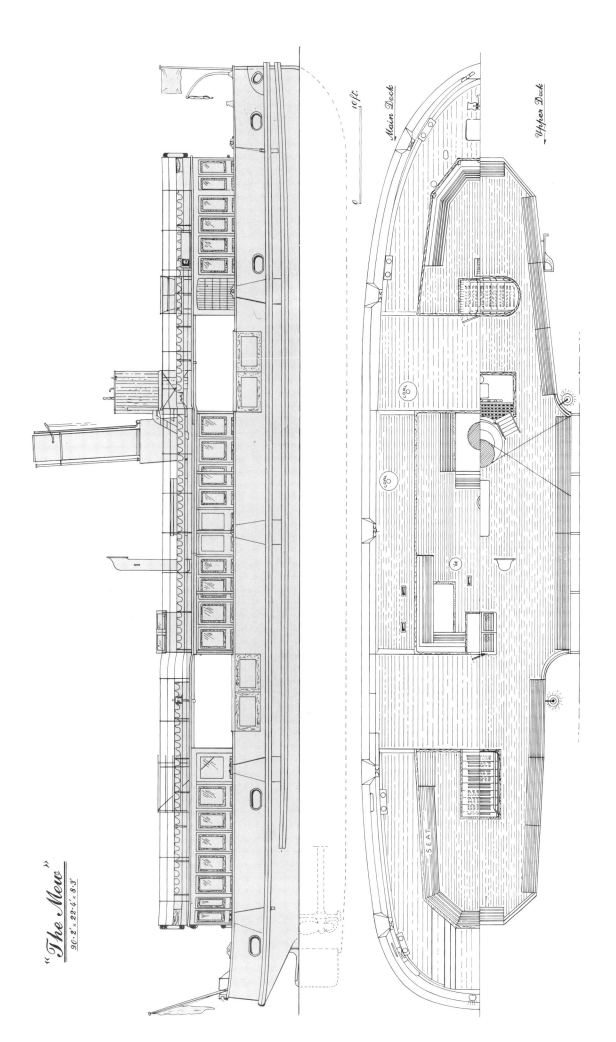

"The Mew"
90.2' x 22.4' x 8.3'

Main Deck

10 ft.

Upper Deck

COAL

COAL

V.R.

SEAT

The Mew. Service: Dart Railway Ferry (1908-1955).
From a plan courtesy National Maritime Museum, Greenwich.

Dart Railway Ferry proved to be the case during the short time when the ferries were owned by the Borough. Local Government Re-organisation came on 1st April 1974 and the ferry thereby passed into the hands of the South Hams District Council who ran it for 4 years during which they declared a loss of between £5,000-£8,000. This was largely due to high administrative costs, but it was sufficient to hoist a large question-mark over the ferry's future.

In October 1976 the 'Western Morning News' reported that the South Hams District Council were considering selling the ex-Railway Ferry and that Messrs. Padden and Crews (Dart Pleasure Craft) wished to buy it or run in competition with it: but that after talks between the parties the latter course had been decided against. The following month, however, the ferry was put out to tender by the Council. Tenders were invited for the complete set-up, or both boats and pontoons separately. Dart Pleasure Craft tendered for all possibilities. After much political in-fighting, the two **Gilbert** ferries were sold to a Cornwall firm for use on the St. Mawes ferry and the pontoons were bought by the Dart Harbour & Navigation Authority for a nominal sum. The Authority was instructed to see that an adequate ferry service was run between the pontoons. Dart Pleasure Craft tendered to do just that and were granted a licence to run from 1st January 1977.

The two **Gilberts** being no longer available, the new operators used one of their river cruisers on the ferry, **Queen Boadicea II**, an ex-Thames pleasure craft, with her sister ship **Queen Boadicea** as relief boat. This arrangement continued for eighteen months. Meanwhile, down in Cornwall, the two **Gilberts** had proved totally unsuitable for the long-haul ferry across the Fal Estuary and their disappointed owners had managed to sell them back to British Rail! According to local rumour, their disappointment was assuaged by a considerable profit which they made on the deal! Readers who are taxpayers may find it difficult to smile at what followed. British Rail discovered the boats were also unsuitable for the work they had in mind (on the Thames) and re-sold them at a loss! It was early in 1978 that the Gilbert vessels came on the market again. Dart Pleasure Craft purchased the **Adrian Gilbert** and she went back into service on her old 'run' in July 1978, with **Queen Boadicea** remaining as the relief boat.

The **Humphrey Gilbert** seemed unlikely to return to the West country. Both vessels had originally gone to the Thames to work the Tilbury-Gravesend ferry, for which they were not retained, and the **Humphrey Gilbert** after spending some months laid up at Newhaven, arrived at Greenwich in August 1978, having reputedly been acquired by Meridian Line Cruises. She was still lying in a creek at Greenwich fifteen months later when she was purchased by the Millbrook Steamboat Co. to work the Drakes' Island ferry, at Plymouth.

Meanwhile the **Adrian Gilbert** (capacity 150 passengers) maintains the Dart ex-Railway ferry today. Although summer traffic is profitable, this cannot be the case during the remainder of the year. On one sunny October Sunday recently I counted three passengers leave the ferry as I and four others (two were children) went aboard. On the return trip we carried two and only three were awaiting the next crossing. The Torbay Steam Railway, which took over British Rail's

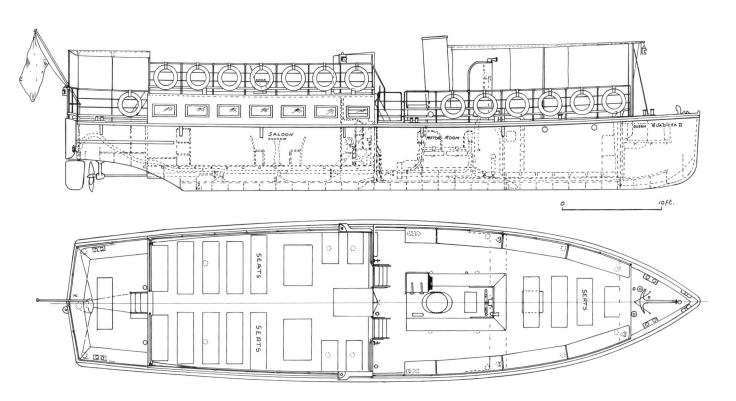

Queen Boadicea II. Service: Dart Railway Ferry since 1976.
From a plan courtesy National Maritime Museum, Greenwich.

Kingswear branch on 31st December 1972, now operates only in the summer. The ferry then meets all trains and benefits from the rail traffic. But unless the railway can secure enough school and commuter traffic to make possible a year-round service, the impartial observer cannot but feel that a single ferry service offering both covered passenger accommodation and greater vehicular deck-space is the real need of the Lower Dart.

DARTMOUTH LOWER FERRY; is certainly as old as Dartmouth itself. The Close Rolls, a series of writs and orders made under the Great Seal by the Sovereign in mediaeval times, show that the ferry was a monopoly as early as 1365, the rights being acquired in that year by one William Carey. The monopoly had been created by the Crown to ensure regular communications to and from Dartmouth. In the Mayor of Dartmouth's Accounts for the years 1531-3 it is noted that as payment for the ferry boat "Master Korn payed at dyvers tymys 4s". In 1540 we find John Leland, Henry VIII's antiquary, recording in his Itinerary: "I ferrid over to Kingswear". We know that a Robert Colyns held the ferry in 1558 (the year of Elizabeth I's accession), and Collins Quay Kingswear still preserves his name. In 1675 John Ogilby, author and printer in Restoration times, explains in his 'Britannia': "You ferry over the Dart (3 furlongs in width here) and on the other side pass through a village (Kingswear) of about 2 furlongs extent." Although it is virtually certain that horseriders and cattle were carried, there appears to have been no provision for wheeled traffic until the mid-nineteenth century. Certainly Fanny Burney, the diarist, got to Kingswear in a chaise circa 1810 but could get no further.

The Ordnance Survey map of 1809 shows that Kingswear ferry landing transferred to the north side of Waterhead Creek and named Hoodown Passage. In 1863 however, engineering works due to the construction of the Dartmouth & Torbay Railway caused the ferry to be transferred back again, the railway company undertaking to build the present slip for the purpose. By the following year, when the line was opened for traffic, they were in negotiation with Mr. G.F. Luttrell (Lord of the manors of Churston Ferrers and Kingswear) for purchase of the rights of the Lower Ferry, which would be in competition with their own steam ferry. Mr. Luttrell sold these rights in 1873 to the South Devon Railway Company, which had meantime absorbed the Dartmouth and Torbay. The Conveyance of the Company 1873 recites that George Fownes Luttrell became possessed of the ferry under the will of John Fownes Luttrell dated 9th April, 1805 (proved 11th May, 1916) and an indenture between George Fownes Luttrell and Thomas Pensford dated 17th October, 1872. The draft heads of agreement dated 1863 contained a condition that the title thereto be accepted without enquiry or dispute.

The South Devon Railway leased the lower ferry to local operators in 1877, the lease to run until 29th September, 1925. This arrangement was inherited by the Great Western Railway who became owners of the ferry when they absorbed the South Devon by an Act of 1878.

The fifty most glorious years of the lower ferry, when it was run by the Casey family of Kingswear, began in 1897 when bewhiskered John Casey and his brother George leased the ferry from the railway at £73 a year. I have seen the original lease, now in the possession of John Casey's grand-daughter, and its tariff makes interesting reading:- Passenger toll ($\frac{1}{2}$ d.), dog, pram or bag of potatoes (1d.); sheep ($1\frac{1}{2}$ d.); horse, pony, ass, cattle (2d.); pack of wool (4d.); coach and four (4/-). The service was maintained by rowing boats and horseboats propelled by sweeps. The fairly-complete remains of one of these horseboats, which could carry 2 carts and horses, lies today in Waterhead Creek: but it is hidden by trees from the road and you must walk the south foreshore to find it.

Among the early ferrymen who worked up to and during the Great War were Bill Cornish, Tom Squires, Charlie Kelland, Tom Tribble, Eli Escon, Jack Cowlan, George Riddale, and Tommy Howard. John Casey died in 1901, his son Thomas Casey inheriting his interest in the ferry. Thomas Casey and his uncle George ran the service for eight Edwardian years until 1909, when George Casey retired (he died the following year), and Tom Casey took a partner, walrus-moustached Frederick Heal.

In 1911 the Mayor of Dartmouth, Mr. Lort Phillips, complained at a Borough Council meeting of overcrowding of passengers on the Lower Ferry and said he feared a 'frightful calamity'. His remarks were taken up by the Press. Casey and Heal immediately published a spirited denial in the offending newspaper, refuting the charge with professional dignity. For some years the horseboat had been handled by a steam pinnace, the **Forester** (114), named after the ancient order to which Casey belonged, and about 1914 a more powerful tug, the **Hauley**, was acquired as well. Hauley is one of Dartmouth's great names, John Hauley being a local merchant venturer and shipowner, who distinguished himself thwarting a French invasion in the reign of Richard II. The rowboat ferries ceased in 1915 when they were replaced by the steam launch **Relief** which had a capacity of about 25 passengers.

Great pride was taken in the appearance of these three steamers. Former ferryman George Riddals recalls that their brasswork was always gleaming, cleaned with brickdust in winter and 'Brasso' in summer. When the **Relief** was withdrawn for boiler cleaning or repairs, either **Forester** or **Hauley** would take over her duties; but as these tugs had no Board of Trade passenger certificates, they were limited to 12 passengers. With the improved service brought by the steamers, the toll was increased to 1d. When the Caseys' lease ran out on 29th September 1925, the Great Western Railway, who perhaps wished to concentrate on their own Railway Ferry, did not renew it: but they gave no reason. Instead they presented the ferry rights unconditionally to the Dartmouth Borough Council for a nominal sum of £100, with use of the Kingswear slip at a rental of £5 per annum. The then Mayor of Dartmouth (Dr. Henry Campbell) wished Casey and Heal to reapply for the rights, but it was not to be. Tom Casey was an independent character, and when he studied the terms of the Council's lease and the extent of supervision they proposed to exercise, he would have none of it, and refused to tender.

Heal now dropped out of the partnership, but Casey, not to be outdone, used his motor boat **I'll try**, which had replaced the **Relief**, to continue the service in opposition to the regular ferry. He obtained the use of Gibb's Steps, a few yards south of the Kingswear slip, and being a well-

*Harry Evans on the **Forester** and Tom Tribble on Kingswear beach watch drovers getting their cattle aboard the float.
Photo: Kathleen Davis.*

known and much-respected character, enjoyed good patronage for his passenger-only service. The revenue without a horseboat however was much reduced, and after less than two years Tom Casey reluctantly abandoned the ferry which had been his life's work. He died in 1978, aged 95, having never lost his love of the river, nor his pride in the near-fifty years service his family had given to it.

The new lessees of the regular ferry were two partners, Peters and Heselton. The **Forester**, now about 60 years old, was withdrawn, but they purchased the **Hauley** and converted her to a motor-tug. Between the expiry of Casey's lease and the new partnership taking over, there had been a lapse in the operation of the horseboats. The G.W.R. had transported animals with the passengers on their steam ferry **The Mew**. A press report of the time stated, "Since luncheon Mr. H.B. Bartlett had been to the station and there saw the bridge-way filled with 200 sheep. Standing at the land end of the quay were several ladies and passengers waiting to cross and they could not go down on the pontoon. He asked if there was any other town served by G.W.R. where the public were asked to travel with the cattle". There was general relief therefore when Peters and Heselton re-introduced the horseboats, which were gradually coming to be known as 'car ferries'. Diesel tugs, built at Mevagissey, eventually replaced the original **Hauley**, and a new and larger float which was used at this period could still be seen till 1979 in use as a boat pontoon, moored off Dartmouth quay. It now lies in Old Mill Creek. Meanwhile the toll had been increased to 4d. to conform with the toll on the railway ferry. This was much resented by Kingswear residents who crossed regularly to Dartmouth for work or shopping. The motor-tugs **Hauley I** (1930) and **Hauley II** (1932) were introduced during this period.

On 16th December 1932 Messrs. Peters and Heselton obtained the Council's approval to assign their lease to the General Estates Co. Ltd., who took delivery of a third new tug (**Hauley III**) in 1933. In March 1935 the General Estates Company was granted a new lease for 21 years. They operated the ferry up to and during World War II, but became convinced that the ferry was no longer a viable proposition and in 1946 they surrendered the lease back to the Council. From 1946 the Dartmouth Borough Council began to operate the ferry, albeit reluctantly, themselves. The General Estate Company's gloomy expectations of non-viability would seem to have been premature. The ferry was making a profit, and rightly or wrongly the townspeople were ill-satisfied with the public ownership and voices were raised that the ferry profits were being used to subsidise other Council projects instead of being applied to the improvement of the undertaking. However, two new diesel tugs, **Hauley IV** and **Hauley V**, built by Philip's of Noss, were put into service in 1965 and 1966 respectively, and the evidence is that the ferry manager and his crews were providing a very reliable service.

In the meantime the railway steam ferry **Mew** had been altered to accommodate some vehicular traffic on the afterdeck, with consequent reduction of passenger space. The Council then introduced a passenger motor-launch service to augment their own car-float ferry. The **Reliance** (purpose-built at Bideford) was followed by the **Perseverance** and **Newcomin**. In effect they were providing the service which had once been handled by Casey's **Relief**. However when in 1957 the **Mew** was replaced by the passenger-only ferries **Humphrey Gilbert** and **Adrian Gilbert**, all vehicular traffic reverted to the Lower Ferry, and the Council agreed to withdraw their passenger-launches, thereby surrendering most of the pedestrian traffic to the railway. The launches were sold out of service to private owners, but can still be seen locally, engaged in crabbing.

On 1st April, 1974 Local Government Reorganisation transferred the ownership of the ferry to the South Hams District Council. Assuming control on All Fools Day was not the most auspicious start, but in fact the actual running of the ferry was in unchanged hands, so the transfer was smooth. It has never been one of the easiest passages to operate; on either side, traffic approaches the slip from a sharp angle; and in a strong sou'esterly wind the floats require skill to handle. From time to time the ferry finds its way into the local newspapers. The Western Morning News reported in October 1976 that the Council were considering providing a passenger-shelter on the car-floats; and in November 1977 that Dart Pleasure Craft (Messrs. Padden and Crews) were negotiating to buy the Lower Ferry from the Council. However, neither of these reported aims were realised.

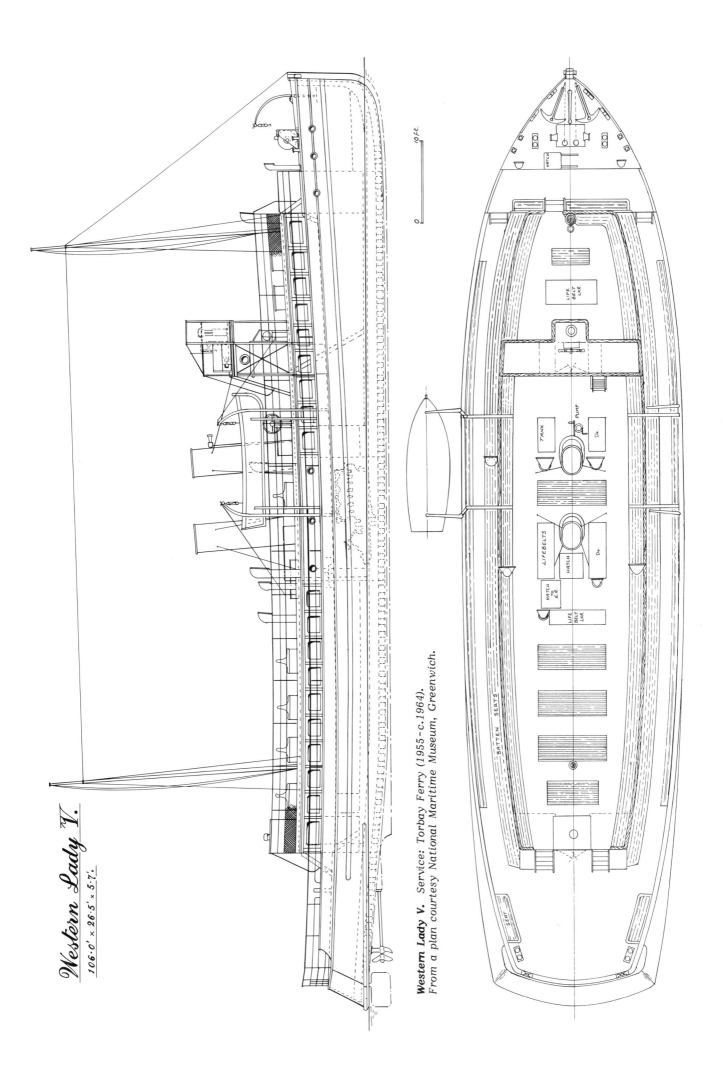

Western Lady V.

106·0' × 26·5' × 5·7'.

Western Lady V. Service: *Torbay Ferry (1955 – c.1964).*
From a plan courtesy National Maritime Museum, Greenwich.

10 Ft.

0

Castle Ferry

The best stories associated with this passage date from the end of the last century when one Charles Kelland was a rowboat-ferryman for the Caseys. Charlie was a loyal servant and a muscular oarsman, but he was a simple soul, and when others were not making a fool of him, was well able to do it for himself. A customer on the last ferry of the evening found that Charlie had, in the dark, given him a florin for a penny in his change and walked back to return it. "Thank'ee" said Charlie "I thought'ee felt white when I gave un to 'ee". Boys delighted to tease Charlie into making fast crossings, as on this occasion:- "Yer, Mr. Kelland, d'yer know what? Mr. Tribble rowed us over in one minute yesterday!" Charlie rose to the bait. "Did'ee, now? Then I'll row yer over in 'arf a minute!" Whereupon he bent to his oars and hurtled the boat across in response to the challenge.

In those days the ferrymen worked for wages until 9pm. and after that could keep the fares if they cared to work on. One night Mr. Casey, needing to return from Dartmouth after nine, asked our hero: "I'm sorry, Charlie, but could you work on till 9.30 tonight?" "Yus, alright" said Charlie, "but yer won't be long, boss, will yer?" A group of lads hauled Charlie's boat out of the water one night and pulled it up into a field. It was hard work, for watermen's boats were heavy. They got up early next morning to witness Charlie's discomfiture. "Wheres' yer boat, Mr. Kelland?" "Ah daun't knaw. I left 'un yer." "Could that be 'un, Mr. Kelland?" (pointing to the field above). "Well, I'm mazed" said Charlie "us must've 'ad a mortal 'igh tide las' night to get 'un up there!" No doubt the ferry still provides its occasional moments of humour to lighten the lives of crew or passengers, but Charlie Kelland was a character and we cannot hope to see his like again. In November 1979 passengers on the ferry were shaken when they saw the naked body of an apparently drowning girl floating in the river. The ferry was hove-to as the crew hauled the dripping body aboard. It then transpired, as the 'Sunday Independent' explained that 'the passengers' fears had been blown up out of all proportion'; for the corpse was a life-size inflatable doll!......you find some funny things floating in the Dart!

Death did come to the Lower Dart not many weeks later however. After closing down the ferry for the night on 2nd June, Tugmaster Bob Floyd and Floatman Bill Farrand boarded the 16ft. motor tender and set off for home in the gathering darkness. Bob Floyd dropped off his colleague at Kingswear and started for Dartmouth. He never arrived. Bill Farrand later told the inquest: "At the top of the hill I turned round to have a look and saw the boat going round in circles in the middle of the river". There was some evidence of a heavy wash from a passing vessel which would have rocked the ferry tender, possibly causing non-swimmer Bob Floyd, who was standing at the tiller, to fall overboard. A verdict of accidental death was recorded.

What does the future hold in store for the Lower Dart, which is now one of three services compet- within a mile of tideway? It is anybody's guess whether the status quo will continue, but it is certain that to those old enough to remember, it will always be 'Casey's Ferry'.

CASTLE FERRY: The only purely-seasonal ferry on the Dart is that which runs in summertime from Dartmouth Quay to Stumpy Steps below Dartmouth Castle. Its origin is unknown, but it is thought to have been operating for seventy years, perhaps longer, providing visitors with the most direct route to the fifteenth century castle in its uniquely beautiful situation. More than 50 years ago this was a rowboat service, in spite of the just-over-a-mile distance and it was a ferryman named Deacon who was the first to use a boat with a petrol-paraffin engine. As the years passed, the general use of the motor car brought the castle to within a few minutes journey of the town centre and made the ferry unable to provide its owner with a living.

Since then it has been run by a working partnership of three men as a part-time activity. The first trio were W. Hedges, Bill Allen and Alf Pine. Hedges' place in the partnership was later taken by Bob Crews, now a director of Dart Pleasure Craft Ltd. The present-day partners are Dave Griffiths, pilot (from 1968), Bob Stevens, shipwright (from 1976), and Jim Distin, fisherman (from 1978). The three motorboats in use are:- **Veryn Bay, Achieve,** and **Y Worry?**; all have light blue hulls, are powered by Lister Diesels and have a passenger capacity of twelve. Larger boats would be unsuitable for the service, as a reef of rock narrows the berth at Stumpy Steps. The service operates from 10am. to 5pm. and the fare is very reasonable at 25 pence.

To enable would-be returning passengers at Stumpy Steps to summon the ferryman, a mirror was installed there three years ago, marked on the reverse side 'To call ferry, turn mirror'. Light reflected by the mirror was visible at Dartmouth Quay, but it seems many passengers did not understand this, and through being moved about, the mirror was broken. A white-painted board- the idea of Alf Pine - was substituted and still does duty today. Bob Stevens recalls how one day his passengers included a Labrador dog. Soon after leaving Stumpy Steps the dog decided on a swim and plunged over the side. Unfortunately he was secured by a chain around his master's wrist and, for a few tense moments, it was uncertain whether the master would be following his dog before the latter could be hauled inboard! All ended happily, but it was a trip to remember.

I asked Dave Griffiths if he could recall any incident of special interest. 'Every trip is interesting' he replied 'because every trip you are meeting people, and people from every part of the world come to Dartmouth'. Some evidently appreciate what they see and find. One foreign visitor, leaving the ferry regretfully, declared 'This is the last civilised country left on earth'.

15.

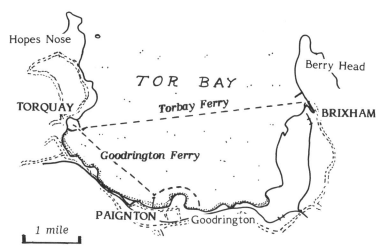

Hopes Nose

TOR BAY

Berry Head

TORQUAY

Torbay Ferry

BRIXHAM

Tor Bay

Goodrington Ferry

South Devon.

PAIGNTON
Goodrington

1 mile

THE TORBAY FERRY: No one, it seems, has ever recorded the history of this coastwise ferry service. True, it has been 'mentioned in despatches': guide books have made casual reference to it, and the Torquay 'Herald Express' newspaper has published photographs and reminiscences of the ferry in its heyday, but available information is fragmentary. Before the motor car became ubiquitous, this ferry was incomparably the best route between Torquay and Brixham. Four and a half miles by water, eight miles by land. In modern summers, when holiday traffic congests the roads, it is still the more pleasant route and no doubt often the quicker. Paignton, which the ferry also serves, is half a mile nearer Torquay (pier to pier) by water than by land, and one and three quarter miles nearer to Brixham.

The earliest service sufficiently regular to be classed as 'Ferry' seems to have begun towards the end of the last century when William Mellor of Torquay put the small steamer **Kiwi** on to the service and later added the **Pioneer**. Retired ferryman Les Woodward can recall seeing the **Pioneer** in his boyhood days and thinks that she continued to run until the Great War. The Torquay Directory of 23rd June, 1915, recorded that on the order of the Admiralty the service of Torbay steamers plying between Torquay, Paignton and Brixham was to be discontinued until further notice. It is likely that the **Kiwi** had been withdrawn some years previously but the ultimate fate of both steamers is unknown. There were no sole rights on the service and, soon after the turn of the century, Mellor's ferries had to face stern competition from a much superior vessel.

In 1901 the Devon Dock, Pier, & Steamship Co. of Exmouth took delivery of the twin-screw steam ferry **King Edward** from Philip's of Dartmouth. The **King Edward**, with a passenger 'Steam 4 certificate' for 149 passengers, a speed of nearly 10 knots, and a small licensed bar in her cabin, ushered in a new era on the Torbay ferry. At Torquay she worked from Princess Gardens Jetty (long demolished); at Paignton she used the Promenade Pier landing-stage; while at Brixham she berthed at the Eastern Quay of the inner harbour. In 1915, when the Admiralty stopped the ferry service, the **King Edward** was requisitioned for war work. According to the late William Pearse, her engineer in post-war days, she was used by the Navy on the north-east coast and was stationed at Newcastle. The Admiralty released her in May 1919 and she resumed work on the ferry service that summer, under Captain Davis of Teignmouth, a former deep-water man, gruff and taciturn. A modern diesel ferry of the same size could be run by three men, but the **King Edward** had a crew of six: Skipper, two deckhands, engineer, fireman, and a steward. 'Dido Bradford, retired Exmouth pilot, remembers joining the ship as a young and entirely untrained fireman. "I got a fire of sorts going" he recalls "but I didn't understand the damper. When the engineer came aboard there was no steam and we were too late at the jetty to run the morning ferry!"

Pioneer off Brixham prior to World War One, packed with Holidaymakers. Photo: P.N. Thomas.

Tor Bay Ferry:
King Edward,
*built 1901, of
the Devon Dock
& Pier Co., on
the company's
patent slipway.
Photo:
P.N.Thomas.*

These were halcyon days for the Torbay service and the following year the Devon Dock, Pier & Steamship Company began using the former tug **Lord Kitchener** as consort or relief to the **King Edward**, as required. The **Lord Kitchener**, a twin-screw steam tug fitted for passenger carrying, had been acquired from Southampton. Of 61 tons gross to the **King Edwards'** 52, and 81ft. in length to the **King Edward**'s 70 feet, she carried two boats in davits and had a tall 'Woodbine' funnel. She was renamed and re-registered in 1921 as the **Countess of Devon**. Her skipper was Captain Allen of Paignton and her engineer Bill Pearse of Exmouth. By 1926 the **Countess of Devon** had been sold to James Voysey, a Topsham shipowner, but her eventual fate is unknown. Allen and Pearce then transferred to the **King Edward**, Captain Davis and his engineer having retired. Some time after this the **King Edward** gained some unwelcome notoriety in connection with a murder. Her then captain was consorting with the wife of a local coal-merchant. When this worthy discovered his wife's infidelity there was an angry scene and he shot her. At that moment the **King Edward**'s skipper, who had been in the habit of carrying the lady as 'supercargo', was delaying his departure from Torquay when she had not turned up as expected!

Meanwhile the service to and from Paignton had been discontinued, due, it is believed, to destruction of the pier landing-stage by fire. Bus services and private cars were threatening to make the ferry uneconomic, but the Torquay-Brixham service continued to run at a fare of 1/- return. The end, however, was in sight, as far as the Devon Dock Co. were concerned. At the end of the 1930 season they abandoned the ferry service, laid up the **King Edward** in Exmouth Dock and put her on the market. But fate had decreed that the **King Edward** should return to her former 'stamping ground'. She was bought by the Dartmouth Steam Navigation Company and operated from Princess Pier, Torquay. In the mornings she did a single 'ferry' run to Brixham and back, but then did short sea excursions to Dittisham or Teignmouth, limited by a Steam 5 certificate to 99 passengers. She was skippered variously by the brothers Agland and Ross Taylor, directors of the small company and a Scotsman was engineer. William Peddle of Brixham was deck hand, and Harry Uglow of Torquay was fireman. The Scot did not sign on for the 1934 season and Harry Uglow was promoted to Engineer, with Les Woodward as fireman. The regular ferry service was no more and was not recommenced until after World War II. Prior to the 1935 season the **King Edward**'s boiler failed to pass the Board of Trade survey, and the Taylors sold her for scrap. In 1939 your author was crossing Stonehouse "ha'penny" bridge Plymouth when his attention was caught by the legend **King Edward, Exeter** on the stern of a rusting hull in a shipbreaker's yard. This was the last I saw of what had been the most graceful steamer of her size that I can recall.

It was not until 'the captains and the Kings' of Kipling's Recessional had departed from the scene of World War II that Torbay had its ferry restored; but, as it transpired, former instruments of war were to provide the service! In 1946 the proprietor of a Totnes bakery, Mr. Edhouse, in partnership with his son, inaugurated the 'Western Lady' ferry service, using ex-Fairmile 'B' naval motor launches. Purchased from the Admiralty, they were converted and re-engined at Brixham. While one maintained the ferry, the others were used on short sea excursions. No less than 672 of this class of M.L. had been constructed between 1940 and 1947, of which 75 became war casualties. Those acquired by the Edhouses were chosen from the sub-class of Rescue Motor Launches (RMLs 492-500 and 511-553) because these had the distinction of a funnel and an upper-deck saloon space amidships, which had been the sick-bay. Three of Edhouse's original four vessels are still in use. Measuring 112ft. in length by 18ft. 3ins. beam, having a passenger capacity of 220 and powered by Thornycroft or Gardner diesels giving them a speed of over 14 knots, the 'Western Ladies' revolutionised travel on the Torbay Ferry as decisively as did the **King Edward** at the turn of the century.

The four boats were named **Western Lady, Western Lady II, Western Lady III,** and **Western Lady IV.** In 1955 the **Western Lady II** was sold to Nice in the south of France and replaced by the **Brightlingsea Belle** (ex-**Southend Britannia**) from the Thames, which was renamed **Western Lady V**(120). This vessel, built by Thornycrofts at Woolston in 1924, was (despite 6ft. less length) a larger vessel than the Fairmiles, while she boasted twin funnels. Her greater passenger capacity (250) provoked a letter of complaint from the Torquay Waterman's Association to the Borough Council Harbour Committee, but without result. In 1963, after 17 years of reliable operation and excellent public relations, Edhouse sold out to the Torbay Boat Construction Co. Ltd., of the Dolphin boat yard, Galmpton whose Directors are M.J. and E.D.W. Perrett; and it is this company which operates

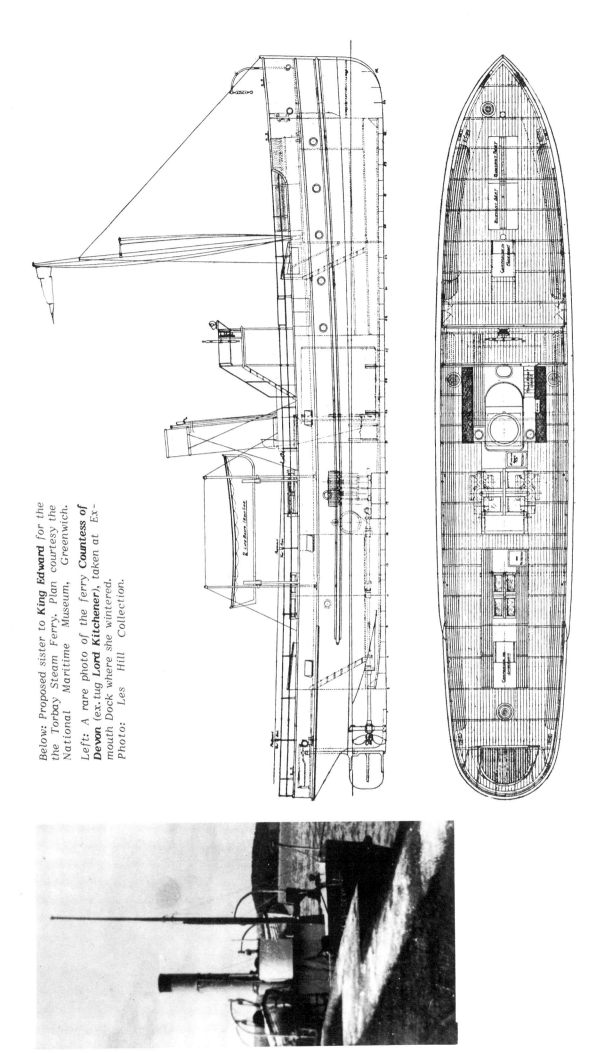

*Below: Proposed sister to **King Edward** for the Torbay Steam Ferry. Plan courtesy the National Maritime Museum, Greenwich.*

*Left: A rare photo of the ferry **Countess of Devon** (ex. tug **Lord Kitchener**), taken at Exmouth Dock where she wintered. Photo: Les Hill Collection.*

Dunkirk veteran **Western Lady V** *leaving Brixham in October 1978. Photo: R.L.E. Edhouse*

the service to-day. They were to receive an unsolicited testimonial a few years later when a foreign government, looking for someone to operate a ferry service in their own country, picked the Western Lady service as the best of its kind in the whole of Britain and invited them to take on the job.

Meanwhile Howard Thomas, managing director of ABC (now Thames) Television, was looking for a likely vessel to be a floating restaurant at their Teddington Lock studios on the Thames. The search for a suitable vessel compassed Devon, and one of the Western Lady Fairmiles was considered but found unsuitable. Then **Western Lady V**, the former Thames ferry, was noticed and inspected, and the Company was persuaded to sell. On her passage up-Channel **Western Lady V** had to weather a gale, but arrived safely in London River. Her new owners removed her funnels and superstructure to accommodate a large deck restaurant, and renamed her **Iris**.

In January 1967 a cloud hovered briefly over the future of the ferry when Brixham Council considered introducing a competing service, to force down the fare which had (not unreasonably one might think) reached 40p. A local firm, the South Western Steam Navigation Co. Ltd., were willing to operate the rival ferry. At Torquay however the Harbourmaster advised the Borough Council that he had no available facilities for an additional ferry service. It was as well, for the trade over the whole season was quite insufficient to support a second service. That same year **Western Lady III** crossed the Irish Sea and by invitation and under sponsorship of the Eire Government carried out cruises around Dublin Bay during the summer season. In November 1967 Torbay County Borough Council debated the proposal of a man named King to operate a hovercraft ferry across Torbay. Councillors were unhappy however about 45mph crossings of the bay and the constant noise. The matter was shelved until a demonstration could be arranged and little has been heard of the suggestion since.

On Tuesday, 9th July 1968 the **Western Lady I**, while running the 10.30am. ferry from Torquay, ran aground off Elbury Cove in thick fog, on a falling tide. Bathers were apprehensive as she loomed suddenly into close view out of the mist and came to rest uncomfortably near. The vessel was on a sandy bottom and in no danger, though some of the passengers appeared uneasy as she began to rock gently on her keel. Torbay lifeboat **Princess Alexandra of Kent** was alerted and took off 122 passengers - and one dog!

Today the ferry operates from May to October and the call at Paignton pier is included when the tide serves. Starting at 10.15am. and running at intervals of 45 minutes, ten return crossings are made daily at the height of the season and eight in early or late summer. The boats have ample covered accommodation for inclement weather, and a licensed bar on the upper deck also dispenses tea, coffee and snacks. In spite of rising fuel costs, harbour dues and pier tolls, the fare has been kept low in comparison with some services and includes a passenger's quay toll at Brixham. It remained static at 50p. from 1977-79. At Torquay the service is from Princess Pier and at Brixham from the New Pier in the outer harbour.

TORQUAY - GOODRINGTON: A summer Ferry which was sorely missed by holidaymakers when it ceased to run was the Torquay-Goodrington Sands service of the 'fifties and 'sixties. A Birmingham business man named Addis started this Ferry in the Summer of 1952 and ran it for two seasons. Worked by motorboats, it operated between North Quay, Torquay (by the Pavilion), and Cliff Promenade Landing Steps at Goodrington, with latterly an intermediate call at Paignton Pier jetty. Summer traffic congestion on the roads was such that it could take a car driver up to two hours (!) to make this short journey, so the ferry route had much to commend it. The financial return however did not come up to Addis's expectations and in early 1954 he sold out to a new operator, Jack Hunkin, an ex-Cornishman.

Hunkin used two motor launches: the **Bluebell** (licensed for 48 passengers) and the **Margaret Anne** (capacity 50). Like his predecessor, Hunkin persevered for just two seasons before giving up. His successor, Denis Job of Paignton, took over in 1956: and it is with his name that this ferry will always be associated. He worked the service for ten years and says today "The Ferry has many happy memories for me and I made a lot of friends who used the ferry every time they were on holiday: some of them still keep in touch now, after all this time". Three boats were put on the service: the **Plingie** (Scots for 'Seagull') licensed for 44 passengers; the **Seacrest** (capacity

48); and the larger **Endeavour**, carrying 72 (121). The first boat of the day left Torquay at 9am., and apart from a 60 minute lunchbreak, ran a half-hourly service till the last boat left Goodrington at 6pm. It was a 7-day week service from 1st June till the end of September. The fares charged were 1s.3d. single, 2s.6d. return, Torquay-Goodrington and remained constant the 10 years.

Torquay - Goodrington

Restrictions imposed by the local authority, and stepped-up Board of Trade requirements were however combining to reduce profitability, and Denis Job reluctantly decided to 'call it a day'. In 1966 Godfrey Hudson (from the Midlands) took over the ferry and worked a 40 minute service with two motorboats; the **Plingie** (purchased from Denis Job) and the **Dragonfly**. First boat from Torquay was now 9.30am., and last boat from Goodrington 5.40pm. The intermediate call at Paignton was introduced at this time, and the revised fares were as follows: 2s.6d. single, 3s.6d. return, Torquay-Goodrington; 1s.6d. single, 2s.6d. return, Paignton-Goodrington. Hudson withdrew after the 1968 season and the ferry has not run since.

Today, in his home overlooking Torbay, Denis Job recalls that timetable running of the ferry was frequently dislocated by errands of mercy, as amateur sailors were so often in distress. On one occasion he chased a large inflatable tented raft on which a party of students were being blown very rapidly seawards. A small army of press and T.V. reporters had gathered on the beach by the time the raft had been overhauled, made fast and towed in. Among many capsized dinghies and their occupants that he rescued was one whose crew consisted of a 70 year-old proprietor of Chemist shops, and his son. The old man "did not look in a very good way" says Denis today, "and I gave him a stiff tot of brandy". Some days after this rescue the son left an envelope for their rescuer with the Goodrington Beach Inspector. Inside.......a 10/- note!

At the height of the season, when the ferry cleared Roundham Head in the late afternoon, over 300 waiting passengers might be visible on Goodrington Beach. On these occasions time was saved by mooring one ferry offshore, to which successive loads were ferried by a rowboat tender, while the other two ferries worked a shuttle service between the moored boat and Torquay. Despite elaborate precautions for transferring the passengers, one very stout woman contrived to fall between the moored boat and tender into 18 inches of water, but was immediately hauled out. Her furious husband ("Done your best to drown my wife!") claimed she had lost a solid silver wrist watch in the process. Whether the watch had in fact been lost in the water will never be known, but it transpired that in fact it was a chrome-plated watch valued at under £3.

Summers brought the stars of entertainment to Torbay Theatres and many household names became regular patrons of the ferry, including Ken Dodd, Vince Hill, and Bert Weedon. It was often necessary to accommodate celebrities aft in the engine-space, to afford them some respite from autograph hunters. These are but a few random glimpses of a ferryman's life. They show that there is more in ferrying than steering a boat from A to B; and they help confirm one's belief that ferries are best run by local men, who despite limited capital and low profit margins stay with the job, know their customers, and meet the needs of the locality. Too often in recent years local proprietors have given place to entrepreneurs from outside the South-West.

*Goodrington Ferry: Red duster flying, **Endeavour** clears the moored craft in Torquay inner harbour, and Dennis Job notches her up. Photo: D. Job.*

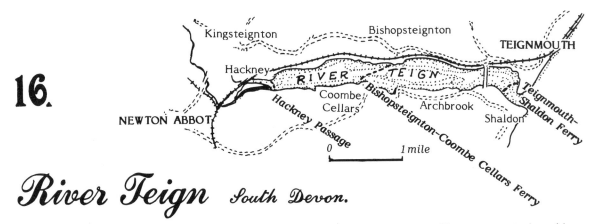

16.

River Teign *South Devon.*

HACKNEY - BUCKLAND: This ferry which has not run since the Great War was centuries old at its close. An old Roman road crossed the Teign by a tidal ford at this point and a ferry was needed when the ford was not negotiable. The landing point below Buckland is now scarcely identifiable, but at Hackney the Passage House Inn (1761) is thriving and its patrons' cars now throng the bank from which the ferry once plied. A larger tavern was built in Victorian times a few yards from the first, and this in turn has been superseded by a modern inn with a restaurant, though both earlier buildings are still standing. An old print (copied on the inn signboard) shows ferrymen poling off with their passengers and a horseboat alongside (122).

The name Hackney derives from the type of fishing net used locally in the fourteenth century, and the hamlet was home to many of the lightermen who worked on the Hackney and Stover canals. Travellers came down an old Pack Horse lane to cross the ford, or take the ferry; and from Roman times an inn has stood here where they could rest till the tide turned or lodge for the night if the last ferry of the day had run. Mosaic pavements have been discovered under the inn, and two of the original fireplaces have been unearthed and restored.

In mediaeval times the crossing was used by the clergy on their travels between Bishopsteignton and Torre Abbey. A costrel (clay drinking vessel), such as might have been carried by a bishop or prosperous pilgrim in the late fifteenth century, was dredged up from 7 feet under the river bed by Mr. George Vallance of Kingsteignton some years ago. Evidently it had been lost overboard from the ferry in mediaeval times. It is now on display in Torquay Museum.

In later years the ferry was chiefly patronised by ball-clay workers crossing from the Torquay road to the Kingsteignton clay-pits and men employed on the canals by which Dartmoor granite and clay reached the River Teign at this point. One of today's senior citizens told me that he believed the landlord of the inn when the ferry closed down was a man named Booth. It is likely that the ferry rights had long been held by the innkeeper.

BISHOPSTEIGNTON - COMBE CELLARS: Combe Cellars is a low-lying foreland on the south bank of the Teign, boasting a tavern, the Smugglers Inn, and a narrow landing-jetty. Today it has been discovered by the motorist, the powerboat enthusiast and the water-skier, but at the turn of the century it was a quiet and charming place, which S. Baring-Gould made the scene of his novel 'Kitty Alone'. The inn had a tea-garden which was famed locally for cockles - and - cream and Devonshire junkets. In the earlier years of this century a 'summer only' ferry used to work between the north shore at Bishopsteignton and Combe Cellars jetty. The village of Bishopsteignton lies three-quarters of a mile from the river and the occupants of the few chalets and houses on the river bank had an uphill trudge to fetch supplies. The ferry seems to have been initiated to give them a link with Combe Cellars and Come-in-Teignhead village, across the river. It also provided holidaymakers in Bishopsteignton with a direct and pleasant route to the delights of Combe Cellars.

Hackney-Buckland Ferry: The innkeeper's dog barks encouragement as Hackney ferrymen pole a well-laden ferry into the tideway. Photo: Passage House Inn, Kingsteignton.

*Hackney -
Buckland
Bishops -
teinton -
Combe
Cellars
Teign-
mouth -
Shaldon*

Shaldon Ferryboat No.3 at Teignmouth Harbour Beach in August 1931. She was eventually sold for conversion into a cabin cruiser. Note the canvas splash-cloths rigged along the sides. Photo: Rosina Langley.

The ferry can only have run for about three hours either side of high water, when the crossing would have been over a thousand yards. Today it is remembered by few, and seems to have been recorded by none. Retired Teignmouth boat proprietor Fred Drew, has told me that the ferryman during the early twenties was one George Sharland; and that he achieved some fame locally by rowing a boat stern-foremost from Shaldon to Newton Abbot and back, for a wager. Mrs. Jessie Bulley of Bishopsteignton says "At the time I remember it, the ferry only ran occasionally, for holiday people". Mr. George Vallance of Chudleigh Knighton recalls that latterly there was a ferry-woman, a Mrs. Boon, but that the service was not very regular.

The small beach from which the ferry worked at Bishopsteignton was known to local boatmen as 'Bridge': this was with reference to the footbridge over the railway which gives access to the shore. Under the trees overhanging the shore at Netherton lie the remains of a waterman's boat which could possibly be the one-time ferry.

> "From Bishopsteignton's shore beside the Teign
> The ferry man bends o'er his dipping oars;
> Abeam, the swans from Archbrook glide serene,
> Aloft, in startled flight, a heron soars.
>
> The passengers gaze down through waters clear
> On banks the falling tide will soon expose;
> Their minds on cockles, cream, and sparkling beer,
> As now Combe Cellars jetty nearer grows".

TEIGNMOUTH - SHALDON: Until the building of the first Shaldon Bridge in 1827, the ancient ferry passage between Teignmouth and Shaldon saved a 14 mile journey round by Newton Abbot. Probably the earliest reference we have to this passage is in the The Earldom of Cornwall Accounts, 1296-7, where it is shown that the Earl, one Edmond, had a ferry across the Teign which was used by travellers making for Dartmouth, but was worth only 6s.8d. a year. The actual landing points then used are not known, but quite certainly the crossing was near the river mouth. A 1759 map of Teignmouth shows the Point (opposite the Ness) marked as 'Passage Point'; while an 1805 map has the same, with a dotted line leading towards the Point, and marked 'Road to Passage'. It seems therefore that in earlier times the ferry operated in the very mouth of the river, where although the distance is shortest, the tide-race is severe.

It is known that by 1795 there was a 'Passage House Inn' on the Shaldon side; and the Vestry minutes of St. Nicholas record that the Easter Vestry was held in 'The Passage-house Inn' in 1821. By 1843, though still called 'Passage House' it had become a private dwelling, and was let to one William Stephens at £20 per annum. The building had disappeared by the turn of the century, but it is thought to have stood somewhere between the present 'Ferry Boat Inn' and Shaldon House, pro-bably at the seaward end of Horse Lane which was the route westward from the beach. Certainly long before 1900 the ferry was following virtually the route it follows today. During the reign of Charles II the rights of ferry were bestowed by Royal Grant on the first Lord Clifford of Chudleigh; and it was from the Cliffords that the Teignmouth and Shaldon Bridge Company purchased them in 1827, when the bridge was opened, and became the ferry operators for 122 years. In Teignmouth Museum can be seen a poster of 1833, which shows that the Company were not insensitive to passengers' complaints. It reads as follows:- SHALDON FERRY. Notice is hereby given that in order to prevent passengers from being delayed on quitting the FERRY BOAT IT IS ORDERED THAT the ferryman do receive the TOLL from each person on GETTING INTO THE BOAT.

HOURS FOR PLYING THE FERRY-BOAT:

	Morn.		Even.
From 1st of April to 1st of October	6	to	9
During February and March)	7	to	7
" October and November)			
" December and January	8	to	6

Dated August 9th, 1833

Teign-mouth - Shaldon

The Bridge Company used heavily built 17-foot rowing boats, equipped with mast and lugsail, and painted with black and white 'gunports' on either side. These have remained the distinctive mark of the Shaldon ferries ever since. Bill Westlake, recently retired Leading Helmsman, and whose uncle, father and grandfather were on the ferry before him, tells me that the Bridge Company obtained Royal sanction for the sole right to use the gun-port markings, and that all the ferrymen of his father's time and before knew this. I have not been able to confirm this, but certainly the markings are worn by no other ferries in the south-west of England (123). Painted ports were frequently used by merchant ships after the Napoleonic wars to create an impression of fire-power they did not possess, to deter aggressors, and remained popular long after as a form of decoration. On small open boats such markings were uncommon, but the Bridge Company perpetuated the custom when the larger motor ferries were introduced in 1907. For some time both the rowboats and motorboats were in use, the former starting the service at 5am. daily, and the latter taking over at 9am. In the years between the wars, three (later, two) of the old rowboat ferries could be seen moored off Shaldon beach, and were used as tenders to and from the motor ferries by the crews. The last rowboat ferry was broken up about 1960. In the London Inn, Shaldon, is a framed photograph, date about 1883, showing Harry Moule, one of the best-known ferrymen of the rowboat days, standing in the ferry, which has the mast stepped.

Other ferrymen whose names have come down to us from the earlier years of the twentieth century were 'Shrimpy' Moule (brother of Harry), Joe Onion (remembered for his huge beard), his brother George Onion (handicapped by a wooden leg), Fred Westlake (one of six Westlakes in four generations on the ferry), 'Plum' Morritt (before and after the Great War), Fred 'Tich' Drew (served at the Dardanelles and returned to become a well-loved boat proprietor), and Helmsman Ward, who drove the first motor ferry on its first crossing. The Teignmouth & Sheldon Bridge Company owned and ran the ferries until 1949, the year after the takeover of the bridge by the Local Authority, In the years between the wars 'Plum' Morritt was joined by his stepson, Walter Walker, while Sid Wolf, George Tothill and Charlie Soaper all belong to this period. Charlie Soaper, who was Leading Helmsman and maintained the ferry engines, holds the record for service on the ferry at 33 years.

In 1949 the ferry rights were acquired by Mr. W.J. Powell of the Green, Shaldon. "He was a good boss", Bill Westlake remembers, "but he died in 1951, and his widow did not want the responsibility of the ferry. It was put on the market and taken over by Teignmouth Urban District Council in August 1952, and they ran it under the Surveyor's Department. One of our ferrymen in Mr. Powells' time was Ted Cummings, who had been a Master-at-Arms in the Navy". The first day of public ownership was celebrated by all four ferries crossing the river to the accompaniment of sirens from ships in harbour, and the hooters of local pleasure craft. An unusual feature of the ferry during the T.U.D.C.'s time was a 'passenger' clock. This was installed as the Council's reply to complaints received about the ferry's timekeeping which the Manager considered were unjustified. Thenceforward passengers could watch the clock and see for themselves how well the advertised times were kept!

During World War II the U.S. Forces took over the section of river beach on the Teignmouth side where the ferry landed: this was at the end of the road below the car park, where there was a small ferry-shelter. As a result the ferry was diverted to run to Bobbetts Quay, Gales Hill. When the Americans vacated the river beach, the ferry could have reverted to its original landing; but instead the present site was chosen, a few yards to the north, at the end of Lifeboat Lane. The roll of post-war ferrymen includes George Tothill and Walter Walker (both returned from H.M. Forces), Fred Delbridge (1954-64), Sammy Sampson (a retired yacht skipper), Bill (Curly) Westlake (second longest service 29 years), and Norman Williams.

On 1st April 1974 the powers of the T.U.D.C. were taken over by the newly-constituted Teignbridge District Council, who thereby acquired the ferry and ran it under the Entertainments and Seafront Department, which is still the case today. In 1972 a new boathouse and concrete slipway with rollers, was built at Shaldon. The boathouse comprises a workshop with a hand winch for hauling up the boats, a small lock-up store, and an exterior paint and oil store. Its provision has greatly facilitated the maintenance of the ferries.

There have been only four motor ferries since their inception in 1907, and they have been distinguished by numbers instead of names. Ferry No.1 was built in 1907 at Dartmouth, of pitchpine on oak and teak. She had slightly less freeboard than the boats that followed her and her bow was squared above the waterline to support the foredeck. Pilot Alf Brook recalls that she was fitted with a Fayen-Bowden single-cylinder engine, which was started up by pulling over a flywheel. Her passenger capacity was about 30. During the 1950s she was sold out of service to a local Customs Officer, who resold her, when she became a sand barge. A crewman, "Little" Dodd, was drowned from her when he tripped on a coil of rope and went overboard.

Ferry No.2, also built at Dartmouth (1908) of similar materials to No.1, cost £38 without the engine. She was originally driven by a 24hp. 'Atlanta' motor, but today has a two-cylinder Lister engine. When this engine was installed in 1961 she was given a major refit and the bow was raised a strake higher. About 1965 a helmsman's shelter was built in her by Bill Westlake. She is still in service as the 'winter boat' and runs for 10 months of every year. During the remaining two months she has her annual refit and then stands by as relief boat so that the service can be doubled if required. She has a passenger capacity of 33.

Ferry No.3 was built at Devonport, Plymouth, in 1927. She had slightly more freeboard than her predecessors, but was narrower in the beam. Her builders did not adhere strictly to the specifications ordered and the Company would not at first accept her. For months she lay on the beach at the bottom of Ivy Lane while negotiations continued. Eventually the builders agreed to make certain alterations and No.3 was put into service (123). As delivered, she had an 'Atlanta' 24hp. engine, later replaced by a Thornycroft diesel. I can remember two occasions between the wars when No.3 suffered an engine breakdown while running. About 1964 she was sold for a 'knockdown' price to Mr. W.G. ('Pixie') Matthews, who resold her, minus her engine, for conversion to a cabin cruiser. Her passenger capacity as a ferry was 32.

Ferry No.4 was built of larch by Bulley's of Teignmouth in 1946. The original Thornycroft engine was replaced the following year by a 30hp. Lister. She has a greater beam than the earlier boats and her capacity is 46 passengers. She is regarded as the 'summer boat' and works in July and August when the traffic is heaviest, being used in winter only as a relief. Her draught is the same as the others, 3'9" aft. As built, she had a complete wheelhouse with hinged doors, but this was removed when it was found that the helmsman's all-round vision was obstructed and that there was insufficient room to work the poles. For years a conspicuous feature of the Shaldon Ferries was the long and heavy fir pole lashed to the engine-compartment gunwale, and used for holding the ferry in position at the beach in a strong tide. These fir poles rotted at the point of friction with the gunwale and were costly to replace when broken. At Bill Westlake's suggestion metal scaffold-poles were substituted and are still used.

Since the **Darlwyn** disaster, safety regulations for passenger motorboats have been greatly stepped up. Whereas the Shaldon ferries once carried six life jackets and one small fire-extinguisher, today the requirement is four lifebelts, three large fire-extinguishers, and liferafts to support 18 people. Two of these rafts are 'buoyant apparatus' seats and occupy the space amidships which was formerly standing-space for passengers. There is no record of any passengers' lives being lost, despite the long history of the ferry, but the years have not been without incident. During World War II Charlie Soaper had just embarked a ferryload of schoolchildren at Shaldon when he sighted an enemy aircraft streaking towards the estuary. Quickly he bustled all the children ashore and made them lie down in the lee of beached boats. On another occasion he had a full load on the ferry when a German bomber roared in low overhead. "I didn't like the look of things a bit" he recalls with masterly understatement, "but he never dropped anything".

When a yacht capsized off the Ness in 1956, Fred Delbridge defied regulations by taking the ferry out to the bar to help save the crew. About 1958 Matthew's pleasure boat **Britannia** became disabled when nets fouled her propellor. Sealey's **Princess Mary** was in difficulties trying to tow her in, having inadequate power. Bill Westlake went to the rescue in Ferry No.4 and took over the tow, but they were caught by the ebb. No.4 stranded on the bar and had to await the next tide.

In October 1964 Fred Delbridge died aboard No.3 whilst crossing from Teignmouth to Shaldon. He had a heart attack and collapsed, but managed to knock the engine out of gear first and thus saved his passengers from a possible serious collision. The ferry drifted, near the end of an ebb tide, and fouled moored boats off the Teignmouth shore. Fred Drew and others went off in a boat to investigate and found Fred Delbridge dead. His ashes were later scattered in the river mouth from the ferry. At that time the ferries carried no bowman when on winter service, a practice that was reversed after this.

Such incidents show that ferries 'have their moments' and are occasionally plucked from obscurity into limelight. But it is their daily service to the community, generation after generation, that secures their place in local history. The Shaldon Ferry has served its people for at least 700 years and will surely do so for many years to come.

*The second sea tram nicknamed **Puff**, which performed the duties of ferry for over 20 years, and the now-disused embarkation jetty. Looking on is the author's daughter Brenda. 1968.*

17.

River Exe

South Devon.

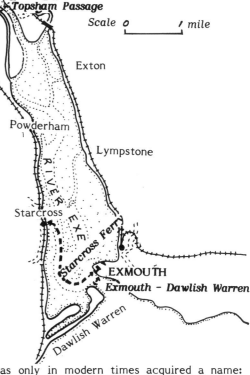

EXETER — Butt's Ferry

Cyst St. Mary

EXETER CANAL

TOPSHAM
Topsham Passage

EXMINSTER

Scale 0 — 1 mile

Exton

Powderham

Lympstone

RIVER EXE

Starcross

Starcross Ferry

EXMOUTH
Exmouth - Dawlish Warren

Dawlish Warren

'Old John' Carder awaiting passengers at Dawlish Warren for Exmouth about 1910. The use of sails was later prohibited. From an old postcard. Photo: Les Hill Collection, Exmouth.

BUTT'S FERRY: This is an ancient passage which has only in modern times acquired a name: a ferry known to few people outside Exeter until the founding of the Maritime Museum brought visitors and gave the ferry a new raison d'etre. The origin of this centuries-old service between Exeter Quay and Haven Banks is unknown. The Deputy Town Clerk of Exeter in 1974 conjectured that the right to operate a ferry was acquired with the grant of Exe Island to the City in the sixteenth century by Edward VI.

However, in the "Letters and papers of John Shillingford, Mayor of Exeter 1447-50" there appears a petition from this Mayor for aid to repair Exe Bridge because the ferry was dangerous: 'where of longe tyme and withynne tyme of mynde was nother brigge ne way bot by right and perillous ferybote; by the whiche fery as hit is seid and like that of olde tyme puple were in grete perill and meny perrished and lost". This is evidence that a ferry was working in the fifteenth century, and that it had already been the scene of fatal accidents.

The danger to the ferry arises from Trew's Weir, some way downstream. At spring tides the river at Exeter Quay is sometimes flowing at four knots, and at that speed the water in the vicinity of the ferry goes over Trew's Weir in five minutes. For this reason the ferry has long been worked by a fixed-rope system, to eliminate any danger of it being swept over the weir. Stanchions on the boat carry sheaves through which is passed a wire cable across the river, and the ferryman hauls on the wire with gloved hands to propel the boat, which is fitted with small platforms for end-loading. Though the wire is an obstruction to shipping, it can be lowered to the river bed in 30 seconds for passing vessels, and be immediately raised by winch afterward.

In 1750 a 21 year lease was agreed with William Chard for £12 per annum. Chard however did not quite complete his lease and in 1769 it was assigned to Benjamin Ash on the same terms. He was followed by William Sercombe. The ferry house, built early in the nineteenth century, is first referred to in a lease of 'dwelling and ferry' to John Mitchell in 1821. The 'Exeter Flying Post' newspaper records the death of ferryman Mitchell's wife on 14th February 1828. John Passmore succeeded the widowed Mitchell in 1842 for four years and was followed by Charles Edwards. J.G.R. Gooden took up a 7 year tenancy in 1878; and his successor James Percy had his lease renewed four times - the last in 1902. The original leases to all these eight ferrymen mentioned here are among documents relating to the ferry held by the Devon Record Office.

A local Act of 1835 relates to the removal of the ferry and the establishment of another ferry or a footbridge, but this move came to nothing. In 1970 however Exeter City Council determined to rid themselves of the legal obligation to continue the service, and promoted a private Bill in the Commons to this end. In the meantime the Council gave notice in the Press that from 1st June that year the ferry hours would be restricted to: 7am.- 10am., 12 noon - 2pm., and 4pm. - 6.15pm. It was intended to discontinue services after 30th September 1972, but there was vigorous local opposition led by Mr. George W. Butt, an Exeter citizen, and Major David Goddard of the Maritime Museum. (The museum, opened in 1969, occupies three warehouses on either side of the Exe, so that virtually all its visitors have to make use of the ferry).

Initially the City Council were successful in obtaining Parliamentary permission for closure, and there seemed little hope for the ferry when 30th September 1972 dawned; the 'Western Morning News' reporting as follows: "The early-morning milkman's mist lifted, but there seemed to be a mist of sadness surrounding the ferry as Mrs. Constance Sheppard of Claremont Grove, St. Leonard's, made what will almost certainly be one of her last journeys on it with her Labrador dog, Judy. Her daily walk with Judy always includes a ferry crossing. "I will miss it" she said, "I will just have to stay on my own side of the river now". Sad, too, was the ferryman, 63 years old George Hancock of Isca Road, Exeter. He has had the job for four years, taking it after being farm bailiff for the Earl of Devon."

Last-ditch efforts to save the ferry however brought a reprieve, for the Environment Minister ordered a planning enquiry into Exeter City Council's decision to close it. The Council argued that the ferry had lost nearly £4,500 in the past 5 years, and that its wire was an obstruction to sailing activities on the river. George Butt maintained that the ferry was an environmental asset, was essential to the existence of the Maritime Museum for whom it transported about 50,000 passengers annually: and that the Museum authorities were willing and able to run the ferry on licence at no cost to the City Council. The outcome was that George Butt won the day, and the grateful Museum, who have worked the ferry since, have named the passage after him.

In 1978 a flat-bottomed and larger ferry boat was constructed by the Museum and brought into use on 8th December for an official visit of H.R.H. Prince Philip, who was the new boat's first passenger. Harry Andrews, aged 68 and ferryman when he was 14, was joined by his colleague, Reg Lyons, to take the Prince across the river. He told pressmen "I've taken thousands of people across the river, but this was the most important trip of my life". His father Gerry Andrews had been ferryman at Exeter Quay before him.

Today the future of the ferry is as secure as it has ever been. The service is daily throughout the year, till 5pm. in winter and 6pm. in summer. On the Haven Banks side can still be seen slight remains of the original ferryman's house, demolished in the mid-seventies. Ferryman Alf Hemens told me that the name of one of the last ferrymen to occupy the house was Gregory, and that he had a profitable side-line with boats for hire on the river. Today a hut with electricity supply for heat and cooking, shelters the duty ferryman between crossings. Three men now share the work of the ferry between them: Harry Andrews and Reg Lyons cover Monday to Fridays, while Alf Hemens does the weekends.

The present ferryboat carries two chromium-plated plaques which commemorate the Duke of Edinburgh as first passenger and a second which reads: Butt's Ferry. This ferry was saved in 1972 for the convenience of all by Mr. George Butt of Exeter. "The condition upon which God hath given liberty to man is eternal vigilance." John Philpot Curran 1750-1817.

TOPSHAM PASSAGE: This ferry was anciently attached to the manor of Exminster. Exeter City Council have a record of a licence granted by the lord of the manor in 1736 to two men named Buttell and Wear to operate the ferry from the Exminster side. The passage is certainly much older than this, however, for Topsham had been a considerable port from the tenth century, and continued to flourish even after the building of Exeter Ship Canal in 1564. In 1847 the main line of the South Devon Railway (later absorbed by the G.W.R.) was laid through Exminster and the opening of Exminster station made the ferry accessible to railway passengers.

By the earlier years of this century the Ferry rights had been acquired by the Heavitree Brewery and thenceforward the ferry operated from the Passage House Inn at Topsham, successive licensees being responsible for working the crossing or employing local boatmen. From the early 1920s, when the ferry toll was still $\frac{1}{2}$ d., a memorable character named Bill Bolt, one of the publican's several sons, was ferryman until about 1930. When Bill had started a drink, he was loath to put it down. The Rev. P. Longridge (retired Rector of Highweek) recalls that passengers walking across the fields after alighting from a train at Exminster had to shout lustily to draw Bill Bolt's attention; and might be obliged to shout for some time until he saw fit to leave the bar. He kept a twin-barrelled shot gun with him in the boat and often alarmed more nervous passengers by suddenly throwing down his sculling oar, and letting fly at passing snipe or other feathered target! The publican who followed Bolt in the 1930s was named Davies, and he also had sons who worked the ferry.

In 1943 Heavitree Brewery sold the ferry to St. Thomas Rural District Council. The steady pro-liferation of the motor car had been making the ferry uneconomic, but it was a statutory passage and could not be closed. One of the successive ferrymen employed by the Council was Bill Edworthy, who had been Bos'n of the S.S. **Duchess of Devonshire**, wrecked on Sidmouth beach in 1934, and was by this time a pensioner. Your author was a young quartermaster in the **Duchess** in her last seasons, and I can testify that Bill was a great character, a good shipmate, and a first-class seaman. He died, pint-mug in hand, a few years ago, in Topsham's Salutation Inn.

The greatest blow to the ferry was the closure of Exminster Station under the 'Beeching Axe'. For Topsham folk, Exminster was the outlet to Plymouth and the West, saving time, expense and change of trains via Exeter. (As late as 1947 Exminster station was served by 11 down and 13 up trains). The path between ferry landing and the station, over the canal and across the water meadows was always pleasant in reasonable weather. With the closure of Exminster station, the ferry became little more than a convenience for ramblers and people at leisure. In 1966 Topsham was incorporated in Exeter, and control of the ferry passed to Exeter City Council, who are the present-day operators. For many years before this and until 1969, the ferryman was 'Dolly' Gray, and he was in his seventies when he retired. Year in and year out for seven days a week, 'Dolly' Gray, had never taken a holiday. His employers were taken aback when at the age of 70 'Dolly' requested that he might have the next day off. "Certainly", he was told "but why?" "Oi be gettin' married tomorrer" was the reply, and he did.

Stan Pym, the present ferryman, started on the ferry in 1974. Within a year he had an unusual emergency call. It was October, and the ferry had reverted to short-day service, so Stan was home.

in his slippers, shaving. About 8pm. a knock on his door heralded four firemen, who wanted Stan to ferry them (with their portable pump) to a fire on the opposite bank. The unoccupied lock-keeper's cottage between Exminster slip and the Ship Canal was mysteriously on fire! Stan rushed down in his slippers and unmoored the ferry, and the firemen heaved their heavy pump aboard. The boat's freeboard nearly disappeared under the weight! The crossing accomplished, one fireman rushed to the scene of the fire leaving his comrades too short-handed to carry the pump! Stan therefore, still in carpet slippers, took over as fourth man to manhandle the pump to the fire. (Anyone who has walked the canal bank at Exminster in Autumn will realise that Wellington boots are a first requirement!). The fire was soon under control and Stan was able to return to his shaving.

Today's ferry is a 12ft. clincher-built boat with a Johnson outboard motor, and it is kept quite busy in the summer, though winter traffice is very light. "It's not exactly a well-paid job", Stan says cheerfully, "but it's healthy. Out here I never get a day's illness."

STARCROSS FERRY: In 1978 the steel hull of a small steamboat which had long lain derelict at Millbrook in the Port of Plymouth, was floated off the mud and towed to Mashford's yard at Cremyll for scrapping. There were no spectators to witness her departure, nor did a single line appear in West country papers. Yet her name, still decipherable, was **Starcross**; and her framed photograph had appeared above ferry timetables for twenty years on railway stations all over the Great Western system (128). Her active years had seen the heyday of the Exmouth-Starcross ferry passage which has since dwindled to a summer-only service. In recent years a car ferry has been proposed for the Exe estuary, to work between a jetty at Cockwood and a marina planned for the Exmouth side. Should this dream become reality, the Starcross ferry may know another heyday; but at the time of writing the glories belong strictly to time past.

Time Past is considerable for the Starcross ferry, one of the oldest in the south-west. There may have been a ferry here even before the Norman Conquest, for in AD 705 the Bishop of Sherborne was given land at Exmouth and, at a date thereafter which is unrecorded, established a ferry across the estuary to Starcross. Today's Exeter Road in Exmouth, and all the land lying now to the west of it, had not been reclaimed from the river; and the Bishop's ferry station must have been somewhere near the present junction of Chapel Street and Market Street, a site which lay in the parish of Littleham, in a locality anciently known as Prattishide. The earliest specific reference we have to the ferry, dates from 1122 when the Abbey of Horton in Dorset (whose properties included Littleham) was annexed to Sherborne, together with the rights of ferry across the Exe. The first we hear of Littleham is in 1042 when Edward the Confessor granted the manor to his thane Ordgar. By this time the Bishop of Sherborne had most probably been operating his ferry for some time, so that the reference to the ferry in the proclamation of 1122 was perhaps only ratifying an existing situation.

From what we know of post-Conquest coastal craft, we can conjecture that the early ferries were of barge-like appearance, beamy, up to 30ft. in length and rigged with a single mast and lugsail. Besides carrying passengers, there would have been room perhaps for a couple of horses or a number of smaller animals such as sheep and pigs. From the embarkation point on the Exmouth side, the ferry would have sailed - or been poled - down a narrow waterway between the Point and the Fowley sand-bank, and thereby reached 'the antient channel', following it to Woolcombe's Island on the West bank of the Exe. Here was a flight of stone stairs for a landing-place, while nearby was the ferry house and a stone cross set up by the Bishop of Sherborne. The 'stair' and 'cross' eventually gave the place its present name of Starcross.

In 1227 Henry III gave the city of Exeter to his brother Richard, Earl of Cornwall, to whom the citizens paid an annual rent of £13. The grant included the River Exe and estuary and all shipping and toll rights. In practice, however, there was an exception to the city's rights - the Bishop of Sherborne's ferry. After forty years of dispute between city and bishop, agreement was reached in 1267 that the rights of ferry should be transferred to Exeter Corporation, and that the Bishop of Sherborne, his convent and dependants should enjoy for ever free passage on the ferry. Disputes continued however for another 200 years, until, according to local historian Captain Peacock, Sherborne's privilege was abolished in 1473. Although the original departure-point for the ferry had lain in Littleham, it appears that Exeter Corporation bought the quay at Pratteshide, and re-sited the ferry station there, in the parish of Withycombe.

The earliest known lessee of the ferry is recorded in 1287. This was John Pycard, who paid

Starcross Ferry: **Starcross** *on her speed trials in 1923 with skipper George Prowse at the helm. Photo: Devon Dock, Pier & S.S. Co.*

the mayor and bailiffs of Exeter 44s. a year rent, and had to accept responsibility for upkeep and repair of the ferryboats and ferry house: the ferry is referred to as "our passage of Pratteshide". Pratt is considered to have been the name of a man who at one time worked the ferry, one of Sherborne's sub-tenants. The name Pratteshide (Pratt's place) became attached to the ferry landing, ferry house, and adjoining cottages. Exeter Corporation had paid 4d. a year rent for Pratteshide ferry station to the Uppehille family until 1327 when the family renounced their rights.

Robin Bush, Assistant County Archivist of Somerset, who has researched the early history of Starcross ferry thoroughly and to whom I am greatly indebted for information, states that "there can be no doubt that the quay from which the ferry or passage boat left, and the buildings attached to it, occupied the triangular site of the old public conveniences in Exeter Road, outside Glenorchy Chapel". In 1329 a chapel was built near the ferry station, presumably for the use of intending passengers who sought protection and for the thanksgivings of those who had crossed in safety. The chapel was licensed for service by the Bishop of Exeter at the request of one John de la Wille, who was probably the tenant ferryman. Remains of what is very possibly that building (St. Margaret's Chapel) can still be seen in Chapel Street.

Exeter Corporation accounts record the names of the tenant ferrymen in the sixteenth century as follows:- John Brownryng (1507-13), John Coweryng (1513-19), John Browne (1519-42), John Drake (1542-58), Gilbert Drake (1558-89), Robert Drake (1589-1624). John Browne appears to have given rise to dissatisfaction, possibly through sub-letting the tenancy unwisely; for it is recorded in April 1528 that a deputation from the Corporation was despatched to 'ryde to Exmouth and there to discharge the tenant of the passage boytt (boat) and to sett the sayd passage agene after their discretion'. Browne however survived this inspection and held the lease until 1542 when it passed to the Drake family of Pratteshayes. John Drake, who became ferryman on 28 April that year, was the eldest of at least three brothers. When he died without an heir 16 years later, Gilbert, the third brother, took over the ferry lease. (It appears that the second brother had died in 1554 probably through having been shot through both cheeks by an arrow in the Prayer Book rebellion!). Gilbert Drake held the lease for 31 years during which time the ferry house and garden which had been in a neglected state were repaired and leased separately from the ferry. Gilbert's son, Robert Drake, succeeded him in 1589 and retained the lease for 35 years, until 1624. The seventeenth century ferrymen were as follows:- John Watts (1625-26), Richard Watts (1626-86), Thomas Watts (1 month), Edward Woodward (1686-1743).

In 1603 Exeter Corporation again had cause to investigate complaints about the ferry, and sent representatives "to repere unto the ferrye of William Helion to lerne the contents". Evidently Helion was a sub-tenant of Robert Drake. The following year there was trouble of a different kind when the Lord of the Manor of Littleham, Sir Thomas Denys, claimed that he owned the land at Pratteshide on which the ferryhouse stood. Exeter Corporation, anxious to avoid a second bout of litigation over the ferry, seem to have come to some amicable agreement with Sir Thomas, and no more is heard of this claim. In 1625 John Watts obtained a 99 year lease of the ferry, only to die the following year; and on 31st January 1626 the lease was taken up by Richard Watts and held by him for 60 years. It proved to be a rather turbulent period in the ferry's history. Local boatmen began poaching on the trade of the authorised ferry, and from 1633-34 a Mr. Hele claimed a right to convey travellers across the river, basing his claim on a loophole in the lease granted to Watts. Exeter Corporation took up the matter with Hele and by October 1634 had settled the affair out of court. Meanwhile the unfortunate Watts had to cope with the trauma of a fatal accident.

On 4th September, 1633 the passage-boat was wrecked on a rough crossing and three passengers lost their lives. They were Andrew Putty, John Rynnicke and William Walter; and Walter's body was not found for five weeks. A decade later, armed with a musket at the expense of the parish, Watts was in charge of the ferry throughout the troubled years of Civil War, and would have witnessed the six weeks siege by Fairfax of a fort on the Warren which was held by the Royalists. When Watts died in 1686 his son, Thomas, took charge for a month while the tenancy was being advertised. Edward Woodward was the new lessee, taking over on 8th November with a 99 year lease. The two cottages and garden on the ferry quay were let separately at the same time to John Hall, a thatcher. In 1689 Exeter Corporation suspected that Woodward had a casual attitude to his duties, and an alderman was asked "to give a check to ye keeper of ye fferry at Prattishead for neglecting his duty". The alderman must have reported favourably, as Woodward continued as ferryman well into the next century and eventually served for 57 years (until 1743). Later in the eighteenth century the ferry lease was held by:- George Bussell (1751-58), Andrew Perriam (1758-66), John Wyett (1766-?), Thomas Elson (?-1827). Woolcombe's Island at Starcross was washed away in 1703 and the ferry landing resited at a position north of the present Courtenay Arms Inn. In 1745 the local watermen were warned by the Town Clerk of Exeter that they must not poach on the ferry.

George Bussell took out three successive leases between 1751 and 1753, the second in partnership with another ferryman, John Mason, who disappears from the records without explanation after about twelve months. Bussell's successor, Andrew Perriam, had to pay a £10 rental, but evidently business fell off in his time for when he handed over to John Wyett about twelve years later the rental had been reduced to Twenty shillings. In 1774 a complaint was made that the ferryman was not always in attendance when passengers needed his services. In the last decade of the eighteenth century there are references to John Richards (Mine Host at the Passage House Inn), and to Thomas Elson, the ferryman who angered the locals and the Exeter Corporation by raising the tolls to increase his profits. The Corporation stepped in and fixed a scale of tolls, as follows:- Passenger (2d.), 4 wheel carriage (1/6), Horse (4d.), More than 1 horse (3/-), 2 wheel carriage (1/-), All tolls double after sunset. Elson was the ferryman when Fanny Burney, the novelist, made the crossing to Starcross in 1791. In her 'Diary and Letters' she wrote that as she disembarked she saw local women 'with feet and legs entirely naked, straw-bonnets of uncouth shapes tied in their heads......strolling along with mannish strides to the borders of the river, gathering cockles......"

Between 1808 and 1845 William Hull, a prominent Exmouth landowner, built a lengthy embankment from north of the Point, and drained the forty acres of land thereby enclosed. This left the old quay and ferry station high and dry, but it is thought that silting of the ferry channel had already caused a new passage house and ferry station to be built on the outer face of the Point near the Old Customs House. Reproduction of contemporary prints of this picturesque ferry house can be seen in 'The Book of Exmouth' by Robin Bush (Barracuda, 1978). After Elson's death in 1827 there seems to have been no regular ferryman until John Pyne was granted the lease in 1835. In December the following year both ferryboats were sunk, when a hurricane ravaged the South coast. Pyne's appointment was at the expense of Sir Diggory Forrest who had also applied for the lease, and the Corporation may have felt cause to regret this during the following years. Although a new scale of increased tolls had been drawn up in 1838, they received complaints that Pyne was overcharging, so they obliged him to exhibit the authorised fares on a tollboard at the ferry station. The following year he complained that local boatmen were running unauthorised ferries, and in 1842 a boatman that Pyne was then employing complained that he had not been paid. Worse was to follow; in August 1843 the ferry was crossing from Starcross when, in hoisting the sail, the ferryman accidentally knocked a man's hat into the river. He and his three passengers rushed to the lee gunnel to retrieve the hat, and the boat was swamped and capsized. The local Revenue cutter's boat came to the rescue and picked up three of those in the water, but a young servant girl lost her life. This disaster provoked an outbreak of criticism of the ferry and ferrymen: one complaint being that the boats were unsuitable for carrying vehicles, and that carriages were laid athwart-ships with two wheels overhanging one side and the other end balanced by large stones slung in nets over the other gunnel. The accident and the public outcry that followed did not reflect well on the management of the ferry, and in 1845 Exeter Corporation were probably not sorry to sell the undertaking for £1,000 to the South Devon Railway Company.

The signs of change were not at first apparent. For the South Devon Railway, traversing the west bank of the river from Exeter to Newton Abbot, the newly-acquired ferry to Exmouth was the least of their worries. They were experimenting expensively - and unsuccessfully - with atmospheric traction until September 1847, and the ferry continued at first to operate as before. As late as 1899 Freeman's Handbook to Exmouth was recording 'a pontoon for conveyance of horses and carriages and other vehicles also crosses the river to Starcross'. Clearly an important date in the history of the passage is when the sailing vehicular-ferry was replaced by the steam passenger ferry: but it is a date that seems impossible now to fix with certainty, and if Freeman is taken as correct a few years must have elapsed when both steam and sailing ferries were plying simultaneously. Steam ferries were certainly operating in 1892 and probably earlier. The entrance to Exmouth Docks (opened 1864) became used as the departure point for the steam ferries, which were pedestrian-only. On the Starcross side the South Devon Railway built the wooden pier adjacent to the station in 1846. Vehicular traffic across the Exe thus came to an end, but by the time the steam ferries were plying, the South Devon Railway had long been absorbed (in 1876) by the Great Western, while the ferry rights had been sold on 1st June 1869 to the Exe Bight Oyster Fishery and Pier Company Ltd.

The steam ferry service began when the Exe Bight Company sold the rights during the 1880s to a Finnish sailor named Gronberg. Gronberg owned a twenty-eight foot sailing drifter called the **Melita** in which he installed a high-pressure engine with a vertical boiler, and so ushered in a new era on the ferry. The **Melita** was joined on the service by the **Pioneer**, a small paddler of uncertain age. The **Pioneer** was found unsuitable for the work and was eventually beached just above Starcross. There she remained for many years, during which her tophamper and paddleboxes were removed. She sank in the mud and was visible only at low water springs when her ribs showed above water.

In 1891 the Exmouth & Great Western Ferry Company, a subsidiary of the Exmouth Dock Company acquired the ferry rights from Gronberg. His son, Freddy Gronberg, however continued to work on the ferries for years until he died. The new company ordered a purpose-built ferry from Messrs. Simpson & Strickland of Dartmouth. This was the **Prince**, delivered in 1891 and named after the Company's former excursion steamer which had been sold that same year to Lee-on-Solent. The **Prince** was a distinctive steamboat, open-decked with relatively high freeboard, and she set the pattern for future construction. Her narrow funnel carried the steam exhaust pipe on the after side, and she was, for thirty years, the only Starcross ferry to have twin-screw engines.

Before the Great War, **Prince** was followed by two generally similar steamboats, the **Zulu**, presumably named after the G.W.R. express of that name which stopped at Starcross station, and the **Melita**, named after Gronberg's original ferryboat, which she replaced.

The **Zulu** built by G. Lavis & Co., Exmouth, was commandeered by the Navy during the Great War. After return to service she was cut in two (c.1920) by Lavis's, and lengthened. **Zulu** had a single screw driven by a triple-expansion engine. Her exhaust pipe was on the foreside of the funnel, and she was also distinguished by her square bow and straight stem, and her cast-brass helm wheel. The **Melita** had a cutter bow, with a curved stem. Her steam-exhaust pipe was abaft the funnel, and she had slightly more freeboard than **Zulu**. Mr. R.F. Rew of Exeter recalls that the skipper of **Melita** during the Great War and for a while after was named Pearce - "a lean, taciturn individual very efficient at his job, but seldom known to smile". Installation of the engines in both steamers was carried out by (another) Mr. Pearce, of the Lavis Shipyard. **Prince, Zulu**, and **Melita** were all wooden-hulled, with transom sterns.

In March 1898 the newly-formed Devon Dock, Pier & Steamship Company acquired the assets of the Exmouth & Great Western Ferry Company, as well as the Dock and Ironworks, and the excursion steamers of the Devon Steamship Company. They took over the ferry rights and reached agreement with the G.W.R. that they should receive 5% of all rail tickets booked by them. The ferry has remained with this company to the present day. On the Starcross side the ferries met all trains, calling at the timber-piled pier built by the South Devon Railway which had direct access to Starcross Station. As originally built, the pier terminated at the point where the tin shed stands. From the ferry steps at the end, a very low jetty of duckboards about 12 inches above the river bed led out toward a ferry-mooring in the channel. At the turn of the century and until 1904 Bill Diaper, a Starcross station porter, had the task of keeping this extension-jetty swept clear of mud and weed, seeing passengers safely along it at low water, and then putting them aboard the ferry by rowboat. Reg Cowell, Starcross octogenarian, can recall, as a boy, seeing Bill Diaper at work. The

Great Western Railway extended the pier in 1904, so that the ferries could berth at low water. In those days ferries on passage passed the old fever hulk which lay off Cockwood, and near Exmouth dock entrance the river tug **Queen of the Exe** (skipper Mitchell), which for many years was moored here at the edge of the fairway. Boats getting out of control in the strong tides often fetched up alongside **Queen of the Exe**. Mr. R.F. Rew of Exeter recalls the ferry **Melita** being unable to combat a spring tide when approaching Exmouth dock one day in the 'twenties, and being assisted in by one of the others going out and securing alongside. The 'twenties and 'thirties were the heyday of the ferry, when 'STARCROSS FOR EXMOUTH' really meant something, and passengers could usually reach Exmouth more quickly by G.W.R. and crossing the river than by the Southern (ex L.S.W.R.) route to Exmouth station. Two boats were required to work the service in summer, while the third ferry ran river excursions to off Turf.

In 1923 the Company decided to invest in a fourth ferryboat, to be steel-hulled. She was built on the Exmouth dockside, with their own labour under the supervision of foreman-shipwright Bill Peters, and fitted with a powerful twin-screw triple-expansion engine by Sissons of Glasgow. Like her predecessors, the **Starcross** (128) was steered from the bow, the helmsman giving hand signals to the engineer. Her regular engineer was Sid Seymour, while for many years her skipper was Dan Horne. Present day ferry skipper Bert Mellish recalls: "As soon as Dan had turned the **Starcross** outside the dock entrance he would light up his pipe. He was always dressed in collar and tie, and you would never hear him swear". Dan was a 'key' man in the Company's service, and was responsible for the operation of the patent slipway when the excursion steamers or ferries were hauled up for repair. Sadly, not long after retirement, Dan Horne lost his sight. The patent slipway (designed by Cosens of Weymouth in 1896) was demolished in 1932.

The **Prince** was withdrawn in the mid-twenties and sold to a private owner who eventually allowed her to rot away near Topsham Lock. The **Melita** was sold in the early 'thirties, to become a small houseboat in Exmouth dock. **Starcross** and **Zulu** were joined in 1933 by the rather ugly **Tamar Queen**, an open motor boat with a high foc'sle enclosing a small fore-cabin. She was soon irreverently nicknamed "the codshead". Retired ferry skipper Ted Game recalls that the **Tamar Queen** was re-engined in 1934 with a 40hp. Ruston-Hornsby motor and became thereby the first diesel boat working out of Exmouth. Her capacity was 73 passengers. About 1937 the Port Authority decided to shift the remains of the old **Pioneer** on Starcross beach. The Exeter dredger came down-river and pulled her apart. Steve Ball, retired Exeter pilot, recalled in a letter to 'Ships Monthly': "I went down inside the **Pioneer** and slung the parts of the old horizontal engine, the shafting and so forth. They were sold for scrap."

Railways were still the pre-eminent form of transport and hence the ferry retained its importance and continued to be busy. The G.W.R.'s 1939 summer timetable shows sixteen crossings each way daily, with passage time twenty minutes. Parcels traffic remained important, as it had always been, the Company's own van (driver Bill Lindsey) carrying out prompt deliveries in Exmouth. The G.W.R.-and-ferry route remained in keen competition for the Exmouth traffic with the S.R. line from Exmouth station. For some time a Saturday morning express - with two coaches reserved for Starcross and Exmouth passengers - was halted at Starcross with Paddington the next stop. In all connections at Starcross the ferry had to await the arrival of the train, even if it was late. A level crossing (now removed) obviated the need for ferry passengers to use the platform footbridge. Meanwhile the **Zulu** had been withdrawn in 1934 and sold to Holman's the boatbuilders, who dismantled her. She had been replaced by the purpose-built **Diesel Comet**, which although motor-driven was structurally very much in the tradition of Starcross steam ferries. In her earlier seasons she had a funnel, which was later removed when her engine was re-mounted further for'ard. Built of $1\frac{1}{2}$ inch pitchpine by Messrs. Lavis, she was 46ft. in length and fitted with twin-screw Lister engines.

With the outbreak of World War II the **Starcross** was requisitioned by the Admiralty and went to Devonport Dockyard, where it was probably intended to use her as a liberty boat or tender: but it is said that she was in fact used to convey vegetables to ships at the buoys. At the end of hostilities her condition was poor and the company did not want her back. She was acquired by the Millbrook Steamboat & Trading Company, who however did not recondition her, and her end came as noted at the beginning of this narrative. The **Diesel Comet** and **Tamar Queen** (latterly renamed **Tamar**) had seen the ferry service through the war years, but the **Starcross** had to be replaced, and the Company ordered a purpose-built ferry from Lavis's in 1947. This was the 55ft. **Exonia** (1), fitted with Hotchkiss internal cone propellors which enabled her to operate in hardly two feet of water, when the other ferries could not reach Starcross pier at low water spring tides. Her passenger capacity of 172 made her the most commodious boat yet used on the service. After 26 years she was withdrawn in 1973 and sold the following year to a Torquay owner who converted her to orthodox propulsion and is belived to have been sold since to Manchester owners.

A replacement for the time-expired **Tamar** was obtained in 1954. The new vessel delivered by Lavis that year was the **Orcombe**, orthodox twin-screw with a passenger capacity of 123. Her arrival completed the modernisation of the ferry fleet and signalled its readiness to handle an increased volume of traffic which, it was soon clear, would not be forthcoming. The years of decline had begun, and were to continue. In 1968 - a sad year in the ferry's history - the service was downgraded to summer-only. This was consequent on the fall of the 'Beeching Axe' on British Railways, which involved the withdrawal of the parcels trains and made the winter ferry service uneconomical.

In 1972 the **Diesel Comet** was sold to a Budleigh Salterton buyer for about £100, and taken to Exeter. The **Orcombe** is still in service today. Early in 1981 she was lifted out of the water for the first time since entering service and placed on the dockside for complete overhaul. Since 1976 she has been partnered on the ferry by a new **Exonia** (2), a fibreglass hulled open boat which offers little comfort to her unfortunate passengers in inclement weather. The ubiquity of the motor car has largely negatived the importance of the rail-ferry link at Starcross: and since the service had become summer-only, the value of the ferry pier to British Rail had been much diminished. By 1981 considerable expenditure on repair work was necessary: indeed an estimate was tendered for £100,000. In February that year British Rail sold the pier to Exeter Marine Ltd., who planned to restore the structure and run it as a commercial enterprise, without prejudice to its use by the ferry.

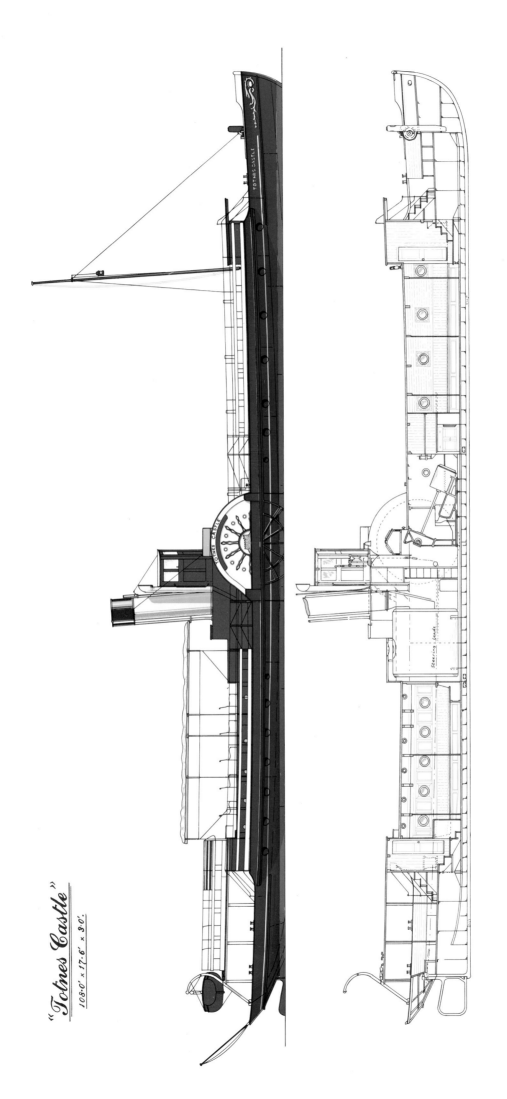

"Totnes Castle"

108·0' × 17·6' × 3·0'.

Totnes Castle *of 1921. Service: Totnes Boats (1923–1929).*
Plan courtesy National Maritime Museum, Greenwich.

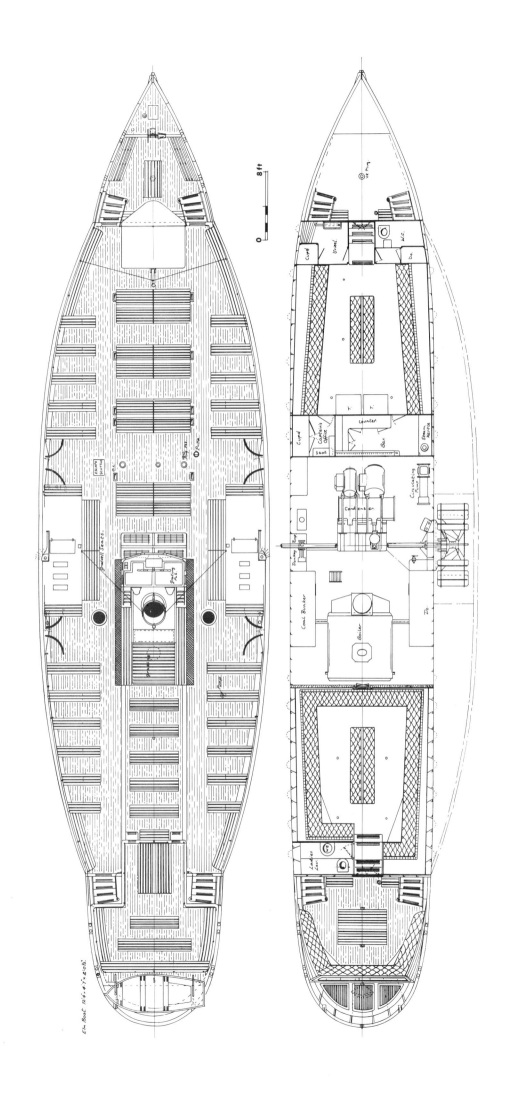

Starcross Pier lies approximately north-west from Exmouth Dock Steps, but the ferry has to steer a sou'westerly course until the Great Bull sandbank has been rounded. In winter fog it could be a hazardous business, especially in ebbing spring tides. Skipper Tommy Kettle recalls one morning when he would have waited for the fog to lift, had it not been for 22 workmen anxious to land at Starcross. After leaving the dock entrance, **Diesel Comet**, giving the Great Bull a wide berth with no landmarks visible, failed to respond quickly enough to the helm in the swift tide and stranded on the Warren. Ten minutes later the fog lifted and Tommy wished he had delayed departure; the more so when a press photographer arrived to record their discomfiture. "We've crossed here hund'ds of times wi'out a hitch and no sign o' you", Tommy complained. "First time we have a spot o' trouble, an' here you are!"

The winter of 1961 was one the crews would not easily forget. Much of the river iced over, the channel buoys were displaced and the ferries maintained the service with great difficulty, as the opportunity offered. When the weather was not the aggravation, it could be the passengers! Passengers' bicycles were accepted on the ferries but were very unpopular with skipper Bert Page, as they cluttered deck space. Bert, formerly mate of the sea-going excursion steamer **Duke of Devonshire**, was used to broad decks. On one occasion he tripped over a carelessly placed bicycle, bruising himself. He gave immediate vent to some sailorly language which was unappreciated by the bike's owner, a local doctor. He reported Bert at the Dock office after berthing!

Bert Mellish recalls a London couple who were leaving Exmouth to catch the train at Starcross. Two ferries were at the steps, the one berthed inside displaying a board advertising River Trip and Ferry. They took seats on this boat, but Bert asked them if they were for Starcross. When they said 'yes' he directed them to the ferry lying on the outside. They were unimpressed and remained seated. "This one is marked RIVER TRIP AND FERRY, as clear as a London bus,' they replied. 'Well' said Bert with a kindly smile, 'you might see a London bus advertising HP sauce, but you wouldn't expect the driver to have a bottle!' Retired railwayman Reg Scott tended the ferries at Starcross pier for many years from 1924 and recalls that constant silting in the river prevented ferries berthing at low water in spite of the pier extension. Two open boats, one 35ft., the other 25ft., were kept handy for transferring passengers and goods between pier and ferry. The 25ft. boat was latterly fitted with a JAP air-cooled engine, to avoid delay to trains.

One foggy evening a voice was faintly heard screaming 'Help!' from somewhere across the river. Reg Scott jumped into the 25ft. tender, accompanied by Ted Game and Ted Kerswell from the ferry, which was at the pier awaiting a train. They rowed out into the mists, searching, hailing, and listening; but the piteous voice was not heard again. Next day they learned that an angler, out on the sandbanks in waders, had lost his bearing in the fog and been swept away by the tide.

About 150 yards north of Starcross Station can still be seen a stone groyne abutting into the river from the railway embankment. On its extremity once stood a tall post supporting a lamp bracket. It was Reg Scott's duty after dark to place a lighted lamp here and another on Starcross pier. The ferry skippers kept these lights in line to be sure of keeping in the deepwater channel. Today Starcross Station has been downgraded to an unstaffed halt and there is no railwayman to tend any lights: nor are they needed, for today the ferry does not run after dark. Fog and darkness were not the only adversaries of the ferrymen: it could be rough in the estuary. On one such day the ferry was unable to lie alongside Starcross pier, and packages were being thrown across the gap. Finally the ferry closed briefly to enable a passenger's trunk to be lugged on to the steps and left for Exmouth. The trunk 'stayed put' when Reg Scott had to hurry to meet a down train, but before he had a chance to return, it had floated off! It was observed bobbing wildly in the troubled waters and promptly chased and recovered by boat. A Starcross porter took it home, opened it and dried all the contents. It was then despatched by rail on its intended journey. Amazingly, no complaint was received! Every ferry has its tall story, but this one is certainly true.

EXMOUTH – DAWLISH WARREN: The ferry between the north-eastern tip of Dawlish Warren and Exmouth Point is known to have been in existence by 1797. It was worked as an extension to the Starcross passage run by Exeter Corporation, and conveyed by them to the South Devon Railway in 1845. The Railway subsequently sold it to the Exe Bight Oyster Fishery & Pier Co. Ltd. in 1869. In 1862 there was high drama when a passenger mysteriously disappeared after crossing to the Warren and the police suspected Ferryman Trim of his murder, with robbery as a motive. It was not until the missing traveller's body was washed ashore, with his wallet intact, that Trim was cleared of suspicion. In those days the ferry would have run from the north side of the Point.

The service from the pier beach at Exmouth is believed to have been started by John Carder in the 1880s. He used an open boat with lug'n mizzen rig and was the sole ferryman until his death. View postcards of Exmouth circa 1910 included one of bewhiskered John and his boat, awaiting passengers at the Warren (126). He was over 80 when one morning, shortly after the end of the Great War, he was found drowned in Exmouth Dock. After 'old John's' time, the service was worked by a succession of local men in competition with each other. The families principally involved were the Bradfords, the Hockings and the Holmans. Since those days the end of the Warren has largely washed away: the river mouth was then only 500 yards wide at high water and on the Warren were about 70 dwellings, mostly bungalows, but also some grounded houseboats, used as holiday homes. This created a need for the daily delivery of bread, milk, papers, etc. There was plenty of work for the ferrymen, who started at 6am. delivering necessities, and saw to it that there were boats for passengers till as late as midnight, if required.

At the height of the trade there were up to eight boats working on the ferry, including **Pansy** (W. Holman), **Mayfly** (A. Bird), **Jehovah Jireh** (J. Bradford), and **Rosemary** (W. Parker). Other ferrymen included two W. Hockings who were not related, but the names of their boats are not remembered. A. Martin and 'Dido' Bradford were among the last ferrymen to ply. The return fare, 2d. in John Carder's time, was increased to 3d. and finally to 4d. The use of sails when carrying passengers was eventually prohibited by bye-laws, and thereafter ferrymen rowed their clients across, in 14ft. skiffs. The trade decreased very much in the late 1930s when much of the Warren and the bungalows were washed away, and the ferry came to an end at the outbreak of World War II.

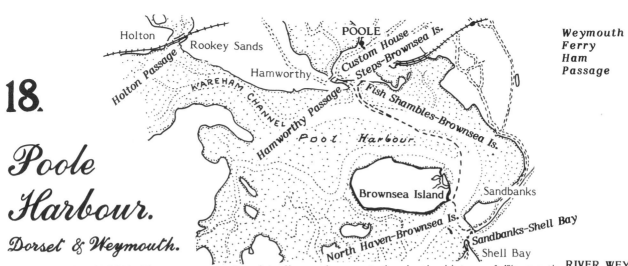

18.

Poole Harbour.

Dorset & Weymouth.

WEYMOUTH FERRY: There seems to be virtually no documentation in the history of Weymouth ferry, but it must certainly have been operating as long as Weymouth and Melcombe Regis have existed on opposite sides of the River Wey. There are references to a "passage boat" in Tudor times, but this would have been higher up the Wey than today's ferry and before the building of the original bridge in 1593. Today the ferry runs from the Nothe Steps on the Weymouth side to the Melcombe Regis quay adjacent to the seaward end of Devonshire Buildings. The site of the landing on the Melcombe Regis side did not exist prior to about 1800. Locally it is believed that the ferry has certainly operated in this position since the opening of the Nothe Gardens on the Weymouth side during the 1870s. Mr. J.A.C. West, Curator of Weymouth Museum, makes the point "It is a logical position, being the furthest point from the Harbour Bridge which is regularly used by pedestrians. A site any nearer the Harbour Bridge would automatically increase the likelihood of passengers walking round, rather than paying the toll!"

It is a summer-only service, and is run for the benefit of anyone wanting to avoid the long walk round via the bridge. In practice, the greater proportion of passengers are holidaymakers and tourists and the ferrymen have been veteran fishermen of the district. The Local Authority grants the licences and at present the number of active ferrymen is four. It is probably one of the least-known ferries of the West country but came briefly into the public eye in March 1979 when the local press reported that ferryman Warren of Weymouth had been missing without trace for eight weeks and had last been seen in the early hours of one morning in Yeovil. Frederick 'Darkie' Warren, aged 76, was an ex-fisherman and a well-known local character on the ferry. However, the mystery did not have an unhappy ending, for the Dorset Evening Echo reported on 6th April that he had been found "alive and well but does not want his whereabouts to be known".

We have been unable to trace any recorded accidents connected with the ferry, which seems to have an unblemished record in this respect within living memory, a tribute to the men who have worked the service. Ferryman Alf Pavey remarked "Of course, over the years there have been one or two passengers overboard, but never a fatality". The men who work the ferry believe that there is more glamour attached to its history than is commonly assumed. "It has been handed down, generation to generation" says Alf, "that Queen Elizabeth I gave the local seafaring men a charter to work the harbour ferry in their latter years as a source of income when they were retired, in token of their service for England against the Spanish. No one has seen this charter, and we can't prove its existence, but we are sure the ferry has legal protection. When extra berths were being built for the cross-Channel boats in the 1930s, an attempt was made to close down the harbour ferry but it failed because of our rights". Also one local boatman told me "It's always been a rowing-boat ferry and always has to be. You mayn't use a motor-engined boat on it".

Before the building of the first Town Bridge (the present bridge is the fifth) the ferry, on its old site, must have been of considerable importance. Merchants, ships' crewmen, tradesmen and market-bound housewives would all have needed to use it. Yet despite its decline through removal many years ago to its present site, there were as many as 32 ferrymen at work in the 'twenties and early 'thirties. Today the financial lot of pensioners is happier and the hard work of ferry seems correspondingly less attractive. A number of fishermen have ferry licences but only four are actively working the service:- Bobby Gray, Arthur Gumm, Alf Pavey and Dick Sargent. The season is from Easter to the end of October, daily from 9am. to 8pm. The fare, 1d. before the Great War, 2d. in the 'twenties, 3d. in the 'sixties, is now 5 decimal pence. The rowboats used are clinker-built, 14ft. in length, and each has a passenger capacity of nine.

The occasional passenger whose name is a household word is usually a 'show-biz' personality appearing in summer shows. Alf Pavey recalls Hughie Green (of Opportunity Knocks fame) boarding the ferry without his purse. "I'll have to owe you the 3d!" he said to Alf.

HAM PASSAGE: Hole's Bay, an extensive inlet on the north side of Poole Harbour, has a narrow mouth which once formed a barrier between the Hamworthy peninsular and the town of Poole. Today the A350 road crosses this gap, which was first bridged in 1837, but prior to the bridge the only passage was by a ferry, the origin of which is not known. The ferry was propelled by the ferryman hauling on a fixed rope, a method no longer used in the West country today except by the ferry over the canal basin at Exeter. Leland (Henry VIII's antiquary) seems to have used Ham Passage and we have this reference in his Itinerary: "There lyith agayn the kay ('opposite Poole Quay') a point of land, as a causey, after the facion of a brode swerd....the poynte is agayn towards the town, and the broad part hangynge up to the land, and by this causey men cum from Litchet to the fery". It is thought that Leland passed this way about 1540-41, so this is possibly the earliest reference to Hamworthy ferry.

*Ham or Hamworthy Passage: George Davis rowing from Poole Quay to Hamworthy
with a light load, in the late 1920s.   Photo: Poole Museum Service.*

However, we have also the record of the lease of the ferry to a John Henbury on 22nd May, 1541, by the Mayor and Corporation of Poole, as follows: "Grant from John Notherell and all his brethren for fifty one years of the Passage House and Passage to John Henbury, merchant, to pay yearly, one couple of capons". An annual rent of two neutered cockerels was apparently preferred to cash! Henbury and his successors were allowed to collect 4d. annual rate from Poole families, and charge strangers $\frac{1}{2}$ d. a crossing; but his unwieldy craft had a capacity of 70 passengers, so he (or his employee) needed plenty of muscle to maintain the service. In the terrier of the town of Poole's lands made in 1561 is a reference to "the passage purchased and maintained by the town and belonging unto the same stright over against the great Key letten under John Henbury by lease and now in the tenure of Robert Wright. The yearly rent of the same is one couple of capons of antient time accustomed to be paid unto the Baylie of the Town for the year being."

In 1787 the historian Hutchins describes "a passage boat large enought to hold 80 persons, which continues to ply all day and is hauled by a rope stretched from one side to the other, for which every family (in Poole) pays only 4 pence a year and every stranger a halfpenny each time."

The town's archives contain many references both to the condition of the passage boat and to the conduct of the ferryman. In 1770 John Osman was presented that "Notwithstanding he has been frequently presented for not appointing a proper person for plying Ham Boat many complaints have been made of his persisting in his neglect and this day the said boat was adrift and several people waiting to go over being a great nuisance." In 1784 the boat was described as being in a "leaky condition and not fit for passengers to go over in her". In 1792 the state of the ferryboat was such that some passengers "complain'd that they have nearly lost lives in crossing the water". An act of vandalism was punished in 1828 when a customs' clerk named Thomas Bristowe was convicted in that he did "Wilfully and maliciously cut and injure a certain Rope called the Ham Passage Rope extending across the ferry or passage leading from the Quay at Poole to the Quay at Hamworthy.....the Rope being the property of Jos. King, the Younger, and James King of Poole aforesaid, Brewer". Bristow was fined £1 and ordered to pay this sum plus costs within seven days.

A wooden bridge was constructed privately over the crossing in 1837, and replaced by an iron bridge in 1884. The ferry was now faced with competition, but the tolls charged by the Poole Bridge Company were probably higher than the ferry toll. The Poole Corporation had been resistant to the bridge project because they received a rent for the ferry; but the demands of increasing motor traffic could not be ignored, and in 1927 the third bridge was built by the Corporation and bridge tolls discontinued. Thenceforward the ferry catered for pedestrian traffic only and its story became one of decline. In its latter days the ferry was chiefly of benefit to the patrons of the Shipwrights Arms Inn, which until its demolition in 1978 stood at the end of Ferry Road, Hamworthy. This inn was originally the Old Passage House - home of the ferrymen of many generations. After the Great War, the ferry rights were only intermittently let and only occasionally exercised.

Joe Matthews (grandfather of Fred wills of the Brownsea Ferry) was followed in the 1920s by a one-legged ferryman named George Davis (136), whose disablement was due to a shotgun accident. He ran the ferry for a number of years and is still remembered by many. Then followed Bill Elkins, who left to work at the Power Station and was succeeded by Tom Russell. The last lease was in the late 1930s to a man named Baker, who introduced a motorboat service. The ferry ceased to run when the public were excluded from the quays for military purposes in World War II. Today the ferry steps on either side, still maintained and still so-called, are the only visible relic of this ancient passage. The ferry rights have belonged to Poole Corporation from time immemorial.

HOLTON PASSAGE: A long-forgotten ferry of Poole was that which used to ply across the narrow neck of Lychett Bay between Holton and Rockley Sands. An ancient route from Wareham to Poole involved the two crossings at Holton and Hamworthy. When John Leland visited the area in the sixteenth century he recorded this ferry although it would seem he did not use it:- "From Wareham to Lytchet village by somewhat low and moorish ground, there cometh a small gut as in a fenny ground out of the haven of Poole on to the town of Lytchet before I entered into it......there lay a way to Poole by a ferry against Poole self.....". Today the route between Wareham and Poole is via the A351 and A35, passing half a mile to the north of Lytchett Bay and a ferry at Holton would not be relevant. In 1847 the Southampton & Dorchester Railway was opened under the chairmanship of A.L. Castleman and adopted roughly the route of the old Wareham-to-Swanage road, crossing Lytchett Bay at the site of the ferry, by Holton Viaduct. Although the five trains daily in each direction were for the first few months only lightly loaded, the route soon became popular and the L.S.W.R. absorbed the line in the following year.

Although the actual year of the ferry's closure is unknown, there seems little doubt that it was the victim of rail competition, and probably did not long outlive the coming of the trains. (This railway, although sufficient to kill the ferry, did not fulfil its promoters' hopes of becoming a trunk road, and by reason of its winding course and crossings of tidal inlets acquired the nicknames of 'Castleman's Corkscrew' and 'The Water Snake'). The former east landing of the ferry is now adjacent to the Rockley Sands Holiday Camp; and had the old road from Wareham continued in use.

CUSTOM HOUSE STEPS - BROWNSEA ISLAND: With four independent ferry services operating from different points in Poole, Brownsea Island would appear to be one of the most accessible and well served locations in Britain during the summer months!

The Custom House Steps service is a 'Combine' ferry, run by three operators with a boat apiece: takings are pooled, there is no competition and passengers need not return by the same boat as they made the outgoing trip. It is known as the Fred Wills Boat Service and like the other Brownsea ferries commenced running in 1964 as soon as the island was open to the public. Fred Wills started 'Round the Island' trips in 1945, when he was 'demobbed' from the Services, with the motorboat **Boy Philip**; and it was with the **Boy Philip** that he inaugurated the ferry in 1964. He formed a syndicate with other boat proprietors, but the others later withdrew and he engaged in a working arrangement with Bob Hale, owner of the **Water Gipsy** (38' capacity, 53 passengers) and J. Harvey & Sons, who contributed the **Neried** (31' capacity 57) to the service. In 1970 Fred Wills sold the **Boy Philip** and replaced her with the larger **White Heather** (36' capacity 55) which had been built at Teignmouth, Devon and had been employed there on sea and river fishing trips by Hockin and Pittaway. The service operates daily from Good Friday or 1st April (whichever is earlier) until the end of September; hourly until the Spring Bank Holiday and half-hourly for the remainder of the season.

A large proportion of every season's passengers are Boy Scouts from all over the world, as Brownsea is used by the Scout movement as a training centre and jamboree venue. Fred Wills recalls that on one occasion there was a force 10 gale raging when a party of 120 Scouts on Brownsea Island were due to leave to catch the cross-channel steamer to the Continent. The ferry service had been suspended because of the weather, but Fred Wills arranged with the Harbourmaster to make the necessary crossings to fetch the Scouts so that they would not miss their connection.

Bob Hale told me that the **Nereid** was formerly on the ferry under different ownership and was then named the **Lady Betty.** In those days it seems she had an uneviable reputation for collisions and her then owner was several times engaged in lawsuits. On one occasion his son was accompanying him and suddenly shouted "Dad, there's a man on the bow!" The skipper walked for'ard to investigate (without throttling down!) and saw the white knuckles of a pair of hands gripping the gunnel feverishly. A man was hanging on for dear life! "Wotta you doin' there?" asked the skipper. "You've run down my b..... boat!" said the desperate owner of the hands; and sure enough, the skipper could see, astern, the flooded remains of a dinghy in his wake!

Also using Custom House Steps is the motorboat **Castella**, which is owned by John Lewis Stores and runs a ferry service for their staff and holiday guests at Brownsea Castle. The **Castella** has a capacity of 38 passengers and leaves the quay at 12, 3 and 6 daily in the season, running a triangular service which includes North Haven: but this is not a public ferry. The National Trust also run a year-round service for their staff. Their ferry, the **Brownsea**, is a fibreglass boat of about 36ft., with a Lister engine and has a Board of Trade licence for 48 persons. A name from the past that should not go unrecorded is that of boatman Harry Dean, who was the island ferryman throughout the 1914-18 war.

FISH SHAMBLES STEPS - BROWNSEA ISLAND: The ferry to Brownsea Island which runs from the Fish Shambles Steps at Poole Quay is operated by J. Harvey & Sons (Poole) Ltd. They are the largest passenger-carrying concern in the harbour and have been established for a hundred years. Their Brownsea Island Ferry (summertime only) commenced running on the 16th May 1963, as soon as the island was thrown open to the public by the National Trust. The distance from Fish Shambles Steps to Brownsea Island jetty is over a third of a mile but involves only a part-crossing of Poole Harbour, which is seven miles long by four-and-a-half broad.

Six motorboats are variously employed on the ferry. Three of these are 30ft. open boats with passenger capacities between 50 and 60 - the **Ferry Naiad, Ferry Sprite,** and **Nereid.** Two are 50ft. part-covered boats accommodating about a hundred - the **Northern Angler** and **Maid of the Harbour.** Also appearing sometimes on the ferry is the 50ft. completely covered **Maid of the Islands,** which is principally used for cruises around the harbour and islands and is designated the Water Bus. The 30ft. **Nereid** normally works on the Fred Wills 'combine' ferry from Custom House Steps. Harvey and Sons' association with Brownsea Island goes back much further, however, than the inauguration of the present ferry; for in 1907 William James Harvey took Lord Baden-Powell and twelve Boy Scouts to Brownsea for the first Scout camp held on the island. The boat in which

*North
Haven -
Brownsea
Island
Sandbanks
Shell Bay
Ferry*

the Chief Scout was ferried was named **Hyacinth**, and later came to a premature end. She was stolen by some boys one night and was wrecked near the Isle of Wight.

NORTH HAVEN - BROWNSEA ISLAND: North Haven Ferries are owned by D.E.F. Kingsbury, who took over the boats and business of the Davis ferry which had previously run to Shell Bay with Harvey's boats and had also been involved in the litigation with the Floating Bridge Company. Kingsbury started his Brownsea Island service in 1964. The island had become the property of the National Trust in 1961 on the death of its former owner, elderly recluse Mrs. Bonham Christie. It was then an overgrown wilderness and much clearing had to be done before opening to the public.

Three motor boats were employed from the start but one was usually sufficient to maintain the service and all three would only be in use together on rare occasions. These boats were:- **Felicity** (35'), **Sandbanks Queen** (40') and **Gerton** (26'), the last-named having a cutaway bow below the waterline to facilitate beaching. Although ex-ferries, these boats had been adapted by Davis & Co. as Fire Tenders, and had to be reconverted. The **Felicity** and **Sandbanks Queen** had played their part in British history when they joined the armada of small vessels which went to Dunkirk in 1940 to evacuate the British Expeditionary Force. In the early 1970s all three were sold out of service and replaced by the craft operating today. The **Felicity** is now at Keyham (Plymouth), the **Sandbanks Queen** at Fleetwood (Lancs.) and the **Gerton** is still at Poole but employed on fishing and not as a passenger boat.

The boats now in service on the ferry are the **Privateer** (40', capacity 70), the **Buccaneer** (32' capacity 70), and the **Rockhopper** (22' capacity 26). **Privateer** and **Buccaneer** were acquired from Padstow, Cornwall, where they were running on the ferry to Rock. The **Rockhopper** also hails from Padstow, but was employed there as a pleasure boat. The ferry operates daily from April to September during the hours of admission to Brownsea - 10am. to 8pm. or dusk - giving a half-hourly service, and the crossing occupies approximately ten minutes. When not engaged on the ferry the boats are available for private charter, coastal or harbour cruises and fishing trips. In summer Poole harbour is thronged with private craft, both sail and motor, and spring tides reach a speed of seven knots. Therefore although the crossing is short, it is not necessarily uneventful, and many amateur sailors have cause to be thankful that the ferry is in the hands of true professionals.

SANDBANKS - SHELL BAY FERRY: The desirability, if not necessity, of a ferry across the quarter-mile wide mouth of Poole Harbour from the earliest times is evident from a glance at the map. It appears that local fishermen provided an as-required service in bygone days. Their right to do so however was disputed in the days of Elizabeth I, when the Governor of Brownsea Island, Admiral Sir Christopher Hatton, appears to have claimed the rights of toll and sent armed officers to halt the ferry boats and demand the takings. In Calendar 24 of the Poole Borough Archives it is recorded that a complaint was made against the gunner and his men who had been appointed to strengthen Brownsea Castle against a possible Spanish invasion. It was alleged that they were interfering with the rights of passage which 'for tyme out of mynde hath been used for everyman to sett over passengers from pointe to pointe'. This was in the mid-1560s. More than ten years later it seems that the local ferrymen were still worried about their position: as witness a document which refers to this ferry in the series of 93 questions put to and answered by 'Our Counsel' following the Great Charter of Elizabeth I in 1568. (It dates from about 1573). The question concerning the North Haven ferry asks: "Who ought man to sett over persons from pointe to pointe, and now the Castle will permit no man to sett over any butt those of the castle?" The answer given by learned counsel states: "Every man may use as heretofore hath been accustomed, If any do disturb him he may bring his action of trespass against him that doth disturb him".

Yet in 1575 there was a further complaint that the gunner was insisting on ferry rights for conveying the 'friends or acquaintances or other' of the shipmen. At last the Mayor and Corporation of Poole championed the cause of the ferrymen and on 25th August 1581 laid the following complaint before the Court of Admiralty: "That the gooner of Brankseye Castell doth moleste the inhabitants of the towne and will not suffer them to passe any persons from northhaven point to southhaven pointe butt doth threaten them to shoote att them and vyolentlye doth take their moneys from them, wh' is not onlye a greatt hinderaunce to poore men that were wont to gayne monye that wayes butt also an infrynginge of our lyberties, wher-fore we thincke ytt verye necessarye to be remedyd". The Court decided that the garrison of Brownsea were exceeding their rights, and upheld the ferrymen's complaint.

Dispute over the rights of ferry was however to come again to the Courts, in the present century. Meanwhile in 1906 a rowboat ferry for foot passengers was begun by James Harvey, founder of J. Harvey & Sons (Poole) Ltd. It is said that it was Harvey's ferrymen who, with an eye to business, encouraged the use of the name Shell Bay for Studland or South Haven, on account of the rich variety of shells to be found there.

Although a statutory power for Poole Harbour Commissioners to establish a vehicular ferry subject to them acquiring any franchise rights, was granted in 1914, it was never implemented. But the growth of the motor car traffic increased the pressure for a vehicular ferry, and in 1923 a private Act of Parliament established the present car ferry of the Bournemouth-Swanage Motor Road and Ferry Company. On 15th July 1926 the first steam-driven 'floating bridge' of this company commenced operation. An attempt to establish a monopoly however roused considerable local opposition and led to a mass meeting being held in the hall of Parkstone Grammar School. It was soon clear that there was strong support for the previous ferry operators, particularly Harvey & Sons and Davis, who were now using motorboats, and working by agreement with Bankes Estates. A legal battle ensued between the statutory company and those exercising the ancient customary rights of ferry. The Law Case (Public right of way) between Harvey's and the Floating Bridge Company was taken to the London Law Courts on 16th May 1928, and then to the House of Lords. Here Harvey's won the case on 30th May 1930, when the Court of Appeal ruled that the statutory ferry did not oust customary rights. It was stipulated however that the slipway and jetties constructed under the private statute could not be used by other than the ferry company, and accordingly

*North Haven - Brownsea
Island: **Privateer** with
almost a full load of
passengers lies at the
North Haven jetty, while
beyond, the Sandbanks-
Shell Bay chain-ferry
approaches Sandbanks.
Photo: C.V.Waine.*

private ferries have since used their own jetties alongside. This lawsuit made legal history and is now a leading case on the law of ferries. For Harvey's however, the victory was dearly won. The case cost so much that all their assets had to be mortgaged. The large house at Sandbanks where James Harvey, the founder, had lived was sold, and the small ferry boats were run by Mr. Charles Harvey, the son. After World War II vehicular traffic increased considerably while pedestrian traffic dwindled and Harvey's withdrew their ferry between Sandbanks and Shell Bay in 1967. Among their longest-serving boatmen were the late ferryman Scott (nearly 60 years) and Frank Hewett (40 years) and the still-thriving Terry Luff (24 years). Many well-known personalities had been among their passengers, including the motorboat racing drivers Scott Payne and Sir Henry Seagrave.

At the time the law case was proceeding, a substantial block of shares in the Bournemouth-Swanage Company was offered to Poole Corporation, but the offer was refused. In 1930 the company produced plans for a bridge between North and South Haven points to replace the chain ferry, and introduced a private bill in Parliament to implement them. The Bill was strongly opposed by Poole Corporation and ultimately failed. The history of the vehicular ferry is an interesting story in its own right. More than two years of hectic activity took place following the passing of the Act, for a long ferry road had to be built over wild heathland on the Swanage side, as well as the landing-hards on both sides of the estuary. The Motor Road Construction Company was formed to carry out the necessary works, with Mr. G.J. Aman as Manager and Mr. Fookes as resident Engineer and Surveyor. Mr. F.L. Gosney was appointed office clerk to the Company and his son, Mr. R.H. Gosney, was later engaged to supervise the weighbridge, where many thousands of tons of stone from local quarries were checked in. Thus began a remarkable association of the Gosney family with the Sandbanks ferry, which was to encompass more than 60 years and still continues today.

At either end of the course of the road ex-Great War accommodation huts were erected to house imported labour, while workmen from Poole arrived daily by motor boat and from the Swanage end by covered lorry. Construction began at both ends and worked towards the halfway point. At Shell Bay a bungalow was erected for the Foreman of Works. Much of the unskilled labour was done by small gangs of navvies who worked sometimes for only a few days before moving on. One workman, who was employed in cutting down the heather, had a profitable sideline in trapping adders, bottling them and selling them to research scientists!

When the work reached the stage of road-surfacing, steam rollers and motor rollers were brought by rail to Swanage Station and thence to the scene by road. One of these motor rollers eventually came to grief on the hill into Swanage, when it ran out of control, overturned and blocked the road for some hours. Sentinel steam wagons and four-wheel drive motor lorries which brought the quarried stone, were a familiar sight. Mr. R.H. Gosney can still remember these lorries trundling off on the last return trip of the day with their exhaust pipes glowing red hot in the twilight. At Studland and Shell Bay the remains of the old timber buildings which accommodated the navvies can still be seen, while the one-time foreman's bungalow now serves as the Company office. When the ferry eventually commenced running, Mr. F.L. Gosney continued as clerk to the Ferry Company, his son, Mr. R.H. Gosney becoming a toll collector, while Mr. G.J. Aman remained as Manager. An additional bungalow was erected at Shell Bay for the Ferry Engineer.

Ferry No.1, which had a capacity of twelve average-size cars, was constructed by Samuel White of Cowes. She was delivered early in 1926 and put on the chains for trial. It was found that she did not cope too well when the tide was doing its worst at $5\frac{1}{2}$ knots, so was returned to Cowes for engine modification, and thereafter gave no trouble, opening the service as stated on 15th July 1926. Her appointments included two tiny cabins, with adjoining toilet, so that the navigator and engineer of the duty crew could sleep aboard. This arrangement has been continued to the present day, and is unique in the West country. Ferry No.1 was later modified to accommodate an extra three cars. When the annual overhaul became due each January (lasting two weeks) the ferry was towed by a Poole tug to the refitting yard, usually Bolsons. A large motorboat was hired from Harvey's to handle pedestrian traffic and cycles. The Bournemouth-Swanage buses, which normally crossed on the ferry, ran to and from the hards, their passengers being crossed by the motorboat.

Sandbanks In the mid-'thirties a lady driver just missed the ferry at Sandbanks, and stopped her car on
Shell Bay the slip. Realising that she had a few minutes to spare before the ferry returned, she left the car and crossed the road to the Haven Inn. But the car's handbrake had a defective ratchet. On-lookers stared in wonder as the handbrake slipped and the car ran into the water. Filling rapidly, it moved down the hard and disappeared from sight! Ferry No.1 was not able to berth until a Poole harbour crane was brought up to move the obstruction!

In the late 'thirties the Territorial Army carried out a landing exercise at Shell Bay from a troopship. An offshore wind sprang up after the landing and the troopship prudently stood out to sea. As the wind did not abate soon enough for her to return, the troops and all their equipment were ferried to Sandbanks for dispersal from Poole. The army officer who signed the forms for the Company to reclaim the fares from the War Department was none other than H.R.H. Prince Henry, Duke of Gloucester!

When World War II began in 1939, the ferry continued its normal service until 23rd June 1940, when Shell Bay and most of the South Haven peninsular became a battle-training area. The road was then closed, the public excluded, and the ferry reserved for military traffic only. Live ammun-ition was frequently used as battle-conditions were simulated, and the ferry road suffered constant damage and make-shift repair during the run-up to the Normandy invasion. H.M. King George VI, Prime Minister Winston Churchill and General Montgomery all visited Shell Bay during this period. As essential military traffic could not be suspended for two weeks during ferry refits, arrangements were made to bring over a chain ferry from Cowes, as relief boat.

Ferry No.2 had long been working between East and West Cowes, across the River Medina. She also had been built by Samuel White's but was a smaller craft accommodating only 6-8 average cars. When, the war over, the ferry road was eventually reinstated and public service was resumed (31st January 1946), the company purchased this Cowes ferry, and kept her in reserve at moorings in Poole Harbour. The reinstatement of the ferry road was no light task, as apart from poorly-repaired potholes and craters due to Normandy preparations, there were earlier anti-invasion forti-fications, barriers and concrete blocks to be demolished. Ferry No.2 was retained during the early 'fifties, but it was then decided that her very occasional use hardly justified twelve months' harbour dues and maintenance costs, so she was sold. The Sandbanks passage is very exposed and in bad weather the prows of the ferry may lift and drop as much as two feet on the hards, so that the service has to be suspended. Ferry No.2 was once crossing in a westerly gale when one of the harbour navigation buoys broke adrift from its moorings and, dragging its chain, was swept across the ferry's path. The buoy mooring cable became entangled with one of the ferry chains and immobilised the ferry until it could be freed.

In the early 1950s Mr. Aman died. He was succeeded as manager by Mr. F.L. Gosney, whose son R.H. Gosney became office clerk until the early 'sixties when he was promoted to Traffic Supervisor and was to serve the company for 50 years. Meanwhile another son, L.A. Gosney, had joined the staff about 1953 as a Navigator. (He became Traffic Supervisor in 1975 when his brother retired). Mr. F.L. Gosney was succeeded as Manager about 1963 by Mr. F.V. Smith, who had been Company Secretary for some years previously. Mr. R.H. Gosney's son, N.R. Gosney, joined the Company as a Navigator in the late 1970s and is still serving in that capacity today.

In the early years traffic had been light, especially in winter; but as the new Bournemouth-Swanage route became popular and the private car multiplied, Ferry No.1 was seen to be too small to keep the traffic flowing (Plate 2). An order for a new boat was placed with Bolson's of Poole, and when it arrived No.1 was placed on the market. Ferry No.3, delivered in 1958, is still in service today. She is diesel-electric powered and has deck space for 28 cars. No.1 was sold for £500 to become a pile-driving pontoon at Poole: it is believed she is still in service for this purpose, at Southampton. Early in 1960, just before the introduction of diesel-electric vessels on the Torpoint ferry at Plymouth, No.3 became for a while a training-ground for the Torpoint crews. They came to Sandbanks to observe the time required for stopping and re-starting, the handling of the bridge controls and the approach to the slipway during strong spring tides.

Today the ferry is busy at all times of the year. Two full-time crews and two reserve crews are needed to guarantee the service. A crew consists of Navigator, Engineer, and one or more Ticket collectors according to the season and the Navigator and Engineer work a 24 hour shift which commences at 2pm. Each crew has two rest-days a week. Ticket Collectors do day-work, a forty-hour week with occasional overtime. The first boat from Sandbanks is at 7am. and the last boat of the day leaves Shell Bay at 11.10pm. during the summer: but in the winter the last boat is at 9.10pm. except at weekends.

Blackwater Ferry: The rope-worked punt and the thatch-ed ferry house. An idyllic scene at the turn of the century.

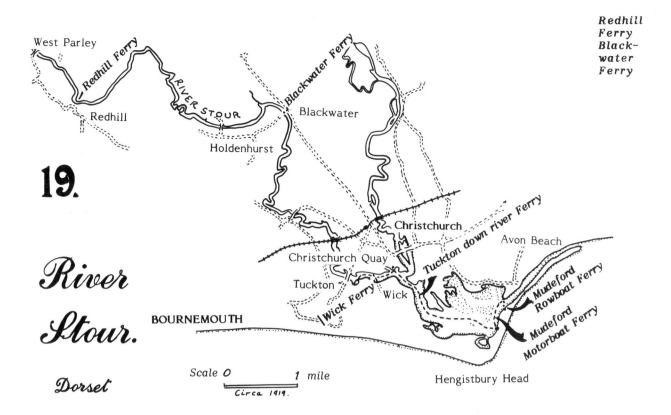

19.

River
Stour.

Dorset

West Parley

Redhill

Holdenhurst

Blackwater

Christchurch

Christchurch Quay

Tuckton

Wick

BOURNEMOUTH

Avon Beach

Mudeford Rowboat Ferry

Mudeford Motorboat Ferry

Hengistbury Head

Scale 0 ————— 1 mile
Circa 1919.

REDHILL FERRY, now no more, was once important as the only link between West Parley and Bournemouth. Before the building of the New Road Bridge, road traffic had to travel via the ancient Dorset Bridge at Longham. The ferry was sited at Redhill on the River Stour, about half a mile downstream from West Parley, where the Wimborne Road runs very close to the river. Here, in earlier times, was a ford, once known as Riddlesford (Red Hill ford), and this place name appears on several maps dating from 1791. The recent $2\frac{1}{2}$" Ordnance Survey map of Bournemouth (sheet 40/09) marks the ford. At this point the Roman Legions under Aulus Plautius are said to have crossed the Stour on their way to attack the Britons at Badbury Rings, c. AD 46. The ferry plied at the site of the ford, and must have been in operation from early times.

By Victorian times the ferry was well patronised by courting couples and others who enjoyed its romantic setting. Now, more than 40 years after closure, it is hard to visualise the scene as it must have been at the turn of the century. Marshalls' Riverside Tea Gardens flourished then on the south bank and offered 'strawberry tea' in season. Passengers were poled across in a punt, but in later years the ferry was worked by rope. A lease of the ferry tea gardens dated 18.7.1931 is in Bournemouth Library. This five-and-a-half years agreement between landlord Mrs. Florence Lamey and tenant ferryman William Bannerman provides for an annual rent of £50 in respect of the Tea Gardens with building and two tennis courts, the landing-stages and the ferryboat: subject to the lease of the ferry right being confirmed by Colonel Prideaux Brune.

The ferry carried 6,000 passengers in 1931, 8,000 in 1932 and 14,000 in 1933. Yet it was closed in March 1934 in the face of strong local protest. Petitions were signed, and arguments for and against appeared regularly in the local newspapers. The petition to re-open was opposed by the Rector of West Parley and the tenant of the adjacent farmland, and the ferry stayed closed. My curiosity was aroused by the closure of a ferry which the public wanted and which was paying its way. Mr. Sansom, the verger, who had held that office for more than 50 years, remembers the ferry and the manner of its closing. It appears that the wife of the influential yeoman who farmed the land by the ferry came one day across a party of people cavorting in the nude at the river bank, after (presumably) having crossed on the ferry from Bournemouth, which she regarded as Vanity Fair. Outraged, she demanded of her husband that he persuade the Rector, who also had a right in the ferry, that it should be closed down in the public interest. Rector and farmer found themselves in agreement, and public outcry was in vain. Certainly, an unusual story for a ferry closure.

BLACKWATER FERRY derives its somewhat ominous name from the village just north of Christ-church. It connected the east bank of the Stour, where the road to Hurn runs very close to the river, with the west bank opposite, where the right of way from Holdenhurst village meets the Stour. It was vested in the Heron Court Estate and the rights belonged to successive Earls of Malmesbury. A receipt in the possession of Bournemouth Library, dated 12th December 1909 acknowledges half a year's rent (£4.1.3.) paid to the Earl of Malmesbury by ferryman Alfred Chalk; this was in respect of land at Ringwood Road, the ferry boat, and the old ferry cottage and garden. The receipt includes a reference to a contra account for ferrying estate workmen.

The ferry cottage was most picturesque, a stone, two-storied house with a fine thatched roof. The rustic porch was half-overgrown with honeysuckle and the leaded windows had diamond panes. There was a stable at one end (140). In the early years of this century the ferry was particularly busy in June, bringing admirers to the Earl of Malmesbury's nearby rhododendron plantation, described by Ward, Lock & Co.'s guide as "one of the finest sights that even lovely Hampshire can afford".

In 1905 the 'Bournemouth Graphic' was only mildly enthusiastic about this scene at Blackwater passage. The issue of 16th February stated '.....a cottage and an old punt is what you will see. It sounds uninteresting, but if you are thirsty you will be interested to know that you can get within that tiny cot a nice tea for 4d. or 6d., or even a bottle of ginger beer'. A couple of years earlier a correspondent to the same newspaper was lavish with praise:- 'In this quiet secluded spot there is no sound save the singing of birds.... or the lapping of water on the stones.....the whole atmosphere seems to be filled with natural music....A girl with handsome face and figure, well developed by work and exercise in the open air, often takes the passengers across the ferry in the absence of her brother, and is accompanied by two pet cats, who seem to think that the boat could not go without them, and accordingly take their places at her feet as she stands holding the rope to guide the boat upon the surface of the clear water...."

There were times of course when the scene was less entrancing, for in winter the Stour could overflow its banks, and make it impossible to work the ferry. This was awkward for farm labourers who crossed daily to get to their work. In its earlier days Blackwater was very much a farmer's ferry, as Thomas Miller's poem reminds us:-

"Now moves the ferryboat across the river,
Bearing the wealth produced by many a farm!
Oxen and sheep and fruit and mid them all
The sun brown cultivators of the soil".

It is sad that the thatched ferry cottage (140) was pulled down about 1934, while the ferry ceased to ply during or shortly after the first World War. The remains of the ferry steps are all that can be seen today.

WICK FERRY: A passenger ferry has undoubtedly existed at Wick for centuries as the natural communication between the village and the town of Christchurch. No direct road nor bridge connected Southbourne and Christchurch until a private company built the first bridge at Tuckton in 1882. Very probably the early ferries were run by local residents using their own boats to travel from Wick to the Quomps - the five-acre meadowland on the Christchurch side. For the greater part of its history the ferry must have been vested in the lords of the manor but research has uncovered nothing prior to the eighteenth century. Mrs. Arthur Bell in her book 'From Harbour to Harbour' (1916) writes of Wick ferry: "The ferry across the Stour must have been in use before the college of Augustinian canons was founded" (i.e. prior to Domesday Book).

The first ferry service of which we have any detailed knowledge was started in 1814 or 1815 by a farm worker named Marshall. He was employed on a farm tenanted from John Sloman of Wick House, but had broken his leg and was unable to resume farm work. Mr. Sloman provided him with a boat and gave him land on the Wick side of the river which has been the ferry landing-place ever since. Sometime after this, a rival ferry was established by Eli Miller, based on the Christchurch side, and it remained in his family till 1903. The Millers then sold out to a Mr. J.C. Edmonds, who did not retire till 1946. Writing the following year in the 'Bournemouth Times' of 4th July, he recalled that in his early days the ferry began running at 5.30am. and continued till 11pm. In the Miller family's time and in Edmonds' earlier days, there was an old houseboat moored on the Wick side, beneath overhanging willow trees, where teas were served. Mr. Pope, a senior citizen of Christchurch, recalls that at the beginning of this century a square ended punt (as now) was used in the summer, and poled across. In the winter a salmon punt was substituted and was rowed with oars.

From 1900 to the 1920s the regular ferryman was Jack O'Brien, who was paid fixed wages, first by Eli Miller's widow and later by Mr. Edmonds. Jack O'Brien was a big built man, and it is on record that he required outsize boots which were made for him by his devoted sister! But Jack himself was clever with his hands. Mr. Pope recalls that one of his specialities was making working model windmills of wood, which he erected and displayed by the ferry waiting-hut. His Christmas dinner was always a cygnet - "beats all yer turkeys" he would say. Mr. Pope tells how perhaps on a miserable foggy night one would whistle for the ferry and hear Jack's "O-er!" (over!) through the gloom as he unhesitatingly rowed across for a single $\frac{1}{2}$ d. passenger. Jack O'Brien was a favourite subject of artists, and his portrait appeared several times in the Royal Academy. In 1927 Mr.Edmonds built a Boathouse on the Christchurch side and started a caravan camp which he sold after giving up the ferry. In 1947 an outboard engine was fitted to the ferry punt for the first time and the crossings made in half the time. On the 1st February 1954 Wick ferry was put out of action by ice on the river for the first time since 1855. After an hour, ferryman 'Brigham' Young cut a channel in the ice and restarted the service; but he became frozen in, later that afternnon and had to be 'rescued'. On the Southbourne side the ice was four inches thick at the landing slip and landings were made on the adjacent bank.

On 28th September 1957 the ferry temporarily closed down. Wick ferry Holiday Camp declared they had made a loss of £267 over the past year and did not propose to restart the service till the demand increased in the Spring. There was considerable public outcry, and the matter was discussed by the local authority. After nearly five weeks of closure, on the first of November the ferry was restarted by Christchurch fisherman Bob Bishop, using a salmon punt. He ran daily from 8am. - 1pm. and 2pm. - 4.30pm. and said he hoped to use a larger boat in course of time.

In 1958 the previously used ferry punt was given a Lister engine and a tunnel stern, and was mostly worked by Bob Bishop's daughter, Dawn. In the early 1960s the ferry was bought and run for awhile by Tuckton Riverside Services (owners of the Funnel Boats).

Today the former Wick Ferry Holiday Camp of 1965 has become a self-catering chalet camp run by the Warner Organisation (Pontin Group). They own the ferry rights, but the tenancy is held by Bournemouth Boating Services, who also operate the Tuckton Tea Garden Down-River Ferry. Since 1963 the Wick ferry service has been summer-only. The ferry crosses the Stour from a pontoon landing stage (with toll-hut) on the Christchurch side to the old stone slip inherited from Marshall's time on the Wick side. The punt, which has a green hull with red waterline, is the same that was fitted with an outboard engine in 1947. Since then the sides have been raised to increase freeboard, *Tuckton* space has been made on the foredeck for carrying buoyant apparatus, and a 6hp. Lister engine *Ferry* installed and given an air-inlet funnel. Capacity is limited to twelve passengers.

THE TUCKTON FERRY: The Christchurch down-river ferry was started by a Mr. Hodges in 1910 with two motor-boats, the **Pioneer I** and **Pioneer II**, both petrol-engined. Ralph Elliott put a boat on the service in 1919, followed by his brothers Ben and Frank. Frank ran only for a short time but held the licence until the early 'fifties; Ralph operated till the end of 1953 and died in January 1954. No attempt was made to form a company: boats remained individually owned, but worked together as a 'combine'. Ted Stride was working the service from 1926, and three more boat-owners - Thornton, Keynes and Kendall were taking part from 1927. George Derham was another early starter, but left a few years later to run an independent service based at Convent Walk on the River Avon. About 1930 Ted Budden, Bert Stride and W. Croucher joined the original combine which henceforth traded under the name of United Service Motor Boats. A reputation was established for smart, clean boats, and good timekeeping.

The Convent Walk service, started in 1930, changed hands in 1933 when George Derham sold out to new owners. This concern ultimately had five boats on the ferry:- **Venture** (1930), **Avon Belle** and **Lady of Avon** (1932), and **Avon Vanity** and **Ocean Queen** (1935). It survived the interruption of World War II but eventually closed down in the early 'fifties. The United Service faced further competition when 'The Funnel Boats' began running in the mid-thirties. This venture, run by Edwin Mens and his son Norman, worked from the Christchurch side of the river at Tuckton Bridge, and ran to Mudeford beach. By 1939 it had a fleet of seven 12-seater boats, each of which had a dummy funnel on the engine-box. The Funnel Boats service (together with a boatyard) changed hands about 1949, and again about three times before its closure in 1968. During the 1950s it had a fleet of four 48-seaters and two older boats with a capacity of 22, and made an intermediate call at Wick Holiday Camp (now Pontin's). From 1955 they worked from the Bournemouth side of Tuckton Bridge. Their fleet latterly included **Tuckton Belle, Tuckton Maid, Stour Queen, Stour Belle;** and the **Avon Belle** and **Lady of Avon** bought from Convent Walk when that service closed down c. 1953.

Originally the ferries of Hodges and his United Service successors ran from Christchurch Quay to Mudeford Beach (Sandbanks). At the Mudeford end all three concerns had their own landing-stages, while two of them (United Service and Convent Walk) had tea-boats converted to floating Cafes, with hulls approximately 45ft. x 20ft. beam. Between 1930 and the outbreak of World War II the United Service had about 9 boats (all 12-seater) working between Christchurch Quay and Mudeford Beach under licences issued by Christchurch Council.

Their long, two-pontoon landing-stage at Mudeford adjoined a two-deck teaboat which served locally caught salmon, lobster and prawn teas. The teaboat was owned by Mr. Croucher, one of the ferryboat owners. Trade was blossoming and in 1931 five of the operators decided to invest in a larger boat to be owned between them. This boat, the **Unity**, was the first large passenger boat designed for and fitted with Hotchkiss cone propellers, the patent of a Poole engineer. Convent Walk boats already had the small 12-seater **Venture** with this new form of propulsion, but the **Unity** represented a considerable advance on her, and was sometimes used by Donald Hotchkiss for demonstrations before the R.N.L.I. and other interested parties. On one occasion a trip was made to Mudeford through reed beds and over weeds, returning all the way in reverse! The arrangement however utilised valuable seating-space in the boats and after a few years they were converted to diesel, with single-screws.

In 1934 trade was still on the increase and five of the operators decided on a design by Eric French for a 50-seater boat with the propeller in a tunnel and a draught of 15 inches when loaded. Five of these sister-craft were built and named with a **Headland** prefix, e.g. **Headland Queen**, the **Headland** being presumably a reference to Hengistbury. All fares were collected on the boats, return tickets being sold initialled on the back so that the skipper who brought the passengers back sold the tickets back to the seller for half the return fare: this system continued until 1954, when, as will be seen, the service was worked to and from Tuckton Tea Gardens.

During World War II, Christchurch Harbour and river were closed to traffic from 1940 to June 1945, but the ferryboats went on 'Active service'. **Headland Pal, Headland Queen, Headland Princess** and **Avon Vanity** served with the R.A.F. at Chichester, Beaulieu River, and Poole: while the **Headland Maid** went to the west coast of Scotland. What had been a freak boat was bought by Ted Budden soon after the war, and was later acquired by the combine in 1963 and converted for use on the ferry. This was the **Chunky**, originally built in Hull in 1935, and was a hull bearing an Armstrong-Siddeley car body and engine, complete with car seats and doors! At Mudeford, after the war, the Christchurch Council provided a public landing-stage for the 19 boats working the service (144). Today there are only five United Boats, and the Mudeford motor ferry making use of the landing stage. The teaboats have long disappeared. The boom years of pre-war were not to return. Trade declined, Covent Walk ferries disappearing in the mid-fifties and Funnel Boats in the late 'sixties.

In 1954 the name of the combine was shortened to United Motor Boats. That year the proprietor of Tuckton Tea Gardens asked that the service might run from there. As the potential of Tuckton for trade was unknown, it was decided that all the United boats would share a toll box on Christchurch Quay and at Tuckton Tea Gardens and pool all the takings. During the 'sixties two further calls were added to the ferry route - Double Dykes from 1964, and Pontin's (Wick ferry) from 1969. Today there are five boats working the ferry, owned by John and Richard Elliott (sons of Ralph) and Robin Stride (son of Ted Stride). They own their fathers' three Headland boats and share the **Headland Pal** and the ex-Convent Walk **Avon Vanity**. They also own the self-drive boating business at Tuckton Tea Gardens and the Wick ferry under the name of Bournemouth Boating Services.

Over the years many well-known personalities have travelled on the Tuckton ferry, especially actors appearing in Bournemouth summer shows. But the ferry has had its own personalities who

*Tuckton Ferry: The 25ft. **Sally** at Christchurch Quay in the 1960s. A photo by
E.T.W. Dennis of Scarborough.*

have given long service and become very well-known locally. One of these was Reg Keynes. The
Keynes family have run a boat business at Christchurch Quay since 1906. They ran a 12-seater ferry
from 1927-1933 and owned the **Headland Pal** from 1934-70. (The **Pal** was sold to Keyhaven but
bought back for the ferry by the present operators). Reg skippered a boat for 5 years but was
chiefly occupied on the quay. He died in 1979. Another personality of the ferry was Ralph Elliott,
owner of the **Sally** and the **Headland Maid** from 1919 to 1954.

The service had had a remarkably accident free record, but there was universal sorrow when,
during the 'fifties, one of the skippers died of a heart attack while at the helm. The varnished
ferryboat **Sally**, going to Mudeford to pick up people for shopping in Christchurch, had left at
9.15am. empty, with Archie Frampton as skipper. When the next boat went down-river about twenty
minutes later, the **Sally** was found circling out of control in the harbour, with Archie (who was
in his sixties) lying dead beside the wheel. Although the heyday of this ferry service is in the past,
and the number of boats employed is much less than fifty years ago, trade is still brisk in the
holiday season, and the reputation for smart, clean boats and good timekeeping has been conscien-
tiously maintained.

MUDEFORD FERRY: This service crosses the dangerous Mudeford 'run' at the entrance to Christ-
church Harbour, between Mudeford Quay and Mudeford Sandbank. Notes we examined in Christchurch
Library state 'this ferry is by right of custom operated by the Derham family', while the book
"Ferries and Ferrymen" declares unequivocally "the Mudeford Ferry, for years a perquisite of the
Derham family". Our investigations, however, do not bear this out. In fact it would appear that the
Derhams, Cokes, Strides, Edgells and indeed other fishing families were all concerned with this
ferry for many years up to about 1975. In later years ferrymen Ron Foster (now, sadly, deceased)
and Mike Parker have been regular operators.

The boats used have traditionally been flat-bottomed salmon punts of about 15 foot length,
and broad in the beam. They were fitted with thole pins and supplied with three oars. In rough
or very strong tide conditions two men would row. In the home of fisherman Parker at Haven
Cottages, there is a fine sepia photograph of rowboat ferries dealing with a long queue of intending
passengers on the Sandbanks side. By the mid-1960s demands were being heard for a motor boat
which could deal more rapidly with the crowds, and provide greater comfort and security for its
passengers. The safety factor began to be raised, in spite of the excellent record of the rowboat
ferrymen. These arguments came to a head from 1969 to 70 when the local press reported constantly
on the ferry issue.

In March the Christchurch Council appear to have granted a concession to run a motor ferry to
a Mr. John Gelsthorpe and partners; and in April the Council were taken to task by Mr. K. Derham
in the local paper in no uncertain manner: "I think the council have made a wrong decision in granting the concession to operate a motor ferry by persons who have little or no experience of operating
in the Run. This job entails very expert experience of boat handling as can be obtained only through
years of rowing to and fro across the Run under all conditions of wind and tides. Wind in excess of
20 knots and tide 4-5 knots and even more when the rivers are in flood". A week later the local
panel of three who normally granted the ferry licences refused to meet to consider the application,
and the Town Clerk suggested that the matter might have to be referred to the Christchurch magis-
trates. In addition, opposition was being voiced by the rowboat ferrymen. The following month the
matter appeared to be closed when the applicants said they could not afford the £60 required to
cover the ferry's insurance, so they were withdrawing and putting their £600 motorboat up for
sale. It next appeared that the Council had 'jumped the gun' in assuming the ferry would be
motorised, for a metal landing-stage had been delivered to the Sandbank side, and ferryman Mike
Parker enquired of the Mudeford and Sandpits Residents' Association how much money the Council
had spent on it? No direct answer was forthcoming to this question and Mr. E.I. Grace changed
the subject to the matter of safety, and overcrowding of the rowboats.

There was no evidence of overloading, but the rowboat ferry came under further attack when Councillor M. Lynk, Chairman of the Safety Committee commented that it was a 'potential catastrophic disaster', and persuaded his committee to request the Beach Committee to re-examine the possibility of a motor ferry, and to emphasise 'in the strongest possible terms' their opposition to the rowboat ferry continuing under the long-standing conditions. Thus, within a matter of weeks, discussion over a possible motor ferry had led to an extraordinarily fierce attack on the established rowboats, in spite of their excellent safety record. Ferryman Mike Parker objected to an attack by a councillor 'who admits he hasn't any specialised knowledge of rowing or boats'; while Councillor Freestone told the Committee 'it had not been intended to do away with the rowboat ferry, but to supplement it'. A few days later however Alderman Bell stated at a council meeting, in reply to a question, that the Council would prefer a motorised ferry, firstly on the grounds of safety and secondly because it would facilitate the running of a timetable service. In November that year an Editorial in the local paper urged a get-together between Council and local boatmen to resolve the problem - but at the same time declaring it would be unfair to run a motor boat in competition with the established ferry.

Christmas intervened and it was February 1970 before the ferry was really in the news again. At last the Christchurch Council and the local boatmen held joint discussions. It transpired that the Council were willing to spend £3,000 on a suitable motorboat and hire it to the rowboat ferrymen. The ferrymen however showed a distinct lack of enthusiasm for working such a boat as 'employees of the Council'. A breakthrough came to the deadlock in the April, when two experienced Mudeford fishermen, Andrew Russell and William Watson, applied for permission to run the ferry with boats purchased by the Council. The application came as a surprise, both to the ferrymen and the Councillors. Mr. Ken Derham also admitted surprise, but he added "They are two good men. There is no question about that. They have had years of experience of the run, and I think the council is lucky to have them interested in the ferry".

The arrangements were for the Council to buy two 21ft. Cheverton Champ heavy duty glass fibre workboats with 15hp. Lister diesels at £1,756 each, and to sell them to the partners with repayments by instalments over 2 years. Their right to run the ferry would be for 10 years, and the boats would be licensed for 12 passengers and comprehensively insured. New landing steps at the quay for the exclusive use of the ferry, were to be provided at a cost of £425. The service would operate in the summer months and the adult single fare was agreed at 1/-.

That summer the motor ferry commenced running, and the rowboat ferry continued in opposition; the former worked from the new ferry steps to the Sandbanks jetty upstream, while the rowboats worked from the public steps straight across the Run to the beach. Trouble arose when the Council authorised a conspicuous notice advertising the motor ferry on Mudeford quay, but demanded the removal of a smaller sign exhibited by the rowboat ferrymen. This simply said "THIS IS THE FISHERMEN'S ROWING FERRY" but it had not been authorised and the quay superintendent requested it be pulled down and taken to the Council's depot. "The Council is definitely trying to force us out of business" said ferryman Mike Parker. "It is most unfair. We realise that the motor ferry will get the bulk of the trade, but we see no reason why we should not continue to operate".

Time, however, is a Great Healer and the motor ferry has now come to be both accepted and appreciated. At the end of June 1970 the service began with the two 21ft. Cheverton launches, **Ferry Lass** and **Ferry Girl**. The following year a 22ft. clinker-built relief boat, the **Wally**, was acquired but was replaced after some months by an 18ft. Cheverton, **Champ**. In 1973 William Watson withdrew from the partnership, and the **Champ** and the **Ferry Girl** were both sold. In their place was purchased a 25ft. clinker-hull Ramsgate passenger launch (built at Deal) and named **Ocean Dawn**. In 1977 this boat was sold and replaced by the **Ferry Lady** (145), built by Treeve at Hayle and fitted out by Andy Russell himself. Her passenger capacity is 32 and she carries a crew of two.

Over the past ten years, stress of weather has caused the ferry to be suspended on about four days. An 'as-required' rather than a timetable service is provided and the ferry does not run in winter except at fine weather weekends when a need seems indicated. Since the end of the partnership a regular crew of at least two has been employed on a part-time basis. One August evening in 1980 we watched **Ferry Lady** at work on 'The Run'. Nearby the salmon-punt rowing ferry lay keel uppermost on the beach and had apparently not run that season. **Ferry Lady** was being expertly handled with ex-rowboat ferryman Mike Parker at the helm. The old adage was proving true: "If you can't beat 'em, join 'em!"

Mudeford Ferry: **Ferry Lady** *southbound with Mike Parker at the helm, August 1980. Photo: Edwina Small.*

Index

Castle Ferry: **Achieve** heads upstream from Stumpy Steps with Dave Griffiths at the helm.

Photo: Edwina Small.

Boat Names.

King Harry Ferry: **Ferry No.3.** at Philleigh in 1934.

Photo: P.N.Thomas.

ACKNOWLEDGMENTS

Appledore Maritime Museum; Antony Estate, Cornwall; Braunton Museum; Bristol Harbourmaster; Bristol Library; Bristol Record Office; British Rail, Exeter; British Waterways Board; Dart Pleasure Craft Ltd.; Dartmouth Borough Museum; Dartmouth Harbourmaster; Devon Dock, Pier & S.S. Co. Ltd.; Devon Record Office; Exeter Library; Gloucester Library; Harvey, J. and Sons, Poole; H.M. Customs & Excise; The Kilvert Society, Hereford; King Harry Steam Ferry Co. Ltd.; Looe Harbourmaster; Moorings Supt., Christchurch; Noah's Ark Museum, Fowey; Old Cornwall Society, Fowey; Penzance Museum; Philip & Sons, Dartmouth; Plymouth Library; Plymouth Museum; Poole Library; Poole Museum Service; Port Eliot Estate, St. German's; Rector and Verger of West Parley; Redruth Library; St. Michael's Mount Estate; South Hams District Council; Tamar Bridge & Torpoint Ferry Joint Committee; Toms, C. & Sons, Polruan; Torbay Harbourmaster; Torquay Museum; Truro Library; Weymouth Museum Service.

Mrs. Clarice Adams of Morwellham; Vic Anderson of Dartmouth; Percy Andrews of Dittisham; A.S. Ashmole of Salcombe; Mr. & Mrs. Askew of Newnham; Max Barnes of Aust; Roy Barnes of Dartmouth; Mrs. Sadie Bayliss of Claverton; P.S. Bebbington of Plymouth; Mrs. Elizabeth Bennett of Mylor; Fred Bennett of Feock; Jack Birch of Plymouth; Ralph Bird of Carnon Downs; Jack Blight of Flushing; L.J. Bonstow of Duncannon; Frank Booker of Plymouth; Fred Bowker of St. Just-in-Roseland; H. ('Dido') Bradford of Exmouth; R.J.Bray of Brixham; Peggy Bridges of Bath; T.J. Broad of Torpoint; Mrs. Brookman of Saltford; Bob Brown of Chepstow; Fred Bunt of Bodinnick; Len Carter of Newton Ferrers; Chris Cockran of Gunnislake; Frank Cook of Restronguet; Mr. & Mrs. Clutterbuck of Twerton; George Cornell of Andover; Arthur Cowell of Reading; Reg Cowell of Starcross; M.A. Critchley of Looe; Jack Crossley of Antony; Ben Curtin of Plymouth; E. Darch of Combwich; Paul Dash of Falmouth; Norman & Kathleen Davies of Kingswear; Mrs. F. Delbridge of Shaldon; Fred Drew of Teignmouth; Sam Dungey of Plymouth; W.J. Dunstone of Millbrook; R.L.E. Edhouse of Paignton; D.G. Eley of Cotehele; Harry Elford of Plymouth; Percy Elford of Plymouth; David Elliott of Bristol; Dick Ferris of Truro; Gordon Ferryman of Brean; Martin Findlay of Plymouth; John Fishwick of Appledore; Cecil Foster of Newton Ferrers; Edgar Foster of Newton Ferrers; E.M. Fry of Botherick; Ted Game of Exmouth; R.H. Gosney of Swanage; Ivor Gregory of Plymouth; Dave Griffiths of Dartmouth; John Grimshaw of Bristol; J. Guilfoyle of Warleigh; Mervyn Habgood of St. Michael Penkivel; Harold Hannaford of Dartmouth; E. Hannaford of Salcombe; W.C.J. Harvey of Poole; Alf Hemens of Exeter; Les Hill of Exmouth; Sydney Holloway of Saltash; Geoff Holman of Exmouth; Harold C. Jewell of Saltash; Denis Job of Paignton; Alistair Johns of Flushing; Norman Johns of Instow; W. King of Botherick; D.E.F. Kingsbury of Poole; Jack Kingston of Torpoint; Mac Knapp of Littleton-on-Severn; Douglas Langford of Calstock; Will Langworthy of Kingswear; Harry Lavis of Exmouth; Fred Lewis of Looe; Bill Lindsey of Padstow; Tom Marshall of Millbrook; Rev. Frank Martin of Mylor; J. Matthews of Marazion; Len Matthews of Teignmouth; T.E. Mattocks of St. Just; Bert Mellish of Exmouth; Ian Merry of Bere Alston; R.J. Moore of Plymouth; Fred Mills of Dartmouth; Nancy Moule of Shaldon; Peter Moule of Kingsbridge; W.G. Neale of Bristol; Jim Newman of Bristol; Peter Newman of Tolverne; W.H. Newman of Topsham; Bernard Norsworthy of Plymouth; G.A. Northey of Newquay; Dick Oxland of Plymouth; Percy Palmer of Chepstow; Mr. & Mrs. Pedlar of Bere Ferrers; A.J. Pengelly of Looe; J.C.W. Perrett of Galmpton; Frank Peters of St. Mawes; Mrs. Pickering of Fowey; Mr. Pope of Christchurch; Albert Powe of Appledore; Gilbert Putt of Salcombe; Stan Pym of Topsham; Don Rawe of Padstow; Bill Rendle of Dittisham; R.F. Rew of Exeter; George Riddels of Dartmouth; Bert Roach of Bristol; Mrs. Dorothy Roach of Lelant; Andrew Russell of Christchurch; S.W. & W.E. Ryder of Kingsbridge; C. Scarrot of St. Germans; Albert Sharp of Pill; Len Slade of Fowey; F.V. Smith of Poole; Charles Soaper of Shaldon; W. Spiller of St. Germans; I.D. Spreadbury of Fowey; R.J. Stride of Christchurch; Ken Stuckey of Wick St. Lawrence; Herbert Symons of Gunnislake; Denis Thorne of St. Germans; Douglas Tiller of Poole; George Tothill of Shaldon; Gerald Truscott of Saltash; Harry Uglow of Torquay; George Vallance of Kingsteignton; D.C. Vosper of Saltash; Walter Walker of Teignmouth; Ivor Waters of Chepstow; Jack Webb of Gerrans; Sam Webber of Plymouth; Bill Westlake of Shaldon; Harold White of Dartmouth; Sam Willcox of Cremyll; Bernard Y. Williams of London; Harry Williams of Plymouth; John Williams of Chepstow; Norman Williams of Teignmouth; Tom Williams of Dartmouth; Fred Wills of Poole; Reece Winstone of Bristol.

BIBLIOGRAPHY & PRESS SOURCES

Ancient Ferry at Saltash, The, by D.C. Vosper. Bath Chronicle (files). Bath Herald (files). Beloved St. Ives by Cyril Noall, 1957. Book of Exmouth, The, by Robin Bush (Barracuda 1978). Bournemouth Graphic (files). Bournemouth Times (files). Brean Down by L.M. Dulton, 1921. Christchurch Echo (files). Christchurch Times (files). Coasts of Devon and Lundy Island, The, by J.D. Page. Coleridge & Wordsworth in Somerset by Berta Lawrence, 1970. Dartmouth by Percy Russell (Batsford Press). Dartmouth Chronicle (files). Devon by W.G. Hoskins (1954 David & Charles 1972). Diary and Letters by Fanny Burney (1791). Drake's Island (Penwell Press). Essays in Cornish History by Charles Henderson, 1935. Evening Post (files). Evening World (files). Ferries and Ferrymen by G. Bernard Wood (Cassell 1969). Ferries in Great Britain, M. of T. Comm. Report, (H.M.S.O. 1948). From Harbour to Harbour by A. Bell, 1916. Guide to the Tamar by W. Hearde. Handbook to Exmouth by Freeman, 1899. Harveys, 200 years of Trading by Cyril Noall (U.B.M. Harvey). Herald Express (files). History & Antiquities of Somerset by Collinson. History Around the Fal by Fal History Group (Exeter Univ. 1980). History of Borough & County of Town of Poole by H.D. Smith (J. Locker, 1951). History of Exmouth (Peacock). History of Saltford Village, A by Percy Sims (Sims and Mawdett). History of the Cremyll Ferry by P.L. Hull (Camborne Pub. Co.). Industrial Archaeology of the Bristol Region by Buchanan & Cossens (David & Charles). Lake's Parochial History of Cornwall by J. Polsue (E.E.P. Ltd.). Life in Edwardian Truro by Rex Barrett (Rooster Books). Maid of Sker, The by R.D. Blackmore (1872). Mercantile Navy List, The, (H.M.S.O.). More Chapters from the Kilvert Saga (Kilvert Society publication). Notes on the Parish of Mylor by H.P. Oliney (Barnicott & Pearce). Old Cornish Inns by H.L. Douch (Bradford Barton 1966). Padstow 1895-1925 by Claude Berry (Lodenek Press 1976). Poole Bay & Purbeck by Cochrane (Longman's 1970). Poole Borough Archives. Plymouth: A New History by Crispin Gill (David & Charles). Plymouth, Stonehouse & Devonport by Whitaker. Plymouth Extra (files). Plymouth Times (files). Regional History of the Railways, A, by D. St. Thomas (David & Charles 1960). Roseland, The, by Laurence O'Toole (Lodenek Press). St. Anne's Ferry and Path. Pamphlet by Father Grant. Sea Breezes (files). Sea Board of Mendip, The, by Dent (1902). Severn Enterprise by Chris Jordan (A.H. Stockwell 1977). Shining Ferry by A. Quiller-Couch, 1905. Ships Monthly (files). Somerset County Herald (files). Somerset Countryman, The, (files). South Devon & South Cornwall by Ward & Baddeley (Nelson 1915). South Devon Times (files). Sunday Independent (files). Tale of Gordano, The, by Eve Wigan (Chatford 1971). Tamar Bridge (TB & TF Joint Committee 1962). Tamar Valley at Work, The, by E. Paige. Teignmouth Post (files). The Cornishman (files). The Falmouth Packet (files). The Kingsbridge Branch by A.R. Kingdon (Oxford Publishing Co.). The Pride of Poole by Beamish (Poole Boro. Corp. 1974). Times and Mirror (files). Victorian Maritime Album by Basil Greenhill. Ward, Lock & Co's Guide Books. Westcountry Passenger Steamers by G. Farr (Stephenson & Sons 1967). West Briton & Cornwall Advertiser (files). Western Daily Press (files). Western Evening Herald (files). Western Morning News (files). Weston Mercury (files). Weston-super-Mare Gazette (files). Yealmpton Branch, The by A.R. Kingdon, (Oxford Pub. Co. 1974).

Stonehouse Passage: *Ferry and ferryhouse, c. 1765. Ferry replaced by the 'Ha'penny Bridge' in 1773.*
Sketch - Terry Duggan.

Tolverne Passage: *Tolverne ferryman about to pull in for a passenger, just below Smuggler's Cottage. Tregothnan Hall visible in background. Early 1900s.*
Sketch - Terry Duggan.